THE AFRICAN DIASPORA AND THE DISCIPLINES

THE
AFRICAN
DIASPORA
AND THE
DISCIPLINES

Edited by TEJUMOLA OLANIYAN

and JAMES H. SWEET

INDIANA UNIVERSITY PRESS

Bloomington and Indianapolis

This book is a publication of

Indiana University Press
601 North Morton Street
Bloomington, Indiana 47404-3797 USA

www.iupress.indiana.edu

Telephone orders   800-842-6796
Fax orders   812-855-7931
Orders by e-mail   iuporder@indiana.edu

Manufactured in the United States of America

Library of Congress Cataloging-in-Publication Data

The African diaspora and the disciplines / edited by Tejumola Olaniyan
and James H. Sweet.
     p. cm.
   Includes conference papers.
   Includes bibliographical references and index.
     ISBN 978-0-253-35464-8 (cloth : alk. paper) — ISBN 978-0-253-22191-9
(pbk. : alk. paper) 1. African diaspora—Study and teaching (Higher)—
Congresses. I. Olaniyan, Tejumola. II. Sweet, James H. (James Hoke)
   DT16.5.A326 2010
   909'.0496—dc22

                                                          2009043095

1 2 3 4 5 15 14 13 12 11 10

CONTENTS

PART THREE. ARTS AND CULTURE

PART FOUR. DIASPORA CONTEXTS

ACKNOWLEDGMENTS

The editors incurred many debts in the funding, planning, and execution of this volume. Most of the book's chapters derive from a two-day international symposium held at the University of Wisconsin–Madison in March 2006. This symposium brought together more than a dozen scholars from around the world. Without the generous financial support of our sponsors, such an event could not have been possible. Our major benefactors were the African Diaspora Cluster, the Office of the Provost, the College of Letters and Science, the African Diaspora and Atlantic World Research Circle, and the African Studies Program. Co-sponsors included the Department of African Languages and Literature, Department of Afro-American Studies, Anonymous Fund, Department of Anthropology, Department of Art History, Department of English, Department of French and Italian, Department of Geography, the Harvey Goldberg Center for the Study of Contemporary History, Department of History, the International Institute, Latin American, Caribbean, and Iberian Studies, School of Music, Department of Philosophy, and Department of Theater, all of the University of Wisconsin.

Although financial support is crucial, the dedication and labor of colleagues, students, and administrative staff ultimately allow projects like this to come to fruition. We would first like to thank all of the contributors, whose collective energies provide a new vision for conceptualizing the African diaspora across the disciplines. Their collegiality, creativity, and timely delivery of the chapters made the task of editing an enjoyable one. We would also like to thank the members of the African Diaspora and Atlantic World Research Circle, particularly the graduate students, whose dynamism and energy are crucial to the circle's day-to-day functioning. Indeed, one could justifiably argue that graduate student pushing and prodding prompted the interdisciplinary inquiries that animate much of this volume. Finally, a few individuals deserve special thanks for their contributions. Our colleague, Madeleine Wong, played a crucial role in the early planning and organization of the symposium. Jim Delehanty, the associate director of The African Studies Program at UW, offered his usual wise counsel and planning skills. And last but certainly not least, Toni Pressley-Sanon worked indefatigably on this project from beginning to end. She organized the travel and accommodations for all of the symposium attendees, served as conference coordinator, and administered the details of bringing this volume together. Without her diligence, efficiency, and good cheer, our task would have been much more difficult.

We are also very appreciative of the support and understanding of Dee Mortensen, our editor at Indiana University Press, in taking on this publication. Her unflagging enthusiasm, in many ways, was catalytic from the start of our imagining the post-conference book phase of our project. Laura MacLeod, assistant sponsoring editor, expertly managed the important details. The anonymous readers offered probing and very insightful comments; scholars truly ought to celebrate themselves when they can take for granted such detailed and dispassionate attention from peers.

THE AFRICAN DIASPORA AND THE DISCIPLINES

Words

- Ebulliance

- opprobrius

INTRODUCTION

Tejumola Olaniyan and James H. Sweet

The African diaspora has become a most vibrant area of research and teaching interest across the disciplines in the past two decades in the American academy. The larger context of this boom is the rise of varieties of minority, postcolonial, transnational, and migration studies. Institutional units or subunits dedicated to African Diaspora Studies have multiplied across universities, and scholarly books, journals, special issues of journals, and articles continue to be published on the topic.[1] Much of the scholarship is devoted to the primary work of excavation, interpretation, and analysis. Within those frames, we can affirm that the yield of insight so far has been truly substantial. There is a glaring lack, however, in our existing body of conceptual and definitional knowledge. Most scholars of African Diaspora Studies have been trained in one particular discipline, but the area of study to which they are such committed champions is evidently vaster than particular disciplinary boundaries. African Diaspora Studies, in its most robust and enabling conception, covers the African world comprehensively conceived: Africa and its diaspora populations wherever we find them, from all disciplinary perspectives. It is obviously a tall order, if not impossible, for one scholar to master the protocols of more than a few disciplines. So how does one, solidly based in a discipline as is still the hegemonic norm, practice African Diaspora Studies, an inherently interdisciplinary enterprise?[2] The current ebullience of the field notwithstanding, there is a deafening silence on this crucial matter. Little effort has been made to clearly situate, delineate, and reflect on the *practice* of diaspora scholarship within the possibilities and constraints simultaneously afforded and imposed by the disciplines. Interdisciplinary dialogue on the theoretical contours of the African diaspora is even rarer. By identifying and speaking of this lack in the field, we are calling neither for encyclopedic knowledge of the disciplines nor for the abandonment of rigorous disciplinary training and specialization as a condition for African diaspora scholarship. On the contrary, our goal in this volume is more modest but potentially widely transforming and transformative:

to *begin* a serious conversation on the intersections of African Diaspora Studies and the disciplines.

The central goal of the book is twofold: (1) to theorize and define methods, problems, and conflicts of "doing" African diaspora research and scholarship from various disciplinary perspectives, and (2) to initiate and facilitate interdisciplinary and cross-regional dialogues and debates on African Diaspora Studies. We aim to illuminate the ways that the African diaspora is understood, produced as an object of study, enabled, and constrained in and by the various disciplines. Rather than an emphasis on primary research and analysis, we tasked our authors with the appropriately self-reflexive and challenging meta-level scrutiny of the practice of African Diaspora Studies within and at the interstices of disciplines. Here then are some of the specific foundational questions we posed to the authors:

1. Is the African diaspora seen as a discrete field within your discipline? If so, how is it distinguished from other fields like African American Studies, Migration Studies, etc.? In short, how does your discipline define the African diaspora?
2. What are the major methodological conventions of your discipline, particularly as they relate to the African diaspora? Are these methodological conventions consistent across fields in your discipline, or does the study of the African diaspora require different kinds of approaches/ questions?
3. Are there conflicting approaches to African Diaspora Studies within your discipline? Does the diaspora include Africa, or does it include secondary migrations like those from Brazil to Nigeria, or Jamaica to England or Canada? Are there any theoretical/methodological tensions between those who study earlier streams of the diaspora (like those associated with the Atlantic slave trade) and those who study more recent streams (like those of contemporary African migrants to the United States)?
4. What is the relationship of your discipline to other disciplines as it relates to the study of the African diaspora? Does your discipline draw heavily from the approaches and methodologies of other disciplines? Is your discipline in conflict with another discipline over approaches to diaspora?
5. Has the practice of African Diaspora Studies impacted your discipline in any way? What are the constraints and possibilities of doing African diaspora in your discipline?

In addition to the broad questions outlined above, we also gave contributors the freedom to address more specific issues that are germane to their particular disciplines.

Apart from our central emphasis on disciplinary and area coverage intersections, we also specifically commissioned more or less discipline-anchored "state of the field" studies of a more global reach, particularly in regions where the study of the African Atlantic diaspora is not so obvious, namely, Europe and South Africa. For these authors, we asked how the peculiarities of race, region, and politics impact the production and dissemination of research on diaspora. If we are appropriately self-conscious about the possibilities and constraints of the study of the African diaspora within the disciplines, we must also recognize that differing spatial and temporal configurations impact heavily on the practice of diaspora studies. We should not expect the African diaspora to be understood and practiced similarly in the United States, Europe, and Africa, places where academic-institutional, socioeconomic, and political imperatives often diverge. Differing imperatives frequently result in differing conceptualizations and institutional iterations, challenging us to recognize that the disciplines are not the only obstacles toward a more illuminating theory of praxis.

We want to stress that this book is not exhaustive in its coverage of the possible disciplinary and regional perspectives on the African diaspora. Our original goal was to cover as much ground as we could, and indeed, the conference from which this volume is derived did much more in this direction.[3] In addition to the essays found in this volume, there were papers on literature, religious studies, archaeological chemistry, and the study of the African diaspora in Brazil. Lamentably, some of the papers were already committed to other venues; in other instances, we were unable to secure revisions from the authors. Such is the peril of edited volumes. To be sure, we recognize these gaps, as well as others (including only passing references to the African diaspora in Asia and the Indian Ocean). Nevertheless, even in the absence of these crucial perspectives, the essays in this volume finally begin to critically articulate the difficult intersection of the disciplines and African Diaspora Studies and to suggest methods and practices most applicable to that endeavor. This self-conscious reflection on *how* we study the African world from within our specific and narrow disciplinary perspectives raises new questions, new methods, new theories, and new institutional formations that move beyond the confines of the disciplines, while at the same time acknowledging their boundaries.

Scholars have long discovered that in *doing* African Diaspora Studies, they frequently needed to alter some of the entrenched canons of their disciplines. For example, African and African Diaspora Studies have moved away from traditional fixations on the literate archive, toward an array of nondiscursive sources, including oral history, art, popular culture, embodied and ritual memory, etc. Likewise, African Diaspora Studies often eschew theoretical perspectives drawn from European intellectual and philosophical traditions, favoring questions and paradigms more pertinent to African experiences. The authors in this volume view these challenges to the disciplinary canons as a reflection of the health and vigor of African Diaspora Studies as an emergent field. At the same time, there is little indication that African Diaspora Studies should become a discipline unto itself. Indeed, precisely because of the overlapping and intersecting methods, languages, literatures, and institutional configurations of the various disciplines, it is absolutely imperative that students and scholars of the African diaspora first anchor themselves in their respective disciplinary canons and then branch out from this foundation. If anything, students of the African diaspora bear a greater burden in "disciplining" their scholarship, lest it become haphazard and ungrounded. Neither scholarly method as a crucial arena of meta-level inquiry, nor the African diaspora as area coverage, would be served well by superficiality. Mastery remains crucial for both intellectual and practical reasons, such as the increasing diversity, multiplicity, and complexity of areas of inquiry, limitations of graduate training, and a job market still ruled by disciplines.

Once a disciplinary baseline has been established, what then constitutes the African diaspora as an interdisciplinary field? How does one expand from within a traditional discipline to engage broader interdisciplinary African diaspora perspectives? The authors in this volume make at least four major suggestions: First, Africa must be the intellectual starting point of African Diaspora Studies. Research questions centering on Africa, whether as a real or imagined homeland, reconfigure many of our traditional disciplinary understandings. In some instances, the very sanctity of the discipline is called into question by such inquiries. For example, the idea of African "philosophy" represents a revolutionary idea in a discipline which sees itself as largely European in provenance. In other instances, explicit references to "Africa" sometimes disappear from debates, obscured by overlapping expressions of race, class, gender, sexuality, and so on. Nevertheless, Africa remains intertwined out of context. This intertwining of "Africa" with a complex globality brings us to the second suggestion: The African diaspora is mutually constitutive of other political formations such as race, class, gender, sexuality, and environment, and must therefore be studied from an overlapping, comparative perspective. Though adhering to differing local configurations, all of these political formations traverse the boundaries of the disciplines and therefore demand global, interdisciplinary analysis. Third, there must be a renewed emphasis on an African diaspora intellectual genealogy, focusing on the pioneering works of scholars like W. E. B. Du Bois, C. L. R. James, Aimé Césaire, Eric Williams, Oliver Cox, George Padmore, Frantz Fanon, and Walter Rodney. Again, this emphasis is not to the exclusion of traditional canons. Rather, a consideration of an African diaspora intellectual tradition offers ways of conceptualizing a new field as well as pushing the boundaries of traditional disciplines. For instance, instead of viewing Walter Rodney simply as a "Marxist," as many sociologists or political scientists have done, perhaps it would be better to trace the impacts of George Padmore on C. L. R. James or James on Rodney. Fourth, scholars must be open to the multitude of nondiscursive expressions that constitute "sources" for the study of the African diaspora. In some instances, African diaspora political formations create these new sources. For example, only recently have politically conscious scientists pushed the discipline of Genetic Biology to see DNA as a potential tool for mapping the African diaspora. In other instances, sources are inscribed in some of the most unexpected places—objects, memories, shrines, and even bodies. For example, scholars now read gesture and body posture to outline new ways of understanding African diaspora history and popular culture.

Taken together, these four suggestions constitute a core of general guidelines on a theory of praxis for African Diaspora Studies. Ultimately, the essays in this volume demonstrate how African Diaspora Studies is beginning to create its own unique set of scholarly imperatives; they also show how African Diaspora Studies is challenging disciplinary traditions from within. In this way, the intellectual vitality of the African diaspora and the disciplines is mutually reinforcing.

The book is divided into four sections that run roughly from histories and the sciences to arts and cultural studies. Part 1 addresses those disciplines most closely related to the peopling, ethnography, and history of the African diaspora. Kim Butler explores "history's possibilities as a component of many disciplines for research on the African diaspora and how work in the discipline stands to expand our understanding of diasporas in general." In the process, Butler "historicizes" diaspora history, tracing its roots to the late nineteenth century and following it through its various scholarly iterations in the twentieth century. Though ideas about "diaspora" and "Africans abroad" circulated from early in the twentieth century, it was not until 1965, when George Shepperson drew attention to the specific term "African diaspora," that the idea gained greater traction in the historical profession. By the 1990s, almost anyone researching the descendants of African peoples could define himself or herself as a historian of the "African diaspora," without any critical inquiry into exactly what the field entailed or how it should be conceived. According to Butler, demands for greater clarity on the meaning of the "African diaspora" resulted, to some extent, in a decline of the field. As scholars realized the limitations and demands of African diaspora history, some moved on to similarly ill-defined fields such as Atlantic history and global history. Ultimately, Butler views the study of comparative and overlapping diasporas, employing interdisciplinary methods and ideas, as the path to a fuller, more complete understanding of the processes by which the African diaspora was forged.

Richard Price's essay on Anthropology echoes some of Butler's concerns about charting the *process* of identity formation in the African diaspora. In particular, Price highlights recent debates over the meaning of "creolization," critiquing the utility of these debates and pointing to future directions for research. Price takes special issue with an "influential group of scholars, who style themselves 'African-centrists.'" According to Price, these African-centrists often overly generalize historical particulars of time, space, and power, rendering the processes of cultural change static. In addition to his methodological critique, Price argues that debates over creolization are overtly marked by present-day realities of North American racism, with African-centrists often articulating "ethnic" or "nationalist" political positions through their scholarship. Price does not completely reject the importance of Africa to the diaspora. Rather, he calls for a more subtle, complex, and historically informed rendering of the "miraculous" process by which Africans and their descendants forged cultures in the Americas.

Fatimah Jackson and Latifah Borgelin take up the role of genetics in explaining the biological history of African diaspora roots and routes. They summarize the scholarship of mtDNA and Y chromosome analysis in various diasporic locations, concluding that a determination of ethnic or regional location of one's oldest maternal and paternal ancestors is theoretically possible; however, precise pinpointing of "ethnic" homelands is simply not feasible at this time, due to deficiencies in data collection in Africa. To date, only a miniscule portion of the African continent has been genetically mapped, reducing potential American-to-African homeland matches to just a small number of African "ethnic" possibilities. Thus "these databases can only give us, at this time, a partial and incomplete interpretation of African diversity." Perhaps more egregiously, some scientists ascribe present-day ethnic identities to the partial genetic matches elicited from this incomplete database. Even if a fully complete database existed, the genetic variants that mark African origins are tens of thousands of years older than the ethnic identities now associated with particular African geographies. Genetic science might demonstrate that an African American shares direct ancestry with a person in Yorubaland, but their shared ancestor lived in a time well before the Yoruba, as a people, ever existed. Ultimately, scientific findings are not often in accord with popular and some scholarly perceptions about the centrality of genetics as a key to unlocking the African American past. Difficulties with such popular perceptions, and even uncertainties in the science, are demonstrated in the television series *African American Lives* by Henry Louis Gates Jr. Indeed, Jackson and Borgelin state that genetics "entrepreneurs . . . have misrepresented the data and deceived their customers." Nevertheless, despite deficiencies in data and poor interpretive outcomes, genetics can indeed answer many important questions related to the population history of the African diaspora. The authors conclude that, in sustained collaboration with historians, ethnographers, linguists, and archaeologists, geneticists will eventually help us better understand and detail the migratory patterns of the African diaspora.

In chapter 4, Judith Carney demonstrates how the discipline of Geography bridges "the social and biological sciences . . . offer[ing] a holistic approach to contemporary and historical problems." Carney finds that Geography has been slow to embrace ideas and methods of African diaspora scholarship; however, the discipline is slowly changing. In particular, cultural geographers and biogeographers have begun demonstrating the ways that Africans and their descendants shaped American landscapes. According to Carney, these African influences include foods (rice), medicines (healing plants), and spatial settlements (runaway slave communities). Carney concludes that African cultural-environmental contributions are just now receiving the attention they deserve from geographers. She holds out hope that African systems of environmental and botanical knowledge in the Americas will soon command the same respect as Amerindian ones.

The discipline of archaeology is the subject of Theresa Singleton's chapter. Contrary to the marginal place of the African diaspora in Geography, Singleton finds that the proliferation of recent research on the diaspora has led some archaeologists to conclude that the African diaspora constitutes a separate field of study within the discipline, one that encompasses a broad geographic range across five continents. Singleton points out that the methods employed by archaeologists of the African diaspora center on identity (ethnic and racial) and diaspora (comparing various sites of peoples emanating from the same homeland). These inquiries are inherently interdisciplinary in scope, particularly drawing on History. However, as Singleton reveals, the relationship between Archaeology and History is not without its difficulties. Singleton explores in detail these interdisciplinary tensions and points to ways that future scholars can transcend old geographic and disciplinary boundaries.

Part 2 shifts away from explicitly historical concerns toward the more presently focused disciplines of sociology, politics, and philosophy. In chapter 6, Paget Henry reflects on the emergence of Africa and the African diaspora as fields of inquiry in Caribbean sociology. It was not until the 1960s and 1970s that Caribbean sociologists, often collaborating with their American mentors, began to examine the Caribbean, through the lens of either culture contact theory or modernization theory. According to Henry, these scholars tended to overlook the seminal contributions of W. E. B. Du Bois and the Atlanta school of sociology, not to mention local Afro-Caribbean intellectuals such as Antenor Firmin and C. L. R. James. In the late 1970s, dependency theory and other Marxist-leaning approaches largely supplanted culturalist and modernization approaches, but this era was short-lived. By the 1980s, neo-liberal economic theory displaced ideas about culture and development, thereby pushing Africa and the diaspora to the extreme margins of American sociological concerns. Henry argues that the fields of Africa and African diaspora sociology are still suffering the effects of the "cleavages and contradictions" of this period and have "not produced . . . books and articles to match the quality of the output of the earlier period." In order to remedy this problem, Henry urges a more explicit engagement between Caribbean sociology and its Africana "intellectual tradition." Instead of viewing Africana thinkers in terms of Western schools of thought—existentialist, Marxist, post-structuralist, etc.—Caribbean sociologists should consider the influences of their own scholarly lineage—George Padmore's impact on James, Aimé Césaire's impact on Frantz Fanon, and so on. Henry concludes that only by engaging this "local intellectual stream" will Caribbean sociology reclaim a central place in the discipline.

Robert Fatton argues similarly to Henry that the discipline of Political Science has no subdisciplinary field devoted to the African diaspora. Rather, African diaspora concerns are usually articulated through "race or minority studies within the field of American politics" or through "comparative politics." These disciplinary subfields reflect some of the same "modernization" imperatives that drove the discipline of sociology. Indeed, those working in comparative politics, or "area studies," "simply assumed that all countries went through the same sequence of development that had led to Western industrialization and liberal-democracy." Mirroring the same trajectory described by Henry for Sociology, Fatton argues that the neoliberal economic model became even more entrenched in the late 1980s after the fall of the Soviet bloc. In essence, the West had won. History ended. There was no alternative to capitalist modernity, certainly not in the African diaspora. Characterizing the discipline's obsession with Western models as "provincial," Fatton calls for new approaches that "reject the benignity of existing arrangements of power and wealth." Like Henry, Fatton calls on political scientists to return to "radical and critical traditions of left-wing scholarship," particularly that produced by Africana figures like Du Bois, Cox, Fanon, James, Cabral, and Rodney. Fatton goes one step further, arguing that "the politics of the belly"— economic dependency, forced migration, racism, and class warfare— manifest similar symptoms in Africa and the diaspora. The same conceptual tools utilized to understand political modalities in Senegal or Congo can be used to better understand politics in Haiti, but only through a serious engagement with local forms of knowledge. Fatton does not romanticize the "local." Like Kim Butler, he sees the promise of African diaspora politics in the shifting and overlapping identities that are at once local, national, and global.

Olúfémi Táíwò's essay on the discipline of Philosophy reflects many of the same concerns raised in Henry's and Fatton's chapters. Taiwo notes that the African diaspora claims no discrete field in the discipline of Philosophy; however, the recent emergence of black or African American philosophy opens potential spaces for thinking diasporically. As Táíwò sees it, the problem is not so much one of intellectual production. Rather, it is the discipline's propensity to reject African-descended thinking as "philosophical." Black and African American philosophy are thus deemed to be outside the discipline's boundaries, most often categorized as "history or area studies." Like Henry and Fatton, Taiwo views the last thirty years as crucial ones in the silencing of African diaspora concerns. In his rendering, once Africans and their descendants achieved freedom from colonialism and state-sanctioned white power, "philosophical interchanges between Africa and its diaspora declined in importance, and the cross-fertilization of ideas that used to mark their common relations almost ceased." Ultimately, Táíwò calls for a diaspora philosophy that explicitly engages discourses of freedom and ideological struggle in a comparative context that includes Africans, African Americans, and Caribbeans.

Part 3 examines theater, music, art, and cultural studies. Sandra Richards's chapter on drama, theater, and performance studies unravels important differences between the academic pursuits of theater and performance studies, on the one hand, and actual performance, on the other. According to Richards, the African diaspora does not exist as a separate field in theater studies, despite texts and criticism that fall under apparently promising categories like "postcolonial" and "intercultural." In each of these instances, the categories of analysis tend to reify colonial categories, "Orientalizing" the African diaspora, rather than revealing it. Richards finds performance to be one venue where a broader diaspora consciousness might be expressed—as say in the similar sociopolitical reading of Wole Soyinka's play *The Beatification of Area Boy* in Nigeria and Jamaica. Contemporary social, economic, and racial conditions often reflect shared histories of oppression, but Richards asks, how do we separate "ethno-transnational" identities from identities based on "post/neo-colonial status"? Ultimately, she agrees with other authors in this volume that race, class, gender, sexuality, etc., overlap and cleave in ways that complicate notions of a singular African diaspora. Thus "black globality" challenges static notions of community centered on race alone, demanding cooperative, cross-cultural, interdisciplinary research and scholarship.

Melvin Butler's chapter on Ethnomusicology demonstrates the multiplicity of ways that African diaspora music is taught and researched in the academy. Some institutions have departments of ethnomusicology; others offer diaspora content through various subdisciplines of Music, such as the "Anthropology of Music." According to Butler, regardless of approach, "there is broad institutional consensus that ethnomusicological training must involve study across academic disciplines." Until the middle of the twentieth century, African and African-descended musical forms were often characterized stereotypically as "primordial," "rhythmic," and "emotive." However, anthropological research like that of Melville Herskovits began to challenge these stereotypes in profound ways. Emerging as it did in the 1950s, ethnomusicology has been shaped by the Herskovitsean model. Indeed, Butler argues that "the musical link between Africa and its diaspora has been one of the most prevalent themes throughout the history of ethnomusicological thought." At the same time, some ethnomusicologists have begun to move beyond questions of African musical "retentions" and "creativity" in slave communities, noting that intraregional dialogue, like that between African-descended peoples and Indian-descended peoples in the Caribbean, shapes and transforms musical production. Some of the most recent scholarship in ethnomusicology concentrates explicitly on "intradiasporic" musical practices, for instance, examining the ways that the music of recent African immigrants is played and performed in traditionally "black" spaces in New York City. Here, Butler points to some of the same possibilities for overlapping and conflicting performances raised by Richards in her essay. Again, the relationship between the local and the global remains most salient.

In chapter 11, Moyo Okediji also calls attention to the overlapping "contentions of race, gender, class, and religion" in Africana art history. According to Okediji, Africana art history is divided into three categories—historical African, contemporary African, and diaspora. Each of these is separated by a veil "that dismembers the object on view from the subject that is viewing it." For historical African art history, this veil is slavery; for contemporary African, the veil is colonialism; and for the diaspora, it is immigration. Tracing the historiography, Okediji reveals the hidden and silenced expressions of slavery, colonialism, and immigration in Africana art. He also shows us how art history maps these erasures onto other contentious categories such as gender, class, and so on. Ultimately, like many of our authors, Okediji views Africana art history as deeply contested political terrain that articulates oppressive elements of slavery, colonialism, and immigration, even as it systematically silences them as explicit categories of analysis. He calls for new methods and theoretical approaches to address the asymmetrical power of Western "relativist traditional art history." In particular, he prescribes a semiological system that highlights the values of equity and justice, reading context and subtext equally to provide a balanced political assessment of visual culture.

Grant Farred's essay on Cultural Studies, elaborates on the political concerns raised in Okediji's chapter and in nearly all of the chapters in this volume. In his opening sentence, Farred asserts, "The singular claim of Cultural Studies is that there can be no project of the political, no thinking of the political, without culture, without the study of culture at its core." Cultural studies' dependence on explicit political projects as its raison d'être forces its practitioners to think outside of "orthodox" disciplinary contexts. Thus cultural studies becomes a series of dislocations, mirroring those of the African diaspora. In Farred's rendering, African diaspora subjects are always "out of context . . . articulated to, disarticulated from, and rearticulated through a context that is outside of the place from where the subject speaks." Likewise, cultural studies lies squarely outside of "pure" disciplinary contexts, even as it capaciously draws from them, responding to the political imperatives of the moment. For Farred, "cultural studies and the African diaspora can do more than learn from each other. . . . Thinking them together demonstrates how these two modes of critical thinking, this poacher's discipline and this political condition that is increasingly crucial to the lives of people throughout the world, are conceptually constitutive of each other." Through his analytical braiding of cultural studies and African diaspora, Farred reinforces the demands for a diaspora scholarship that is politically driven, considering local, national, and global forces, as well as overlapping ones related to race, gender, sexuality, and the environment.

In keeping with Farred's theme of the African diaspora as "out of context," the final section of this volume considers the impact of diaspora scholarship in spaces outside the American institutional and political spheres of influence. Carolyn Cooper's chapter on the African diaspora in the Creole-Anglophone Caribbean follows Farred's call to read diaspora "out of context." In the first half of her essay, she analyzes Jamaican dancehall culture as a ritualized form of African female sexuality and fertility. Rejecting representations of dancehall as "obscene," "vulgar," and "pornographic," Cooper "recontextualizes" working-class women's roles in dancehall to cohere with Yoruba fertility rituals and celebrations of sexuality, allowing these women to "assert the freedom to play out eroticized roles that may not be available to them in the rigid social conventions of the everyday." She then turns to more practical matters of the way the African diaspora is conceptualized and taught in Jamaican universities. The African and African Diaspora Studies program at the University of the West Indies emerged out of the already existing Institute for Caribbean Studies. No new courses were added, and no attempt was made to distinguish African and African Diaspora Studies from African American Studies or Caribbean Studies. Rather, extant courses on themes related to Africa and the Caribbean were brought together to create a new comparative, interdisciplinary major.

Xolela Mangcu reminds us that the concept of the African diaspora is not merely an "oceanic" phenomenon; it retains salience on the African continent, too. The notion of an "African Renaissance," articulated most

forcefully by former South African president Thabo Mbeki, bears a striking resemblance to scholarly articulations of the African diaspora. Indeed,
Mbeki often invoked the history of the diaspora to contextualize South
African struggles. Yet Mangcu asks whether Mbeki and others like him,
who forged their consciousnesses in exile, could actually achieve a "syn-
thesis of diasporic and continental" identity. Tracing an intellectual history of diaspora identity in South Africa from the nineteenth century,
Mangcu concludes that the current expression of diaspora identity—the
African Renaissance—is devoid of cultural content, betraying an earlier
Pan-African tradition in the country. According to Mangcu, the African
Renaissance is little more than a proxy for economic development discourse, a tool selectively wielded by the state to define an essential "African" in lockstep with the ruling party's economic and political agenda.
Like many of our authors, Mangcu calls for more active involvement of
civil society in defining the contours of diaspora politics and scholarly
production.

In the final chapter of the volume, Jayne Ifekwunigwe turns our at-
tentions to perhaps the least likely venue for expressions of African diaspora intellectual production—Europe. In the popular and scholarly imagination, nothing could be further "out of context" than diaspora subjects
in Europe. Ifekwunigwe explains this not simply as a problem of assert-
ing transnational "African-ness" but also as a problem of locating a singular "Europe." Afro-Europeans are often divorced from the potent political formations that emerged out of the common American experience
of the African slave trade. Internal to "Europe," they also grapple with differing national expressions of racism, sexism, class discrimination, and
religious intolerance. This is to say nothing of the profound national divisions of language, culture, and history. In this way, "Europe" is no more
stable than "Africa." Still, Ifekwunigwe shows how "strategic identification with 'Blackness'" is sometimes utilized to forge transnational diasporic projects like the Black European Studies Program (BEST). In Europe, especially, Ifekwunigwe argues for conceptions of diaspora that are
"dynamic, interlocking, interdependent global networks of geopolitical
spheres each of whose localized intersectional constituencies are also sensitive to and impacted by the political machinations of the nation-states
of which they are a part." In short, diaspora is a process of overlapping local, national, and global interests. In her analysis of contemporary African
migrants to Europe, Ifekwunigwe reminds us that this process is ongoing,
intimately connected to the politics of the past, but expressing new racial,
gendered, and class configurations. Finally, Ifekwunigwe raises the important question of whether the institutional power of U.S. universities dic-
tates the contours of African diaspora "centers" and "peripheries." Indeed,
she criticizes the editors of this volume for reifying the "already margin-

alized status" of African Diaspora Studies outside the United States, gathering the "international" dimension of the diaspora under a single banner.

Ironically, our rationale for examining international responses to the African diaspora accords exactly with Ifekwunigwe's concerns. The United States has become the institutional hub for study of THE African diaspora, often absent the voices of the diaspora "subjects" American scholars claim to represent in their research. Thus we thought it imperative to draw upon some of those voices "out of context," beyond the boundaries of American "institutional might." As Cooper shows, Caribbean institutional engagement with the African diaspora largely mimics the American, albeit with strong Caribbean inflections. Likewise, Mangcu demonstrates that the African diaspora, in the guise of the African Renaissance, is actually a political liability for broader civic engagement in South Africa. Ideally, we would have liked more essays such as these, ones that call into question the very efficacy of the American intellectual project of African Diaspora Studies and its powerful (or not so powerful) impacts on local actors. To assume that the study of the African diaspora has similar valences in the various spaces that constitute the diaspora is to ignore the diverse intellectual and political traditions of those spaces. Take, for example, Brazil. Despite boasting the largest population of African-descended peoples outside of the African continent (more than 75 million people, nearly 45 percent of the total population), the *idea* of the African diaspora is only just beginning to register on the Brazilian academic radar. One of the preeminent scholars of the Afro-Brazilian experience, João José Reis, recently stated, "The idea of an African diaspora is primarily a discourse associated with black militant discourse in Brazil and has yet little conceptual resonance in our historiography. In Brazilian historiography, the 'black diaspora' is used more as a catchword than an elaborated concept. This is interesting given the enormous preoccupation with 'African origins' in the fields of history and anthropology in Brazil."[4]

Until recently, the explicit study of Africa and its diaspora was all but nonexistent in Brazilian universities, with the exception of three research centers, located in Bahia (CEAO), São Paulo (CEA), and Rio de Janeiro (CEAA). In large part due to pressure from Brazilian scholars and activists, this situation is beginning to change. In 2003, the federal government passed legislation requiring the teaching of African and Afro-Brazilian culture and history in all elementary and middle schools. As a result, enrollment in Africa-related courses at Brazilian universities has risen dramatically; likewise, graduate programs in African studies have surged.[5] Some would argue that these new developments are little more than American racial concerns artificially and ahistorically implanted onto the Brazilian landscape as a new form of cultural imperialism.[6] Others see a direct correlation between expressions of African diaspora con-

sciousness and broader global struggles against social, economic, and political inequalities that rend Brazilian society in very unique and peculiar
(often racialized) ways.[7] Thus, just as with other political projects of the
African diaspora, local, national, and global imperatives overlap in ways
that inform scholarship and activism, often "out of context."

Ultimately, whether in Brazil, South Africa, Europe, or even Asia,
Ifekwunigwe is correct that "any comparative interrogations of African
diasporas . . . must be interdisciplinary, historically grounded, ethnographically situated, and mindful of institutional hierarchies and infrastructural
deficits that contribute to the perpetuation of hegemonic discourses." The
United States claims no monopoly on the intellectual production or political contours of the African diaspora. As this volume demonstrates, no
discipline can claim a monopoly on the diaspora either. The diaspora is
often silenced in disciplines such as geography, sociology, political science, and philosophy. Part of this erasure relates to the influence of neoliberal philosophies of the past thirty years, which all too easily lend
themselves to reifying old patterns of racism and colonialism, as much as in
the academy as in the larger global community. Yet this marginalization
is not inevitable. On the contrary, the potential exists at an interdisciplinary and international level for politically informed scholarship that
challenges dominant epistemologies, centering an Africana intellectual
tradition in cooperation with local, national, and global actors. To that
end, this volume invites scholars with interests across disciplines and
across geographic space to engage one another "out of context," in the diasporic space that is at once liminal and potentially liberating from the
boundaries of space and "discipline."

NOTES

1. See, for example, the following handy library of monographs, articles, collections of essays, and journal special issue: Hamilton (2006, 2007), Gomez (2004,
2006), Akyeampong (2000), Byfield (2000), Butler (2002), Gilroy (1993), Harris
(1982), Hunwick and Powell (2002), Hine and McLeod (1999), Palmer (1998), Okpewho, Davies, Manning (2003, 2009), Mazrui (1999), Lovejoy (1997), Patterson and
Kelley (2000), Thompson (1987), and Terborg-Penn and Rushing (1996). Diaspora
studies, conceived as a general umbrella for the study of various dispersed populations, is itself now a growing field. In 1991, *Diaspora: A Journal of Transnational
Studies*, the first academic journal of its kind, began publication. See also Cohen
(1997) and Radhakrishnan (1996).

2. In a very interesting way, the rise of transnational studies such as diaspora
studies has also coincided with an usually renewed vigor in the critique of the disciplines and disciplinarity: their inherently provincial focus, their sometimes too-
easy slip into methodological rigor mortis, and their immense capacity for cynical
self-reproduction and preservation through the now almost divine perception of
"departments" as the only time-proven and most effective method of organizing

the production, management, and dissemination of knowledge. Terms such as "interdisciplinary," "multidisciplinary," and "transdisciplinary" have emerged as alternative and supposedly more enabling approaches. The most used and misused of these terms is "interdisciplinary," to which is applied every routine gesture against every perceived stricture by the disciplines. "Multidisciplinary" gives too much of an impression of a jolly collection or meeting of different and separated disciplines, while "transdisciplinary" suggests too fancifully that it is possible and desirable to get beyond the disciplines. Notwithstanding its overly common use to the point of being merely gestural, we are working here with "interdisciplinary" and insist that it has hardly exhausted its critical possibilities. The inherent ambiguity of the prefix "inter-" as capable of simultaneously signifying both connection and separation best suits our stated modest goal of initiating serious dialogue across the disciplines on African Diaspora Studies from the vantage point of deep knowledge of our particular disciplinary locations. "Interdisciplinary" in this case authorizes critical dialogue and enables the production of a knowledge that may be but is not necessarily bound by the disciplines, a sort of knowledge that makes for simultaneous and multiple disciplinary identification and disconnection. On debates and discussions about disciplines and disciplinarity, see Moran (2006), Klein (1990, 2005), Feller (2007), Frodeman and Mitcham (2007), Somerville and Rapport (2002), and Messer-Davidow, Shumway, and Sylvan (1993). See also the useful site www.interdisciplines.org.

3. The two-day conference in March 2006, sponsored by the African Diaspora and Atlantic World Research Circle at the University of Wisconsin–Madison, brought together scholars representing more than a dozen disciplines.

4. Caulfield (2008), 20.

5. Zamparoni (2007).

6. See, for instance, Bourdieu and Wacquant (1999).

7. The Bourdieu and Wacquant article engendered a number of responses from American and Brazilian scholars alike. See, for example, French (2000, 2003), Healey (2003), and the special edition of the Brazilian journal *Estudos Afro-Asiáticos* 24, no. 1 (2002) devoted entirely to this debate.

BIBLIOGRAPHY

Akyeampong, Emmanuel. 2000. "Africans in the Diaspora: The Diaspora and Africa." *African Affairs* 99.395: 183–215.

Bourdieu, Pierre, and Loic Wacquant. 1999. "On the Cunning of Imperialist Reason." *Theory, Culture, and Society* 16: 41–58.

Butler, Kim. 2002. "Defining Diaspora, Refining a Discourse." *Diaspora* 10: 189–219.

Byfield, Judith, ed. 2000. Special issue on the diaspora. *African Studies Review* 43, no. 1 (April).

Caulfield, Sueanne. 2008. "In Conversation with . . . João José Reis." *Perspectives on History: The Newsmagazine of the American Historical Association* 46. Accessed at www.historians.org/Perspectives/issues/2008/0801/0801con1.cfm.

Cohen, Robin. *Global Diasporas: An Introduction*. Seattle: University of Washington Press, 1997.

Feller, Irwin. 2007. "Interdisciplinarity: Paths Taken and Not Taken." *Change* 39, no. 46–51.

French, John D. 2000. "The Missteps of Anti-Imperialist Reason: Bourdieu, Wacquant, and Hanchard's *Orpheus and Power.*" *Theory, Culture, and Society* 17: 107–28.

———. 2003. "Translation, Diasporic Dialogue, and the Errors of Pierre Bourdieu and Loic Wacquant." *Nepantla: Views from the South* 4: 375–89.

Frodeman, Robert, and Carl Mitcham. 2007. "New Directions in Interdisciplinarity: Broad, Deep, and Critical." *Bulletin of Science, Technology, and Society* 27, no. 6: 506–14.

Gilroy, Paul. 1993. *The Black Atlantic: Modernity and Double Consciousness.* Cambridge: Harvard University Press.

Gomez, Michael. 2004. *Reversing Sail: A History of the African Diaspora.* New York: Cambridge University Press.

———. 2006. *Diasporic Africa: A Reader.* New York: New York University Press.

Hamilton, Ruth Simms, ed. 2006. *Routes of Passage: Rethinking the African Diaspora.* East Lansing: Michigan State University.

———. 2007. *Routes of Passage: Rethinking the African Diaspora.* Vol. 1, pt. 2. East Lansing: Michigan State University.

Harris, Joseph, ed. 1982. *Global Dimensions of the African Diaspora.* Washington, D.C.: Howard University Press.

Healey, Mark Alan. 2003. "Powers of Misrecognition: Bourdieu and Wacquant on Race in Brazil." *Nepantla: Views from the South* 4: 391–402.

Hine, Darlene Clark, and Jacqueline McLeod, eds. 1999. *Crossing Boundaries: Comparative Histories of Black People in Diaspora.* Bloomington: Indiana University Press.

Hunwick, John, and Eve T. Powell, eds. 2002. *The African Diaspora in the Mediterranean Lands of Islam.* Princeton, N.J.: Markus Wiener.

Klein, Julie Thompson. 1990. *Interdisciplinarity: History, Theory, and Practice.* Detroit: Wayne State University Press.

———. 2005. *Humanities, Culture, and Interdisciplinarity: The Changing American Academy.* Albany: State University of New York Press.

Lovejoy, Paul. 1997. "The African Diaspora: Revisionist Interpretations of Ethnicity, Culture, and Religion under Slavery." *Studies in the World History of Slavery, Abolition, and Emancipation* 1: 1–23.

Manning, Patrick. 2003. "Africa and the African Diaspora: New Directions of Study." *Journal of African History* 44: 487–506.

———. 2009. "The African Diaspora: A History through Culture." New York: Columbia University Press.

Messer-Davidow, Ellen, David R. Shumway, and David J. Sylvan, eds. 1993. *Knowledges: Historical and Critical Studies in Disciplinarity.* Charlottesville: University Press of Virginia.

Moran, Michael. 2006. "Interdisciplinarity and Political Science." *Politics* 26: 73–83.

Okpewho, Isidore, C. B. Davies, and Ali A. Mazrui. 1999. *The African Diaspora: African Origins and New World Identities.* Bloomington: Indiana University Press.

Palmer, Colin. 1998. "Defining and Studying the African Diaspora." *Perspectives* 36.

Patterson, Tiffany R., and Robin D. G. Kelley. 2000. "Unfinished Migrations: Reflections on the African Diaspora." *African Studies Review* 43: 11–50.

Radhakrishnan, Rajagopalan. 1996. *Diasporic Mediations: Between Home and Location.* Minneapolis: University of Minnesota Press.

Somerville, Margaret A., and David J. Rapport, eds. 2002. *Transdisciplinarity: Re-Creating Integrated Knowledge.* Montreal: McGill-Queen's University Press.

Terborg-Penn, Rosalyn, and Andrea Benton Rushing, eds. 1996. *Women in Africa and the African Diaspora: A Reader.* 2nd ed. Washington, D.C.: Howard University Press.

Thompson, Vincent B. 1987. *The Making of the African Diaspora in the Americas, 1441–1900.* White Plains, N.Y.: Longman.

Zamparoni, Valdemir. 2007. "A África e os Estudos Africanos no Brasil: Passado e Futuro." *Ciência e Cultural* 59: 46–49.

PART ONE
HISTORIES

1

CLIO AND THE GRIOT: THE AFRICAN DIASPORA IN THE DISCIPLINE OF HISTORY

Kim D. Butler

Given the multiplicity of expressive languages with which African peoples have encoded, remembered, and recovered their experiences, it may seem at first glance counterintuitive to separate the ways of knowing imparted by specific disciplines. Yet, upon closer consideration, it presents an opportunity to assess the analytical tools of those fields to better understand their unique contributions and potential for enhancing the future study of the African diaspora. What follows, then, is not an overview of the historiographic literature but rather an exploration of history's possibilities as a component of the collaboration of many disciplines for research on the African diaspora, and how work in the discipline stands to expand our understanding of diasporas in general.[1]

Upon embarking on this task, I was immediately confronted with a host of challenges faced by historians of the African diaspora. The scope of the historian's work is profoundly shaped by place and timing of training; the types of majors, geographic specializations, and research questions vary greatly by region and era. For scholars of my generation training in the United States in the early 1990s, it was generally necessary to choose a geographic concentration informed by geopolitics and Euro-American cultural constructs.[2] Trained as a Latin Americanist, I therefore come to the project of considering the African diaspora and history with limitations on my ability to fully examine sources and dialogues emerging around the world and in various languages. Rather than attempt to cover all historical literatures, my commentary draws primarily from the examples with which I am most familiar to consider how the discipline has contributed to the study of African diasporas. Specialization in training versus a syncretic analysis of diaspora is a widespread challenge to be discussed in greater detail below, but it is just one of the philosophical problems posed by a project such as this. To consider *the* discipline requires some determination of what constitutes professional history—is it exclusively the academy, or do griots, shamans, and artists inscribe and interpret historical memory in equally valid ways?

THE DISCIPLINE OF HISTORY AND SHIFTING AGENDAS

In an eloquent reflection on the discipline of history, anthropologist Michel-Rolph Trouillot details how the Haitian Revolution, so transformative in world history, has been virtually erased from collective memory.[3] Far from an innocent retrieval of "the past," history is a decidedly political endeavor with significant implications for making or destroying mechanisms of power and social control. Whether practiced by professionals within the griot, imbongi, gnawa, or Western academic traditions, the work of historians has always reflected contemporary concerns and contexts.[4] Historians access the past to resolve issues in the present (including the creation of social ideologies) and to provide direction for future action. The present also helps determine who gets to become professionalized and what types of research questions are institutionally supported.

The American Historical Association published a report in 2004 describing the discipline of history as the use of empirical evidence as a basis for "the imaginative construction of narratives that are explicitly referential." It went on to speak of history's primary agenda "to examine the human experience over time, with a commitment to the explanatory relevance of context, both temporal and geographical."[5] Historiographic philosophies differ in their interpretation of what constitutes valid evidence and the individual historian's relationship to that material as well as his or her audience. What is constant across cultures and approaches is that the way history is practiced and disseminated reveals much about the structure, power relationships, and pressing issues of a given society. One can read shifts in the profession as indicative of changes in society at large.

In that regard, the writing of African diaspora history is also a record of changing realities. Developments within the African diaspora itself were to affect the ways it entered the written historical record. The dissolution of slavery in the Americas and the Caribbean, the partitioning of Africa, and the encroachment of colonialism thereafter led to a major series of relocations among the people touched by those developments. Africans and African descendants flocked to new "diaspora capitals"—urban centers of industrial and manufacturing employment; cosmopolitan hubs such as New York, London, Paris, and Rio de Janeiro, where domestic work was plentiful and the economy diverse; and remote sites of capitalist entrepreneurship like the Panama Canal and transcontinental railroad projects. Unlike the dispersals of the slave era, these secondary migrations occurred at a time when travel and communications were greatly facilitated. Not only were people legally owners of their own bodies, but steamships, newspapers, photography, and telegraphs were allowing communities to become and remain interconnected in unprecedented ways.

The question of whether these factors alone may have been enough to engender a diaspora consciousness throughout the global African world speaks to a fundamental debate about diaspora. If diasporas exist based simply on culture and shared history, such opportunities for transnationalism would be sufficient to sustain a vibrant diaspora. However, there is also an intrinsically political aspect of diaspora, a particular type of mobilization utilized to effect a particular activist agenda. As opportunities for communication increased, it became easier to rally in common cause against atrocities visited upon African peoples which could not help but demand redress. Examples abound. The Panama Canal project consumed countless black bodies working on a discriminatory wage scale. King Leopold's agents were lopping off black hands in a gruesome count of the price of turning a sovereign land into his personal rubber export venture. The partitioning of Africa and the rise of colonial regimes, the lynchings in the United States, the legal barriers to post-abolition opportunities, the substitution of immigrant labor to displace blacks, the establishment of apartheid—these were all understood within a race logic that inseparably linked Africa and its descendants. Ironically, this was also a time when American and Caribbean peoples of African descent were seeking to articulate their "rightful share" as citizens of the nations they had helped create, but which were now seeking to marginalize their blackness.[6]

These combined factors (diaspora capitals, communication, common political cause, and racial exclusion) gave rise to a flourishing of pan-Africanist consciousness, within which specific diasporas also came of age. The period from the late nineteenth century through the first decades of the twentieth century produced the first significant corpus of African diaspora history, preceding by several decades the wide usage of the term "African diaspora."

DEFINING DIASPORA IN THE PAN-AFRICANIST ERA

At the 1965 meeting of the International Congress of African Historians in Tanzania, Joseph E. Harris introduced a session with a talk titled "Introduction to the African Diaspora." That session included George Shepperson's paper, "The African Abroad or the African Diaspora," frequently cited as the first widely circulated usage of the term within the discipline of history. The proceedings suggest that the term was already gaining popularity; Harris commented that the original title of their session was to be "The African Abroad," and Shepperson noted that the term "African diaspora" was increasingly circulating as a way to describe the dislocations and resettlements of the Atlantic slave trade.[7] Shepperson's juxtaposition of the phrases as interchangeable harkens back to much earlier conceptualizations of an interrelated global African community. As early as 1913, the term "African Abroad" appeared in the title of a work by an African American lay historian, William H. Ferris.[8] Africa had long figured prominently in the imagination of its departed millions; the importance of the Dar es Salaam meeting was that it situated the diaspora as essential to the understanding of African history.

As pan-Africanism emerged as a transnational political agenda, so too did diasporic historiography. Much of this work emerged in cosmopolitan diaspora capitals, where artists and intellectuals from the continent and the diaspora converged.[9] Self-taught and professionally trained historians alike produced a wealth of literature documenting the ongoing relationships, interrelated histories, and shared concerns of Africans both on the continent and abroad. This literature is perhaps best seen as a product of an emerging diaspora consciousness and politics rather than an examination of the phenomenon of diaspora community formation. Their work, with strong implications for both local and international contemporary politics, emphasized themes also associated with what came to be known as Afrocentricity by the 1980s, but whose roots reached back to the nineteenth century.[10] These themes included the need to prove African civilization and the dignity of its ancient heritage, a mandate to reinsert Africa into the canon of "Western" antiquity as the source of Western traditions, and a call to argue for the global African community's role in the continent's future.[11] This was history with an explicit agenda, as Charles V. Roman expressed in the title of his 1911 volume, *A Knowledge of History Is Conducive to Racial Solidarity.*

While some of this early literature was explicitly pan-Africanist, it may also be understood broadly as a global African historiography framed by race. It may be argued that "black" history in the United States has always been considered within the framework of diaspora. The first three professionally trained black historians in the United States (W. E. B. Du Bois, Carter G. Woodson, and George Haynes) all assumed an interrelated black/African world. Woodson, who often had less than fraternal relationships with fellow historians throughout his professional life, played a major role in setting African American history within a global context. His book *The Negro in Our History* had nineteen editions, to include new research being published in the *Journal of Negro History*, and it was the most definitive textbook on African American history prior to the publication of John Hope Franklin's *From Slavery to Freedom* in 1947.[12] The *Journal* was a fount of information on global black history.[13] Woodson was the founder and guiding light of the Association for the Study of Negro Life and History (ASNLH), organized in 1915, and the creator of Negro History Week (now Black History Month).

Because history is not a discipline requiring extensive equipment, laboratories, or complex computer programs, there was also a vibrant and influential lay historical tradition alongside the work of university-trained historians. Professional history had ignored or misrepresented the black subject, compelling African descendants to rely on their own inscriptions and interpretations of their past. In 1897, Alexander Crummell founded the American Negro Academy with the aim of fostering the study of Africa and its descendants. By the 1880s, there already existed what Ralph Crowder has described as a "thriving Black history movement," which considered the histories of Africa and the diaspora outside the United States as parts of an integrated whole.[14] Though undoubtedly focused on justifying respect and equity in the local context, the positing of transnational community is itself a defining gesture of diaspora politics.[15] What is significant here is that, in the process, it also generated a significant diaspora historiography. The flagship publication of the era was George Washington Williams's *History of the African Race in America* (1883); other titles also set African American history in a global context.[16]

Four years prior to ASNLH, Arturo Alfonso Schomburg and John Edward Bruce, among others, had founded the Negro Society for Historical Research. Although not trained in the academy, its members were among the most prolific and widely read authors on the black experience. Significantly, they were themselves products of diasporic encounters who then extended their global sensibilities to a wider public through their writings in popular community newspapers. John Edward Bruce (known by his newspaper byline of Bruce "Grit") was an ardent advocate of transnational solidarity. In a 1905 article, he declared, "There are Negroes and colored men in America who hold with white men—alleged scholars— that no good thing can come out of Africa, or has come out of it. . . . We ought to be like the white man, claim everything good, useful, or great, animate or inanimate that originated with the black race."[17]

It is important to note that the racialized conceptualization of the diaspora held most sway among those it most marginalized.[18] It was also useful as a rallying point for mobilizing potential power. One sees an explicitly black African diaspora historicized in the black popular press in locations where racial pressures were high, most notably in the *Negro World*, the publication of the Universal Negro Improvement Association. Also significant is that transnational community was articulated from centers where African peoples of diverse origins encountered each other, as was the case with the seminal pan-Africanist writings out of Paris. The political orientations of these early expressions of diaspora consciousness encompassed a range from local claims of citizenship to global black/ African nationalism.

The dislocations that created the modern African diaspora were so vast in scope that the notion of "Africans abroad" has long been quite vivid in historical memory and representation. In the West, racialized practices, and slavery in particular, tied to a pan-continental conflation of Africa, sustained identities and identifications of succeeding generations as Africans-in-diaspora rather than as assimilated immigrants to their respective destinations. Thus there has always been an awareness of an African diaspora in the writings of both professional and lay historians. Also, history has been a significant tool used to support the political project of alliance-building between communities of Africa and the diaspora, as well as with other groups of common interests. The forging of diaspora cannot be separated from its representation and usage by historians; the very act of writing diaspora history has helped formulate diaspora consciousness and, by extent, a popular understanding of what diaspora is.

To illustrate this point, it is instructive to compare the historiography of the African diaspora in the Atlantic Ocean with that of the Indian Ocean/Asia branch. Until recently, very few works framed African dispersals to Asia as "diaspora"; significantly, their experiences also varied in the ways in which race and ethnicity were framed. In January 2006, a major conference on the African Diaspora in Asia set in motion a host of new research initiatives, including participation in an Asian division of the UNESCO Slave Routes Project. One report noted the differing agendas of the scholars and the Siddi (Indians of African descent) delegates, commenting, "Participation in a conference on the African diaspora in Asia no doubt invites expressions of 'diasporic identity.'" The report suggests that UNESCO's involvement will add the Asian branch to the history of forced migration to the Atlantic world and throughout Africa, raising the issue of how institutional priorities (in this case on slave routes) may de-emphasize other modalities of African dispersals.[19]

CONVERGENCES

The emergence of the African diaspora as a specialization within history is a result of the convergence of several developments within the discipline, along with scholarship in other disciplines that would influence the work of historians. The Dar-es-Salaam conference in 1965 was a call to Africanists to incorporate the diaspora as a component of the continent's history, and indeed, much of the new generation of scholarship emerged from Africanist circles. That same year, the preeminent School of Oriental and African Studies in London created the Centre of African Studies. As those institutions were reframing their work from their imperialist origins in the era of African independence, a new cadre of scholars was emerging in the United States.[20]

From their base at the University of Wisconsin–Madison, Jan Vansina and Philip D. Curtin spearheaded professional Africanist history in the

United States and, along with regional specialists such as Thomas Skid-more, helped produce global framings of African history relevant to di-aspora studies. Curtin's 1969 book, *The Atlantic Slave Trade: A Census*, proved to be a seminal text for studies of the diaspora in the Americas in that it provided a quantitative portrait of the origins and destinations of Africans in the Americas (though it also provoked great debate). Wis-consin's significance was not just the scholarly production of students and faculty but also the development of a well-placed intellectual com-munity. In the acknowledgments of his book, *Recreating Africa*, histo-rian James H. Sweet tells of an encounter with Philip Curtin, who had taught Sweet's professor, Colin Palmer. When Curtin greeted Sweet as one of his "grandchildren," he called to mind the familial structure of pro-fessional historical circles.[21] Academic mentors create lineages through which particular approaches and ideas circulate to successive "genera-tions." When supported with institutional backing (i.e., scholarships and professorships), some of these lineages can grow into influential profes-sional networks; in this case, scholars connected to Wisconsin were to con-tribute significantly to the shaping of African diaspora historiography.[22]

Those who trained at Wisconsin during this time published a series of important works in African diaspora history. As Sweet notes, what distin-guished these students, as well as a widening circle of other young histo-rians, was their sensibility to the global scope of African histories. With a solid foundation in African history applied to research both on the con-tinent and in the diaspora, they gathered extensive empirical data on the nuts and bolts of Africa's evolving roles within the modern world system, particularly as related to the Atlantic slave trade.[23] It was this circle of scholars that began popularizing the construct of diaspora in relation to the migrations and communities they were documenting in African ex-perience.

The work of these scholars represented the convergence of several areas of scholarship. In anthropology, Melville Herskovits had elaborated theories of culture change and regeneration that both shaped and antici-pated later works on diaspora. He mapped diasporic movements through his outline of African "culture zones" that were discernible in Afro-American communities, which he saw as an integral and interrelated unit.[24] Such a context informed the work of Arthur Ramos, Roger Bastide, and Zora Neale Hurston, among others. Caribbeanists were also devel-oping a comparative Afro-Atlantic analysis as reflected in Eric Williams's seminal *Capitalism and Slavery* and *The Negro in the Caribbean*.

The construct of the "Atlantic world" opened new possibilities for framing the work of U.S. historians, shifting the field away from the pre-viously popular trope of the frontier. It began emerging during the world wars as a rationale for U.S. allegiances to Western Europe, and consoli-dated with the creation of transatlantic organizations such as NATO. This global perspective was also reflected in the development of a "world his-

tory" subfield and the founding of the *Journal of World History* in 1953.
In 1961, the Atlantic Council of the United States was formed to promote
Atlantic cooperation. This organization founded the *Atlantic Community Quarterly* in 1963 and began promoting Atlantic Studies in American
academies "to make certain that the 'successor generation' of leaders was
similarly devoted to the idea of the Atlantic Community." The original deployment of the "Atlantic" was essentially Euro-American. Bernard Bailyn
credits Philip Curtin's *Atlantic Slave Trade* as the turning point for the
serious inclusion of Africa.[25] Curtin later became one of the core faculty
of the Program in Atlantic History, Culture, and Society at Johns Hopkins University, jointly administered by the Departments of History and
Anthropology. The Hopkins program, and a book series at the Johns Hopkins University Press, supported a flurry of scholarship on the Atlantic
world. The Atlantic framework created a space for historians working on
the transcontinental interconnected nature of the Afro-Atlantic diaspora,
previously constrained by geographic fields of specialization.

World history is another emergent new framework within the discipline well suited to the transnational nature of African diaspora research.
However, as an emerging field, its practitioners grapple with many of the
same issues faced by scholars of the African diaspora.[26] History students
are still primarily trained within national and regional constructs that
limit the global literacy necessary for transnational studies. Nonetheless,
all these new specializations represent attempts to break free of such intellectual borders and provide multidisciplinary venues for historians to
enrich their work on the African diaspora.

Around the world, distinct agendas have influenced the trajectory of
African diaspora historiography. In Latin America, it was necessary to
document an African presence to counteract attempts to minimize and
marginalize their impact. That literature was necessarily set within a national context to support their rights as citizens, especially vis-à-vis what
was typically characterized as "backwards" Africa.[27] On the continent,
Donatien Dibwe dia Mwembu describes how a young generation of African scholars faced a different set of pressing agendas in the post-colonial
era. Upon gaining access to the academy, they took on the task of decolo-
nizing the historiography, only to discover how their training and institutional locations were leading them to replicate many of the premises
they had been taught.[28] The relative importance of national versus transnational history was recalled by an African scholar working outside his
home country. As one interviewee asked him, "Okay: you're non-Shona.
Have you finished studying the history of your own country? Why did you
choose Zimbabwe?"[29]

These are some of the academic developments that converged to stimu-
late a dialogue on the African diaspora and possibilities for appropriate
theories and methodologies for its study. The African diaspora session at
the 1965 Dar-es-Salam conference may be considered a turning point for

beginning to consolidate diverse frameworks of analysis into a coherent field of African Diaspora Studies.

THE EMERGENCE OF AFRICAN DIASPORA STUDIES IN HISTORY

Comparative diaspora theory was relatively undeveloped at the time African diaspora began to emerge as a framework in history.[30] However, the very process of doing this work forced scholars to grapple with essential questions concerning diaspora itself, and this is reflected in the theoretical scholarship focused on African Diaspora Studies. Emerging as it did alongside the Black Studies movement, one of the fundamental issues in the field was whether it was "African" or "Black" diaspora at stake. The terms were often used interchangeably, and though there were implicit questions about race and essentialism, relatively little debate ensued in the literature. Each represents a distinct project of interrogation.

As the African diaspora monolith moved toward increasing sophistication, historians developed important tenets of diaspora theory. For example, the methodological demands to examine discrete communities forced scholars to probe the relationship between overarching meta-diaspora constructs and locally lived experience. Also of concern was how Diaspora Studies might better illuminate the histories of women of African descent.[31] Such efforts have helped propel further development of diaspora theory.

Shepperson's early use of diaspora established from the start a comparative perspective that was to characterize African diaspora analysis. Diaspora had been studied most prolifically as a phenomenon of Jewish history, although groups such as Armenians had also applied the concept to their specific experiences. As with others who borrowed diaspora as an analytic framework, Shepperson made the case for its relevance by emphasizing parallels with the Jewish experience of forced migration. He wrote that not all migrations from Africa comprised the African diaspora, which he specifically defined as "the study of a series of reactions to coercion, to the imposition of the economic and political rule of alien peoples in Africa, to slavery and imperialism."[32] Joseph Harris, who chaired the 1965 African diaspora conference session at which Shepperson presented his paper, outlined a more comprehensive view of African Diaspora Studies when he convened the First African Diaspora Institute in 1979. In his introduction to the first edition of the landmark conference volume, *Global Dimensions of the African Diaspora*, he defined African Diaspora Studies as analysis of

> the voluntary and forced dispersion of Africans at different periods in history and in several directions; the emergence of a cultural identity abroad without losing the African base, either spiritually or physically; the psycho-

logical or physical return to the homeland, Africa. Thus viewed, the African diaspora assumes the character of a dynamic, ongoing and complex phenomenon stretching across time and geography.[33]

Eleven years of scholarship, some of which was incorporated in the second edition of *Global Dimensions*, published in 1993, reinforced and expanded this view.

> The African diaspora concept subsumes the following: the global dispersion (voluntary and involuntary) of Africans throughout history; the emergence of a cultural identity abroad based on origin and social conditions; and the psychological or physical return to the homeland, Africa. Thus viewed, the African diaspora assumes the character of a dynamic, continuous, and complex phenomenon stretching across time, geography, class, and gender.[34]

What is significant about Shepperson's and Harris's definitions is that they emphasize the dynamic processes of diaspora—reactions to political oppression, migrations, identity formation, and relationships with homeland(s)—rather than defining African diaspora study in terms of a fixed subject (i.e., *the* African diaspora or, more recently, "diasporic subjects").[35] Indeed, the extraordinary scholarship produced from the 1980s onward documents in rich detail the multiple ways in which diaspora consciousness and politics have been deployed in the history of a global African community.

In the rush of empirical work, attention to epistemological issues lagged behind. A rich canvas was emerging with little guidance on developing diaspora as an alternative analytical frame. Historians, who had long borrowed from scholarship in such fields as anthropology, turned to interdisciplinary efforts to shape an African diaspora epistemology. Beginning in 1988, Harris, along with Mildred Fierce and João José Reis, represented the discipline of history in the interdisciplinary International Advisory Committee of the African Diaspora Research Project, spearheaded by sociologist Ruth Simms Hamilton of Michigan State University. Hamilton's objective was to move to a "more advanced or mature state of diaspora studies" by comprehensively addressing its epistemologies and methodologies.[36]

Paul Gilroy's much-heralded book, *The Black Atlantic*, in 1993 gave visibility to the new framings of African Diaspora Studies, although Gilroy himself did not claim diaspora as his project. Rather, his focus was on black contributions to modernity. Nonetheless, Gilroy provoked historians to stress that African Diaspora Studies were not limited to the Atlantic world, but included multiple diasporic "streams."[37]

Despite these efforts, by 1998, Colin Palmer noted that there had still not been any "systematic and comprehensive definition of the term 'Af-

rican diaspora.'" He proposed a chronological and historical disaggrega-
tion of the diaspora into discrete segments.[38] His approach defined the
modern African diaspora as a population group.

> The modern African diaspora, at its core, consists of the millions of peoples
> of African descent living in various societies who are united by a past based
> significantly but not exclusively upon "racial" oppression and the struggles
> against it; and who, despite the cultural variations and political and other
> divisions among them, share an emotional bond with one another and with
> their ancestral continent; and who also, regardless of their location, face
> broadly similar problems in constructing and realizing themselves. This
> definition rejects any notion of a sustained desire to emigrate to Africa by
> those of its peoples who currently live outside of that continent's bound-
> aries.[39]

Palmer's article helped inform the 1999 annual meeting of the American
Historical Association, which had taken as its theme "Diasporas and Migrations in History." This was, perhaps, the height of diaspora history in
vogue as reflected in the numerous conferences being organized on the
subject.[40] In an attempt to press for further epistemological discussion,
historian Judith Byfield invited a group of scholars to contribute to a special issue of the *African Studies Review*, titled "Africa's Diaspora." The
April 2000 issue featured a forum on an article by historians Tiffany Patterson and Robin Kelley outlining African Diaspora Studies, with a set of
other works engaging diaspora approaches. Patterson and Kelley refrained
from proposing a fixed definition of African diaspora, opting instead to explore the multiple uses of diaspora.[41]

The proliferation of scholarship and projects that explicitly invoked
diaspora in the late 1990s used the concept in diverse ways. On the one
hand, this opened new possibilities for diaspora. On the other, as it was
deployed more and more broadly, it began to lose the specificity necessary
for practical application as an analytical tool. Although scholars from all
disciplines were engaged in the struggle to clarify the uses of diaspora, it
may be useful at this point to address how the particular disciplinary perspective of history informed that ongoing conversation.

THE AFRICAN DIASPORA AS SUBJECT

Colin Palmer's proposed definition challenged historians to clearly identify their subject, a fundamental mandate of a discipline that narrates. Because so much existing scholarship had been identified by conventional
historical specializations as "African" or "African American," there arose
a tendency to define diaspora history as the study of black populations
outside Africa or the United States, distinguishing that corpus of work
from the established subfields. With the vast majority of populations dis-

persed through the Atlantic slave trade residing in Latin America and the Caribbean, those geographic specializations also became an important institutional site for diaspora study.[42] Thus the location of the subjects of study designated such research as "African diaspora."

As *the* diaspora became increasingly understood as a historic subject, questions arose as to exactly who was included in such a term.[43] Not only did this static definition have intellectual limits as an artificially reified construct, but it was not clear how work on specific diasporic communities and movements should relate to considerations of the overall diaspora.

A second issue at stake was the orientation of work defined as African diaspora—did its research questions engage both African peoples and the phenomenon of diaspora? With much of the scholarship centered on negotiations within the swirling currents of race, questions about diaspora in a generic sense were rarely taken up explicitly. One possible distinction between diaspora and "Black" Studies is the centrality of diaspora processes as the analytical focus of study.

The question of defining a diaspora subject, however, cannot be avoided in the discipline of history. With growing awareness of the multiplicity of diasporas in African experience, a critical challenge of African Diaspora Studies became how to engage diaspora constructs at multiple levels simultaneously—an alternative understanding of Earl Lewis's "overlapping diasporas." As new waves of African migration wash onto shores around the world, there are ever more layers of diaspora in which peoples of African descent exist.[44] Whereas individuals may emphasize particular affiliations in their personal lives, they are nonetheless implicated in the pan-diaspora context of race and attitudes about Africa imposed upon them.[45] This point was written in blood on the streets of the Bronx in 1999 when police officers in search of the perennial black male suspect shot forty-one bullets into the body of Amadou Diallo, a newly arrived Guinean immigrant, as he reached for his wallet.[46]

If the twentieth century's problem of the color line has persisted into the twenty-first, diaspora offers an opportunity to place the multiple communities of African transnational experience alongside race, recognizing the disjunctures and unities that, together, comprise the African diaspora. What Du Bois portrayed as a double consciousness in the stark contrast of the Jim Crow/lynching era is today a more fluid ebb and flow of overlapping identities, especially when we take into account the countless regional and individual framings evidenced by all "Africans abroad."

Understanding diaspora as an interplay between sameness and difference provides a vehicle for historians of particular empirical specializations to illuminate a diaspora's common history. As Thomas Holt wrote in 1999,

There is, however, another dimension to the concept of diaspora that is important to our efforts to pursue it in our scholarship. For students of the black diaspora it is the differences among the experiences of differently situated black peoples that is important as well as, or perhaps even more than, the unities or commonalities that define their peoplehood. In other words, invoking the framework of "a diaspora" presupposes that through a comparative analysis there is something to be learned from experiences that unfolded for *different* black peoples in *different* places and times. There is, of course, an obvious tension between these two frameworks—a *sameness* of experience suggested by the political requirements of diaspora and peoplehood, and the *difference* of experience which any analysis and understanding of those experiences requires.[47]

HISTORICAL SUBFIELDS AND THE DISAGGREGATED DIASPORA

The African diaspora is perhaps the most complex of all diasporas. Departures from Africa began at the dawn of human history, and the mother continent has been sending new waves abroad from that time onward. It is a diaspora of multiple destinations from multiple points of origin, such as the Afro-Atlantic, Indian Ocean, and Afro-Caribbean branches.[48] It is also migration from points as discrete as a country or even a specific town.

The scope of pan-diaspora research is so vast that it is most commonly addressed in anthology form, addressing diaspora experience through multiple disciplinary lenses.[49] Historians have been actively involved in those projects. Among the few attempts at a history of the entire diaspora are Michael Gomez's *Reversing Sail* and Patrick Manning's *The African Diaspora: A History through Culture*. However, several single-authored works provide comprehensive treatments of some of the larger segments of the African diaspora, complex diasporas in their own right as multiple origin sites scattered to multiple destinations. Joseph E. Harris's *The African Presence in Asia* and the work of Edward Alpers, among others, cover the eastward movements into the Indian Ocean.[50] In the Afro-Atlantic, Leslie Rout's *The African Experience in Spanish America* addressed its themes in hemispheric perspective, as do several other more recent works.[51] The fact that most pan-diaspora work is anthologized is not simply a reflection on the impossibility of a single person having that degree of expertise (life is not that long!); it speaks also to the fact that diaspora at the meta level is generally most meaningful as context for more local and personal realities.

While it is possible to think broadly about diaspora, the work of historians necessarily requires topical, temporal, and geographic specificity. The particular ways in which those dimensions are framed reveal quite different perspectives on the African diaspora. What follows is a brief consideration of some of the diverse configurations used to frame African diaspora history.

The first follows the contours of the empires involved in African dispersals. This approach fit well within the structure of most history departments and was the framework within which records were generated and archived. A series of seminal texts chronicled the development of the major economic, legal, and social systems through which Africans would travel (although far less attention has been paid to the Ottoman Empire than those based in Western Europe).[52] Much valuable work on the African diaspora put this framework to good use. Alison Blakely, for example, traced African experience in the Dutch world through the lens of racial imagery, framing a portrait depicting figures as diverse as the slaves of Peter Stuyvesant in what would become New York City and Suriname native Otto Huiswood, who became a leading black radical in that same city centuries later.[53] As Africanist scholarship progressed, it became possible to center Africa as distinct diasporas were set in motion within the imperial construct, as illustrated by the work of James Sweet.[54] The imperial framework facilitates consideration of the ongoing relationships of the diverse peoples brought together under these administrative and linguistic rubrics. However, because individuals circulated across empires, and control over certain territories frequently shifted, there are inherent limitations to this approach.

A second framing of African diaspora history focuses on the many African origins of a single destination community. Although this has been used primarily to explore creolization in the Americas, it is equally applicable anywhere. Insofar as these studies examine the migration and transposition of cultures, technologies, and ideologies, they engage that part of diaspora analysis which looks at the dispersal and its implications and the consolidation of a distinct branch or community of the diaspora. What is significant is that scholars working in this field resisted conflating a generic "African" past.[55] Important debates have taken place in this area in regards to the Americas, where constructions of national identity arose from essentialist positings of European, African, and indigenous elements. Also, the degree to which transplanted peoples retained or lost African cultures, argued prominently by Melville Herskovits versus E. Franklin Frazier, continues to figure as a problematic for Americanists. The close analyses of historians into individuals' lives has illuminated the many ways they constructed their own identities within the context of imposed categorizations.[56] Such an understanding of each African diaspora community as a layered yet integral unit is vital for pushing beyond assumptions of monolithic "black" communities to probe their diversity and, in so doing, more accurately reflect the complexities of black experience.

Increased attention to specificity and better empirical data is now permitting yet another framing of diaspora history, whereby a particular African diaspora can be traced to its multiple destinations. By comparing the trajectories of distinct branches, scholars are gleaning new insights into long-standing conundrums such as the reasons for the greater adaptability and successes of certain groups over others. The Yoruba, for example, have been profiled as an individual diaspora.[57] A regional diaspora approach to Central Africans in the Americas offers much needed insight into a large population group whose legacy was less immediately visible than that of more recent arrivals.[58] Their importance, however, was significant.[59] For the Indian Ocean branch, the UNESCO Slave Routes initiative promises to clarify the distinct diasporic streams that took Africans to Asia and the Middle East.

The examples cited above may be considered configurations, or mappings, based on the *structures* of diaspora: homelands, destinations, and branches. It is also possible to frame research projects based on the *processes* of diaspora. With this approach, scholars may highlight such dynamics as return, homeland/diaspora relationships, the mutually influenced evolution of identities in the diaspora and the homeland. Scholarship on homeland/hostland relationships is a rapidly growing field given the rate of recent emigrations from the continent and its implications for African economic policy and development as well as transnational politics.[60] While much of the emerging literature focuses on African-born émigrés, historians offer a longer view of this dynamic.[61]

This is by no means an exhaustive list of possibilities, nor are these categories mutually exclusive. For example, the anthology on the Yoruba diaspora is organized according to its geo-historical structure, but its content closely analyzes diaspora processes. They are highlighted because history requires a narrative contained within some sort of framework, and each of these illuminates distinct perspectives on diaspora experience.

THE INSTITUTIONS OF THE DISCIPLINE: INSCRIBING DIASPORA

Because the material support for research and intellectual dialogue resides primarily in universities and funding agencies, these institutions have played a considerable role in shaping African diaspora epistemology. It is, therefore, useful to examine how particular institutional interventions have channeled the direction of African diaspora work in history. Although there are many aspects that could be examined here, I will simply take a brief look at graduate education, professional activities (conferences, organizations, seminar series), and publishing.

As mentioned above, most graduate programs are organized into traditional geographic, topical, and temporal subfields (e.g., Modern Europe, Latin America, Africa). Because of the relatively smaller faculties in African, Latin American, and Asian history, those fields are rarely subdivided as is common with European history. This facilitates broader ranges of focused training for graduate students, but each of these fields have established tropes into which African diaspora must carve its own niche.

Because the nature of African peoples' history in the modern era is so profoundly marked by diaspora and transnationalism, diaspora questions being explored in any one subfield often demand extension into others. African Diaspora Studies defined in this way required an alternative to the imperial framework that had become a fixture within the discipline. Scholars seeking to trace diasporas from their sites of origin often found it necessary to learn new historiographies as they went along. For dissertations, this usually meant having to rely on recommendations "for further research" outside one's primary area of training.[62] Melina Pappademos, a graduate student in the 1990s, noted that the traditional subfield designations limited the ability of centering African peoples themselves as historical subjects. Addressing the epistemological limitations of colonial boundaries, she wrote:

> The primary [stumbling block] was that academe grouped African descended people by their European and colonially derived relationships (ex: North America, Latin America, South America, and the Caribbean) and not by their Black derived positions. I may have been naive but this seemed problematic to me. Using these categories as points of departure automatically privileges the historical perspective of colonials and national elites and relegates the view(s) of African-descended people to the margins of the very diasporic discourse in which they are supposed to be centered. This process not only shapes the ways in which African Americans are referenced and researched but it totally undermines Diasporic-wide comparative studies. Students are forced to research Blacks solely within a region or nation-state even as they are told they can study "the Diaspora.[63]

Most of the current generation of diaspora scholars have trained outside their areas of graduate work in order to develop a comparative framework that includes the full scope of African Diaspora Studies. That experience is now informing the creation of both individual courses and new subfields that will facilitate graduate training in African diaspora history.

Further complicating diaspora graduate study were the de facto subdivisions within the formal concentration fields. Latin America and the Caribbean are home to the largest African diaspora populations, yet many departments cannot support more than one or two faculty members in the field. This often marginalizes the Caribbean in favor of the "big" countries and topics in Latin America; Haiti is routinely shortchanged despite its importance as the only successful revolt against American slavery.[64] Also, linguistic borders separated the Spanish Americas from other political units and smaller networks such as the once-powerful ambit of the Dutch West India Company (which left a legacy of Dutch-speaking populations in Suriname, Curaçao, St. Maarten, etc.). The transnational reality of the modern world from the colonial era on does not conform so neatly with such boundaries, so it has been necessary for scholars to cross the discipline's divides to follow their subjects. For example, Florida now falls within United States or "African American" history, but African diaspora communities first formed there in Spanish colonies, requiring familiarity with the canon taught in Latin American history.[65]

While the African diaspora is a rapidly developing historical concentration in the United States, the availability of diaspora courses, concentrations, and full majors varies around the world. Perhaps the most extensive academic center for African diaspora history at present is the Harriet Tubman Resource Centre on the African Diaspora within the Department of History at York University in Toronto. The School of Oriental and African Studies in London, given its continental orientation, did not at this writing offer courses specifically dedicated to the diaspora in the discipline of history. In continental Africa, relatively few history departments offer courses on the African diaspora.[66] In Latin America, the participation of African descendants in the academy is disproportionately low; in Brazil, the abysmal rate of African descent representation in universities has persisted for decades.[67] However, important sites of diaspora research have flourished at Bahia's CEAO (Centro de Estudos Afro-Orientais), Rio de Janeiro's Faculdade Candido Mendes, and the Diaspora Studies Program at the Centro de Investigaciones Históricas de América Central at the University of Costa Rica, among others.

Professional activities such as conferences, research centers, and seminar series have been especially central to the development of African diaspora history, particularly because they provide a forum for communication across branches of research. One of the most influential has been what began as the Nigerian Hinterland Project in 1995 under the directorship of Paul Lovejoy. With a generous grant from UNESCO, this project to research slave routes has blossomed into numerous projects around the world, conferences, volumes, and institutions. Conferences on the African diaspora number too many to list here and have led to the publication of anthologies, as well as to the formation of organizations such as the Association for the Study of the Worldwide African Diaspora (ASWAD). Professional groups such as the Association for the Study of African American Life and History and the Association of Black Women Historians have actively sponsored African diaspora scholarship through their publications and activities. One of the oldest institutions for African diaspora history is the Schomburg Center for Research in Black Culture, which offers several research fellowships. In publishing, diaspora series in history have greatly benefited book production. African diaspora history now regularly appears in multidisciplinary journals, and "diaspora" is a standard index term in the principal disciplinary journals.[68] Each of these venues, as it makes its selections, establishes criteria, and defines priorities, contributes to the forging of a canon of African diaspora history.

METHODOLOGY

History has many subfields—not just regional but also in specializations like quantitative and economic history that require distinct methodologies. The discipline has been enriched in recent decades with the methodological tools pioneered for the study of peoples of African descent on the continent and abroad, such as oral history and social history. Diaspora Studies has inherited many of these tools. Social history focuses on the average people, interactions, and institutions that comprise a given community, often referred to as history "from the bottom up." Its techniques have been particularly relevant for Diaspora Studies, because it has helped reconstruct the lives of peoples in conditions of slavery and disenfranchisement for whom the conventional record is scarce.

The lives of those who travel and, in the process, help forge diaspora are an important part of Diaspora Studies that is written primarily through the methodology of biography. Biography, in probing people's motivations and the psychology behind their actions, helps illuminate the imaginings that make and unmake diaspora. For example, the Marcus Garvey Papers project, encompassing the *Negro World* and other UNIA-related contributions of individual members, is compiling a biography of a movement.[69]

Cliometrics, or quantitative history, is a subfield of particular relevance to Diaspora Studies because it has been used to store and analyze the copious extant records on the slave trade. With the advent of accessible computing, it became possible to quantify ships and human cargo using data from all possible sources. Massive databases listing ports of origin and arrival, trade routes, ship names, data on the captives, and other documentation have recently been published by historians.[70] The suddenly available information began to reveal far more detail about the trade and was the most significant development in slave trade documentation since the publication of Curtin's *Atlantic Slave Trade*. Historians have had to be careful not to fall under the spell of numbers that have their interpretive limitations. If a plantation had fifty unimposing Minas and two charismatic and knowledgeable Kongos, the Kongo influences could be far more profound than numbers could reflect, particularly given that culture and tradition can be inherited by future generations.[71] The seductive lure of copious data and research resources centered on the slave trade led to an overemphasis on slavery in early understandings of African Diaspora Studies, but this is now shifting to include other forces that continue to generate African diasporas.

Art history has evolved as a distinct field with its own important literature on the diaspora, such as Robert Farris Thompson's *Flash of the*

Spirit.[72] However, because art history is commonly separated from general history departments, most PhD candidates never receive formal training in the field.

While professional history offers a variety of subfields, scholars studying the African diaspora find that multidisciplinarity is imperative. But does this simply mean reading works by nonhistorians, or is it something more encompassing? Each discipline, both within and without the academy, inscribes its own "way of knowing" that can potentially be tapped to enrich the historian's work. As this volume discusses many of the contributions of many disciplines to African Diaspora Studies, I will limit my remarks to just a few areas for consideration.

First, beyond the scholarship focused on African descendants, there is a large and growing field of Diaspora Studies more generally that is informed by the discipline of history. Originating as disparate bodies of work organized by the group under study (i.e., Jewish, Basque, Armenian, etc.), that work is now cohering as diaspora is considered comparatively as a recurring form of human community. With diasporas becoming increasingly viable as virtual communities, there has been much contemporary scholarship on the economic and political implications of new diasporas and on the migrants themselves.[73] History's orientation toward the past offers an opportunity to consider diaspora in the long *durée*. Such a view allows us to understand the processes that sustain a diaspora over time or that contribute to its dissolution—in other words, the full trajectory of particular diasporas.

Second, the historian probing the archives of the African diaspora will have to venture beyond the word and into the fields of expressive arts. While much important work has been done to situate the arts of the diaspora as a repository of philosophy, social thought, and even political action, it remains a challenge for historians to shape a language and methodology for incorporating expressive culture as source material beyond textual analysis.[74] Dance anthropologist Yvonne Daniel utilizes the term "embodied knowledge" to describe a branch of knowledge, or way of knowing, in which "many African principles and moral values continue to vibrate, and often where other domains of interest—botany, mathematics, philosophy, economics, history, religion, ethics—are revealed and reinforced."[75] Such embodied knowledge, reflected not only in dance but also in facial and corporeal expression, ritual movement, and the martial arts, is a valuable complement to the often scant documentary sources available to historians.

Finally, perhaps one of the greatest challenges for historians will be reconciling Euro-American disciplinary traditions with quite different historical philosophies represented throughout the African diaspora. For example, if the past is understood as the lived experiences of those who are now ancestors, one may take a quite different approach to the inquiry of that past if there are tools available to obtain information directly from those ancestors. The concept of ancestor worship may overshadow what, for historians, is the more fundamental function of ancestor *access*. In his dissertation on the *engolo* martial arts traditions of Central Africa that moved into the diaspora through the Atlantic slave trade, T. J. Desch-Obi discussed how the ancestors' assistance (through mediation) allowed him to probe well beyond the limitations of the written record. After repeatedly being told that "*engolo* comes from the ancestors," Desch-Obi confronted the issue head-on:

> How could I interview the ancestors? I certainly had no written sources I could consult for any time periods earlier than the seventeenth century. When an African wants to find answers to a question that eludes explanation through direct observation, one option is to consult a diviner who can bring these questions directly to the ancestors. Of the many forms of divination in West Central Africa, the most potent and esteemed form is human divination, in which ancestors are called back through ritual processes to enter a medium [*kimbanda*] and speak directly to the client/seeker of answers. . . . Once seated in a medium's head, the ancestors could then literally speak to the living through the medium and answer questions posed by the *kimbanda*'s clients. Although I learned much from Kahavila [a *kimbanda*], the ancestors also answered many of my pressing historical questions through historical linguistics.[76]

He goes on to describe his initiation into a "process that would lead me directly to the thoughts and historical experiences of an ancestral community through the vocabulary of their descendants."[77] In this case, the ancestors guided the historian to an appropriate methodology, but one quite outside the realm of Euro-American conventions. Other interactions with ancestors are somewhat more difficult for the profession to accept as "legitimate." When the ancestral female warrior Mbuya Nehanda was invoked and embodied in a medium during the Zimbabwe independence struggle, was the figure talking and acting Mbuya Nehanda herself or a modern woman merely representing herself as the ancestor?[78] Indeed, African systems of accessing ancestral knowledge are themselves diasporic subjects insofar as practitioners have carried them abroad and have created transnational communities of circulating knowledge.

PUBLIC HISTORY

Throughout recent decades, an emphasis on collegiate professional circles has tended to overshadow the world of public history within the discipline.[79] However, public venues such as museums, television and radio broadcasts, and even popular culture constitute important sites for the representation of African diaspora community and history. Because public history venues need to be responsive to specific audiences, there are sometimes tensions between national exigencies and transnational con-textualizations. The case of slave trade history at Ghana's coastal slave ports, for example, highlighted the quite different needs of Ghanaians and foreign visitors from the diaspora.[80] The extent to which public sites in-scribe commonality or difference, and the ways this is done, is an impor-tant factor in establishing popular sensibilities of diaspora and should be carefully considered as a space for the making of diaspora.

CONCLUSION

Why does African diaspora history matter? Any formulation of commu-nity identity is political; it declares allies, objectives, and foes. A century ago, radical black activists dissatisfied with the hand they were dealt bore witness to the common ills suffered by Africans on the continent and abroad. Today, transnational alliances hold the potential of improving the lives of African peoples and their descendants. There are many fronts to forge such relationships, of which history is but one.

In the end, African diaspora history can only move ahead in the con-text of the combined work of all the disciplines. Professional history has flourished because it continues to adapt new methodologies as was the case with the emergence of Black Studies. Unlike clearly defined ethnic or national subjects, diaspora combines topical, regional, and ethnographic dimensions. Historians face the challenge of claiming subjects who do not themselves identify in the same way and through the same commu-nities, such as African descendants in Asia, the Middle East, and Latin America. Despite the voluminous extant literature, much work remains to be done on the centuries of slave trading that dislocated millions of African peoples, the ways in which those processes forever changed the histories of all peoples, and the continued implications today. Countless other questions remain to be explored.

As old as African diaspora history is, the work of African diaspora his-tory is still quite young.

NOTES

1. Because of the interdisciplinary nature of African diaspora research, a focus on history alone will shortchange significant works in other fields. There are sev-eral excellent overviews of the broader literature, as well as specific subfields of history, including Kelley, "'But a Local Phase of a World Problem'"; Zeleza, "Re-writing the African Diaspora"; Akyeampong, "Africans in the Diaspora"; Vinson, "African (Black) Diaspora History, Latin American History—A Comment"; Pat-terson and Kelley, "Unfinished Migrations"; Patrick Manning, "Africa and the Af-rican Diaspora"; Harris, "Expanding the Scope of African Diaspora Studies."

2. The conventional choices of the United States, Latin America/Caribbean, Africa, and Europe for African diaspora scholars have given way to an increasingly broad range of specialization options at U.S. universities. See discussion later in this chapter.

3. Trouillot, *Silencing the Past.*

4. See, for example, Kaschula, "Imborgi and Griot," and El Hamel, "Constructing a Diasporic Identity."

5. Bender, Katz, Palmer, and the AHA Committee on Graduate Education, *The Education of Historians for the Twenty-first Century*, 4.

6. The phrase is borrowed from Helg, *Our Rightful Share.*

7. The proceedings of the 1965 congress were published as T. O. Ranger, ed., *Emerging Themes of African History.* See Harris, "Introduction to the African Diaspora," in Ranger, *Emerging Themes*, 147, and Shepperson, "The African Abroad or the African Diaspora," in Ranger, *Emerging Themes*, 152. On earlier usages, see Dufoix, *Diasporas*, 11–13.

8. Ferris, *The African Abroad; or, His Evolution in Western Civilization.* Dufoix notes Charles V. Roman's explicit usage of the term "diaspora" to draw a parallel with the Jewish experience in 1917. Dufoix, *Diasporas*, 12.

9. See, for example, Edwards, *The Practice of Diaspora.*

10. Moses identifies early strains of Afrocentrism as early as the seventeenth century in *Afrotopia: The Roots of African American Popular History.*

11. For a more detailed discussion of how diaspora discourse evolved vis-à-vis pan-Africanist discourse and activism, see Edwards, "The Uses of Diaspora."

12. Gates and West, *The African-American Century*; Goggin, *Carter G. Woodson.*

13. Kelley, "'But a Local Phase of a World Problem.'"

14. Crowder, *John Edward Bruce*, 93.

15. Khachig Tölölyan argues that a diaspora's success is contingent, in part, on its ability to direct transnationality to address local concerns. Tölölyan, "Elites and Institutions in the Armenian Transnation."

16. See, for example, Augustus Straker, *Reflection on the Life and Times of Toussaint L'Ouverture* (1885) and Pauline Hopkins, *Primer of Facts Pertaining to the Early Greatness of the African Race* (1905), cited in Crowder, *John Edward Bruce*, 93, 96; Ferris, *The African Abroad* (1913).

17. Cited in Crowder, *John Edward Bruce*, 97–98. Crowder provides a detailed and much-needed account of the work of early lay historians on 91–133, as part of a comprehensive analysis of Bruce's life and work. See also Seraile, *Bruce Grit.*

18. My own research has shown that even in the same country, African descendants deployed race as a political identity primarily when it became a barrier to political, social, and economic mobility. Butler, *Freedoms Given, Freedoms Won.*

19. Van Kessel, "Goa Conference on the African Diaspora in Asia."

20. SOAS was the outgrowth of a long tradition of "orientalist" studies in Britain as a concomitant of the nation's imperial interests. Michael McWilliam analyzes this in regard to Asian scholarship in "Knowledge and Power: Reflections on National Interest and the Study of Asia." An African alumnus reflects on SOAS past and present in Goodwin, "SOAS, a Long 40 Years Ago . . . ," 34.

21. Sweet, *Recreating Africa*, xi.

22. On this phenomenon, see Collins, "Toward a Theory of Intellectual Change."

23. To cite but a few of these works: Knight, *The African Dimension in Latin American Societies*; Palmer, *Slaves of the White God*; Schuler, *Alas, Alas Kongo*; Karasch, *Slave Life in Rio de Janeiro, 1808–1850*; Miller, *Way of Death*; Manning, *Slavery and African Life*. Paul Lovejoy, one of UW–Madison's most prolific alumni, has contributed significantly to the field of African Diaspora Studies through his stewardship of the UNESCO Slave Routes Project and the Harriet Tubman Resource Centre based at York University, Toronto.

24. Herskovits, *The Myth of the Negro Past* and *The New World Negro*.

25. Bailyn, *Atlantic History: Concept and Contours*, 7–11, 32–33.

26. Manning, *Navigating World History*; Dunn, *The New World History: A Teacher's Companion*.

27. See, for example, Garcia, *Afrovenezolanidad e inclusión en el proceso Bolivariano Venezolano*; Duncan and Melendez, *El Negro en Costa Rica*.

28. Mwembu, "History and Memory," 440–48. A highly critical assessment charged that "many [first generation African] historians, inheritors of the professional method, are involved in universities, colleges, and schools, peddling what has been bequeathed to them." Ture and Swai, *Historians and Africanist History*.

29. Mothibe, "Fieldwork among Neighbors."

30. Extensive theoretical work on comparative Diaspora Studies did not appear until the 1990s. See, for example, Hall, "Cultural Identity and Diaspora"; Safran, "Diasporas in Modern Societies: Myths of Homeland and Return"; Clifford, "Diasporas"; Cohen, *Global Diasporas: An Introduction*. Jana Evans Braziel and Anita Mannur have anthologized a diverse set of readings on diaspora theory, along with an extensive bibliography, in *Theorizing Diaspora*.

31. Harris, *Global Dimensions*; Terborg-Penn, Harley, and Rushing, eds., *Women in Africa and the African Diaspora*. Both of these works grew out of conferences: the First African Diaspora Studies Institute (1979) and the 1983 conference of the Association of Black Women Historians, "Women in the African Diaspora: An Interdisciplinary Perspective." A defining characteristic of African diaspora theoretical scholarship is its interdisciplinarity. So, although historians have participated in, and benefited from, the theoretical work, they have rarely considered diaspora exclusively through the lens of the discipline.

32. Shepperson, "The African Abroad or the African Diaspora," 153.

33. Harris, *Global Dimensions of the African Diaspora* (1982), 5.

34. Harris, *Global Dimensions of the African Diaspora* (1993), 3–4.

35. I have argued elsewhere that defining the diaspora in terms of the fixed subject, what I call an "ethnographic" approach to diaspora, creates an inescapable reified box that permits neither the study of dynamic processes nor the multiplicity of situational identities. Butler, "Defining Diaspora, Refining a Discourse," 193.

36. Hamilton, ed., *Creating a Paradigm and Research Agenda for Comparative Studies of the Worldwide Dispersion of African Peoples*, 16.

37. Zeleza, "Rewriting the African Diaspora."

38. Palmer, "Defining and Studying the Modern African Diaspora" (1998), 1.

39. Palmer, "Defining and Studying the Modern African Diaspora" (2000), 30. Palmer's conceptualization of diaspora took on the implicit positioning of African diaspora as synonymous with blacks abroad. His reference to racial oppression signals a definition that does not necessarily include nonblack African nationals, such as Afrikaners, Ugandan Indians, etc.

40. This flurry of activity included not only conferences but also the creation of seminar series such as the Black Atlantic/African diaspora seminars at Rutgers University. In addition to thematic conferences, professional organizations such as the American Historical Association, the Association for the Study of African American Life and History, and the African Studies Association regularly feature African diaspora topics at their annual conferences.

41. Patterson and Kelley, "Unfinished Migrations: Reflections on the African Diaspora and the Making of the Modern World," *African Studies Review* 43, no. 1 (April 2000): 14–15. See also Edwards, "The Uses of Diaspora."

42. It is only recently that historians working in the Latin American field have begun framing their work comparatively as African diaspora study. Ben Vinson III explains how African Diaspora Studies evolved within a Latin American historiographic canon that dealt only tangentially with the black experience. Vinson, "African (Black) Diaspora History, Latin American History." For Caribbean specialists, C. L. R. James's *The Black Jacobins* (1938) and Eric Williams's *Capitalism and Slavery* (1944) set early precedents for global framings of African diaspora histories; the region has a continuing and vibrant tradition of African diaspora scholarship.

43. Indeed, the organizers of the conference for which this chapter was written asked whether historians understood the diaspora to include Africa, or secondary migrations like those from Brazil to Nigeria, or Jamaica to England or Canada as well.

44. Butler, "Multilayered Politics in the African Diaspora: The Metadiaspora Concept and Minidiaspora Realities."

45. This dynamic is explored in detail in Hintzen and Rahier, *Problematizing Blackness.*

46. Diallo and Wolff, *My Heart Will Cross This Ocean.*

47. Holt, "Slavery and Freedom in the Atlantic World."

48. My use of these terms refers to the dispersals from Africa during the transatlantic and Indian Ocean slave trades (Afro-Atlantic and Indian Ocean branches) and the secondary diasporization of African descendants in the Caribbean who moved in the post-abolition era to new opportunities in Latin America, the United States, Europe, and to other destinations within the Caribbean.

49. To list but a few: Harris, *Global Dimensions of the African Diaspora,* 2nd ed.; Hine and McLeod, eds., *Crossing Boundaries;* Okwepho, Davies, and Mazrui, eds., *The African Diaspora and New World Identities;* Jalloh and Maizlish, eds., *The African Diaspora;* Alli, ed., *Africa and the African Diaspora: Aspects of an Experience.*

50. Alpers, "Recollecting Africa." See also Jayasuriya and Pankhurst, eds., *The African Diaspora in the Indian Ocean;* Hunwick and Powell, eds., *The African Diaspora in the Mediterranean Lands of Islam.* Indian Ocean branch scholarship is developing distinct concentrations in India/Asia and the Arabic-speaking Middle East.

51. See Walker, ed., *African Roots/American Cultures*; Moore, ed., *African Presence in the Americas*; Conniff and Davis, *Africans in the Americas*; Andrews, *Afro-Latin America, 1800–2000*; Thompson, *The Making of the African Diaspora in the Americas, 1441–1900.*

52. See, for example, Boxer, *The Portuguese Seaborne Empire, 1415–1825*; Russell-Wood, *A World on the Move*; Postma, *The Dutch in the Atlantic Slave Trade, 1600–1815.* Some of the earlier works, such as Postma's, treated Africans and colonial enslavement only tangentially.

53. Blakely, *Blacks in the Dutch World.*

54. Sweet, *Recreating Africa.*

55. Examples include Hall, *Slavery and African Ethnicities in the Americas*; Gomez, *Exchanging Our Country Marks*; Karasch, *Slave Life in Rio de Janeiro, 1808–1850.* Although I focus here on historians' work, this line of research employs a high degree of interdisciplinarity given the limitations of documentary sources produced during the slave trading era, with significant publications in a variety of disciplines.

56. To cite just a few examples, see Bennett, *Africans in Colonial Mexico*; Nishida, *Slavery and Identity*; Gomez, *Exchanging Our Country Marks*; Bryant, "Slavery and the Context of Ethnogenesis"; Adderley, *New Negroes from Africa.*

57. Falola and Childs, eds., *The Yoruba Diaspora in the Atlantic World.*

58. Heywood, ed., *Central Africans and Cultural Transformations in the American Diaspora.* Another seminal work on this topic from the field of art history is Thompson, *Flash of the Spirit.* A comparison with literary scholar Warner-Lewis's *Central Africa in the Caribbean* helps illuminate the different types of source materials and analyses resulting from diverse disciplinary approaches to the same topic.

59. Vansina, foreword to Heywood, *Central Africans*, xi.

60. The rapid pace of diasporization has made such issues of increasing concern for countries with significant diaspora populations, such as India. For an African case study, see Pires-Hester, "The Emergence of Bilateral Diaspora Ethnicity among Cape Verdean-Americans."

61. For example, Blyden, *West Indians in West Africa, 1808–1880*; Soumonni, "The Afro-Brazilian Communities of Ouidah and Lagos in the Nineteenth Century"; Turner, "Les Brésiliens."

62. For example, Michael A. Gomez, whose book *Exchanging Our Country Marks* contributed to nuancing the African specifics of African American history in the tradition of such scholars as Sterling Stuckey and Gwendolyn Hall, moved far afield from his initial dissertation research. See Gomez, "Malik Sy, Bokar Saada, and the Almaamate of Bundu."

63. Pappademos, "Romancing the Stone: Academe's Illusive Template for African Diaspora Studies."

64. Trouillot, *Silencing the Past.*

65. Rivers, *Slavery in Florida*; Landers, *Black Society in Spanish Florida.*

66. A search of history programs at 100 African universities yielded courses explicitly focused on the African diaspora at Obafemi Awolowo University (Nigeria), Kenyatta University (Kenya), and the University of Malawi. Courses with units on the diaspora were found at the University of South Africa and the University of the Western Cape. This search is preliminary and does not include the franco-

phone universities, nor an extensive review of all academic offerings at these institutions, but does seem to indicate that history departments have yet to fully incorporate Diaspora Studies as part of the common canon. My thanks to research assistant Corbin Laedlein for his work on this project.

67. Telles, *Race in Another America*. A controversial movement to institute racial quotas at Brazilian universities has sought to address these disparities.

68. Journals explicitly focused on African Diaspora Studies include *Contours* (2003–2005) and *African and Black Diaspora*, founded in 2008.

69. Hill, ed., *The Marcus Garvey and Universal Negro Improvement Association Papers*. See also Lewis's *W. E. B. Du Bois: Biography of a Race, 1868–1919* and *W. E. B. Du Bois: The Fight for Equality and the American Century, 1919–1963.*

70. Eltis, Behrendt, Richardson, and Klein, *The Trans-Atlantic Slave Trade: A Database on CD-ROM*; Hall, *Afro-Louisiana History and Genealogy Database*; Eltis and Richardson, eds., *Extending the Frontiers: Essays on the New Transatlantic Slave Trade Database*. See also www.slavevoyages.org.

71. A fine example of how historians have had to grapple with numbers and their interpretation for Diaspora Studies is Falola and Childs, eds., *The Yoruba Diaspora in the Atlantic World*.

72. Another example of using art to trace the diasporization of philosophy as borne in culture is Drewal and Mason, *Beads, Body, and Soul: Art and Light in the Yorùbá Universe*.

73. Some of this research is anthologized in Koser, ed., *New African Diasporas*.

74. The Harlem Renaissance and Negritude cultural movements, and the scholars of those movements, have situated aesthetics and culture as integral to the sociopolitical understanding of global African cultures, particularly given the importance of arts as a vehicle for intellectual and political expression for oppressed populations. See, for example, Nettleford, "The Aesthetics of Negritude."

75. Daniel, "Embodied Knowledge in African American Dance Performance," 352.

76. Desch-Obi, "Fighting for Honor," mss. (2005), 4–5. See Desch-Obi, "Engolo: Combat Traditions in African and African Diaspora History" (PhD diss., UCLA, 2000).

77. Desch-Obi, *Fighting for Honor* mss, 4; Desch-Obi, *Fighting for Honor*, (2008).

78. Michael-Bandele, "The Role of Zimbabwean Women in Zimbabwe's War for Independence and National Development, 1960–1987."

79. Bender et al., *The Education of Historians for the Twenty-first Century*.

80. Bruner, "Tourism in Ghana: The Representation of Slavery and the Return of the Black Diaspora."

REFERENCES

Adderley, Rosanne. *New Negroes from Africa: Slave Trade Abolition and Free African Settlement in the Nineteenth-Century Caribbean*. Bloomington: Indiana University Press, 2006.

Akyeampong, Emmanuel. "Africans in the Diaspora: The Diaspora and Africa." *African Affairs* 99 (2000): 183–215.

Alli, W. O., ed. *Africa and the African Diaspora: Aspects of an Experience.* Jos, Nigeria: Mazlink Nigeria, 1999.

Alpers, Edward A. "Recollecting Africa: Diasporic Memory in the Indian Ocean World." *African Studies Review* 43, no. 1 (2000): 83–99.

Andrews, George Reid. *Afro-Latin America, 1800–2000.* Oxford: Oxford University Press, 2004.

Bailyn, Bernard. *Atlantic History: Concept and Contours.* Cambridge: Harvard University Press, 2005.

Bender, Thomas, Philip M. Katz, Colin Palmer, and the AHA Committee on Graduate Education. *The Education of Historians for the Twenty-first Century.* Urbana: University of Illinois Press, 2004.

Bennett, Herman L. *Africans in Colonial Mexico: Absolutism, Christianity, and Afro-Creole Consciousness, 1570–1640.* Bloomington: Indiana University Press, 2003.

Blakely, Allison. *Blacks in the Dutch World: The Evolution of Racial Imagery in a Modern Society.* Bloomington: Indiana University Press, 1993.

Blyden, Nemata. *West Indians in West Africa, 1808–1880.* Rochester, N.Y.: University of Rochester Press, 2000.

Boxer, Charles R. *The Portuguese Seaborne Empire, 1415–1825.* London: Hutchinson, 1969.

Braziel, Jana Evans, and Anita Mannur. *Theorizing Diaspora.* Malden, Mass.: Blackwell, 2003.

Bruner, Edward M. "Tourism in Ghana: The Representation of Slavery and the Return of the Black Diaspora." *American Anthropologist* 98, no. 2 (1996): 290–304.

Bryant, Sherwin K. "Slavery and the Context of Ethnogenesis: Africans, Afro-Creoles, and the Realities of Bondage in the Kingdom of Quito, 1600–1800." PhD diss., Ohio State University, 2005.

Butler, Kim D. "Defining Diaspora, Refining a Discourse." *Diaspora* 10, no. 2 (2001): 189–219.

———. *Freedoms Given, Freedoms Won: Afro-Brazilians in Post-Abolition São Paulo and Salvador.* New Brunswick: Rutgers University Press, 1998.

———. "Multilayered Politics in the African Diaspora: The Metadiaspora Concept and Minidiaspora Realities." In Gloria Totoricagüena, ed., *Opportunity Structures in Diaspora Relations: Comparisons in Contemporary Multilevel Politics of Diaspora and Transnational Identity,* 19–51. Reno: Center for Basque Studies, University of Nevada, 2007.

Clifford, James. "Diasporas." *Cultural Anthropology* 9 (1994): 302–38.

Cohen, Robin. *Global Diasporas: An Introduction.* Seattle: University of Washington Press, 1997.

Collins, Randall. "Toward a Theory of Intellectual Change: The Social Causes of Philosophies." *Science, Technology, and Human Values* 14, no. 2 (Spring 1989): 107–40.

Conniff, Michael L., and Thomas J. Davis. *Africans in the Americas: A History of the Black Diaspora.* New York: St. Martin's Press, 1994.

Crowder, Ralph L. *John Edward Bruce: Politician, Journalist, and Self-Trained Historian of the African Diaspora.* New York: New York University Press, 2004.

Curtin, Philip D. *The Atlantic Slave Trade: A Census*. Madison: University of Wisconsin Press, 1969.

Daniel, Yvonne. "Embodied Knowledge in African American Dance Performance." In Sheila S. Walker, ed., *African Roots/American Cultures: Africa in the Creation of the Americas*. Lanham, Md.: Rowman and Littlefield, 2001.

Desch-Obi, T. J. "Engolo: Combat Traditions in African and African Diaspora History." PhD diss., UCLA, 2000.

———. *Fighting for Honor: The History of African Martial Art Traditions in the Atlantic World*. Columbia: University of South Carolina Press, 2008.

Diallo, Kadiatou, and Craig Wolff. *My Heart Will Cross This Ocean: My Story, My Son, Amadou*. New York: Ballantine, 2003.

Drewal, Henry John, and John Mason. *Beads, Body, and Soul: Art and Light in the Yorùbá Universe*. Los Angeles: UCLA Fowler Museum of Cultural History, 1998.

Dufoix, Stéphane. *Diasporas*. Berkeley: University of California Press, 2008.

Duncan, Quince, and Carlos Melendez, *El Negro en Costa Rica*. San Jose: Editorial Costa Rica, 1981.

Dunn, Ross. *The New World History: A Teacher's Companion*. Boston: Bedford, 2000.

Edwards, Brent Hayes. *The Practice of Diaspora: Literature, Translation, and the Rise of Black Internationalism*. Cambridge: Harvard University Press, 2003.

———. "The Uses of Diaspora." *Social Text* 19, no. 1 (Spring 2001): 45–74.

El Hamel, Chouki. "Constructing a Diasporic Identity: Tracing the Origins of the Gnawa Spiritual Group in Morocco." *Journal of African History* 49, no. 2 (2008): 241–60.

Eltis, David, and David Richardson, eds. *Extending the Frontiers: Essays on the New Transatlantic Slave Trade Database*. New Haven, Conn.: Yale University Press, 2008.

Eltis, David, Stephen Behrendt, David Richardson, and Herbert S. Klein. *The Trans-Atlantic Slave Trade: A Database on CD-ROM*. Cambridge: Cambridge University Press, 1999.

Falola, Toyin, and Matt D. Childs, eds. *The Yoruba Diaspora in the Atlantic World*. Bloomington: Indiana University Press, 2004.

Ferris, William H. *The African Abroad; or, His Evolution in Western Civilization: Tracing His Development under Caucasian Milieu*. New Haven, Conn.: Tuttle, Moorehouse, and Taylor, 1913.

Garcia, Jesus "Chucho." *Afrovenezolanidad e inclusión en el proceso Bolivariano Venezolano*. Caracas: Publicación del Ministerio de Comunicación e Información, 2005.

Gates, Henry Louis, Jr., and Cornel West. *The African-American Century: How Black Americans Have Shaped Our Country*. New York: Free Press, 2000.

Gilroy, Paul. *The Black Atlantic: Modernity and Double Consciousness*. Cambridge, Mass.: Harvard University Press, 1993.

Goggin, Jacqueline. *Carter G. Woodson: A Life in Black History*. Baton Rouge: Louisiana State University Press, 1993.

Gomez, Michael A. *Exchanging Our Country Marks: The Transformation of African Identities in the Colonial and Antebellum South*. Chapel Hill: University of North Carolina Press, 1998.

———. "Malik Sy, Bokar Saada, and the Almaamate of Bundu." PhD diss., University of Chicago, 1985.

———. *Reversing Sail: A History of the African Diaspora*. Cambridge: Cambridge University Press, 2005.

Goodwin, Clayton. "SOAS, a Long 40 Years Ago . . ." *New African* 403 (January 2002).

Hall, Gwendolyn Midlo. *Afro-Louisiana History and Genealogy Database*. Baton Rouge: Louisiana State University Press, 2000.

———. *Slavery and African Ethnicities in the Americas: Restoring the Links*. Chapel Hill: University of North Carolina Press, 2005.

Hall, Stuart. "Cultural Identity and Diaspora." In Jonathan Rutherford, ed., *Identity: Community, Culture, Difference*, 222–37. London: Lawrence, 1990.

Hamilton, Ruth Simms, ed. *Creating a Paradigm and Research Agenda for Comparative Studies of the Worldwide Dispersion of African Peoples*. East Lansing: Michigan State University, 1990.

Harris, Joseph E. "Introduction to the African Diaspora." In T. O. Ranger, ed., *Emerging Themes of African History*. Dar es Salaam: University College, 1968.

———. *The African Presence in Asia: Consequences of the East African Slave Trade*. Evanston, Ill.: Northwestern University Press, 1971.

———, ed. *Global Dimensions of the African Diaspora*. Washington, D.C.: Howard University Press, 1982.

———, ed. *Global Dimensions of the African Diaspora*. 2nd ed. Washington, D.C.: Howard University Press, 1993.

———. "Expanding the Scope of African Diaspora Studies: The Middle East and India, a Research Agenda." *Radical History Review* 87 (Fall 2003): 157–68.

Helg, Aline. *Our Rightful Share: The Afro-Cuban Struggle for Equality, 1886–1912*. Chapel Hill: University of North Carolina Press, 1995.

Herskovits, Melville. *The Myth of the Negro Past*. New York: Harper, 1941.

———. *The New World Negro: Selected Papers in Afro-American Studies*. New York: Minerva, 1969.

Heywood, Linda, ed. *Central Africans and Cultural Transformations in the American Diaspora*. Cambridge: Cambridge University Press, 2002.

Hill, Robert A., ed. *The Marcus Garvey and Universal Negro Improvement Association Papers*. Berkeley: University of California Press, 1983–95.

Hine, Darlene Clark, and Jacqueline McLeod, eds. *Crossing Boundaries: Comparative History of Black People in Diaspora*. Bloomington: Indiana University Press, 1999.

Hintzen, Percy C., and Jean Muteba Rahier, eds. *Problematizing Blackness: Self-Ethnographies by Black Immigrants to the United States*. New York: Routledge, 2003.

Holt, Thomas. "Slavery and Freedom in the Atlantic World: Reflections on the Diasporan Framework." In Darlene Clark Hine and Jacqueline McLeod, eds., *Crossing Boundaries: Comparative Histories of Black People in Diaspora*, 33–44. Bloomington: Indiana University Press, 1999.

Hopkins, Pauline E. *Primer of Facts Pertaining to the Early Greatness of the African Race*. Cambridge: P. E. Hopkins, 1905.

Hunwick, John, and Eve Trout Powell, eds. *The African Diaspora in the Mediterranean Lands of Islam*. Princeton, N.J.: Markus Wiener, 2002.

Jalloh, Alusine, and Stephen E. Maizlish, eds. *The African Diaspora.* Arlington: Texas A&M University Press, 1996.

James, C. L. R. *The Black Jacobins.* New York: Dial Press, 1938.

Jayasuriya, Shihan de Silva, and Richard Pankhurst, eds. *The African Diaspora in the Indian Ocean.* Trenton, N.J.: Africa World Press, 2001.

Karasch, Mary C. *Slave Life in Rio de Janeiro, 1808–1850.* Princeton, N.J.: Princeton University Press, 1987.

Kaschula, Russell H. "Imborgi and Griot: Toward a Comparative Analysis of Oral Poetics in Southern and West Africa." *Journal of African Cultural Studies* 12, no. 1 (1999): 55–76;

Kelley, Robin D. G. "'But a Local Phase of a World Problem': Black History's Global Vision, 1883–1950." *Journal of American History* 86, no. 3 (December 1999): 1045–77, special issue: "The Nation and Beyond: Transnational Perspectives on United States History."

Koser, Khalid, ed. *New African Diasporas.* New York: Routledge, 2003.

Knight, Franklin. *The African Dimension in Latin American Societies.* New York: Macmillan, 1974.

Landers, Jane. *Black Society in Spanish Florida.* Urbana: University of Illinois Press, 1999.

Lewis, David Levering. *W. E. B. Du Bois: Biography of a Race, 1868–1919.* New York: H. Holt, 1993.

———. *W. E. B. Du Bois: The Fight for Equality and the American Century, 1919–1963.* New York: H. Holt, 2001.

Manning, Patrick. "Africa and the African Diaspora: New Directions of Study." *Journal of African History* 44, no. 3 (2003): 487–506.

———. *The African Diaspora: A History through Culture.* New York: Columbia University Press, 2009.

———. *Navigating World History: Historians Create a Global Past.* New York: Palgrave Macmillan, 2003.

———. *Slavery and African Life: Occidental, Oriental, and African Slave Trades.* New York: Cambridge University Press, 1990.

McWilliam, Michael. "Knowledge and Power: Reflections on National Interest and the Study of Asia." *Asian Affairs* 26, no. 1 (February 1995): 33–46.

Michael-Bandele, Mwangaza. "The Role of Zimbabwean Women in Zimbabwe's War for Independence and National Development, 1960–1987." M.A. thesis, Howard University, 1988.

Miller, Joseph C. *Way of Death: Merchant Capitalism and the Angolan Slave Trade, 1730–1830.* Madison: University of Wisconsin Press, 1988.

Moore, Carlos, ed. *African Presence in the Americas.* Trenton: Africa World Press, 1995.

Moses, Wilson Jeremiah. *Afrotopia: The Roots of African American Popular History.* Cambridge: Cambridge University Press, 1998.

Mothibe, Tefetso Henry. "Fieldwork among Neighbors: An African's View of Another African Country." In Carolyn Keyes Adenaike and Jan Vansina, eds., *In Pursuit of History: Fieldwork in Africa.* Portsmouth, N.H.: Heinemann, 1996.

Mwembu, Donatien Dibwe dia. "History and Memory." In John Edward Phillips, ed., *Writing African History,* 439–64. Rochester, N.Y.: University of Rochester Press, 2005.

Nettleford, Rex. "The Aesthetics of Negritude: A Metaphor for Liberation." In Carlos Moore, ed., *African Presence in the Americas*, 33–54. Trenton: Africa World Press, 1995.

Nishida, Mieko. *Slavery and Identity: Ethnicity, Gender, and Race in Salvador, Brazil, 1808–1888*. Bloomington: Indiana University Press, 2003.

Palmer, Colin A. "Defining and Studying the Modern African Diaspora." *Perspectives* (newsletter of the American Historical Association) 36, no. 6 (September 1998); reprinted, *Journal of Negro History* 85, nos. 1–2 (2000): 27–32.

——. *Slaves of the White God: Blacks in Mexico, 1570–1650*. Cambridge: Harvard University Press, 1976.

Pappademos, Melina. "Romancing the Stone: Academe's Illusive Template for African Diaspora Studies." *Issue: A Journal of Opinion* 24, no. 2, "African Diaspora Studies" (1996): 38–39.

Patterson, Tiffany Ruby, and Robin D. G. Kelley. "Unfinished Migrations: Reflections on the African Diaspora and the Making of the Modern World." *African Studies Review* 43, no. 1 (2000): 11–45.

Pires-Hester, Laura. "The Emergence of Bilateral Diaspora Ethnicity among Cape Verdean-Americans." In Isidore Okpewho, Carole Boyce Davies, and Ali A. Mazrui, eds., *The African Diaspora and New World Identities*, 485–503. Bloomington: Indiana University Press, 1999.

Postma, Johannes Menne. *The Dutch in the Atlantic Slave Trade, 1600–1815*. New York: Cambridge University Press, 1990.

Ranger, T. O. ed. *Emerging Themes of African History*. Dar es Salaam: University College, 1968.

Rivers, Larry E. *Slavery in Florida: Territorial Days to Emancipation*. Gainesville: University Press of Florida, 2000.

Roman, Charles Victor. *A Knowledge of History Is Conducive to Racial Solidarity, and Other Writings*. Nashville, Tenn.: Sunday School Union Print, 1911.

Rout, Leslie B., Jr. *The African Experience in Spanish America*. Rev. ed. Princeton, N.J.: Markus Wiener, 2003. Originally published by Cambridge University Press in 1976.

Russell-Wood, A. J. R. *A World on the Move: The Portuguese in Africa, Asia, and America, 1415–1808*. New York: St. Martin's Press, 1992.

Safran, William. "Diasporas in Modern Societies: Myths of Homeland and Return." *Diaspora* 1 (1991): 83–99.

Schuler, Monica. *Alas, Alas Kongo: A Social History of Indentured African Immigrants into Jamaica, 1841–1865*. Baltimore: Johns Hopkins University Press, 1980.

Seraile, William. *Bruce Grit: The Black Nationalist Writings of John Edward Bruce*. Knoxville: University of Tennessee Press, 2003.

Shepperson, George. "The African Abroad or the African Diaspora." In T. O. Ranger, ed., *Emerging Themes of African History*. Dar es Salaam: University College, 1968.

Soumonni, Elisée. "The Afro-Brazilian Communities of Ouidah and Lagos in the Nineteenth Century." In Jose C. Curto and Renée Soulodre-La France, eds., *Africa and the Americas: Interconnections during the Slave Trade*. Trenton, N.J.: Africa World Press, 2005.

Straker, D. Augustus. *Reflections on the Life and Times of Toussaint L'Ouverture*. Columbia, S.C.: C. A. Calvo Jr., 1886.

Sweet, James H. *Recreating Africa: Culture, Kinship, and Religion in the African-Portuguese World, 1441–1770*. Chapel Hill: University of North Carolina Press, 2003.

Telles, Edward. *Race in Another America: The Significance of Skin Color in Brazil*. Princeton, N.J.: Princeton University Press, 2004.

Terborg-Penn, Rosalyn, Sharon Harley, and Andrea Benton Rushing, eds. *Women in Africa and the African Diaspora*. Washington, D.C.: Howard University Press, 1987.

Thompson, Robert Farris. *Flash of the Spirit: African and Afro-American Art and Philosophy*. New York: Random House, 1983.

Thompson, Vincent Bakpetu. *The Making of the African Diaspora in the Americas, 1441–1900*. Essex: Longman, 1987.

Tölölyan, Khachig. "Elites and Institutions in the Armenian Transnation." *Diaspora* 9, no. 1 (2000): 113–14.

Trouillot, Michel-Rolph. *Silencing the Past: Power and the Production of History*. Boston: Beacon Press, 1995.

Ture, Arnold, and Bonaventure Swai. *Historians and Africanist History: A Critique*. London: Zed Press, 1981.

Turner, J. Michael. "Les Brésiliens: The Impact of Former Slaves upon Dahomey." PhD diss., Boston University, 1975.

van Kessel, Ineke. "Goa Conference on the African Diaspora in Asia." *African Affairs* 105, no. 420 (2006): 461–64.

Vinson, Ben, III. "African (Black) Diaspora History, Latin American History—A Comment." *Americas* 63, no. 1 (July 2006): 1–18.

Walker, Sheila S., ed. *African Roots/American Cultures: Africa in the Creation of the Americas*. Lanham, Md.: Rowman and Littlefield, 2001.

Warner-Lewis, Maureen. *Central Africa in the Caribbean: Transcending Time, Transforming Cultures*. Kingston: University of the West Indies Press, 2003.

Williams, Eric. *Capitalism and Slavery*. New York: Russell and Russell, 1944.

———. *The Negro in the Caribbean*. Washington: Associates in Negro Folk Education, 1942.

Zeleza, Paul Tiyambe. "Rewriting the African Diaspora: Beyond the Black Atlantic." *African Affairs* 104, no. 414 (2005): 35–68.

2 AFRICAN DIASPORA AND ANTHROPOLOGY

Richard Price

> I think the debate over creativity vs. continuity was mostly bootless, and feel sort of sorry it even happened—lot of trees cut down for that one. . . . But since people keep on having to get tenure, perhaps it is unavoidable.
>
> —*Sidney W. Mintz, 2006*

Although W. E. B. Du Bois apparently wrote of the "black diaspora" in *The Crisis*,[1] anthropology, like its sister disciplines, managed to get along without the term "black [or African] diaspora" until quite recently. Indeed, a French anthropologist has just now published a brave book to introduce her countrymen to this foreign concept, not yet part of French academic discourse.[2]

Despite the absence of the term, which even in the Anglophone academy became common only in the final quarter of the twentieth century, the discipline of anthropology can be credited with having pioneered the study of its signifier within the academic arena. From Franz Boas, whose famous speech at Atlanta University in 1906 so encouraged Du Bois, on through to his student Melville J. Herskovits, who devoted much of his life to the study of the "New World Negro," to more recent generations who specialize in "Afro-American anthropology" or the "anthropology of the African Diaspora," the discipline has left its mark, often at the very center of debates within the academy.[3]

Herskovits's seminal ideas about the diaspora evolved in part from interactions with African American scholars who were usually outside the walls of elite universities—U.S. pioneers such as W. E. B. Du Bois and Carter G. Woodson, Cubans such as Fernando Ortiz, and Haitians such as Jean Price-Mars—not to mention Zora Neale Hurston, who was Herskovits's research assistant at Columbia in 1926.[4] Nonetheless, in part because of his sheer ambition and in part because of the workings of U.S.

racism in the academy, the task of defining the field and training the first generation of academic specialists fell largely on his own shoulders.[5] His first clear formulation—"The New World Negro: The Statement of a Problem," in which he outlined the whole scientific program for the comparative study of Africans in the diaspora (from the Suriname bush to the streets of Harlem)—was published in the *American Anthropologist* in early 1930, only months after he returned from his eye-opening fieldwork among Saramaka Maroons. From there, it was only a small step to the protean debates with Chicago sociologist E. Franklin Frazier that shaped the controversies that still resonate today—to what extent did the Africans brought to the Americas, and their descendants, continue to feel and act in "African" ways, and what might this signify? Or were African Americans simply oppressed, "deprived" Americans?

Like other Boas students (almost all of whom worked with American Indians), Herskovits was trained to search for origins. Theirs was mainly a backward-looking enterprise, trying to reconstruct for science the pristine lives that were once lived by the elders and ancestors of the oppressed and degraded Indians they interviewed and photographed. In 1925, Herskovits wrote that "any given culture is comprised of two elements, a certain amount, probably the smaller, which has originated within the group, and a much larger amount which has been borrowed."[6] Part of every anthropologist's job, then, was to trace traits present in one culture back to an ancestral one. This genealogical imperative, in Herskovits's case the search for the African origins of Negro American traits, when combined with fieldwork with various diasporic populations, led him to theorize processes such as the "retention," "syncretism," and "reinterpretation" of "Africanisms"—all somehow part of the overarching process of "acculturation." These ideas then took on a life of their own, influencing the way anthropologists interested in other parts of the world analyzed their materials and influencing scholars in neighboring disciplines as well.

Soon after Herskovits's death in 1963, his genealogical imperative gained a second life, but from largely independent sources. In the wake of the civil rights movement, ideas that valorized Blackness and Africanity—which had long been an undercurrent in U.S. identity politics (Du Bois, Garveyism, the New Negro Movement of the Harlem Renaissance)—blossomed as never before. From Alex Haley's *Roots* and Robert Farris Thompson's *Flash of the Spirit* to the African-names-for your-new-baby and 100-traditional-African-hairstyles booklets at supermarket checkout racks, from Harvard to the streets of Watts, Black was Beautiful and roots were in. There is no doubt that the staying power, within the academy and out, of Herskovits's diasporic vision, and its revitalization during the past several decades, has as much to do with ongoing identity politics as with its originality or truth.[7]

Through much of the twentieth century, anthropologists worked to defend the status of their discipline as a science, and these efforts accelerated during the scramble for funds and prestige that followed World War II and the development of Area Studies programs. When Whitten and Szwed's landmark *Afro-American Anthropology* appeared in 1970, a lone critic raised the warning flag. Ruth Landes, who had been blackballed by Herskovits for not following his agenda of seeking African connections,[8] wrote a review in the *American Anthropologist* in 1971 in which she notes that all twenty-five contributors "sound like students of Herskovits."

> In my New York City college years [the early 1930s], which acclaimed America's "Negro Renaissance," writers of all origins marveled at the vigor of Black lifeways. In the present volume we have a different order of witness, which prefers to emphasize the *observers'* absorption in professional techniques and concepts. Thus the editors state that the essays pursue "problems in cultural analysis" and "new directions for research . . . of social processes" to reveal the "continuing adaptation" of New World Blacks. . . . The "causes" producing similarities of structures are "sought in . . . similar environing pressures" called "techno-economic." . . . [The contributors] present individuals as functioning like synapses in societal circuits, or as links and conductors totaling enmeshed messages. . . . Perhaps because writers here think in terms of "strategy" rather than "creativity," they do not consider personalities, nor the Black creative arts, including literature. . . . I myself cannot name the Afro-Brazilian world I knew without instantly hearing, seeing, smelling the vivid actors in it. Abstractions from human life plus sensuous personages are complementary data; and both awarenesses fill our worlds.

Landes's laudable call for a kinder, gentler, more humanistic diasporic anthropology understandably exaggerates—some of the contributors to the volume, such as Roger Abrahams and John Szwed, have spent much of their lives studying expressive culture, black literature, and music—but she did catch the oppressive nature of the regnant scientific paradigm, which left practitioners little room for maneuver. Indeed, her critique was echoed twenty years later by David Scott, a postcolonial scholar who questions "the theoretical object" of the Afro-Americanist anthropologist's gaze, which he argues is constructed on the ideological assumption that "peoples of African descent in the New World require something like anthropology, a science of culture, to provide them with the foundational guarantee of an authentic past."[9]

There is, however, a deeply humanistic strain, running from Boas through Herskovits to more recent anthropologists of the diaspora, as Scott acknowledges when he notes that Afro-American anthropology "manifests a deep, humanist inclination toward a story about continuities and embraces the earnest task of demonstrating the integrity and the intactness of the old in the new, and of the past in the present."[10] And this "humanist inclination toward a story about continuities"—this genealogical imperative—is shared without shame by many of the anthropologists and historians concerned with the diaspora today.

Michel-Rolph Trouillot expresses the underlying awe that still drives many of those who seek to understand the African American past in this way:

> From the family plots of the Jamaican hinterland, the Afro-religions of Brazil and Cuba, or the jazz music of Louisiana to the vitality of Haitian painting and music and the historical awareness of Suriname's maroons, the cultural practices that typify various African American populations appear to us as the product of a repeated miracle. . . . Their very existence is a continuing puzzle. For they were born against all odds.[11]

Creativity, continuity, and resistance in the face of unspeakable oppression. . . .

*   *   *

Since there have been several recent and often meaty historiographical-cum-bibliographical surveys of anthropology's contributions to the study of the diaspora, I have chosen not to go over that ground here.[12] Suffice it to note, however, that anthropological concepts such as acculturation, syncretism, and creolization have moved to and enriched other disciplines engaged in Diaspora Studies and, on the other hand, insights from anthropologists engaged in Diaspora Studies (particularly in the Caribbean), involving phenomena such as resistance, colonialism, migration, and transnationalism, as well as the very confrontation with complex, heterogeneous, fully historicized societies, have helped challenge anthropology's own sometimes rigid functionalist models. In this essay, rather than recapitulate these surveys, I would highlight some recent debates and point to future directions. And given the absence of participation in this volume by a linguist, I choose to highlight a major theoretical paradigm that began in linguistics, became the site of the most heated battles in diasporic anthropology and history during the past two decades, and has more recently been appropriated and watered down, perhaps to the point of meaninglessness, by theorists of globalization and transnationalism. I speak of "creolization."[13]

The concept of creolization—the process by which people, flora and fauna, ideas, and institutions with roots in the Old World are born in the New, where they develop and reproduce themselves—migrated from the field of natural history to linguistics and thence to anthropology during the course of the twentieth century. (The earliest usage in English that refers to cultural as opposed to biological processes seems to date from 1928, when Jonkeer L. C. van Panhuys, in a letter to Herskovits, described culture change among the Suriname Maroons as "creolisation.") But it was only in the 1960s that "creolization" became common coin among linguists and anthropologists, particularly following the 1968 University of the West Indies conference that resulted in the pioneering collection *Pidginization and Creolization of Languages*. After that, creolization theory quickly carved out a place as an analytic tool applied to the unusual processes of culture change that first took place in the violent colonial cauldron of the early New World (which had previously been conceptualized in anthropology in terms of now-outmoded theories of "acculturation," "transculturation," or "cultural interpenetration").[14]

More recently, there has been a lively debate in the disciplines of anthropology and history about the continuing usefulness of "creolization" for the understanding of cultural process in the Caribbean and elsewhere in Afro-America. At the center of these polemics is *The Birth of African American Culture*,[15] the scholarly work most closely associated with the theory of creolization among New World slaves, which built on and extended the ideas of Melville J. Herskovits. Recognizing that creolization involves rupture and loss, creativity and transformation, and celebration as well as silencing of cultural continuities and discontinuities, that essay proposed an anthropological *approach* for studying African American pasts. For the study of slavery across the Americas, it tried to lay out the kinds of constants (e.g., the realities of power differences) and the kinds of variables (e.g., demographic, cultural, and geographic specificities) that merited scholars' attention. It assumed that, despite certain commonalities based on relations of power, slavery in nineteenth-century Virginia, for example, was in significant ways a different institution from slavery in seventeenth-century Mexico or slavery in eighteenth-century Saint-Domingue, and it tried to point to the kinds of specific sociocultural processes that brought about these differences. The clarion call of that essay was historicization and contextualization—the same careful analysis of sociohistorical particulars that Mintz had first called for in the study of creole languages at the 1968 conference in Jamaica.[16]

The Mintz and Price essay sought an answer to certain kinds of questions (still hotly debated today), as a way of getting at more general cultural processes. For example, how "ethnically" homogeneous (or heterogeneous) were the enslaved Africans arriving in a particular locality—in other words, to what extent was there a clearly dominant group—and what were the cultural consequences? What were the processes by which these imported Africans became African *Americans*? How quickly and in what ways did Africans transported to the Americas as slaves, and their American offspring, begin thinking and acting as members of new communities—that is, how rapid was creolization? In what ways did the

African arrivants choose to—and were they able to—continue particular ways of thinking and of doing things that came from the Old World? What did "Africa" (or its subregions and peoples) mean at different times to African arrivants and their descendants? How did the various demographic profiles and social conditions of New World plantations in particular places and times encourage or inhibit these processes?

One influential group of scholars, who style themselves "African-Centrists," have criticized those like Mintz and me whom they dismissively label "Creation theorists" for emphasizing the creativity of enslaved Africans and their descendants in the Americas. They write, for example, "An 'African-centric' perspective overcomes a fundamental flaw in the history of Africans in the Americas as analyzed by many historians of slavery, particularly those identifying with the 'creolization' model articulated by Sidney Mintz and Richard Price."[17] However, a number of other scholars across a range of disciplines—History, Anthropology, Folklore, Postcolonial Studies—have found the creolization model analytically useful. As anthropologist Michel-Rolph Trouillot reminds us:

> Theories of creolization or of creole societies, assessments of what it means to be "creole" in turn, are still very much affected by the ideological and political sensibilities of the observers. . . . All seize creolization as a totality, thus one level too removed from the concrete circumstances faced by the individuals engaged in the process. All these models invoke history. . . . Yet the historical conditions of cultural production rarely become a fundamental and necessary part of the description or analyses that these models generate. Calls for a more refined look at historical particulars [and here he points in a footnote to the Mintz and Price essay] remain unheeded. . . . We have not thought enough about what went on in specific places and times to produce a framework sensitive enough to time, place, and power.[18]

On this, I stand with Dell Hymes, who stressed that, from a linguist's perspective, creolization refers to a very particular sociohistorical nexus, representing "the extreme to which social factors can go in shaping the transmission and use of language."[19] That is, as an analytical concept to describe a precise and unusual set of sociohistorical circumstances—in which individuals from diverse societies and cultures are suddenly brought together under conditions of vastly unequal power and then, together, create new social and cultural institutions—creolization continues to be an analytically powerful tool for the study of change.

The finest recent studies of culture change in the diaspora—Stephan Palmié's *Wizards and Scientists*, David H. Brown's *Santería Enthroned*, and J. Lorand Matory's *Black Atlantic Religion*—build directly on creolization to analyze translocal and transnational processes of culture change that are central to an understanding of diasporic history. Indeed, I would argue that creolization remains a privileged analytic concept for describing the special kinds of culture change brought about by African-born slaves (and escaped slaves) and their descendants throughout the Americas during the formative period of Afro-American institutions; that, given the current state of knowledge, generalizations about slave creolization may be less useful than carefully historicized and contextualized analyses; and that the field of Creolization Studies continues to be highly charged politically, with U.S. identity or race politics exercising a powerful (and often counterproductive) influence on scholarly conclusions. A review of some recent historical studies of creolization in North America will help me advance these contentions.

* * *

Immense progress has been made since the pioneering North American slavery studies of the 1960s and 1970s, which for all their significant revisionism tended to view slavery as a monolithic institution and derived its particulars largely from the nineteenth-century antebellum South. More recent studies engage instead in systematic comparison among regions and through time and emphasize the complexity and unevenness of cultural development. Taken together, these recent studies point to the importance of historical particulars—the significance of local and temporal variation—in understanding creolization, which proceeded at different rhythms and paces in different regions. As Ira Berlin has argued for North America as a whole,

> Understanding that a person was a slave is not the end of the story but the beginning, for the slaves' history was derived from experiences that differed from place to place and time to time and not from some unchanging transhistorical verity. . . . Rather than proceed from African to creole or from slavery to freedom, people of African descent in mainland North America crossed the lines between African and creole and between slavery and freedom many times, and not always in the same direction.[20]

We now know, for example, that most of the first generation of enslaved Africans to land in North America did not come directly from Africa but had labored first in other Atlantic regions, where they had learned European languages and other aspects of European culture. In some regions, such as Florida, these cosmopolitan "Atlantic Creoles" and their culture managed to survive into the eighteenth century. But in other regions, such as the Chesapeake, there was a process of re-Africanization, in this case under the harsh new tobacco regime, and there was a consequent reshaping of the culture of the original generation of slaves. Nevertheless, the multiplicity of these new Africans' origins assured that creolization (and inter-African syncretism) would dominate the reshaping process. As Berlin notes, "The slave trade in the Chesapeake operated to scatter men and women of various nations and diminish the importance of African nationality."[21] And then the tide turned again: by 1720 in the Chesapeake,

African Americans once again came to outnumber those who had been born in Africa and, as Philip Morgan writes, it was these African Americans (also called "Creoles") who "set the tone and tenor of slave life in the region remarkably early. Africans learned the ropes from them. . . . The lessons largely flowed from Creoles to Africans."[22] Indeed, by 1780, 95 percent of Virginia slaves were American-born, and by that time, as in other regions of North America, race-consciousness had become a primary factor in identity politics.

To take another example, in the Carolina Lowcountry, the course of creolization was different. The cosmopolitan Creole generation was swamped by new Africans imported directly to labor on the great rice plantations that sprang up at the end of the seventeenth century. (As John Thornton writes of that moment, "African culture was not surviving—it was arriving.")[23] Morgan describes how, during the relatively lengthy period of large-scale African slave arrivals in the Lowcountry, "in Charleston, even the most sophisticated creole slaves lived cheek by jowl with Africans" but that "in the long run, Africans, even in the Lowcountry, were aliens in a strange land."[24] By the middle of the eighteenth century, several decades after the corresponding shift in the Chesapeake, American-born slaves once again held a majority in the Lowcountry. Another significant contrast with the Chesapeake was the overall black majority in the Lowcountry—in 1720, for example, when African Americans formed no more than a quarter of the population in Virginia, they formed two-thirds in the Lowcountry.

It should be clear that these demographic and other local variations had significant cultural consequences (for example, on the languages slaves spoke with one another, the religions they practiced, the way their buried their dead) as well as influencing the ways enslaved Africans and their descendants conceptualized their identities (as "Ibos" or "Congos," as belonging to the Smith Plantation or the Jones Plantation, as husbands and wives and fathers and mothers, and as field hands or skilled workers). In North America as among the Suriname Maroons that I study, creolization based on inter-African syncretism was a driving force, yet in some historical situations in North America, where slave-master contact was strong, there was clearly more influence from the European side on the new African American culture that was emerging. Likewise, in those moments and places when massive importations from Africa demographically swamped those who had been living as slaves, African contributions to emerging culture (once again, often in the form of inter-African syncretisms or blendings) came to the fore.

*   *   *

Studies of North American slavery, like Afro-Americanist research more generally, remain enmeshed in the realities of North American racism. Studies of creolization are no exception and continue to be deeply affected by scholars' ideological and political positions. Nowhere is this influence of the present on the interpretation of the past clearer than in considerations of the role of African "ethnicities" in the development of African American culture and society.

Most recent studies agree that, because of the diversity of labor regimes and the demographic mixes they brought with them, creolization proceeded in different ways at different times in North America but that everywhere there was constant reshaping of African ideas and practices to the necessities of local North American life. Whether they take as their focus the development of slave institutions—material life, work in the fields, skilled labor, exchanges between whites and blacks, family life, religious life, and so forth—or the comparison of regions through time, the best of these studies suggest that African ethnicity was important at certain moments in certain places but was a variable that faded relatively quickly, in terms of the slaves' own identity politics. As Berlin writes of North American slaves,

> For most Africans, as for their white counterparts, identity was a garment which might be worn or discarded. . . . Choice, as well as imposition or birthright, determined who the new arrivals would be. . . . In short, identity formation for African slaves was neither automatic nor unreflective, neither uniform nor unilinear.[25]

There is, however, an alternative perspective that argues forcefully for the long-term persistence of African ethnicities in North America and for their identifiable influences on the lives of African Americans. In line with earlier cultural nationalist positions about North American slavery, this perspective equates creolization with Europeanization (largely dismissing the realities of inter-African syncretism in the Americas). Its adherents, mainly historians of Africa, sometimes call themselves, as noted above, "African-centric" scholars.

Michael Gomez, to take a prominent example, organizes *Exchanging Our Country Marks*, his study of the development of African American society, by presenting chapters devoted to the fate in North America, first of people from Senegambia and the Bight of Benin, then of Islamicized Africans, next of Sierra Leoneans and the Akan, and finally of Igbos and West Central Africans—reflecting a hypothesis of ethnic persistence that remains unproven. He concludes, "The development of African American society through 1830 was very much the product of contributions made by specific [African] ethnic groups."[26] In my view, such an African-centric perspective underestimates both the agency of enslaved Africans and the inherent malleability and strategic uses of ethnicity in identity politics.

John Thornton, another influential Africanist historian, goes so far as to speculate that "on the eve of the revolution in Saint-Domingue, Kikongo was also, in all likelihood, the most commonly spoken first language, or was a close runner-up to French. In fact, the creole leaders of the revolution in 1791 complained that most of their followers could 'scarcely make out two words of French.'"[27]

But from an Americanist perspective, it might be useful to signal that these people's speech options were not simply an African mother tongue or French. Indeed, these Haitians would in great majority have been speaking to each other in *their own shared language*—neither Kikongo nor French—but a new language that they (and the generations of enslaved Africans and their descendants who preceded them) had created in Saint-Domingue: Haitian Creole.[28]

Much of the difficulty with an approach that places such emphasis on African ethnicities in the Americas is the historically contingent nature of these identities in Africa (as elsewhere in the world), which has consistently hobbled efforts to establish an African "baseline" for New World studies. J. Lorand Matory, whose ethnographic work in Nigeria and Brazil is exemplary, writes of Yoruba identity that "To call the self-identified Òyó, Ègbá, Ègbádò, Ìjèbú, and Èkìtì captives of even the late 19th century 'Yorùbá' is, in most cases . . . an anachronism. . . . Calling [these peoples] of the 19th century and their pre-19th century ancestors 'Yorùbá' reads a commonsense reality of the late 20th century back onto a period in which that reality was only beginning to be produced."[29] Ghanaian philosopher Kwame Anthony Appiah has also written eloquently on this issue, citing as an example Chinua Achebe's remarks about the relative recency of the "Igbo" identity in Nigeria: "For instance, take the Igbo people. In my area, historically, they did not see themselves as Igbo. They saw themselves as people from this village or that village. . . . And yet, after the experience of the Biafran War, during a period of two years, it became a very powerful consciousness." Appiah then cautions:

> Recognizing Igbo identity as a new thing is not a way of privileging other
> Nigerian identities: each of the three central ethnic identities of modern
> political life—Hausa-Fulani, Yoruba, Igbo—is a product of the rough-and-
> tumble of the transition through colonial to postcolonial status. . . . Modern
> Ghana witnesses the development of an Akan identity, as speakers of the
> three major regional dialects of Twi—Asante, Fante, Akuapem—organize
> themselves into a corporation against an (equally novel) Ewe unity. . . .
> Identities are complex and multiple and grow out of a history of changing
> responses to economic, political, and cultural forces, almost always in oppo-
> sition to other identities.[30]

Historian Joseph C. Miller offers the example of the complexities hiding behind such "ethnic" labels as "Congo" when he writes:

Central Africans would have discovered new social identities beyond these local, and already multiple, ones along their tortured ways toward the coast. Yoked together in slave coffles with others of unfamiliar linguistic and cultural backgrounds, they must have gained a sense of familiarity with one another and would have created alliances out of it, which the Europeans labeled "Congo." . . . The slaves' further experiences of confinement during the Middle Passage and the specific circumstances they encountered in the Americas created changing incentives for Central Africans to draw on differing aspects of their home backgrounds as they searched for a morally restorative sense of humane community among themselves. The meaning of being "Congo" in the Diaspora changed accordingly.[31]

Such considerations undermine African-centric representations of African American society as a surviving mosaic of African fragments. If, as social science theory teaches, ethnicity is indeed malleable and used strategically by actors, then the African-centric approach must be seen as a form of anachronistic essentialism. Indeed, anthropologist Stephan Palmié characterizes it as a "theme-park approach" which compresses African cultural geography in such a way that someone might imagine that "in certain New World settings the lower Zaire nowadays abuts southwestern Nigeria."[32]

If we are to transcend political and ideological *parti-pris* in studying the diasporic past, we must focus on the historical conditions of cultural production. Indeed, when African-centric historians move from generalizations (where ideological preferences often drive their narratives) to the concrete circumstances faced by the individuals engaged in the process of creolization, their approach can provide provocative insights and raise problems for further study. For example, John Thornton's explorations of the role of Kongo-born slaves among participants in the 1739 Stono Rebellion in South Carolina and in the Haitian Revolution open intriguing new perspectives.[33]

It would appear that the more specific (the more limited in time and space) the African-centric study of American phenomena, the better its chances of being historically persuasive. Studies emphasizing shared African origins clearly make sense in those relatively unusual cases where large groups speaking the same language and sharing cultural understandings landed together in the Americas and, together, shaped a new culture. One such case is the eighteenth-century Danish West Indies. Historian Ray Kea, a specialist on the Gold Coast, has analyzed an eighteenth-century slave rebellion in these Danish islands, in which he teases out the consequences of the "Amina" backgrounds of the slaves involved with considerable subtlety, helping us imagine something of the mind-set (ideologies, notions about authority, ideas about death) held by people being shipped out of a particular port at a particular time because of particular local circumstances in Africa, and he describes how some of these played themselves out in a specific event in the New World.[34] In short, there is little doubt that such an Africanist perspective has its place in our tool-kit for understanding creolization—the ways enslaved Africans and their descendants created communities and institutions in their new homes. If used in the service of greater contextualization and historicization, such perspectives, informed by rich knowledge of African history, cannot but add to our understandings of events on this side of the Atlantic.

*   *   *

Given the variety of historical circumstances in which New World creolization took place and the weight on the field of presentist ideological concerns, our best strategy would appear to be some combination of careful historical contextualization and broader comparisons across the Americas. Three such recent studies emerging from different scholarly traditions help point the way. Each demonstrates that creolization, like the continued transformation of individual and group identities through time, is a complex process and that later nostalgia for Africa (or claims about "African origins") may mask the radical nature of earlier cultural processes.

In *"Chi ma nkongo": Lengua y rito ancestrales en El Palenque de San Basilio, Colombia,* Swiss linguist Armin Schwegler demonstrates that sacred songs sung at the most apparently African of all Palenquero rites, the *lumbalú,* are (in the words of reviewer John M. Lipski) "not the partially decreolized outcome of original African songs, but rather are essentially modern [that is, eighteenth-century or nineteenth-century] creations, based on a combination of regional Spanish and Palenquero [the local creole language], to which African and pseudo-African words and onomatopoeic elements have been added," and "that the active use of spoken African languages in Palenque disappeared very early, if in fact the population ever used an African language as the primary means of communication." This observation about the early development and predominance of a creole language is especially interesting in that Schwegler is able to show that the Africans who founded Palenque were characterized by a relative linguistic homogeneity, with Bantu languages, particularly ki-Kongo, providing the main substratum for the new creole language, Palenquero. In his review, Lipski calls this book "at once a masterful analysis of the elusive *lumbalú* language and a major breakthrough in Afro-creole studies . . . a benchmark against which future studies of creole languages and cultures will be measured."

Wizards and Scientists: Explorations in Afro-Cuban Modernity and Tradition, by German anthropologist Stephan Palmié, is devoted to Cuba, where for much of the history of the island (in the words of David Eltis), "there was no dominant African group."[35] The thrust of his argument, which derives both Afro-Cuban religious "tradition" and Western "modernity" from a single transatlantic historical matrix, is that a "focus on the putative African origins of locally coexisting New World traditions [for example, *regla de ocha*, long associated by anthropologists with Yoruba-speaking slaves, and *palo monte*, similarly associated with speakers of western Central African Bantu languages] both obscures the history of such forms of cultural complexity and fails to address the role of representations of difference as a meaningful component of contemporary practice." "We are dealing," Palmié writes, "with an aggregate formation in which notions deriving from western Central African minkisi cults and Yoruba-derived forms of worship of divine beings known as *orisha* were jointly conjugated through a single New World history of enslavement, abuse, and depersonalization. In the course of this process, Yoruba-derived patterns of *orisha* worship and western Central African forms of manipulating minkisi objects not only underwent parallel changes but also became morally recalibrated in relation to each other." He describes how in the course of the nineteenth century, with the arrival of a large number of Yorubas, a creolization-like process occurred in which "the two traditions [Yoruba and Central African] not only merged into a larger complex of partly overlapping conceptions and practices but came to offer functionally differentiated ritual idioms that spoke—and continue to speak—to fundamentally different forms of historical experience and contemporary sociality." "Neither ocha nor palo," he continues, "could have evolved to their present phenomenology and moralized positions along a spectrum of differentiated ritual idioms without the presence of the other within the same social framework." Like other contemporary anthropologists plumbing the mechanics of creolization in a particular historical context, Palmié stresses shifting social contexts in the shaping of meaning and practice, and he fully expects the course of creolization to be complex as well as extremely difficult, in retrospect, to tease out.[36]

African American anthropologist J. Lorand Matory's *Black Atlantic Religion: Tradition, Transnationalism, and Matriarchy in Afro-Brazilian Candomblé* analyzes the intensely ideological role of African ethnicity and the ongoing creation and redefinition of particular African ethnicities through time in Bahia, Brazil. Set in the context of other recent studies of the early Black Atlantic world that stress transnationalism and the widespread movement of peoples, ideas, and even crops, Matory's study expands on Palmié's remark that "interaction between indigenous and scholarly conceptions of *traditionality* and *African purity* have engendered considerable discursive slippage."[37] Matory explores a case where practitioners' convictions about the history of their Afro-Brazilian religion (and its fidelity to one or another African "nation") can be shown to be discursive formations that emerge directly from historical creolization. In this sense, the several branches of Candomblé, like the Brazilian martial art of *capoeira*, involve an ideology among participants that stands at the other end of a continuum from that of Saramaka Maroons, who stress their ancestors' New World spiritual discoveries more than fidelity to particular African practices. Matory analyzes the often-conflictual historical processes by which certain continuities become privileged and certain discontinuities become officially masked, both in Brazil and on the African coast, over the course of several centuries. Throughout, he stresses the agency of a host of actors on both sides of the Atlantic and their ongoing interactions in ever-changing relations of power and conflict and solidarity, with the emergence of new ethnic identities as one result. He demonstrates, for example, that what many scholars have taken to be "direct African continuities" in twentieth-century Candomblé are the result, in part, of the active agency of priests, traders, and others who, under specific historical circumstances during the nineteenth century, fostered a process of *anagonizacão* (Yoruba-ization) long after Bahian Candomblé had first developed. And in stressing continuing historical relations throughout the southern Atlantic world, he demonstrates the contingency of such identities as Jeje (important in Candomblé), which depended on continuing Brazil-Cuba-Nigeria-Dahomey interactions and culminated in the late nineteenth century with Afro-Brazilian returnees to Africa transforming the Bight of Benin, however briefly, into the Djedje coast. Throughout, Matory insists on the slaves' (and other Africans') strategic practices of self-representation. Creolization and others forms of culture change were ultimately effected by enslaved Africans and their own descendants. "What is often called cultural 'memory,' 'survival' or 'tradition' in both the African diaspora and at home is, in truth, always a function of power, negotiation, and strategic re-creation."[38]

These three studies, placed alongside those on North America and Suriname,[39] strongly suggest that African ethnicity remains *one* (among many) of the ways that enslaved peoples who were brought to the New World thought about (and in some parts of the Americas, continue to think about) themselves, and that it played various roles in different aspects of life for varying periods in different places in the New World.[40] A thoughtful summary of this position may be found in an article by Philip Morgan in which he draws on recent data about the Atlantic slave trade to consider the overall cultural implications for early New World societies.[41]

*   *   *

During the past two decades, "creolization," like a good bit else in anthropology (including "ethnography"), has been appropriated pretty much wholesale by other disciplines, particularly Cultural Studies, Postcolonial Studies, and the like. In the process, the concept has lost much of its vigor and analytical specificity, coming to stand for almost any kind of cultural blending or hybridity. Mimi Sheller, in her book *Consuming the Caribbean*, lays out the case with precision, protesting that the concept "is not simply about moving and mixing elements, but is more precisely about processes of cultural 'regrounding' following experiences of violent uprooting from one's culture of origin. It is deeply embedded in situations of coerced transport, racial terror, and subaltern survival. . . . Creolization is a process of *contention*" (emphasis in original).[42] She writes further of the "theoretical piracy on the high seas of global culture," where "the creolization paradigm" is now used to describe "the ways in which cultural consumers throughout the world creatively adapt in-flowing goods, thereby localising the global and indigenising the universal." In other words, she argues, "Creolization has transmogrified from a politically engaged term used by Caribbean theorists in the Caribbean in the 1970s [she's thinking primarily of Kamau Brathwaite and Rex Nettleford but also mentions Mintz and Price], to one used by Caribbean diaspora theorists located outside the Caribbean in the 1980s [she's thinking of Stuart Hall and Paul Gilroy], and finally to non-Caribbean 'global' theorists in the 1990s [she's thinking of Ulf Hannerz and Jim Clifford]." And she calls for "returning to the Caribbean roots of the concept of creolisation, regrounding it in its specific social and cultural itineraries" in order to "recover the political meanings and subaltern agency that have been barred entry by the free-floating gatekeepers of 'global' culture."[43]

* * *

Readers familiar with my work in Suriname may be surprised to hear that my current research uncovers layers of Africanity among Maroons that even the most ardent Africa-centrists have never dreamed of. My recent *Travels with Tooy* includes literally hundreds of songs and texts in such languages as Apínti, Apúku, Komantí, Luángu, Papá, and Púmbu that have strong affinities with languages of Africa. And in that book, my Saramaka friend Tooy takes me, and my readers, on journeys back through the centuries to the African motherland itself. But he also takes us on trips to the land of forest spirits whom Saramakas discovered only after their escape from slavery in the New World and on visits under the sea to the land of the *Wénti* sea gods, whom they discovered only at the beginning of the twentieth century. My hope in this book—one of the deepest explorations of a New World diasporic cosmology ever—is to join Palmié, Brown, Matory, and other recent ethnographers of the diaspora, but from a wildly eccentric, non-urban (Maroon) perspective, in showing how and why debates about African continuities vs. New World creativity are indeed, in Mintz's words, "mostly bootless."

Creolization, which I take to be that "miraculous" contestational process that took place as the first generation or two of Africans re-created lifeways in each New World colony, quickly led to fully formed cultural institutions, from languages to religions.[44] In the four or five centuries that have followed (depending on the New World site), their descendants have, in the case of many urban dwellers (as with practitioners of regla or Candomblé), kept up active intercourse and dialogue with African home-lands as they have developed and embellished their institutions, and in the case of Maroons (whether in Suriname or, say, in Jamaica)[45] further developed their cultural institutions largely out of their own marvelous diasporic imaginations (without further direct interaction with Africa). *Travels with Tooy* is my own contribution to documenting the second of these diasporic situations.

As the anthropology of the diaspora moves into the twenty-first cen-tury, it is surely time to go beyond debates about cultural memory and forgetting to explore the complex politics of self-representation and iden-tity through time. We must take account of conflict as well as consensus in representing culture and demonstrate its role in shaping and reshap-ing institutions. We must grant full agency to African Americans, mak-ing them the central actors in the construction of their cultures. We must remain focused on process and change, the ways certain continuities be-come privileged, the ways certain discontinuities become masked—the politics of culture through time. Where relevant, we must explore dialogue between people in different class positions and in often distant places all over the Americas and West Africa. Historicization and contextualization remain a primary responsibility. And we must continue to do the kinds of careful ethnography that characterizes the work, for example, of Palmié, Brown, and Matory. For when all is said and done, all of our theories (whether about transnationalism, globalization, creolization, or whatever) depend on the adequacies of that ethnography—long-term immersion in diasporic sites and situations, speaking the relevant languages, and, ulti-mately, earning the trust and respect of our interlocutors.

NOTES

Some of the material in this paper is based on work supported by the National Sci-ence Foundation under Grant No. BCS-0450170. Any opinions, findings, conclu-sions, or recommendations expressed in this material are those of the author and do not necessarily reflect the views of the National Science Foundation.

The epigraph is from Sidney W. Mintz, personal communication, 7 January 2006.

1. Fabre, *La rive noire,* 51. Du Bois's term seems to have been "black diaspora"; Fabre says "diaspora noire."

2. Christine Chivallon suggests that anthropologist Roger Bastide was the first French scholar—in 1967—to use "diaspora" in print to refer to Africans in the New World. Chivallon, *La diaspora noire des Amériques,* 149.

3. At the same time, Afro-Americanists within anthropology have often found it difficult to carve out successful careers for themselves, as their subject has been devalorized by the rest of the discipline. Reasons are complex but include standard

U.S. racism as well as the traditional anthropological premium placed on working with "the real McCoy" (i.e., bare-assed savages). See Sidney W. Mintz's foreword to Whitten and Szwed, eds., *Afro-American Anthropology: Contemporary Perspectives*; Matory, *Black Atlantic Religion*, 275–77. On the complex politics of Afro-American anthropology, see also Willis, "Skeletons in the Anthropological Closet," and Szwed, "An American Anthropological Dilemma."

4. Price and Price, *The Root of Roots; or, How Afro-American Anthropology Got Its Start*; Yelvington, "The Invention of Africa in Latin America and the Caribbean."

5. Herskovits, of course, founded the first program in African Studies established in a U.S. university, at Northwestern in 1948.

6. Herskovits, "Social Pattern: A Methodological Study," 60.

7. The most recent variant is the DNA swabs one can submit to Internet sites to discover exactly where in Africa one's ancestors originated—the confirmation (and commodification) of African identity by means of genetic "science."

8. Landes, who followed Herskovits by a few years as a Boas student at Columbia, was an independent-minded woman with two American Indian books already to her name who wished to study the great black city of Salvador (Bahia, Brazil), but was first sent off for a preparatory year at Fisk University (in Nashville) so that she could "get used to Negroes." She got a little closer than her mentor intended and had to be hurried out before an interracial scandal became public. And after the Bahia fieldwork for her book, *The City of Women*, again showed too much familiarity—Landes became the frequent and fairly public companion of the dapper Afro-Brazilian folklorist and journalist Edison Carneiro—Herskovits (now a full professor) wrote letters to her potential employers to warn them about her "unorthodox" and "unscientific" field methods. Her reward for a book that precociously theorized (or, at the least, foregrounded) race, gender, and sexuality—but largely ignored Herskovits's agenda—was to be barred, throughout a long career, from receiving any permanent job in the United States. Her review for the *AA* was written from Canada.

9. Scott, "That Event, This Memory: Notes on the Anthropology of African Diasporas in the New World," 268.

10. Ibid., 262.

11. Trouillot, "Culture on the Edges," 191.

12. Pertinent examples include Trouillot, "The Caribbean Region"; Mintz, "Enduring Substances, Trying Theories"; Yelvington, "The Anthropology of Afro-Latin America and the Caribbean"; Khan, "Journey to the Center of the Earth"; Thomas and Slocum, "Rethinking Global and Area Studies."

13. In what follows, I draw on several pieces I've written for different audiences: "The Miracle of Creolization: A Retrospective," "Some Anthropological Musings on Creolization," and "The Concept of Creolization."

14. On "acculturation," see Herskovits, *Acculturation*; on "transculturation," Ortiz, *Contrapunteo Cubano del Tabaco y el Azúcar*, and Malinowski's introduction to *Contrapunteo Cubano*; and on "cultural interpenetration," Bastide, *Les religions afro-brésiliennes*.

15. Mintz and Price, *The Birth of African-American Culture* was published in 1992, but originally written in 1973 and widely circulated thereafter.

16. Mintz, "The Socio-Historical Background to Pidginization and Creolization."

17. Lovejoy, "Identifying Enslaved Africans."

18. Trouillot, "Culture on the Edges," 8–9, 20.

19. Hymes, *Pidginization and Creolization*, 5.

20. Berlin, *Many Thousand Gone*, 3, 5.

21. Ibid., 115.

22. Morgan, *Slave Counterpoint*, 460–61.

23. Thornton, *Africa and Africans in the Making of the Atlantic World, 1400–1800*, 320.

24. Morgan, *Slave Counterpoint*, 461, 456.

25. Berlin, *Many Thousand Gone*, 103–5.

26. Gomez, *Exchanging Our Country Marks*, 291.

27. Thornton, *Africa and Africans*, 321.

28. Thornton's consistent use of the phrase "the colonial language" (which he opposes to various African languages) when he writes of the early Americas exposes his *parti-pris*. In his account, creole languages—which in most territories at most times were the most widely used means of communication among slaves—scarcely exist.

29. Matory, *Black Atlantic Religion*, 56–57.

30. Appiah, *In My Father's House*, 177–78.

31. Miller, "Central Africa during the Era of the Slave Trade, c. 1490s–1850s," 42–43.

32. Palmié, *Wizards and Scientists*, 159.

33. Thornton, "African Dimensions of the Stono Rebellion"; Thornton, "'I am the subject of the King of Congo.'"

34. Kea, "'When I die, I shall return to my own land.'"

35. Eltis, *The Rise of African Slavery in the Americas*, 257.

36. The citations in this paragraph are from Palmié, *Wizards*, 25, 26, 27, and 193. David H. Brown's *Santería Enthroned* takes us even farther in demonstrating the essential newness—and marvelous hybridity—of such fundamental Cuban institutions as *regla de ocha* or *abakuá*. As Palmié writes, in a laudatory review, Brown demonstrates (among much else) that "regla de ocha does not represent a diasporic variant of 'Yoruba religion' (something that cannot be said to have existed in Africa even as late as the nineteenth century) that was imported wholecloth by the thousands of enslaved Yoruba-speakers who reached Cuba in the first half of the nineteenth century. Rather, regla de ocha (and specifically the cult of Ifá) was literally cooked up, no earlier than in the last two decades of the nineteenth century, by fewer than a dozen Africans and their creole descendants living in or near the third *barrio* of the town of Regla, and it continued to undergo dramatic and contentious transformations throughout the first half of the twentieth century as it spread through western Cuba's provinces of Havana and Matanzas." Palmié, "Santería Grand Slam."

37. Palmié, *Wizards*, 161.

38. Matory, *Black Atlantic Religion*, 70.

39. See esp. Price and Price, *Maroon Arts*, and Price, *Travels with Tooy*..

40. The studies by Palmié, Matory, and Brown also suggest differences between creolization as it occurred in the early plantation and Maroon context and as it oc-

curred much later within the slave (and free black) sector of such cities as Havana and Salvador (Bahia). In these urban contexts, the arrival of large numbers of enslaved Africans in the mid-nineteenth century meant that processes akin to creolization were ongoing during the late nineteenth and early twentieth centuries, when Santería and Candomblé were largely created. The relative recency of these creolization-like processes in these cases makes them particularly useful for an understanding of processes of initial culture creation and change, and it also gives their cultural products their specific character.

41. Morgan, "The Cultural Implications of the Atlantic Slave Trade."

42. Sheller, Consuming the Caribbean, 189.

43. Citations are from Sheller, Consuming the Caribbean, 188–96. For other recent excursions into creolization theory, see Baron and Cara, eds., "Special Issue: Creolization," and Romberg, "Ritual Piracy or Creolization with an Attitude."

44. In tandem with Haitian linguist Michel DeGraff, who writes persuasively against the idea that creole languages lack certain of the linguistic features and complexities of more "mature" languages, I have long argued that creolization was more often than not rapid and remarkably effective, quickly creating cultural institutions that were "fully formed." See, for example, DeGraff, "Morphology in Creole Genesis"; DeGraff, "On the Origin of Creoles."

45. For a masterful consideration of creolization, history, and memory among the Maroons of Jamaica, see Bilby, True-Born Maroons.

REFERENCES

Appiah, Kwame Anthony. In My Father's House: Africa in the Philosophy of Culture. New York: Oxford University Press, 1992.

Baron, Robert, and Ana C. Cara, eds. "Special Issue: Creolization." Journal of American Folklore 116, no. 459 (2003).

Bastide, Roger. Les religions afro-brésiliennes: contribution à une sociologie de l'interpénétration des civilisations. Paris: Presses Universitaires de France, 1960.

Berlin, Ira. Many Thousand Gone: The First Two Centuries of Slavery in North America. Cambridge: Harvard University Press, 1998.

Bilby, Kenneth M. True-Born Maroons. Gainesville: University Press of Florida, 2005.

Brown, David H. Santería Enthroned: Art, Ritual, and Innovation in an Afro-Cuban Religion. Chicago: University of Chicago Press, 2003.

Chivallon, Christine. La diaspora noire des Amériques: Expériences et théories à partir de la Caraïbe. Paris: CNRS Éditions, 2004.

DeGraff, Michel. "Morphology in Creole Genesis: Linguistics and Ideology." In Michael Kenstowicz, ed., Ken Hale: A Life in Language, 53–121. Cambridge: MIT Press, 2001.

———. "On the Origin of Creoles: Cartesian Critique of Neo-Darwinian Linguistics." Linguistic Typology 5 (2001): 213–310.

Eltis, David. The Rise of African Slavery in the Americas. Cambridge: Cambridge University Press, 2000.

Fabre, Michel. La rive noire: De Harlem à la Seine. Paris: Éditions Lieu Commun, 1985.

Gomez, Michael A. *Exchanging Our Country Marks: The Transformation of African Identities in the Colonial and Antebellum South.* Chapel Hill: University of North Carolina Press, 1998.

Herskovits, Melville J. *Acculturation: The Study of Culture Contact.* New York: J. J. Augustin, 1938.

———. "Social Pattern: A Methodological Study." *Social Forces* 4 (1925): 57–69.

Hymes, Dell, ed. *Pidginization and Creolization of Languages.* Cambridge: Cambridge University Press, 1971.

———. *Reinventing Anthropology.* New York: Random House, 1969.

Kea, Ray. "'When I die, I shall return to my own land': An 'Amina' Slave Rebellion in the Danish West Indies, 1733–1734." In John Hunwick and Nancy Lawler, eds., *The Cloth of Many Colored Silks: Papers on History and Society Ghanaian and Islamic in Honor of Ivor Wilks,* 159–93. Evanston, Ill.: Northwestern University Press, 1996.

Khan, Aisha. "Journey to the Center of the Earth: The Caribbean as Master Symbol." *Cultural Anthropology* 16 (2001): 271–302.

Landes, Ruth. Review of Norman E. Whitten Jr. and John F. Szwed, eds., *Afro-American Anthropology: Contemporary Perspectives. American Anthropologist* 73 (1971): 1306–10.

Lipski, John M. Review of Armin J. Schwegler, *"Chi ma nkongo." New West Indian Guide* 72 (1998): 356–60.

Lovejoy, Paul E. "Identifying Enslaved Africans: Methodological and Conceptual Considerations in Studying the African Diaspora." Paper prepared for UNESCO/SSHRCC Summer Institute, York University, 1997.

Malinowski, Bronislaw. Introduction to Fernando Ortiz, *Contrapunteo Cubano del Tabaco y el Azúcar,* xv–xxiii. Havana: Jesús Montero, 1940.

Matory, J. Lorand. *Black Atlantic Religion: Tradition, Transnationalism, and Matriarchy in the Afro-Brazilian Candomblé.* Princeton, N.J.: Princeton University Press, 2005.

Miller, Joseph C. "Central Africa during the Era of the Slave Trade, c. 1490s–1850s." In Linda M. Heywood, ed., *Central Africans and Cultural Transformations in the American Diaspora,* 21–69. Cambridge: Cambridge University Press, 2002.

Mintz, Sidney W. "Enduring Substances, Trying Theories: The Caribbean Region as Oikoumenê." *Journal of the Royal Anthropological Institute* (n.s.) 2 (1995): 289–311.

———. Foreword to Norman E. Whitten Jr. and John F. Szwed, eds., *Afro-American Anthropology: Contemporary Perspectives,* 1–16. New York: Free Press, 1970.

———. "The Socio-Historical Background to Pidginization and Creolization." In Hymes, *Pidginization and Creolization of Languages,* 481–96.

Mintz, Sidney W., and Richard Price. *The Birth of African-American Culture.* Boston: Beacon Press, 1992.

Morgan, Philip D. "The Cultural Implications of the Atlantic Slave Trade: African Regional Origins, American Destinations, and New World Developments." *Slavery and Abolition* 18 (1997): 122–45.

———. *Slave Counterpoint: Black Culture in the Eighteenth-Century Chesapeake and Lowcountry.* Chapel Hill: University of North Carolina Press, 1998.

Ortiz, Fernando. *Contrapunteo Cubano del Tabaco y el Azúcar.* Havana: Jesús Montero, 1940.

Palmié, Stephan. "Santería Grand Slam: Afro-Cuban Religious Studies and the Study of Afro-Cuban Religion." *New West Indian Guide* 79 (2005): 281–300.

———. *Wizards and Scientists: Explorations in Afro-Cuban Modernity and Tradition.* Durham, N.C.: Duke University Press, 2002.

Price, Richard. "The Concept of Creolization." In David Eltis and Stanley L. Engerman, eds., *World History of Slavery.* Cambridge: Cambridge University Press, n.d.

———. "The Miracle of Creolization: A Retrospective." *New West Indian Guide* 75 (2001): 35–64.

———. "Some Anthropological Musings on Creolization." *Journal of Pidgin and Creole Languages* 22 (2007): 17–36 (special issue, ed. Bettina Migge and Norval Smith).

———. *Travels with Tooy: History, Memory, and the African American Imagination.* Chicago: University of Chicago Press, 2008.

Price, Richard, and Sally Price. *The Root of Roots; or, How Afro-American Anthropology Got Its Start.* Chicago: Prickly Paradigm Press, 2003.

Price, Sally, and Richard Price. *Maroon Arts: Cultural Vitality in the African Diaspora.* Boston: Beacon Press, 1999.

Romberg, Raquel. "Ritual Piracy or Creolization with an Attitude." *New West Indian Guide* 79 (2005): 175–218.

Schwegler, Armin J. *"Chi ma nkongo": Lengua y rito ancestrales en El Palenque de San Basilio (Colombia).* Frankfort: Vervuert, 1996.

Scott, David. "That Event, This Memory: Notes on the Anthropology of African Diasporas in the New World." *Diaspora* 1(1991): 261–84.

Sheller, Mimi. *Consuming the Caribbean: From Arawaks to Zombies.* London: Routledge, 2003.

Szwed, John F. "An American Anthropological Dilemma: The Politics of Afro-American Culture." In Hymes, *Reinventing Anthropology,* 153–81.

Thomas, Deborah A., and Karla Slocum. "Rethinking Global and Area Studies: Insights from Caribbeanist Anthropology." *American Anthropologist* 105 (2003): 553–65.

Thornton, John. *Africa and Africans in the Making of the Atlantic World, 1400–1800.* Cambridge: Cambridge University Press, 1998.

———. "African Dimensions of the Stono Rebellion." *American Historical Review* 96 (1991): 1101–13.

———. "'I am the subject of the King of Congo': African Ideology in the Haitian Revolution." *Journal of World History* 4 (1993): 181–214.

Trouillot, Michel-Rolph. "The Caribbean Region: An Open Frontier in Anthropological Theory." *Annual Review of Anthropology* 21 (1992): 19–42.

———. "Culture on the Edges: Creolization in the Plantation Context." *Plantation Society in the Americas* 5 (1998): 8–28.

———. "Culture on the Edges: Caribbean Creolization in Historical Context." In Brian Keith Axel, ed., *From the Margins: Historical Anthropology and Its Futures,* 189–210. Durham, N.C.: Duke University Press, 2002.

Willis, William S., Jr. "Skeletons in the Anthropological Closet." In Hymes, *Reinventing Anthropology,* 121–52.

Yelvington, Kevin A. "The Anthropology of Afro-Latin America and the Caribbean: Diasporic Dimensions." *Annual Review of Anthropology* 30 (2001): 227–60.

———. "The Invention of Africa in Latin America and the Caribbean: Political Discourse and Anthropological Praxis, 1920–1940." In Yelvington, ed., *Afro-Atlantic Dialogues: Anthropology in the Diaspora*, 35–82. Santa Fe: School of American Research, 2006.

3

HOW GENETICS CAN PROVIDE
DETAIL TO THE TRANSATLANTIC
AFRICAN DIASPORA

Fatimah L. C. Jackson and Latifa F. J. Borgelin

In addition to the major role that genetic data play in elucidating disease susceptibilities, genetic data are increasingly being used to reconstruct ancestral origins and identify familial ties, even when they extend back for hundreds of years. For those interested in the latter, with respect to the transatlantic African Diaspora, genetic data are proving to be valuable adjuncts to historical, linguistic, ethnographic, and archaeological data in these reconstructions. By themselves, however, genetic data are inadequate to provide a complete profile of an individual's or a group's ancestral heritage. Genetic analyses provide data that identify *which* genes are currently present, but such data rarely provide a context or time frame for understanding *when, why,* or *how* the gene entered an individual or group. Geneticists are not known for either confronting the underlying assumptions of their research or investing in a comprehensive review of the historical, ethnographic, or linguistic records of the people under genetic assessment. As a result, many genetic interpretations (circulated primarily among geneticists) frequently resurrect hypotheses of population, ethnic, and group origins that have long been discounted by experts who are more familiar with population history (e.g., the Hamitic hypothesis).

Heritage is too complex to be reducible to simple gene sequences. However, in conjunction with data from other disciplines, genetic information can yield a more robust perspective on the migrations of African peoples, their exposures to various selective pressures (both natural and artificial), evidence for gene flow among Africans from various regions as well as from non-Africans (e.g., Europeans, Native Americans), and opportunities for genetic drift and in some cases founder effects in specific locales. For example, genetic studies of the general African Brazilian population have revealed the notable genetic signature of Senegambia region ancestries, which contrasts with the strong Yoruba cultural signal in this population. Furthermore, demographically detailed genetic studies among spe-

cific groups of African Brazilians indicate different geographical sources
of African slaves for the four major Brazilian regions (Silva et al. 2006).
These genetic data reveal patterns that *differ* from those expected on the
basis of historical registers, thus suggesting the role of regional ethnic
sex differences in the slave trade. Without this genetic information, the
historical record would be neither complete nor accurate in depicting the
heritage of African Brazilians. In other cases, the genetics are able to provide an independent source of data that confirm existing historical reports. An example of this is a recent report among African Brazilians of
Sao Paulo (Gonçalves et al. 2008) which suggests that the relative African
ancestral contributions are from West Central (0.445), West (0.431), and
Southeast Africa (0.123), which supports the historical documents. Merging such valuable genetic data with nongenetic sources (e.g., history, ethnography, and linguistics) can yield important details and specificity to
our reconstructions of the diverse events associated with the transatlantic
African Diaspora and its aftermath. Historically, such events are particularly well suited for quantitative assessment using our current genetic
technology. This chapter is about how such evaluations can be of benefit
in collaborative efforts to understand the implications of this major historical event.

BACKGROUND AND RATIONALE

Between the fifteenth and nineteenth centuries CE, the Atlantic trade in
enslaved Africans resulted in the forced movement of 11 to 13 million
people from Africa, mainly to the Americas (Curtin 1969). Only 9 to 11
million survived the transatlantic Middle Passage, and many more died
in the early years of captivity. The Middle Passage was a genetic bottle-
neck for enslaved Africans in that it severely restricted the initial African genetic diversity. However, the survivors of the Middle Passage were
able to regenerate much of the original diversity, primarily through gene
flow in the New World largely unencumbered by African tribal and regional restrictions and secondarily through gene flow with non-African
individuals. Increasingly, the descendants of those enslaved Africans have
sought to contextualize their ancestry by understanding more about who
their ancestors were, where they came from, what conditions initiated
their movements within the African continent and their forced migrations to the Americas, and what New World genetic events they may have
experienced. Each of these inquiries is ultimately designed to provide a
better understanding of the health status, ancestral backgrounds, and potential disease susceptibilities of contemporary descendants.

Historical records indicate that enslaved Africans came from broad
regions of continental Africa, but it has only been with the advent of anthropological genetics that we have a serious opportunity to determine

their specific regional ancestries. Molecular genetic studies have been used to trace African regional origins of many of their descendants (see Salas et al. 2004, 2005a) and to reconstruct the proportions of ancestry derived from different African regions (see Shriver and Kittles 2004). The more varied types of genes and gene systems that are employed in these reconstructions, the stronger (and more believable) the regional associations.

Reconstructing ancestry to the (African) ethnic level is a different magnitude of effort than are the regional reconstructions. This is because ethnicity is a more tenuous concept than regionality; ethnic groups change in composition and identity with greater frequency than groups migrate from one ecosystem to another. This is due to the fact that the vast majority of the ethnic groups of Africa are subsistence agriculturalists—either horticulturalists or pastoralists—who have developed behavioral and biological adaptations to facilitate their survival in a specific terrestrial biome. Moving out of the local ecosystem to a very different region with very different and new ecological constraints is a serious undertaking.

Research in reconnecting African regional and ethnic roots has been driven by the desire, on the part of many African Americans, for a deeper understanding of their ethnic origins. Conceptually, African Americans seek a tribal origin that is independent of those ethnic groups who enslaved their ancestors. Genetic advances provide the hope for a better understanding of the unique role that ancestry plays in shaping disease susceptibility and modulating disease epidemiology.

THE IMPORTANCE OF GENETICS IN AFRICAN DIASPORA RECONSTRUCTIONS

Genetic analysis has become the single most powerful line of *new* evidence being assessed to bring additional insights into the enormous human migrations that underlie the transatlantic trade in enslaved Africans. This chapter highlights the progress that has been made in identifying regional and ethnic ancestries and examines the prospects for future insights. We also acknowledge the emerging limitations of genetic-based ancestry data, particularly in the effort to link contemporary African Americans with a specific (presumably ancestral) African ethnic group.

All discussions of genetic variation among Africans of the Diaspora to the New World must begin in Africa, the homeland of all humanity (Plaza et al. 2004). This huge and ancient continent presents the most complexity in human genetics of any continent. Three characteristics define the genetics of the African continent:

- First, African genetic studies show that the deepest and oldest genetic lineages among modern humans are found in Africa. This is a reflection of our species origin and long-term residence on this continent. Africa contains the greatest levels of human genetic variation and is the source of the worldwide expansion of all modern humans. This has led some researchers to define non-Africans (e.g., Europeans, Asians) as technically subsets of African peoples. This is because non-Africans are derived from smaller groups of Africans who, after successfully leaving the continent 60,000 to 50,000 years ago, subsequently underwent their own set of evolutionary changes in the ensuing 3,000 generations.

- Second, continental Africans have five times the genetic diversity observed in the rest of the world. There are three main reasons for this increased genetic diversity among Africans, compared to non-Africans:

  Our species (*Homo sapiens sapiens*) and the precursors of our species have lived for the longest period of time in Africa. Modern humans emerged in Africa approximately 200,000 years ago (10,000 generations ago). The precursors of modern humans (bipedal hominids) were in Africa for nearly 7 million years before that. This extended residence has allowed for more mutations and recombination events, as sources of variation, to accumulate in the genomes of Africans.

  Africa is the most tropical of continents and hosts a diversity of ecological niches to which various African groups have adapted. Differences in the natural selection pressures in these niches have promoted variations in the human groups occupying and surviving in these niches. Africa is home to deserts, grasslands, tropical rainforests, steppes, mangrove swamps, and temperate forests.

  For much of human history, the average group size remained fairly small and the bulk of reproductive matings occurred among members of the group. This factor tended to promote genetic diversity *between* groups and increased the homogeneity *within* groups. This increased the magnitude of genetic mosaicism within continental Africa, compared to many other parts of the world. Africa maintained, in the early history of our species, a large number of stratified and regionally substructured indigenous groups. It is from this original African diversity that the bulk of human biodiversity emerges.

- Third, Africa continues to have the highest level of population substructure on a global level. African-descended individuals of the Americas are primarily derived from ancestors who lived in West, West Central, and Southeast Africa. Today, these areas include the countries of Senegal, Gambia, Guinea, Guinea-Bissau, Mali, Nigeria, Niger, Ghana, Sierra Leone, Liberia, Burkina Faso, Côte d'Ivoire, Benin, Togo, Cameroon, Equatorial Guinea, Gabon, the two Congos, Angola, Mozambique, and Malagasy Republic. Additional ancestral contributions may also have come from Central African Republic, northern Namibia, Mauritania, and Chad. This is the conservative list of transatlantic African ancestral regions and represents, among them, notable ecological variation, including areas of deserts, grasslands, and tropical rainforests. This ecological variation contributes to the high degree of genetic substructure in the indigenous populations of these countries. Population clusters throughout Africa are often correlated with self-described ethnicity and shared cultural and/or linguistic properties. Historical records indicate that a great proportion of Africa's substructure was tapped during the process of enslavement, travel to the Atlantic coasts, and transport to the Americas. This tells us that the African Diaspora was an opportunistic sample of diverse Africans, a fact which complicates the genetic reconstruction of New World African communities.

SOURCES OF GENETIC INFORMATION ON AFRICANS

There are several lines of genetic evidence that inform our current understandings of where African-descended peoples of the Diaspora originated. In particular, DNA derived from mitochondria, sex chromosomes, microsatellite and insertion/deletion markers, and autosomal chromosomes has been used to varying degrees to reveal the story of the population disruptions and forced movements of the numerous African ethnic groups. Each of these sources of genetic evidence (nuclear and nonnuclear DNA) contributes to elucidating specific aspects the African Diaspora experience. It is critical to understand some of the major findings within these lines of genetic evidence and integrate this into our historical, linguistic, and ethnographic databases in order to begin to decipher the true population histories. Table 3.1 lists the major sources of genetic information currently in use in ancestry reconstruction and the limits of each.

MITOCHONDRIAL DNA VARIATION

Until recently, large-scale nuclear autosomal genome sequencing projects have been impractical for technical and financial reasons (HapMap 2005). Human geneticists have therefore exploited the abundance of nonautosomal DNA to make inferences about human origins. It is for this reason that the story of the transatlantic diaspora begins in Africa with studies of mitochondrial diversity. The human mitochondrial DNA (mtDNA) genome is approximately 16.6 KB in size and is maternally inherited. Human mtDNA is readily typed by identifying nucleotide sequence motifs in the noncoding and highly mutating hypervariable regions, primarily regions 1 and 2. Mutations in these regions are often shared by related individuals, such as within a microethnic group. These shared genetic

Table 3.1. Sources of Genetic Data Used in Ancestry Reconstruction, with Particular Reference to the Transatlantic African Diaspora

Source of Data	Advantages of This Data	Limitations of This Data	Applications to African Diaspora Studies	References
mtDNA	Identifies oldest female ancestor on maternal side. Abundant in current samples; easiest to recover in ancient samples. Accessible in men and women.	Only reflects the maternal lineage. Many haplotypes do not show significant regional variation within Africa.	Used extensively to determine oldest source of maternal lineages in African American ancestries.	Ely et al.; 2006, 2007 Jackson et al., n.d Salas et al.; 2004, 2005
Y-chromosome	Identifies oldest male ancestor on paternal side.	Only reflects the paternal lineage. Only accessible in men.	Used extensively to determine oldest source of paternal lineages in African American ancestries.	Underhill 2003
Nuclear DNA	Gives more complete information about maternal and paternal lineages.	Reflects mosaic of human ancestry due to recombination.	Used extensively to study disease traits in African Americans.	McIntire et al., 2003

mutations can be termed a haplotype, and the larger group of similar haplotypes is termed a haplogroup. Sequence haplotypes are compared with the universally recognized Cambridge Reference mtDNA Sequence Standard. This allows for the identification of numerous individual haplotypes in the sublineages of African macrohaplogroups L, M, and U. Contemporary African populations are characterized by very interesting patterns of mtDNA variation, including haplogroups located close to the very root or beginning of the human mtDNA tree. This evidence is used to support the idea of a mitochondrial "Eve," the individual representing the common ancestor from which all extant mitochondrial lineages are descended, who lived in east Africa (reviewed in Templeton 2007).

Mitochondrial DNA genetic analyses take us back to our own oldest female ancestor in our maternal lineage. Since the oldest modern human female ancestor lived in Africa at least 200,000 years ago, ultimately our own oldest female ancestor will be traced to our species' "ancestral Eve." However, since the time that "ancestral Eve" lived, her original mtDNA haplotype has undergone mutations as her daughters (and their daughters) migrated around and out of continental Africa. The genetic analysis of our mtDNA actually allows us to identify our oldest female "daughter of ancestral Eve" based on the observed pattern of mutations in a portion of the mitochondrial genome. For most New World Africans, the mtDNA is of African origin, although smaller proportions of New World Africans have mtDNA linking them to Native American and European ancestral "daughters of ancestral Eve." We have recently identified African Americans with mtDNA haplotypes that are very close to the species mtDNA root—that is, close to the original mtDNA that the "ancestral Eve" is hypothesized to have had (Jackson et al. n.d.)—and we have plotted the African geographical distributions of these and about twenty other common mtDNA variants observed in African Americans.

When anthropological assessments of genetic similarity and linguistic similarity are done, they show that mtDNA variation among contemporary Africans is only weakly correlated with both language and geography (Wood et al. 2005). Simply put, language is often not such a good proxy for genetic relatedness. Language can change within a generation, while, under most historical circumstances, genetics is more resilient. For example, the Nubian peoples of Upper Egypt (southern Egypt and northern Sudan) now speak an Afro-Asiatic language (Arabic) but likely originally spoke a Nilo-Saharan language (Dr. Shomarka Keita, personal communication, February 26, 2009). Their genetics did not undergo as dramatic a modification as did their language, although there is also some evidence of the absorption of many Arab lineages into Nubian families. Certain historical events can initiate major alterations in population biology. When Bantu speakers are excluded from the analyses of mtDNA status, Wood and colleagues (2005) found that the concordance of genetics and language increased. This suggests that the expansion and dispersion of Bantu speakers was significant enough to disturb many local regional genetic patterns that were previously in place.

Research on African linguistic and geographical correlations with mtDNA finds that most U.S. African Americans have mtDNA haplotypes found in highest frequency among contemporary speakers of Niger-Congo languages, and indeed this is consistent with the historical evidence of regional sources of human trafficking for the transatlantic trade. Although the mtDNA variants uncovered in U.S. African Americans are predominantly from contemporary Niger-Congo speakers, many of these mtDNA variants are also observed among many Afro-Asiatic speakers and a few lineages of Nilo-Saharan and Khoisan speakers. The extensive linguistic and geographical distributions of these identical haplotypes suggest that African women have been broadly dispersed across the continent for tens of thousands of years, long before the transatlantic trade in enslaved Africans. The dispersal of African women to different African regional and ethnic groups may be a product of ancient population migrations and mixing associated with the formation and establishment of indigenous kingdoms and empires. Such centers of civilization are notoriously affiliated with important demography-affecting events such as militarism and warfare, regional wealth disparities, consolidated resource placement, population displacement, and biocultural assimilation. What is clear is that contemporary U.S. African American mtDNA heterogeneity is not simply a function of more recent colonial or transatlantic slavery admixture. A number of studies agree that African American mtDNA haplotypes contain variation that is consistent with that described in diverse continental African populations. The most common specific haplotype among African Americans is L2a (18.8%), followed by L1c (11%), L1b (9.2%), L3e2 (9%), and L3b (8.1%), all members of the ancient Pan-African L megahaplogroup. According to the African American SWGDAM forensic mtDNA data set, only 8% of the haplogroups observed within African Americans are more common in non-Africans (Allard et al. 2005), suggesting that today, African American maternal lineages most profoundly represent an amalgamation of African mtDNA variants with minimal non-African mtDNA variants in evidence. This diversity in maternal lineages is interesting, since historian Michael Gomez (2004) has reported that the largest percentages of enslaved African women brought to the United States during the time of the transatlantic trade were either ethnic Ibos (coming from the Bight of Bonny region) or ethnic Wolofs (coming from the Senegambia region). This genetic evidence is reconciled with the historical evidence when we realize that the current African diversity observed in U.S. African American mtDNA haplotypes was likely *already present* among the earliest African captives (Ibo and Wolof, among others). Therefore, African mtDNA ends up being a poor indicator today of *specific* African origins for U.S. African Americans and other African-descended peoples of the Atlantic diaspora, in spite of the hyperbole offered by many of the commercial genetics companies.

Y CHROMOSOME VARIATION

The Y chromosome can also be studied to elucidate the ancestral relationship between modern-day African men and African-descended men of transatlantic African Diaspora. The Y chromosome has unique inheritance patterns that make it a useful tool in assessing the history of Africans of the Diaspora. Only males have a Y chromosome, since genes on this chromosome determine male gender in humans. Like mtDNA, the Y chromosome is inherited only from one parent, in this case paternally from father to son, and does not recombine because only one parental copy is present.

Y chromosome genetics reconstructs your male lineage and points to your oldest male ancestor, "ancestral Adam." The oldest male ancestor lived 250,000 years ago in Africa, so your own oldest direct male ancestor was ultimately a "son of ancestral Adam." Most New World Africans have Y chromosome variants that are African; however, about 30% on average have non-African Y chromosome variants, mainly European in origin. This discrepancy with mtDNA origins is largely a reflection of the historical social/political/economic dynamics of enslavement. Under this situation, the status differential of European males allowed them to take sexual advantage of captive females and thus disproportionately contribute to New World African gene pools.

Approximately 90% of Y-DNA is not homologous to the X chromosome and is termed the male specific Y chromosome region. This is because many attributes of Single Nucleotide Polymorphisms (SNPs) and haplotypes are that they appear to exhibit highly nonrandom distributions across geographical space (Zhang et al. 2003). The Y chromosome may be typed by observing the slow evolving biallelic markers or unique event polymorphisms (UEPs). These SNPs may be the product of specific kinds of mutations called insertions or deletions on the Y chromosome. It is these markers that allow Y chromosomes to be categorized into haplogroup lineages. In West Africa, the Y chromosome haplogroup E3a appears to be the most common lineage with fewer contributions from haplogroups A, B, and other E lineages (Underhill et al. 2001). This E3a group can be divided into seven sublineages using a series of PCR-RFLP assays.

MICROSATELLITES AND Y-SNP

Another source of information from the Y chromosome comes from short motif repeat sequences, like $(CCTTCT)_N$, called microsatellites. A high number of repeat sequences are usually shared by related individuals and can frequently provide information about the ancestral relationships between modern-day Africans and contemporary Africans of the Americas. Researchers can identify the sublineages (i.e., subgroups) of the Y chromosome by counting the number of repeat sequence units found at various microsatellite loci. In Northwest Africa, for example, Y chromosome lineages have been subdivided into multiple haplotypes based on a set of seven microsatellite alleles (Bosch et al. 2000). When the two techniques of short nucleotide polymorphism (SNP) and microsatellite detections are combined, it is possible to identify important Y chromosome polymorphisms.

Marked differences in Y-SNP allele frequencies are observed between continental populations (Wetton et al. 2005). This allows us to distinguish between African Y chromosome haplotypes and European and Native American Y chromosome haplotypes. Allelic and haplotype frequencies for loci identified as DYS19, DYS389-I, DYS389-II, DYS390, DYS391, DYS391, DYS393, DYS437, DYS438, DYS439, and the duplicated locus DYS385 have been studied in various African populations south of the Sahara Desert (Rosa et al. 2004). These studies reaffirm that the deepest Y chromosome lineages are in Africa. This means that the evolutionarily oldest human males were Africans. This result is similar to what is observed for mtDNA, which shows that the evolutionarily oldest human females were Africans. Among West Africans there is a dominant presence of four specific Y-SNP-derived macrohaplogroups (Sanchez et al. 2005). These are the same major macrohaplogroups observed in African Americans with African Y chromosome variants.

In Africa, genetic variation in the Y chromosome is partially correlated with linguistic difference but not with geographic distance (Wood et al. 2005). This suggests, as it did for mtDNA, that the linguistic distribution of specific Y chromosome variants is independent of geography. What this infers is that African men show some clustering by language, but not by geography. Most of this clustering has to do with the expansion and dispersion of Bantu speakers. When Wood and colleagues (2005) removed Bantu speakers from their analyses, there was no correlation between African linguistic group affiliation and Y chromosome status. Outside of the Bantu speakers, language has little bearing on the movement of Y chromosome variants in Africa. This suggests that historically either a small number of broadly distributed African males contributed to the distribution of particular Y chromosome variants, a possibility that is consistent with the effects of polygamy, or a large number of African males have been assimilated, in historical times, into diverse African ethnic and regional groups. In either scenario, there is a clear suggestion that African males have travelled and settled extensively throughout continental Africa, obfuscating any significant regional demarcations, within Africa, by Y chromosome status. As is the case for mtDNA, Y chromosome variation within continental Africa ends up being a poor indicator today of *specific* African ethnic origins for African Americans and other African-descended peoples of the Atlantic diaspora, despite the assertions of many for-profit genetics companies. African Y chromosome diversification is evolutionarily too deep, has been around for too long, and is already too geographically diverse to be considered alone to be regionally or ethnically specific.

THE nDNA VARIANTS

Studies of nuclear DNA (nDNA) diversity reveal that important African genetic retentions have persisted among the peoples of the Americas derived from the indigenous groups of the West and West Central regions of Africa. A number of nuclear genes commonly found include the Duffy null allele (Fyo), considered a definitive marker of African ancestry, the sickle cell allele (in its various molecular forms), and certain specific HLA polymorphisms. The persistence of these African genes, such as certain molecular variants of sickle cell, among transatlantic Diasporic groups, in spite of the general absence of the environmental factors thought to select for these genetic traits (e.g., highly endemic malaria), is somewhat surprising (Hanchard et al. 2006). Other genetic traits show similar patterns of retention, including body size and energy stores (Luke et al. 2001), hypertension susceptibilities (linked to rennin-angiotensin genes) (Rotimi et al. 1996), and the HLA-DQAI allele (Zimmerman et al. 1995). These retained nuclear DNA polymorphisms suggest, in conjunction with the mtDNA and Y chromosome evidence, that New World African-descended groups are still strongly linked genetically to Africa, even after 400 years (fifty generations) of separation. In evolutionary terms, 400 years is expected to be long enough to observe some effects on human microevolution, particularly given the disenfranchised and vulnerable state in which African Americans were held for most of these 400 years. Yet a strong African genetic signal persists. The strength of this signal is a reflection of the consequences of such effects as historical positive assortative mating among peoples of African descent as well as the impact of historical residential and economic segregation rules that restricted the opportunities for gene flow (e.g., reduced admixture effects).

LIMITS TO USING GENETICS TO IDENTIFY THE SPECIFIC AFRICAN ETHNIC ORIGINS OF NEW WORLD AFRICANS

Genetic data have long been used successfully to explore population history (MacEachern 2001), and the value of these approaches has generally been recognized by geneticists. However, there are limitations to these techniques when interpreted in isolation of the historical, ethnographic, linguistic, and archaeological data. Some of these problems include the potential for over extrapolation of limited genetic data and the tendency to assume deep and essentialist historical continuity to contemporary names and groups. There has been a great deal of recent speculation about the ability of mtDNA or Y chromosome analyses alone to identify the ethnicity and regional location of one's oldest maternal and paternal ancestors, respectively, and this has led to the birth of commercial enterprises ready to find one's ancestry for a fee and even issue highly questionable "certificates of authenticity." The major limitations to using mtDNA or Y chromosome data to pinpoint the ethnic group of one's ancestors include the following:

- First, contemporary ethnic groups are not the same as historical ethnic groups. Therefore, a genetic test that demonstrates even an *identical* mtDNA or Y chromosome match between an African American and a contemporary African, for example, a modern Yoruba individual, should not be used to imply that the original, oldest common shared ancestor of these two individuals was also of Yoruba ethnicity. The Yoruba today number over 20 million, and they reside in a number of countries in West Africa (primarily southwestern Nigeria, Benin, and Togo). However, like contemporary African ethnic groups, the Yoruba emerged in West Africa as a coherent ethnic group *after* the onset of the transatlantic trade in enslaved Africans. Prior to this, they were not known as a single people, and the historical literature refers to these proto-Yoruba by many names (Anagos, Ana, Nago, Anago, Lucumi, etc.). During the nineteenth century, the Yoruba assimilated many local subgroups into their ranks. This fact reminds us that ethnicity is not a static variable. Ethnicity changes over generational time and across geographical space, yet many gene-based ancestral reconstructions assume an absence of historical change in population composition and structure in Africa. This is both naïve and ahistorical, and it will ultimately cripple the public confidence in the use of genetic data in historical ancestral reconstructions.
- Second, African mtDNA (and Y chromosome variants) currently have very broad geographical distributions on the African continent (and throughout the African Diasporas worldwide). Neither mtDNA nor Y chromosome regionally distinguished West African and West Central African (Ely et al. 2006, Hünemier et al. 2007). The genetic variants recovered from such broadly distributed groups and used to reconstruct ancestry in African Americans are tens of thousands of years (and thousands of generations) *older* than the modern African ethnic groups to which they are being linked. Therefore, many of these genes (mtDNA,

Y chromosome, and nDNA) appear in many different, geographically dispersed ethnic groups. Given that our scientific databases on Africa are all deficient and not representative of the true extent of African diversity, they can only give us a *partial* and *incomplete* interpretation of African diversity. Most of the sampled countries contain hundreds of different ethnic groups, yet our scientific database contains, at best, only dozens of ethnic groups indigenous to each country. This means that while the accuracy of the biochemical analysis of the molecular genetics is not in question, the legitimacy of the interpretation of these results in the reconstruction of ancestry is frequently questionable.

African-descended individuals of the transatlantic African Diaspora are particularly vulnerable to such misrepresentations because of the dearth of pre-emancipation lineage-specific documentation (to both collaborate and refine the interpreted molecular genetics) and the intensified normal human desire to know one's origins. Entrepreneurs who have commercialized such gene-based identities that restrict African American to a specific African contemporary ethnic group have frequently misrepresented the data and deceived their customers, taking commercial advantage of both their customer's vulnerability and the underdeveloped state of the science.

RECENT INNOVATIONS FOR THE FUTURE OF GENETIC ASSESSMENTS OF THE AFRICAN DIASPORA

Fortunately, large-scale SNP typing efforts have recently become both more economical and feasible. These efforts have yielded single run datasets of more than 500,000 typed polymorphisms in multiple individuals. The 1,000 Genomes Project is a current effort to apply the advances in technology to include more genetic information on individuals and groups in their assessment. The general principal is that the more genes that are studied, the more accurate the ancestral reconstructions potentially become. This is especially important for African-descended individuals in the Americas because most such individuals and groups represent the historical amalgamation of African peoples with modest gene flow from Europeans and Native Americans and limited extra-genetic documentation available on any of this. The ancestral profile for African Americans is thus *more* complicated than for less heterogeneous peoples with less complex and geographically diverse biological lineages.

A second anticipated innovation is the increased collaboration, in some circles, of geneticists with various nongenetic experts. These collaborations, such as those spearheaded by Dr. Henry Louis Gates of Harvard University, can begin to accelerate the revelation of insights into the population histories of the people of the transatlantic African Diaspora. The climate has not always been receptive among historians, ethnographers, linguists, or archaeologists for the contributions of geneticists, and vice versa, but one fact to emerge from the Human Genome Project is beginning to open the door to such collaboration, at least on the part of geneticists. This is the observation that the human genome has far fewer genes than was expected and that each coding gene is responsible for producing four or five proteins (only one protein was the traditional dogma). We do not yet understand what factors signal a gene to produce which protein at a specific time, but the strong sentiment is that the control of gene expression is epigenetic. These nongenetic factors in the form of chemicals on the chromosome may influence the patterns of gene expression and the signal for the production of specific proteins. The source of these chemical epigenetic factors is likely environmental—meaning, in many cases, they are socioculturally induced. So history, ethnography, linguistics, and archaeology clearly have something to contribute to genetic interpretations, and genetics is increasingly being integrated as an independent source of confirmation in nongenetic assessments.

THE GENETICS OF THE AFRICAN DIASPORA IN THE AMERICAS

There have been many successive waves of African migration that have created the modern understanding of the African Diasporas. The transatlantic African Diaspora is associated with four centuries of forced enslavement, transport, relocation to the Americas, and internal migrations. Inherent in this significant relocation mega-event was the scrambling of ethnic-based genetic markers (associated initially with the transport and confinement on the African coasts prior to the transatlantic journey), an initial reduction in some African genetic diversity (as a consequence of the often profound physiological and psychological stresses of the Middle Passage), and a subsequent reorganization and some reexpansion of genetic diversity in the New World (as a consequence of exposure to reemerging and new selective pressures, gene flow among diverse Africans and with non-Africans, and certain regional opportunities for genetic drift) (Jackson 1991, 2006). The transatlantic African Diaspora was a major historic event in human history that dramatically changed the genetic landscape of the Americas, affecting the gene pools of both indigenous groups (e.g., Native Americans) and that of other immigrants (e.g., Europeans). The patterns of change were not uniform over the different geographical regions or types of enslavement, and many reports now document the divergent genetic consequences of this Diaspora on the contemporary descendants of these Africans in the Americas.

Based on genetic assessments supplemented with historical data, it appears that the majority of Africans brought to the Americas came from

West Africa. Early genetic evidence suggested that one-third came from West Central Africa (Salas et al. 2005a). More recent comparison of mtDNA sequences from West, West Central, and Southeast Africa with sequences from over 1,148 U.S. African Americans showed that more than 55% of the U.S. lineages have a West African ancestor, and approximately 41% came from West Central or Southeast Africa (Salas et al. 2005a). Our mtDNA database of over 6,000 individuals confirms that most U.S. African Americans have predominant African ancestry linking them to the peoples of West and West Central Africa with a minor component from Southeast Africa. We have also identified a few U.S. African Americans with mtDNA that identically match the mtDNA of Khoisan speakers from Southwest Africa and others that identically match the mtDNA of NiloSaharan speakers from North Central Africa (Jackson et al. n.d.). These Khoisan mtDNA types may have entered the African American gene pool as a relic of Khoisan-speaking populations that inhabited Southeast Africa (Mozambique) prior to their displacement by Bantu-speaking migrants (Pereira et al. 2001), or they may have reached the Americas via individuals originally from the areas of West Central Africa that border on Southwest Africa (Namibia). The presence in U.S. African Americans of mtDNA haplotypes also observed among contemporary NiloSaharan speakers reminds us of the importance of the trans-Saharan trade routes in African history and the fact that these routes transported humans as well as gold, salt, and other valuables. Given the opportunistic nature of the transatlantic trade in enslaved Africans, it is not unexpected that the tentacles of transatlantic slavery might have, on occasion, reached deeply into North Central Africa.

In North America, different constellations of African groups were brought via the transatlantic trade to various staging areas (Jackson 1997, 2003, 2004, Eltis et al. 1999). Three major areas of importation into the United States have been studied extensively: the Chesapeake Bay (includes Maryland, Virginia, Delaware, and Washington, D.C.), the Carolina Coast (includes Lowland North Carolina, Lowland South Carolina, northern coastal Georgia, and northern coastal Florida), and the Mississippi Delta (includes Mississippi, Louisiana, eastern Texas, southern Arkansas, and southern Tennessee). In each of these regions, the founding African regional groups varied significantly, and this has had important implications for the descendant groups from these regions.

AFRICAN ANCESTRAL ORIGINS IN THE CHESAPEAKE BAY REGION

In the Chesapeake Bay, in late 1619, a Dutch ship brought twenty Africans to Port Comfort near Jamestown, Virginia. These Africans were sold into indentured servitude. They were the first Africans in the English North American colonies, and they played a critical role in the development of the colony. During this time, strong communities of indentured servants (African and European) and slaves (African and Native American) emerged, and there was significant cultural interchange and gene flow between the groups as new families formed. Currently, we do not have an adequate sampling of aDNA (ancient DNA) from a representative cross-section of these early Africans to determine their origins in specific region(s) of the continent. After 1700, however, the historical records indicate that large numbers of enslaved persons from West and West Central Africa were brought to the Chesapeake Bay, and the colonial government passed important restrictions mandating the enslavement of free Africans and barring marriages between Europeans and non-Europeans. Enslaved Africans from the Bight of Bonny area of modern-day southeastern Nigeria and western Cameroon were particularly prominent among the early forced immigrants (38%). Among these groups, the Ibo peoples dominated numerically and culturally. Additional ethnic groups brought to this region from the Bight of Bonny are listed in Table 3.2. Africans were also brought from Gold Coast (16% from modern-day Ghana and Burkina Faso), West Central Africa (16% from modern-day Angola, the two Congos, Gabon, Equatorial Guinea, and southern Cameroon), Senegambia (15% from modern-day Senegal and Gambia), and Upper Guinea (11% from modern-day Guinea, northern Sierra Leone, and northwest Liberia). Enslaved African and African-descended laborers became the driving force to harvest labor-intensive tobacco crops grown especially in Maryland's southern and eastern shore regions. Maryland's central location in the then English colonies as well as its establishment as a shipping center soon meant that Africans by the hundreds of thousands were being funneled through the Chesapeake Bay for enslavement in the mid-Atlantic and Southern colonies. The region was also home to a growing free African American population, and geographic distinctions greatly impacted their status. By the 1720s, there were enough native-born African Americans in Maryland to create their own distinctive local culture, one that also received early influences from local indentured Irish workers and Native American prisoners. Genetically, we are still able to recognize a distinctive "Bight of Bonny" signal among the current descendant population that appears to translate into increased susceptibilities for aggressive, early onset, and hormone-resistant forms of breast and prostate cancer (Jackson 2008).

AFRICAN ANCESTRAL ORIGINS IN THE CAROLINA COAST REGION

The Carolina Coast regions of Savannah, Georgia, and Charleston, South Carolina, were also the important arrival points for enslaved Africans during the transatlantic trade. Large numbers of enslaved persons from

Table 3.2. Major Bight of Bonny coastal and hinterland region micro-ethnic groups who contributed to the founding populations of the Chesapeake Bay

Group name (contemporary and/or historical)	Current location in Bight of Bonny region
Bakoko (Basoo)	**Cameroon**, Littoral Province (south of Douala)
Basaa (Mbele)	**Cameroon**, Littoral Province and Central Province
Bubi (Ibhubhi)	**Fernando Po** and **Biombo Islands** and **Gabon**, Ogooue-Lolo Province (west of Koulamouton)
Douala (Duala)	**Cameroon**, Littoral Province (near Wouri River)
Efik	**Nigeria**, Cross River State (near Calabar)
Ejagham (Ekoi, Kwa)	**Nigeria**, Cross River State and **Cameroon**, southwestern region
Fang (Pamue)	**Cameroon**, South Province (near Kribi), **Gabon**, Northwest, Estuary, and Woleu Ntem Provinces and **Equatorial Guinea**
Kwa' (Bakwa)	**Cameroon**, Littoral Province
Ibibo	**Nigeria**, Akwa Ibom State (Cross River area)
Igbo (Ibo)	**Nigeria**, Abia, Anambra, Ebonyi, Enugu, and Imo States
Ijo (Ijaw)	**Nigeria**, Bayelsa State
Malimba (Limba)	**Cameroon**, Littoral Province (near Sanaga River)
Mokpwe (Bakweri)	**Cameroon**, SouthWest Province
Myene (Omyene, Pangwe)	**Gabon**, Ogoone-Maritime and Middle Ogooue Province
Yasa (Yassa)	**Cameroon**, South Province, **Equatorial Guinea** (coastal), and **Gabon**

Source: Modified from Jackson 2008.

West Central Africa (40%) and from West Africa, particularly from Senegambia (23%) and Upper Guinea (18%), were brought to the Carolina Coast in the seventeenth through nineteenth centuries. Africans were intentionally mixed culturally to reduce the possibilities for successful revolts and to facilitate their assimilation into plantation-slave society. Among these Africans of the Carolina Coast emerged the contemporary Gullah/Geechee culture, a local synthesis of various West and West Central African cultures with important Native American and some European influences. Gullah/Geechee culture retains many African elements and extends from southeastern North Carolina to northern Florida along the Atlantic coast. Throughout the Carolina Coast and the southeastern United States in general, the historic intermarriage of Africans and Native Americans was facilitated by the disproportionate numbers of African male slaves to females (3 to 1), their frequent co-enslavement in close proximity, and the decimation of Native American males by disease, enslavement, and prolonged war against the colonists. The genetic consequences include the incorporation of Native American mtDNA into many African American lineages, primarily haplogroups A and B, and the strong genetic imprint of the large number of West Central Africans on contemporary local African Americans. This imprint may be responsible for the enhanced salt sensitivity and elevated risk for hypertension and strokes in this area (Jackson 2004).

AFRICAN ANCESTRAL ORIGINS IN THE MISSISSIPPI DELTA REGION

Africans were brought to the Mississippi Delta along with the early French and Spanish settlers. A large proportion came from Senegambia (32%), Bight of Benin (25% from modern-day Benin and western Nigeria), and Central Africa (25%). Only 8% came from the Bight of Bonny. Here in the Mississippi River Delta region and its hinterlands they interacted with local Native Americans and Europeans to develop a number of unique microethnic groups including the Sabines (a combination of the lineages of Mississippi Delta Africans, Houma Native Americans, and French settlers), Cane River Creoles (from the combined lineages of local African Americans, indigenous Native Americans, and French settlers), Clifton Chocktaw/Appalachee, Tunican Biloxi, African American [black] Creoles, and many others. Like the Chesapeake Bay, the geography of the region facilitated the semi-isolation and relative self-subsistence of many early groups. The genetic consequences in this part of the U.S. African Diaspora are both complex and profound. Here we find African American lineages with highly varied amounts of non-African components, yet pronounced cultural fusion (the use of sassafras for medicinal and dietary purposes, retention of aspects of vodun culture, etc.). The sharing of cultural elements may have had profound effects on the expressed genetics of the integrating groups. The shared use of sassafras, for example, may have served as a novel catalyst, in susceptible individuals, for pancreatic and liver cancers (Jackson 2004).

AFRICAN GENETIC DIVERSITY ELSEWHERE IN THE AMERICAS

The vast, often indiscriminate, and long-standing transatlantic trade in enslaved Africans impacted every country in the Western Hemisphere. In the Caribbean and in Central and South America, the genetic consequences of the African Diaspora are notable. Among the Garifunas of Honduras and the Chocos of Colombia (Salas et al. 2005b), both show a major genetic component (~84%) from African groups living south of the Sahara Desert and a minor genetic component for Native Central/South

Americans. However, the Garifunas show evidence of a founder effect while the Chocos have several mtDNA types in such high frequency as to suggest the action of genetic drift. Clearly a small number of women formed the basis for this regional group in the New World.

In Mexico, a constellation of ancestry informative genetic markers (AIMs) have been used to quantify the African component of the indigenous population. Using 69 autosomal AIMs, Martinez-Marignac and colleagues (2007) estimated the overall African contribution to contemporary Mexicans to be 5%. Yet Mexico's pronounced population substructure suggests that certain areas may have much higher African genetic components, particularly around the regions where Afro-Mexicans established towns, worked the plantations, and labored in the mines.

In Ecuador, the African Ecuadorian population, their genetic contributions to the male line are 44% African, 31% European, and 15% Native American; the last value is the highest percentage reported so far for an African-derived American group. In this same study (González-Andrade et al. 2007), autosomal (non-sex genes) admixture was estimated as 56% African, 16% European, and 28% Amerindian, one of the highest Native American admixture rates among Africans of the New World.

In Uruguay, serological and molecular markers indicate that African Diaspora populations have had an important genetic influence in the current population (Bertoni et al. 2005). Even in Argentina, where there is little of a "visible" sub-Saharan African presence, at least 10% of the current population exhibit African-derived alleles. (In the mid-nineteenth century at least 30% of the Argentina nationals were of predominantly African descent.) In Buenos Aires, Argentina, Martinez Marignac and colleagues (2004) found that the African contribution to the general population gene pool was 6.5% (+/-6.4), while other researchers have suggested an African contribution of around 10% (Fejerman et al. 2005).

In Brazil, the population is remarkably heterogeneous. In a study of four regional African Brazilian groups, most of the Y chromosomes were from sub-Saharan Africa, and the proportion of Y chromosomes of European origin was greater than that of Y chromosomes of Amerindian origin (Abe-Sandes et al. 2004). Many western Bantu associated mtDNA haplotypes (commonly seen in Angola) have been observed among African Brazilians (Plaza et al. 2004) in addition to West African and other West Central variants. The detection of Angolan mtDNA lineages is consistent with the historical record, since Brazil was one of the main destinations for enslaved persons from this region of Africa (Plaza et al. 2004). Among African Brazilians living in Rio de Janeiro and Porto Alegre, their mtDNA data indicates that respectively 69% and 82% of the matrilineages originated from West Central/Southeast Africa (Hünemeier et al. 2007). These estimates are in close agreement with historical records which indicated that most of the Brazilian slaves who arrived in Rio de Janeiro were from West Central Africa. In a study on Y chromosome variation among self-identified "blacks" in Rio de Janeiro, high heterogeneity and a strong European influence was detected along with evidence of population substructuring (Domingues et al. 2007). Among African Brazilians in Sao Paulo, only 48% of the Y chromosomes but 85% of the mtDNA haplogroups were characteristic of sub-Saharan Africa. Within Brazil, there is quite a bit of regional variation in the proportions of African descent in the local population. For example, in Rio Grande do Sul, Brazil, 16% of the mtDNA haplogroups were African, even though all of the individuals tested identified themselves as "white" (Marrero et al. 2005, Hünemeier et al. 2007).

PATTERNS OF EUROPEAN GENE FLOW INTO AFRICAN DIASPORA GROUPS

A great deal of research has gone into studies of the genetic contributions of European males versus European females to the gene pools of the African Diaspora. Researchers know that these contributions have not been uniform for men and women (Parra et al. 2001, Tian et al. 2006). Genetic contributions from European men have disproportionately influenced the genetics of most African American lineages compared with genetic contributions from European women, a clear reflection of the sexual politics and political-economic disenfranchisement associated with slavery. Although more African men than African women were captured in Africa and able to survive the Middle Passage and its aftermath in the Americas, we observe more European male-associated genes (such as Y chromosome variants) in contemporary New World Africans than European female-associated genes (such as mtDNA variants). This pattern is observed throughout the transatlantic African Diaspora. Even in the Cabo Verde archipelago, a chain of seven islands that served as a Senegambian outpost of the Atlantic trade in enslaved Africans, Y chromosome variants found among (male) Portuguese colonizers are clearly evident among the Africans, while mtDNA variants more commonly encountered among the Portuguese are more rarely observed in the Africans. In contrast, the mtDNA types of Cabo Verde are characteristically West African; almost *no* mitochondrial input comes from the female Portuguese colonizers (Brehm et al. 2002). Similar patterns are seen further south on the Atlantic islands of São Tomé and Principe, where a significant heterogeneous distribution of European paternal lineages can be detected in the two major ethnic groups, the Forros and the Angolares (Gonsalves et al. 2007). So this historic pattern of gender-directed gene flow is another characteristic of the genetics of the African Diaspora.

Among U.S. African Americans, the frequencies of European Y chromosomes are relatively consistent, 26.4 +/- 8.9%, in different geographical locations (Hammer et al. 2005). African mtDNA nucleotide sequences have been found at only about 1% in different European populations—

mainly L1b and L3b (Maliarchuk and Czarny 2005). Including M and possibly U6 as African-derived mtDNA variants, however, greatly increases the African component in Europeans. (Olivieri et al. 2006, however, consider these haplotypes to be Eurasian.) Using 2,018 autosomal SNP markers and 6 mtDNA haplogroups for a group of 93 African American men, the European genetic contribution was only 8.5% in the mtDNA (maternal lineages) but 28.5% in the Y chromosome (paternal lineages), and nearly 20% in the autosomal genes (Lind et al. 2007). This demonstrates the gender-based differences in the genetic contributions from male versus females to the genomes of African American individuals. As a direct consequence of transatlantic slavery practices, the genetic contributions of European males dominate those of European females among African-descended peoples throughout the New World. The genetics of the African Diaspora show evidence of strong asymmetric, sex-biased genetic blending in the founding and ongoing history of the New World African population, with the African and Amerindian contribution being highest from maternal lineages (as measured by mitochondrial DNA) and the European contribution foremost from paternal lineages (estimated from Y chromosome haplogroups). This phenomenon has been observed in Brazil and in several other Latin American countries, suggesting that it might constitute a universal characteristic of both the Iberian and English (and probably French) colonizations of the Americas (Gonçalves et al. 2007).

PATTERNS OF AFRICAN GENETIC CONTRIBUTIONS IN U.S. HISPANIC (LATINO/A) GROUPS

In the United States, the African paternal contributions to Hispanic populations are much higher in the Northeast (10.5 +/- 6.4%) than in the Southwest (1.5 +/- 0.9%) or the Midwest (0%) (Hammer et al. 2005). In fact, it is this regional variation in the African component in many Latino/a ethnic groups that accounts for the genetic heterogeneity of New World Hispanic peoples. Hispanic (Latino/a) peoples are regionally biologically distinct, largely as a reflection of their differential amounts of African genetic diversity. Of course, this genetic diversity is further augmented by the cultural (e.g., dietary, linguistic) differences among Hispanic (Latino/a) peoples as well.

SUMMARY

The transatlantic African Diaspora created a fascinating new distribution of African genetic diversity as well as opportunities for new gene combinations through interactions among Africans from various regions and through local interactions with non-Africans. What has emerged from this major population dispersion is an amazingly large number of African genetic retentions, evidence of modest gene flow with Europeans (primarily North Atlantic and Western European males), localized limited gene flow with Native Americans (primarily Native American women from a diversity of ethnic groups), and some regional opportunities for genetic drift and founder effects. African-descended groups in the New World retain pronounced genetic affinities with West, West Central, and Southeast Africans, in spite of 400 years of separation. These genetic links are underscored by the evidence from maternally inherited mtDNA, paternally inherited Y chromosome, and nuclear DNA markers of African ancestry. Undoubtedly the modest presence of non-African genetic variants in New World Africans is a reflection of past cultural preferences (i.e., positive assortative mating practices), social discrimination by non-Africans, and various instances of geographical and economic isolation.

A review of the literature on the genetics of the transatlantic African Diaspora indicates the continuing need for more substantive interactions between geneticists and researchers in other disciplines. This is due in part to a compartmentalization that appears to exist between the life sciences and especially the humanities, where many researchers examining the African Diaspora are housed. There are currently stronger collaborations between the social sciences and anthropological geneticists, but the level of intellectual interaction remains inadequate. The new genetic technology that allows us to study human genetic variation in increasing detail still needs to be contextualized within an appropriate historical and anthropological framework. The editors of this book are to be commended for including a chapter on genetics in a volume that addresses the transatlantic African Diaspora. This is the direction that future endeavors need to take if we are to fully appreciate the consequences of this, the largest human migration in the history of our species.

NOTE

The authors wish to thank Dr. Shomarka Keita for his helpful comments on an earlier version of this chapter. The authors are responsible, however, for all interpretations expressed.

REFERENCES

Abe-Sandes K, Silva WA Jr, Zago MA. 2004. Heterogeneity of the Y chromosome in Afro-Brazilian populations. *Hum Biol.* Feb;76(1): 77–86.
Allard MW, Polansky D, Miller K, Wilson MR, Monson KL, Budowle B. 2005. Characterization of human control region sequences of the African American SWGDAM forensic mtDNA data set. *Forensic Sc Int.* Mar 10;148(2–3): 169–79.
Bertoni B, Jin L, Chakraborty R, Sans M. 2005. Directional mating and a rapid

male population expansion in a hybrid Uruguayan population. *Am J Hum Biol.* Nov–Dec:17(6): 801–8.

Bosch E, Calafell F, Perez-Lezaun A, Comas D, Izaabel H, Akhayat O, Sefiani A, Hariti G, Dugoujon JM, Bertranpetit J. 2000. Y chromosome STR haplotypes in four populations from northwest Africa. *Int J Legal Med.* 114(1–2): 36–40.

Brehm A, Pereira L, Bandelt HJ, Prata MJ, Amorim A. 2002. Mitochondrial portrait of the Cabo Verde archipelago: The Senegambian outpost of Atlantic slave trade. *Ann Hum Genet.* Jan;66(Pt 1): 49–60.

Curtin PD. 1969. *The Atlantic slave trade: a census.* Madison: University of Wisconsin Press.

Domingues PM, Gusmao L, da Siva DA, Amorim A, Pereira RW, de Carvalho EF. 2007. Sub-Saharan Africa descendents in Rio de Janeiro (Brazil): population and mutational data for 12 Y-STR loci. *Int J Legal Med.* May;121(3): 238–41.

Eltis D, Behrendt S, Richardson D, Klein H. 1999. *The Atlantic slave trade: a database on CD-ROM.* Cambridge: Cambridge University Press.

Ely B, Wilson JL, Jackson F, Jackson BA. 2006. African-American mitochondrial DNAs often match mtDNAs found in multiple African Ethnic groups. *BMC Biol.* Oct 12;4: 34–45.

Fejerman L, Carnese FR, Giocochea AS, Avena SA, Dejean DB, Ward RH. 2005. African ancestry of the population of Buenos Aires. *Am J Phys Anthropol.* Sep;128(1): 164–70.

Gomez, MA. 2004. *Exchanging our country marks: the transformation of African identities in the colonial and antebellum South.* Chapel Hill: University of North Carolina Press.

Gonçalves R, Spínola H, Brehm A. 2007. Y-chromosome lineages in São Tomé e Príncipe islands: evidence of European influence. *Am J Hum Biol.* May–Jun;19(3): 422–28.

Gonçalves VF, Carvalho CM, Bortolini MC, Bydlowski SP, Pena SD. 2008. The phylogeography of African Brazilians. *Hum Hered.* 65(2): 23–32.

González-Andrade F, Sánchez D, González-Solórzano J, Gascón S, Martínez-Jarreta B. 2007. Sex-specific genetic admixture of Mestizos, Amerindian Kichwas, and Afro-Ecuadorans from Ecuador. *Hum Biol.* Feb;79(1): 51–77.

Hammer MF, Chamberlain VF, Kearney VF, Stover D, Zhang G, Karafet T, Walsh B, Redd AJ. 2005. Population structure of Y chromosome SNP haplogroups in the United States and forensic implications for constructing Y chromosome STR databases. *Forensic Sc Int.* Dec 1;164(1): 45–55.

Hanchard NA, Hambleton X, Harding RM, and McKenzie CA. 2006. Predicted declines in sickle allele frequency in Jamaica using empirical data. *Am J Hematol.* Nov; 81(11): 817–23.

Hünemeier T, Carvalho C, Marrero AR, Salzano FM, Junho Pena SD, Bortolini MC. 2007. Niger-Congo speaking populations and the formation of the Brazilian gene pool: mtDNA and Y-chromosome data. *Am J Phys Anthropol.* Jun;133(2): 854–67.

International HapMap Consortium. 2005. A haplotype map of the human genome. *Nature* 437: 1299–1320.

Jackson FLC. 1991. An evolutionary perspective on salt, hypertension, and human genetic variability. *Hypertension* 17(1):I-129–I-132.

———. 1997. Concerns and priorities in genetic studies: insights from recent African American biohistory. *Seton Hall Law Rev.* 27(3): 951–70.

———. 2003. Ethnogenetic layering: a novel approach to determining environmental health risk potentials among children from three U.S. regions. *J Children's Health* 1(3): 369–86.

———. 2004. Human genetic variation and health: ethnogenetic layering as a way of detecting relevant population substructuring. *Brit Med Bull.* 69: 215–35.

———. 2006. An anthropological science perspective on the salt-hypertension hypothesis. *Transforming Anthropology* 14(2): 126–30.

———. 2008. Ancestral links of Chesapeake Bay region African Americans to specific Bight of Bonny (West Africa) microethnic groups and increased frequency of aggressive breast cancer in both regions. *Am J Hum Biol.* 20: 165–73.

Jackson FLC, Wilson JL, Jackson BA, Ely B. n.d. African geographical, linguistic, and ecological distributions of common African American mtDNA variants. Submitted.

Lind JM, Hutcheson-Dilks HB, Williams SM, Moore JH, Essex M, Ruiz-Pesini E, Wallace DC, Tishkoff SA, O'Brien SJ, Smith MW. 2007. Elevated male European and female African contributions to the genomes of African American individuals. *Hum Genet.* Jan;120(5): 713–22.

Luke A, Guo X, Adeyemo AA, Wilks R, Forrester T, Lowe W, Comuzzle AG, Martin LJ, Zhu S, Rotimi CN, Cooper RS. 2001. Heritability of obesity-related traits among Nigerians, Jamaicans, and U.S. Black people. *Int J Obes Relat Metab Disord.* Jul;25(7):1034–41.

MacEachern S. 2001. Montagnard ethnicity and genetic relations in northern Cameroon. Comment on the "Peopling of Sub-Saharan Africa": The case study of Cameroon, by G. Spedini et al. *Am J Phys Anth* 114: 357–60.

Maliarchuk BA, Czarny J. 2005. African DNA lineages in mitochondrial gene pool of Europeans. *Mol Biol (Mosk).* Sep–Oct; 39(5): 806–12.

Marrero AR, Das Neves Leite FP, De Almeida Carvalho B, Peres LM, Kommers TC, Da Cruz IM, Salzano FM, Ruiz-Linares A, Da Silva Junior WA, Bortolini MC. 2005. Heterogeneity of the genome ancestry of individuals classified as White in the state of Rio Grande do Sul, Brazil. *Am J Hum Biol.* July-Aug; 17(4): 496–506.

Martinez-Marignac VL, Bertoni B, Parra EJ, Bianchi NO. 2004. Characterization of admixture in an urban sample from Buenos Aires, Argentina, using uniparentally and biparentally inherited genetic markers. *Hum Biol.* Aug;76(4): 543–57.

Martinez-Marignac VL, Valladares A, Cameron E, Chan A, Perera A, Globus-Goldberg R, Wacher N, Kumate J, McKeigue P, O'Donnel D, Shriver MD, Cruz M, Parra EJ. 2007. Admixture in Mexico City: implications for admixture mapping of type 2 diabetes genetic risk factors. *Hum Genet.* Feb;120(6): 807–19.

Olivieri A, Archilli A, Pala M, Battaglia V, Fornario S, Al-Zahery N, Scozzari R, Cruciani F, Behar DM, Dugoujon JM, Coudray C, Santachlara-Benerecetti AS, Semino O, Bandelt HJ, Torroni A. 2006. The mtDNA legacy of the Levantine early Upper Palaeolithic in Africa. *Science.* Dec 15;314(5806): 1767–70.

Parra EJ, Kittles RA, Argyropoulos G, Pfaff CL, Hiester K, Bonilla C, Sylvester N, Parrish-Gause D, Garvey WT, Jin L, McKeigue PM, Kamboh MI, Ferrell RE,

Pollitzer WS, Shriver MD. 2001. Ancestral proportions and admixture dynamics in geographically defined African Americans living in South Carolina. *Am J Phys Anthropol.* Jan;114(1): 18–29.

Plaza S, Salas S, Calafell F, Corte-Real F, Bertranpetit J, Carracedo A, Comas D. 2004. Insights into the western Bantu dispersal: mtDNA lineage analysis in Angola. *Hum Genet.* Oct;115(5): 439–47.

Pereira L, Macaulay V, Torroni A, Scozzari R, Prata MJ, Amorim A. 2001. Prehistoric and historic traces in the mtDNA of Mozambique: insights into the Bantu expansions and the slave trade. *Ann Hum Genet.* Sep;65(Pt 5): 439–58.

Rotimi C, Puras A, Cooper R, McFarlane-Anderson N, Forrester T, Ogunbiyi O, Morrison L, Ward R. 1996. Polymorphisms of rennin-angiotensin genes among Nigerians, Jamaicans, and African Americans. *Hypertension* Mar;27(3:t 2): 558–63.

Salas A, Richards M, De la Fe T, Lareu M-V,Sobrino B, Sánchez-Diz P, Macaulay V, Carracedo A. 2002. The Making of the African mtDNA Landscape *Am J Hum Genet.* 71(5): 1082–1111.

Salas A, Richards M, Lareu MV, Scozzari R, Coppa A, Torroni A, Macaulay V, Carracedo A. 2004. The African diaspora: mitochondrial DNA and the Atlantic slave trade. *Am J Hum Genet.* Mar; 74(3): 454–65.

Salas A, Carracedo A, Richards M, Macaulay V. 2005a. Charting the ancestry of African Americans. *Am J Hum Genet.* Oct;77(4): 676–80.

Salas A, Richards M, Lareu MV, Sobrino B, Silva S, Matamoros M, Macaulay V, Carracedo A. 2005b. Shipwrecks and founder effects: divergent demographic histories reflected in Caribbean mtDNA. *Am J Phys Anthropol.* Dec;128(4): 855–60.

Sanchez JJ, Hallenberg C, Borsting C, Hernandez A, Morling N. 2005. High frequencies of Y chromosome lineages characterized by E3b1, DYS19-11, DYS392-12 in Somali males. *Eur J Hum Genet.* Jul;13(7): 856–66.

Shriver MD, Kittles RA. 2004. Genetic ancestry and the search for personalized genetic histories. *Nat Rev Genet.* Aug;5(8): 611–18.

Silva WA, Bortolini MC, Schneider MP, Marrero A, Elion J, Krishnamoorthy R, Zago MA. 2006. MtDNA haplogroup analysis of black Brazilian and sub-Saharan populations: implications for the Atlantic slave trade. *Hum Biol.* 2006 Feb;78(1): 29–41.

Templeton AR. 2007. Genetics and recent human evolution. *Evolution* Jul;61(7): 1507–19.

Tian C, Hinds DA, Shigeta R, Kittles R, Ballinger DG, Seldin MF. 2006. A genome-wide single-nucleotide-polymorphism panel with high ancestry information for African American admixture mapping. *Am J Hum Genet.* Oct;79(4): 640–49.

Underhill PA, Passarino G, Lin AA, Shen P, Mirazón Lahr M, Foley RA, Oefner PJ, Cavalli-Sforza LL. 2001. The phylogeography of Y chromosome binary haplotypes and the origins of modern human populations. *Ann Hum Genet.* Jan;65 (Pt 1): 43–62.

Wetton JH, Tsand KW, Khan H. 2005. Inferring the population origin of DNA evidence within the UK by allele-specific hybridization of Y-SNPs. *Forensic Sci Int.* Aug 11;152(1): 45–53.

Wood ET, Stover DA, Ehret C, Destro-Bisol G, Spedini G, McLeod H, Louie L,

Bamshad M, Strassmann BI, Soodyall H, Hammer MF. 2005. Contrasting patterns of Y-chromosome and mtDNA variation in Africa: evidence for sex-biased demographic processes. *Eur J Hum Genet.* Jul;13(7): 867–76.

Zhang J, Rowe WL, Clark AG, Buetow KH. 2003. Genomewide distribution of high-freqauency, completely mismatching SNA haplotype pairs observed to be common across human populations. *Am J Hum Genet.* Nov;73(5): 1073–81.

Zimmerman PA, Phadke PM, Lee A, Elson LH, Aruajo E, Guderian R, Nutman TB. 1995. Migration of a novel DQA1* allele (DQA1*0502) from African origin to North and South America. *Hum Immunol.* Mar;42(3): 233–40.

4 LANDSCAPES AND PLACES OF MEMORY: AFRICAN DIASPORA RESEARCH AND GEOGRAPHY

Judith A. Carney

A broad definition of the discipline of Geography begins with the integrated study of people, places, and environments. In bridging the social and biological sciences, Geography offers a holistic approach to contemporary and historical problems. How can this discipline contribute to African Diaspora Studies? As I hope to show, Geography may add reasonable inferences to the gaps in the historical record. The discipline encourages a critical engagement with culture and environment and the food systems and botanical dispersals that accompanied specific human migrations. At the interface of culture and environment, and in the service of history, Geography uses a unique perspective to examine a past whose witnessing remains obscured by centuries of European triumphalist documentation.

THE AFRICAN DIASPORA AND THE DISCIPLINE OF GEOGRAPHY

Interdisciplinary research is the hallmark of Geography. Some of the pioneering work in Geography, which initiated concern with topics now considered germane to African diaspora research, was developed from four of Geography's subfields: biogeography, historical geography, cultural geography, and cultural ecology.

Biogeography examines the distribution of plants and animals in relationship to their physical environment, the routes followed, and periods of introduction. The earliest diffusion studies of species across the Atlantic avoided mention of Africa altogether and focused on the linkages between the Iberian Peninsula and the New World. Edmundo Wernicke's 1938 study of domestic animal introductions to the Americas, for instance, emphasized the role of Europeans using maritime routes. Cattle, sheep, goats, and pigs were left to roam on uninhabited Atlantic islands as live meat for passing ships. By the mid-sixteenth century, livestock numbered in the tens of thousands in plantation economies, where they provided food, draft animals, hides, and tallow. Wernicke traces the routes by which these animals first arrived in the Americas, identifying the crucial role of the Atlantic islands as steps in their diffusion from the Iberian Peninsula.[1] Even though the transatlantic slave trade was already under way, Africa was in his view of little consequence for intercontinental species diffusion in a process later known as the Columbian Exchange.

While the significance of the Cape Verde Islands for the Atlantic economy is noted by Wernicke and later by Alfred Crosby,[2] little attention is given to the role of the African mainland in providing the species that facilitated their settlement. The islands are a mere 500 kilometers from the Senegambian coast, where one of Africa's premier cattle economies is found. Portuguese settlement relied on enslaved people to raise the crops and animals sold to European ships. Most of the food crops grown (millet, sorghum, and rice) were planted under a similar climate on the African mainland. The introduced African species included livestock. Seventeenth-century accounts reveal a considerable trade in live cattle between the islands and Senegambia. Cape Verdean traders repeatedly introduced African cattle, sheep, and goats to the Atlantic archipelago.[3] This mainland cattle economy was also featured in the accounts of slave ship captains. Jean Barbot, who made two slave voyages (1678–79, 1681–82) to western Africa, depicted the transfer of livestock to a slave ship in Senegambia.[4] A considerable literature exists on Iberian livestock introductions to the western Atlantic. However, there is little written on the African animals transported via slave ships, the role they played in stocking the Atlantic islands, and their importance for provisioning ships headed for New World plantation economies.[5]

One exception is the work of geographer R. A. Donkin, who has written on the diffusion of several obscure edible animal species. In a monograph on the guinea fowl, Donkin identifies its African origin and continental distribution and early diffusion to the Americas; he also reproduces an image of this African poultry drawn in seventeenth-century Dutch Brazil. Donkin records elsewhere the introduction of the African bush pig to seventeenth-century plantation economies.[6] But even when the concern is with African species, the spatial and temporal emphasis of diffusion studies places the context for their dissemination in the background. Thus Donkin's research is not concerned with the way African edible animal species crossed the Atlantic (on slave ships), their role in transatlantic dispersal (as live meat), or their significance in New World syncretic religious traditions (by the enslaved).[7] To this day, the African animal component of the Columbian Exchange remains underexplored by scholars.

More headway has been made investigating transatlantic botanical dispersals. Concern with African species developed from biogeographical interest in the floristic components of landscapes surrounding former plantation economies. In a 1972 paper on the "Africanization" of New World tropical landscapes, geographer James J. Parsons referred to the botanical invasion of African pasture grasses to the American tropics, which occurred during the seventeenth through nineteenth centuries.[8] Five species in particular transformed the grazing economies of New World tropical and subtropical regions: Guinea grass (*Panicum maximum*), Pará or Angola grass (*Brachiaria mutica*), Molasses grass (*Melinis minutiflora*), Bermuda grass (*Cynodon dactylon*), and *jaraguá* grass (*Hyparrhenia rufa*). The common names, Guinea and Angola, for two of these grasses suggest unexplored linkages to the transatlantic slave trade. Parsons drew attention to the role of slave ships in transporting cultivated types of African grasses to the Americas, speculating whether their introduction was inadvertent or intentional. However, he did not consider the fact that slave ships also carried live animals on board, which could also have transported the grasses through their feed, bedding, and hooves. Still, his paper broke new ground in the discipline of Geography by considering the impact of African botanical introductions on New World environments during the transatlantic slave trade.

Clarissa Kimber's 1988 study of the changing plant geographies of Martinique also touched on the presence of African species in the Americas.[9] She used the landscape as the principal unit of analysis to identify the botanical signatures of specific settlement eras. In order to see the linkage between history and botanical introductions, Kimber identified the floristic components of the Amerindian, early European, colonial plantation, and modern eras. But in a study largely concerned with the broad environmental transformations wrought by the dominant social group, African species received very little attention as they served chiefly as food crops planted by the enslaved on subsistence plots. The role of African food crops, and New World Africans in establishing them, had not yet emerged as a research concern in Geography.[10]

Jonathan Sauer also touched on African botanical dispersals in his 1993 historical geography of crop plants. He pointed out the African origins of millet and sorghum and brought the continent into discussion of the international journey of the peanut during the Atlantic slave trade. Interested in the diffusion of the peanut from its South American center of origin to southeastern North America, Sauer traced the crop's unusual Atlantic journey. He drew attention to Krapovickas's research, which suggested that the "Virginia" peanut developed from an Amerindian variety introduced to West Africa by the 1560s. It was this variety which was subsequently established along the Atlantic seaboard. A plant of South American origins, which had not reached Mexico in pre-Columbian times, was dispersed to North America via West Africa, where it was introduced during the seventeenth century as provision on slave ships.[11] We now know that it was first grown in garden plots by the enslaved. For such reasons, the peanut became known in the southeastern United States by its African names, *goober* and *pindar*.[12]

Robert C. West used Afro-Colombian settlement as the organizing principle in his cultural geographical study of the country's Pacific lowlands, but failed to see any meaningful African contribution to the area's cultural history. His work built upon an earlier volume on placer mining during Colombia's colonial period and the use of enslaved laborers to carry it out.[13] West's study of the Pacific Afro-Colombian population provided a well-researched ethnographic snapshot of land use and material culture in the region during the 1950s. However, it did not present New World Africans (slaves, maroons, and freed persons) as significant agents in the development of Pacific lowland culture and settlement. West contended that enslaved Africans depended upon Amerindians to learn subsistence agriculture and house construction and the Spanish for introduction of the plantain, which became the region's dietary staple.[14] In his view, Africans were seemingly unpracticed in tropical agriculture prior to being made slaves. Similarly, the Afro-Colombian population only took up cultivation of the plantain as a consequence of Spanish initiative (even though Europeans first encountered its cultivation in West Africa, where it had diffused 1,000 years earlier). Only in the realm of culture did West discern African contributions in the form of musical instruments, songs, and a disappearing cooperative labor group known as *minga*. Apparently aware of Melville Herskovits's work on African retentions in the Americas, West claimed that their Colombian descendants "have lost practically all of their African cultural heritage."[15]

By the 1980s a different view took shape in the work of geographer David Watts, who examined culture and development of the West Indies since 1492. Watts drew attention to the role of enslaved Africans in plant introductions. He identified Africa as the source of the medicinal and lamp oil, the castor bean, and Africans in establishing important food crops such as pigeon pea, sorghum, and yams to the Caribbean.[16]

J. H. Galloway's 1989 historical geography of the sugar cane industry conceptualized the Atlantic Basin as a historical geographical unit.[17] His study is concerned with the key agricultural transformation that forever changed the relationship of three continents. Galloway examines the industry's Mediterranean origins, the significance of São Tomé for European development of sugar plantations, and the key technological changes that facilitated the crop's dissemination across the Atlantic. As the focus is on the significance of technology change for its spread, enslaved African workers remain in the background. However, in contrast to geographers before him, Galloway envisages the Atlantic as a historical geographical unit for understanding the relationship between Europe, Africa, and the Americas.

By the 1990s, interest in the dissemination of plants, animals, and technologies led biogeographers and historical geographers to touch upon several approaches that remain pertinent to African diaspora research. These approaches included a consideration of African contributions in diffusion studies, an examination of the floristic composition of landscapes for illuminating the presence and use of African botanical species, and an emergent view of the Atlantic basin as a bounded historical geographic concept. Over the same period, research in human geography—especially cultural geography and cultural ecology—began to engage the significance of enslaved Africans in the making of the African Atlantic.

Some of the initial research derived from studies of Caribbean plantation societies in the 1970s and 1980s. This work examined the agrarian history and legacy of the plantation complex. When geographer Lydia Pulsipher excavated the eighteenth-century Galways plantation in Montserrat, she saw beyond the restoration of yet another Caribbean "Great House." Instead, she focused on the very people forced to labor on the estate's sugar plantations. In illuminating their lives and culture within the plantation complex, her 1994 paper drew attention to the significance of the dooryard gardens adjoining slave dwellings.[18] On these plots the enslaved raised subsistence favorites, herbs, medicines, and small animals, just as their descendants continue to do throughout much of the Caribbean.

Cultural geographers have advanced scholarly understanding of the significance of dooryard gardens for Caribbean agrarian history. This research includes inventories of the plants that are grown, which can be used to identify crops of African origin.[19] Plantation studies are typically focused on export commodities and the European role in their development. Research on slave household plots, however, reveals plants, cultivation methods, and agricultural implements of African origin. It draws attention to the role of the individual garden plots for crop experimentation and selection. In this sense, dooryard garden plots operated as botanical nurseries of the dispossessed. As hidden laboratories of crop experimentation, they were no less significant than the European scientific societies of the same era that pursued botanical experimentation.[20]

Cultural geographers have long viewed agrarian history as a critical arena for intellectual engagement. In *Geographical Inquiry and American Historical Problems* (1992), Carville Earle draws attention to the profound relationship of culture and environment for understanding agrarian landscapes of the past, where enslavement may have structured the labor process. The geographer's intellectual journey involves "a reacquaintance with the rural worlds of American history, a patient tracing of the manifold agrarian connections between nature and culture . . . a suspension of modernity's disbelief in the extraordinary power of prosaic agrarian systems, and, in the process, an exposition of a new interpretation of the

American past."[21] Several geographers have embarked upon this scholarly challenge.

Karl Butzer brought agrarian history to light in 2002 by emphasizing how agricultural technology, institutional structures, and power relations offer ways to understand the agrarian history of specific regions and environmental transformations. This research breathes fresh perspectives into diffusion studies while overcoming many of its aforementioned perils. For instance, in tracing the cultural origins of wetland reclamation in French Atlantic Canada, Butzer draws attention to French immigrants in the diffusion of an agricultural technology to Acadia with which they were previously familiar. The need to ensure subsistence in the early settlement history acted as a catalyst for this agricultural diffusion. His emphasis on the significance of cultural knowledge for specific environmental transformations presents a second case study for seeing the way cultural heritages informed wetland development in North America. Butzer's work engages similar themes that emerged from studies of enslaved Africans and the transformation of Carolina wetlands to rice fields. In linking cultural knowledge systems to specific subsistence repertoires (for example, wetland cultivation), geographical scholarship can open "a potentially significant window onto the role of a subordinated people in fashioning the agricultural landscape of colonial America." In this way, it offers insights on the ways that material culture shapes counternarratives of environmental history.[22]

In his examination of the European origins of the cattle ranching tradition in North America, Terry Jordan extended to livestock this interest in the linkages between technology diffusion and cultural heritages. He touched upon possible African cultural influences in late seventeenth-century Carolina husbandry practices, even though he supported an Iberian basis for the western ranching tradition that ultimately evolved.[23]

Each of these geographical studies of technology diffusion is informed by cultural ecology. The research draws attention to food systems and ethnic funds of knowledge for tracing the formation of distinctive New World landscape heritages. In linking technology diffusion to specific human migrations, and in placing distinctive cultural traditions within environmental settings, these studies now offer a way of seeing how Africa has contributed to the agricultural development of the Americas.

NEW DIRECTIONS FOR GEOGRAPHICAL RESEARCH ON THE AFRICAN DIASPORA

Much of my academic focus has been on African rice. What, for instance, do I as a geographer see when I look at a grain of rice? I see a narrative of Atlantic slavery, the story of a plant that journeyed across the Middle Passage with the very people who knew how to grow it and for whom the cereal was the dietary staple. It is a story of forced exile, technology transfer, environments transformed, and subsistence. Each rice hull forms a vessel of social memory and identity. In this telling, the cultural-environmental focus of Geography is historically contingent. By integrating space with time, Geography becomes History.

The journey across the Atlantic presented Europeans with new opportunities for wealth, but the tropical environments they settled were essentially alien to them. For enslaved Africans, their journey sentenced them to a life of toil, but the lands in which they were forced to live often resembled those they were forced to leave. Seen in this light, the Neotropics represent a conceptual divide for Europeans and New World Africans. Europeans found themselves in unfamiliar environments in tropical America and turned to indigenous people they encountered to provide them with food. Enslaved Africans found in these same landscapes recognizable Old World plant genera and micro-environments they had left behind. These landscapes could provide or support the familiar foods and medicines upon which their survival depended. Subsistence in plantation economies developed from the tropical farming acumen of both Amerindian and African peoples. In their quest for survival, New World Africans presided over a convergence of these two tropical agricultural heritages.

The vital role of Amerindians in shaping the landscapes of Latin America has remained a significant focus of geographical research for many decades. Studies of indigenous landscape formation, land use practices, resource management strategies, and agricultural systems have profoundly contributed to the achievements of pre-Columbian societies. In his recent book, *1491*, Charles Mann elucidates many of these scholarly contributions.[24] The transformation of diverse environments into agricultural landscapes enabled pre-Columbian populations to reach densities in tropical America that have been only recently eclipsed. Amerindians accomplished this by domesticating crops suitable to distinctive farming conditions and through the reclamation of fertile soil from wetlands. They developed massive earthworks known as ridged fields and, by lifting bottom muck from shallow lakes, created agricultural islands of raised beds known as *chinampas*. From infertile soils native Amazonians even made organic black earth soils by a now lost technique, which involved inoculation with soil microorganisms.[25] In elucidating the underlying principles of Amerindian food systems, geographers have advanced contemporary academic interest in environmental history, historical ethnography, cultural ecology, and indigenous/local knowledge.

Geographers are also at the vanguard of research on the cultural and biological landscapes shaped by European settlement of the Americas. In drawing attention to the nexus between culture, technology, and environment, geographical scholarship has placed post-Columbian environmental transitions in a broader historical-ecological context.[26] Nonetheless, the discipline has yet to engage fully the ways New World Africans shaped landscapes and floristic communities of the Americas. This is surprising, since enslaved Africans accompanied the first Iberian settlers and formed the numerical majority of "immigrants" to the Americas until the 1820s. They would have noticed that many tropical plant genera and micro-environments encountered in the Neotropics were identical to those they knew in Africa. Enslaved Africans were the only new settlers equipped with the special knowledge and skills required for growing food in tropical environments. The knowledge systems that informed their survival—especially the African and Amerindian plants they used for food, medicine, and spiritual needs—offer a promising area for geographical research. It places the cultural concerns of anthropologists and historians working on Africa and the African diaspora within an appropriate environmental matrix. The arrival of peoples from similar agro-ecological environments in tropical Africa may have injected new ideas and species into existing indigenous ethnobotanical systems.

The issue of African contributions to the Americas has not been fully engaged in part because of the difficulty of separating Amerindian from African influences. But in areas where Amerindian populations vanished, enslaved Africans became the custodians of their botanical knowledge systems, including subsistence achievements. They also established the foodways of their own societies. One way to see these accomplishments is by identifying the African botanical components of the Columbian Exchange. This raises questions about how plants of African origin arrived in the Americas, the purposes they served, and the circumstances under which they were established. It draws attention to subsistence and the role of food in provisioning both the willing and unwilling participants of the transatlantic slave trade.[27]

Shifting research attention to the very foods that sustained the trafficking and sustenance of enslaved labor on both sides of the Atlantic brings attention to the significance of African crops as provisions on slave ships and in plantation economies for sustenance. It illuminates the role of different ethnic groups and women in the transfer of foods and processing technologies and the significance of environmental knowledge systems for establishing specific crops, such as rice.[28] A focus on subsistence demands a different conceptualization of the Atlantic from earlier views of it as a medium for the diffusion of European enterprise and presumed ingenuity. Subsistence reveals the centrality of the African Atlantic as a historical geographical unit of identity, memory, and resistance in which knowledge of botanical resources played an extraordinary role.

Botanical research on African domesticates generally avoids discussion of the role of slavery in plant dispersals.[29] Instead, discussion centers on whether the species is native or a "recent" introduction and the area of the world where it was domesticated. Europeans, and especially the Portuguese, are credited with the global plant exchanges of the Columbian Exchange and the introduction to the Americas of several African species that became global commodities (oil palm, coffee, malaguetta pepper). Certainly some African plants owe their diffusion and establishment to European agency, with coffee providing the most notable example. The African watermelon and castor bean plant, which diffused to Europe in antiquity, similarly suggest a Portuguese introduction. Their early appearance in the Americas is illustrated in seventeenth-century paintings of Dutch Brazil.[30] The castor bean served many important purposes during the plantation period. It provided lamp oil and an all-purpose medicinal. The plant was used as a purgative and to kill off head lice. It also served to treat a variety of skin ailments that afflicted the enslaved.[31]

While European agency is responsible for the diffusion to the Americas of some African species, enslaved Africans likely pioneered the establishment of several of the continent's principal food staples (sorghum, yams, African rice).[32] Captains of slave ships routinely purchased African food crops as provision for the Atlantic crossing. Any grains or rootstock remaining from a slave voyage provided the enslaved with an opportunity to reestablish their dietary preferences. European naturalists first encountered many of the continent's plant domesticates in slave food fields. Commentaries from the early colonial period in fact attribute some of these crops to slave introduction.[33]

The role of Africans in adopting species of Asian origin in prehistory and in developing new varieties of them does not receive the research attention it merits. For instance, the banana and plantain were already important food crops in western Africa, where Europeans first encountered them. These plants appeared so early in the settlement history of the Americas that scholars originally thought they were of New World origin.[34] The significance of such crops in African agricultural systems before the onset of the transatlantic slave trade is seldom considered in accounts of plant introductions to the western Atlantic.

While Africans would transform indigenous landscapes for European plantation agriculture, their agricultural acumen and botanical heritage shaped the tropical environment in subtle ways that strengthened survival. Attention to the plants that succored slaves during illness, flight from slavery, and religious practices offers a promising geographical approach. The significance of such plants for providing slaves and maroons a cognitive map for survival in the Americas is still evident in their use for edible, medicinal, and spiritual purposes in key diaspora areas of the Americas, such as Brazil and the Caribbean.

The cultural uses of African plants in diasporic religious traditions such as Brazilian Candomblé, Cuban Santería, and palo monte as well as Haitian Vodou represent another area of geographical scholarship. In discussing the healing plants used in the liturgical practices of Afro-Brazilian Candomblé, Robert Voeks reveals a social memory of their geographical origin in vernacular Portuguese. For instance, the names for African malaguetta pepper (*pimenta da costa*) and the kola nut (*obí da costa*) refer to West African origins (implied by *da costa*). He observes that some African plants are in fact only known in Brazil by their Nigerian Yoruba names (*tapete de Oxalá, espada de Ogun*). Through these vernacular plant names, Afro-Brazilians recognize that botanical elements of Candomblé practices also inhabit their ancestral West African homeland.[35] Research conducted by geographer Erica Moret on the healing plants of Afro-Cuban religions also indicates the importance of New World African medicinal knowledge and practices.[36]

Another way geographers examine African botanical contributions is through the homeopathic medicinal traditions of the New World. The Caribbean is renowned for its "green medicine"—the use of plants for healing. These include cultivated species native to the Americas as well as Africa and specimens found in both regions. Many of these pan-tropical genera are used for the same purposes, and in similar ways, in the Americas and West Africa. This suggests the possibility that enslaved Africans recognized in the New World related species known for their healing properties. An examination of the Caribbean's medicinal plant pharmacopoeia provides a way of seeing the ethnobotanical palette that developed in Africa over millennia and diffused to the Americas. It also draws attention to the intermediary role of enslaved Africans as custodians of medicinal traditions developed by Amerindians. The Caribbean pharmacopoeia includes many plants of New World origin, even though the native peoples who developed them have long since disappeared. Enslaved Africans inherited this botanical legacy, made their own contributions to its evolution, and left it to their descendants as part of the region's enduring homeopathic tradition.[37]

A recent cultural geographical study on the diffusion of West Africa's ackee fruit to Jamaica draws attention to inter-Caribbean migration for its twentieth-century dispersal to mainland Central America. A fruit that defines the national culinary dish of Jamaica—salt fish and ackee—dispersed to Costa Rica with the migration of Jamaican workers, who built railroads in the early twentieth century and labored on banana plantations. Joseph Powell's ethnobotanical research on the diffusion of the ackee tree provides an insight to the past by showing how Jamaicans in the modern era established specific dietary preferences with migration.[38] His research demands consideration of the agency of the enslaved in establishing in an earlier era African food staples for subsistence.

Two other innovative research directions focus on African land use principles implemented in New World herding economies. Andrew Sluyter's research examines the African role in the open-range cattle herding and common-property tenure system that developed on the Caribbean island of Barbuda. The research of Chris Duvall, based on fieldwork on West African land management, is exploring several innovative directions in the Americas. He examines the roles that enslaved African pastoralists had in developing live-fencing for livestock corrals and discusses the ways that live-fencing served the defensive purposes of fugitive slaves.[39]

A focus on rural communities descended from runaway slaves (Maroons), especially in the Guianas and Brazil (where they thrive to this day), offer geographers other venues for examining landscape linkages to Africa. Many of these communities cultivate land communally, grow and process plants in distinctive ways, and practice subsistence to a degree not found among other peasantries. They also recount oral histories that attach specific African crops to their community's memory of enslavement and escape.[40]

In Brazil, reforms to the federal constitution in 1988 gave many Maroon communities the right to petition the government for land they had long held without title. These included communities descended from runaway slaves, known as *quilombos*, and others formed by freed slaves on unclaimed land. The petitions now number more than 1,000. This is the basis of a recent mapping project by Brazilian geographer Araújo dos Anjos (2005), who provides a comprehensive list of the communities seeking legal land title for the entire country and their spatial locations within each state.[41] His work opens up promising directions for measuring the socioeconomic standing of these communities relative to other parts of Brazil.

Archival records of military expeditions sent to recapture fugitive slaves offer another way to understand diasporic land use and agricultural practices. Attacks on maroon settlements were frequent events in seventeenth- and eighteenth-century Brazil, Suriname, Colombia, and Jamaica. Cartographers often accompanied the expeditions, drawing the fields, defensive structures, dwellings, and siting of vanquished settlements. An analysis of these archival records provides geographers with unexplored primary materials on how maroons used landscape features to sequester and defend their communities.

The significance of place for shaping the social memory of enslavement offers another arena of geographical work relevant to African Diaspora Studies. Carney's recent collaborative fieldwork (2005) with geographer Jacque Chase in the colonial diamond and gold mining area of Minas Gerais explored a mountainous region where the poor, white as well as black, identify numerous geomorphological features that are memorialized from the period of slavery (which in Brazil ended in 1888). Places to which fugitive slaves fled and fought reenslavement form part of a landscape of memory, as do sites where especially tragic events unfolded during slavery. Several of the rock formations are even anthropomorphized to commemorate a particular enslaved African whose tragedy or triumph serves as witness to an event that gave the place its name. Such landscape features keep alive a collective social memory of slavery and resistance among the mixed race peasantry encountered in these remote locales. This geographical research draws attention to the ways that places are made and the counternarrative that shapes memory and identity in specific landscape settings.

Cultural geographers have already begun to examine the role of commemorative monuments for shaping the memory, identity, and political awareness of women in the American West. Cartographic representation is being used to bring attention to pressing social, political-economic, and cultural issues. Among the atlases that have received considerable attention are *The Third World Atlas*, which mapped poverty from a comparative international perspective by geographical scale, and the *State of Women in the World Atlas*, which profiles women's "place" cross-culturally. However, this approach has yet to explore the potential for mapping the spatial distribution of issues that pertain to descendants of Africans in the Americas, thereby bringing broader awareness to the African Atlantic.[42]

CONCLUSION

The publication of historian C. L. R. James's *Black Jacobins* in 1938 established the conceptual approach that would guide the burgeoning research interest in the African diaspora evident from the second half of the twentieth century. In setting the struggles of San Domingo's [Haiti's] slaves for freedom against the convulsions of revolutionary France, James moved slaves from the background to the center of his account and placed the freedom struggle within the transoceanic context of challenges to European political-economic domination. His work revealed the value of situating black history and culture within the Atlantic world, which depended on enslaved labor for economic expansion. James's legacy in thinking of the Atlantic as a conceptual and historical-geographical unit gave impetus to numerous studies that chronicled slave resistance and rebellion in plantation societies. Unlike efforts in other social science and humanities disciplines, the burgeoning literature on the African Atlantic failed to find a similar response in Geography.

But this is changing. As geographers working on Amerindian cultural-environmental contributions to the Americas have learned, white political control over indigenous populations in the colonial period did not totally vanquish their environmental and botanical knowledge systems. Nor did it do so with enslaved Africans. The introduction of edible, medicinal, and spiritual plants of African origin—and the role of the enslaved in their establishment and adaptation—is now receiving the attention it deserves from geographers. As a result, geographers have begun to steadily erode the misconception that enslaved Africans were only minor elements in the shaping of the cultural and agricultural landscape of the Americas.

NOTES

1. Wernicke, "Rutas y Etapas de la Introducción de los Animales Domésticos en las Tierras Americanas."

2. Crosby, *The Columbian Exchange.*

3. Carney and Rosomoff, *In the Shadow of Slavery.*

4. Barbot, "A Description of the Coasts of North and South Guinea; and of Ethiopia Inferior, vulgarly Angola," 99, plate E.

5. See, e.g., Rouse, *The Criollo;* Ribeiro, *Aspectos e problemas da expansão Portuguésa;* Crosby, *Ecological Imperialism.*

6. Donkin, *The Muscovy Duck;* Donkin, *Meleagrides;* Donkin, *The Peccary;* Donkin, "A 'Servant of Two Masters'?"

7. The guinea fowl, for instance, is important in Afro-Brazilian *candomblé* rituals. Vogel, da Silva Mello, and Pessoa de Barros, *A Galinha-d'angola: Iniciação e Indentidade na Cultura Afro-Brasileira.*

8. Parsons, "Spread of African Pasture Grasses to the American Tropics."

9. Kimber, *Martinique Revisited.*

10. There was, however, an outstanding exception by a botanist: Grimé, *Ethnobotany of the Black Americans.*

11. Krapovickas, "The Origin, Variability, and Spread of the Groundnut (*Arachis hypogaea*)"; Sauer, *Historical Geography of Crop Plants.*

12. Wilson, "Peaceful Integration"; Smith, *Peanuts.*

13. West, *Pacific Lowlands of Colombia;* West, *Colonial Placer Mining in Colombia.*

14. For contrasting views on the diffusion of African agricultural and architectural forms to the New World, see Carney, *Black Rice;* Mark, *"Portuguese" Style and Luso-African Identity.*

15. West, *Pacific Lowlands,* 3, 130–31, 185–87.

16. Watts, *The West Indies,* 114–15, 162, 194–95.

17. Galloway, *The Sugar Cane Industry.*

18. Pulsipher, "The Landscapes and Ideational Roles of Caribbean Slave Gardens."

19. Berleant-Schiller and Pulsipher, "Subsistence Cultivation in the Caribbean"; Fredrich, "Morphology of Dooryard Gardens."

20. Carney, "Out of Africa."

21. Earle, *Geographical Inquiry and American Historical Problems,* 9.

22. Butzer, "French Wetland Agriculture in Atlantic Canada and Its European Roots," 466; Carney, *Black Rice.*

23. Jordan, *Trails to Texas.*

24. For a review of cultural ecological contributions, see the 1992 special issue of *Annals,* edited by Karl Butzer, "The Americas before and after 1492."

25. Bebbington, "Indigenous Agricultural Knowledge Systems, Human Interests, and Critical Analysis"; Denevan, "The Pristine Myth"; Doolittle, "Indige-

nous Development of Mesoamerican Irrigation"; Hecht and Posey, "Preliminary Results on Soil Management Techniques of the Kayapó Indians"; Sluyter, "Intensive Wetland Agriculture in Mesoamerica"; Smith, "Anthrosols and Human Carrying Capacity in Amazonia"; Whitmore and Turner, "Landscapes of Cultivation in Mesoamerica on the Eve of the Conquest"; Wilken, *Good Farmers*; Prins, "Local Soil Knowledge"; Zimmerer, "Agricultural Biodiversity and Peasant Rights to Subsistence in the Central Andes during Inca Rule."

26. Butzer, "French Wetland Agriculture"; Butzer, "The Americas before and after 1492"; Zimmerer, *Changing Fortunes*.

27. Carney and Rosomoff, *In the Shadow of Slavery*.

28. Carney, "Rice and Memory in the Age of Enslavement"; Carney, *Black Rice*.

29. Carney and Hiraoka, "*Raphia taedigera* in the Amazon Estuary."

30. These are paintings by artist Albert Eckhout, who accompanied the Dutch governor Johan Maurits to Recife, Pernambuco (1637–44), as part of a scientific expedition.

31. Weiss, *Castor, Sesame, and Safflower*, 4–9; McClellan, *Colonialism and Science*, 69; Watson, *Agricultural Innovation in the Early Islamic World*, 58–61. See commentary in Slenes, "African Abrahams, Lucretias, and Men of Sorrows," 157.

32. Carney, *Black Rice*.

33. Carney and Rosomoff, *In the Shadow of Slavery*.

34. West, *Pacific Lowlands*, 136–37.

35. Voeks, *Sacred Leaves of Candomblé*; Carney and Voeks, "Landscape Legacies of the African Diaspora in Brazil."

36. Moret, "Afro-Cuban Religion, Ethnobotany, and Healthcare in the Context of Global Political and Economic Change."

37. Carney, "African Traditional Plant Knowledge in the Circum-Caribbean Region."

38. Powell, *The Ackee Fruit Tree in Costa Rica*.

39. Sluyter, "The Role of Black Barbudans in the Establishment of Open-Range Cattle Herding in the Colonial Caribbean and South Carolina"; Duvall, "A Maroon Legacy?"

40. Carney. "'With Grains in Her Hair'"; Carney and Rosomoff, *In the Shadow of Slavery*.

41. Descendants of fugitive slaves are referred to as Maroons, in recognition of their contemporary identity as a people. Araújo dos Anjos, *Territórios das Comunidades Quilombolas do Brasil*.

42. Heffernan and Medlicot, "A Feminine Atlas?"; Crow and Thomas, *Third World Atlas*; Seager, *The Penguin Atlas of Women in the World*.

REFERENCES

Araújo dos Anjos, Rafael Sanzio. *Territórios das Comunidades Quilombolas do Brasil*. Brasilia: Mapas Editora & Consultoria, 2005.

Barbot, Jean. "A Description of the Coasts of North and South Guinea; and of Ethiopia Inferior, vulgarly Angola; Being a New and Accurate Account of the Western Maritime Countries of Africa." In Awnsham Churchill, *A Collec-*

tion of *Voyages and Travels, Some Now First Printed from Original Manuscripts, Others Now First Published in English*, vol. 5. London: printed from Messieurs Churchill, for T. Osborne, 1752.

Bebbington, A. "Indigenous Agricultural Knowledge Systems, Human Interests, and Critical Analysis: Reflections on Farmer Organization in Ecuador." *Agriculture and Human Values* 8 (1991): 14–24.

Berleant-Schiller, Riva, and Lydia Pulsipher. "Subsistence Cultivation in the Caribbean." *New West Indian Guide* 60, nos. 1/2 (1986): 1–40.

Butzer, Karl W. "French Wetland Agriculture in Atlantic Canada and Its European Roots: Different Avenues to Historical Diffusion." *Annals of the Association of American Geographers* 92, no. 3 (2002): 451–70.

———, ed. "The Americas before and after 1492: Current Geographical Research." Special issue of *Annals of the Association of American Geographers* 82, no. 3 (1992).

Carney, Judith A. "African Traditional Plant Knowledge in the Circum-Caribbean Region." *Journal of Ethnobiology* 23, no. 2 (2003): 167–85.

———. *Black Rice: The African Origins of Rice Cultivation in the Americas*. Cambridge: Harvard University Press, 2001.

———. "Out of Africa: Colonial Rice History in the Black Atlantic." In Londa Schiebinger and C. Swan, eds., *Colonial Botany: Science, Commerce, and Politics in the Early Modern World*, 204–20. Philadelphia: University of Pennsylvania Press, 2005.

———. "Rice and Memory in the Age of Enslavement: Atlantic Passages to Suriname." *Slavery and Abolition* 26, no. 3 (2005): 325–47.

———. "'With Grains in Her Hair': Rice History and Memory in Colonial Brazil." *Slavery and Abolition* 25, no. 1 (2004): 1–27.

Carney, Judith, and Mario Hiraoka. "*Raphia taedigera* in the Amazon Estuary." *Principes* 41, no. 3 (1997): 125–30.

Carney, Judith, and Richard N. Rosomoff. *In the Shadow of Slavery: Africa's Botanical Legacy in the Atlantic World*. Berkeley: University of California Press, 2009.

Carney, Judith, and Robert Voeks. "Landscape Legacies of the African Diaspora in Brazil." *Progress in Human Geography* 27, no. 2 (2003): 139–52.

Crosby, Alfred W. *The Columbian Exchange: Biological and Cultural Consequences of 1492*. Westport, Conn.: Greenwood Press, 1972.

———. *Ecological Imperialism: The Biological Expansion of Europe, 900–1900*. New York: Cambridge University Press, 1986.

Crow, Ben, and Alan Thomas. *Third World Atlas*. Philadelphia: Open University Press, 1983.

Denevan, W. M. "The Pristine Myth: The Landscape of the Americas in 1492." *Annals of the Association of American Geographers* 82 (1992): 369–85.

Donkin, R. A. *Meleagrides: An Historical and Ethnogeographical Study of the Guinea Fowl*. London: Ethnographica, 1991.

———. *The Muscovy Duck: Carina moschata domestica: Origins, Dispersal, and Associated Aspects of the Geography of Domestication*. Brookfield, Vt.: A. A. Balkema, 1989.

———. *The Peccary—With Observations on the Introduction of Pigs to the New World*. Philadelphia: American Philosophical Society, 1985.

———. "A 'Servant of Two Masters'?" *Journal of Historical Geography* 23, no. 3 (1997): 247–66.

Doolittle, W. E. "Indigenous Development of Mesoamerican Irrigation." *Geographical Review* 85 (1995): 301–23.

Duvall, Chris S. "A Maroon Legacy? Sketching African Contributions to Live Fencing Practices in the Neotropics." *Singapore Journal of Tropical Geography* 30 (2009): 232–47.

Earle, Carville. *Geographical Inquiry and American Historical Problems*. Stanford: Stanford University Press, 1992.

Fredrich, Barbara E. "Morphology of Dooryard Gardens: Patterns, Imprints, and Transformations in St. Lucia, West Indies." PhD diss., Geography, University of California, Los Angeles, 1976.

Galloway, J. H. *The Sugar Cane Industry: An Historical Geography from Its Origins to 1914*. Cambridge: Cambridge University Press, 1989.

Grimé, W. E. *Ethno-botany of the Black Americans*. Algonac, Mich.: Reference Publications, 1979.

Hecht, S., and D. Posey. "Preliminary Results on Soil Management Techniques of the Kayapó Indians." *Advances in Economic Botany* 7 (1989): 174–88.

Heffernan, Michael, and Carol Medlicot. "A Feminine Atlas? Sacagewea, the Suffragetes, and the Commemorative Landscape in the American West, 1904–1910." *Gender, Place, and Culture* 9, no. 2 (2002): 109–31.

Jordan, Terry G. *Trails to Texas: Southern Roots of Western Cattle Ranching*. Lincoln: University of Nebraska Press, 1981.

Krapovickas, A. "The Origin, Variability, and Spread of the Groundnut (*Arachis hypogaea*)." In P. J. Ucko and J. W. Dimbleby, eds., *The Domestication and Exploitation of Plants and Animals*, 427–41. Chicago: Aldine, 1969.

Kimber, Clarissa Thèrèse. *Martinique Revisited: The Changing Plant Geographies of a West Indian Island*. College Station: Texas A&M University, 1988.

Mann, Charles S. *1491: New Revelations of the Americas before Columbus*. New York: Knopf, 2005.

Mark, Peter. *"Portuguese" Style and Luso-African Identity*. Bloomington: Indiana University Press, 2002.

McClellan, James E., III. *Colonialism and Science: Saint Domingue in the Old Regime*. Baltimore: Johns Hopkins University Press, 1992.

Moret, Erica. "Afro-Cuban Religion, Ethnobotany, and Healthcare in the Context of Global Political and Economic Change." *Bulletin of Latin American Research* 27, no. 3 (2008): 333–50.

Parsons, James J. "Spread of African Pasture Grasses to the American Tropics." *Journal of Range Management* 25 (1972): 12–17.

Powell, Joseph B. *The Ackee Fruit Tree in Costa Rica: An Ethnobotanical Dimension of the African Diaspora*. MS thesis, Department of Geography and Anthropology, Louisiana State University, 1991.

Prins, A. M. Winkler. "Local Soil Knowledge: A Tool for Sustainable Land Management." *Society and Natural Resources* 12 (1999): 151–61.

Pulsipher, Lydia. "The Landscapes and Ideational Roles of Caribbean Slave Gardens." In N. Miller and K. L. Gleason, eds., *The Archaeology of Garden and Field*, 202–22. Philadelphia: University of Pennsylvania Press, 1994.

Ribeiro, Orlando. *Aspectos e problemas da expansão Portuguésa*. Lisbon: Junta de Investigações do Ultramar, 1962.

Rouse, John E. *The Criollo: Spanish Cattle in the Americas*. Norman: University of Oklahoma Press, 1970.

Sauer, Jonathan D. *Historical Geography of Crop Plants*. Boca Raton, Fla.: CRC Press, 1993.

Seager, Joni. *The Penguin Atlas of Women in the World*. New York: Penguin, 2003.

Slenes, Robert W. "African Abrahams, Lucretias, and Men of Sorrows: Allegory and Allusion in the Brazilian Anti-slavery Lithographs (1827–35) of Johan Moritz Rugendas." *Slavery and Abolition* 23, no. 2 (2002): 147–69.

Sluyter, Andrew. "Intensive Wetland Agriculture in Mesoamerica: Space, Time, and Form." *Annals of the Association of American Geographers* 84 (1994): 557–84.

———. "The Role of Black Barbudans in the Establishment of Open-Range Cattle Herding in the Colonial Caribbean and South Carolina." *Journal of Historical Geography* 35 (2009): 330–49.

Smith, Andrew F. *Peanuts: The Illustrious History of the Goober Pea*. Urbana: University of Illinois Press, 2002.

Smith, N. "Anthrosols and Human Carrying Capacity in Amazonia." *Annals of the Association of American Geographers* 70 (1980): 553–66.

Voeks, Robert A. *Sacred Leaves of Candomblé*. Austin: University of Texas Press, 1997.

Vogel, Arno, Marco Antonio da Silva Mello, and José Flávio Pessoa de Barros. *A Galinha-d'angola: Iniciação e Indentidade na Cultura Afro-Brasileira*. Rio de Janeiro: Editora Universitária, 1993.

Watson, Andrew M. *Agricultural Innovation in the Early Islamic World*. Cambridge: Cambridge University Press, 1983.

Watts, David. *The West Indies: Patterns of Development, Culture, and Environmental Change since 1492*. Cambridge: Cambridge University Press, 1987.

Weiss, E. A. *Castor, Sesame, and Safflower*. New York: Barnes and Noble, 1971.

Wernicke, Edmundo. "Rutas y Etapas de la Introducción de los Animales Domésticos en las Tierras Americanas." *GAEA: Anales de la Sociedad Argentina de Estudios Geográficos* 6 (1938): 77–83.

West, Robert C. *Colonial Placer Mining in Colombia*. Baton Rouge: Louisiana State University Press, 1952.

———. *Pacific Lowlands of Colombia: A Negroid Area of the American Tropics*. Baton Rouge: Louisiana State University Press, 1957.

Whitmore, T., and B. L. Turner. "Landscapes of Cultivation in Mesoamerica on the Eve of the Conquest." *Annals of the Association of American Geographers* 82 (1992): 402–25.

Wilken, Gene C. *Good Farmers: Traditional Agriculture and Resource Management in Mexico and Central America*. Berkeley: University of California Press, 1987.

Wilson, Mary Tolford. "Peaceful Integration: The Owner's Adoption of His Slaves' Food." *Journal of Negro History* 49, no. 2 (1964): 116–27.

Zimmerer, K. S. "Agricultural Biodiversity and Peasant Rights to Subsistence in the Central Andes during Inca Rule." *Journal of Historical Geography* 19 (1993): 15–32.

——. *Changing Fortunes: Biodiversity and Peasant Livelihood in the Peruvian Andes.* Berkeley: University of California Press, 1996.

5

AFRICAN DIASPORA IN ARCHAEOLOGY

Theresa A. Singleton

Archaeology is unique among the social sciences and humanities because of its ability to examine periods hundreds and thousands of years ago. Consequently, archaeology has the potential to investigate the earliest diasporas out of Africa assuming that sites associated with these migrations and resettlement can be rediscovered. As the cradle of humanity, Africa witnessed its first migration of early hominids from Africa to Eurasia approximately 1.8 million years ago, a phenomenon termed Out-of-Africa 1. Around 100,000 years ago, the earliest anatomically modern humans are found beyond Africa in Europe and Asia and later colonizing Australasia and the Americas, a process known as Out-of-Africa 2.[1] While these migrations are important to understanding cultural developments associated with human biological evolution, they are best described as Great Diasporas of all humankind, not African diasporas.[2]

In current archaeological practice, African diaspora refers to worldwide dispersal of Africans and their descendants usually of the last two millennia, particularly those diasporas emanating from slave trading. Although there were African diasporas originating from conditions other than slaving, these have not been the focus of archaeological investigation. Slavery and the slave trade have a long history in Africa dating over 2,000 years and are therefore important topics in the cultural history of Africa, whether one is interested in the transatlantic, trans-Saharan, Indian Ocean, or domestic slave trades.[3] Moreover, slave trading, particularly the raiding for enslaved people, leaves archaeological signatures in the landscape that other kinds of diasporas may not. Thus the slave trade serves as a critical point of departure, not only for understanding the extraction process of these forced migrations but also for providing direct evidence of how the slave trade impacted parts of Africa. Most archaeological study of the African diaspora focuses on the transatlantic slave trade and its impact on West and West Central Africa, but work has begun in earnest in other parts of Africa.

Unlike academic disciplines that adopted the concept of African diaspora in the 1960s and 1970s, the term "diaspora" has only been used in archaeology since the 1990s to refer to the study of people of African descent.[4] Prior to that time, such research was simply labeled Afro-American and then African American archaeology if undertaken in the United States. Outside the United States, a particular diaspora community was designated by an appropriate term such as "Afro-Jamaicans," "Afro-Canadians," "Afro-Caribbean," and so forth. As more investigations were undertaken on sites in the Caribbean, Central, and South America as well as sites associated with the rise of the transatlantic slave trade in Africa, it became obvious that a term was needed that embraced research taking place on both sides of the Atlantic associated with African diasporas derived from the transatlantic slave trade, hence the emergence of archaeology of the African diaspora. With archaeological research beginning on African diasporas by way of the Indian Ocean and East African slavery and the slave trade, archaeologists are now rethinking and redefining what constitutes the African diaspora for archaeological studies, raising questions such as: What are the spatial and temporal dimensions of this research? Does this research comprise an area specialty or a separate field of archaeology? Should special methodologies and analytical frameworks be developed for this research? What lies ahead for it in the future? This essay examines these issues by looking at the kinds of research that have been undertaken as well as the potential for future archaeological study.

ARCHAEOLOGY OF THE AFRICAN DIASPORA

Spatial Distribution and Limits

Archaeology of African diaspora covers a period of at least 2,000 years and spans five continents—Africa, Asia, Europe, North America, and Central and South America. In practice, however, archaeological study of the African diaspora has been uneven and limited to research in Africa and the Americas. Little or no archaeological study has been reported from Asia or Europe, although the potential to study African diasporas certainly exists on both continents. Sociopolitical factors may account for the lack of interest in both Asia and Europe. Africanist archaeologists Jonathan Walz and Steven Brandt suggest scholars in the Americas and Europe suffer from Atlantic tunnel vision and have been unconcerned with African diasporas to Asia for several reasons: (1) lack of familiarity with eastern languages (Arabic, Swahili, and Urdu among others), literatures, and cultures among Western scholars, (2) the general absence of strong Pan-African sentiment in Afro-Asian communities, (3) nation-states may inhibit outside researchers from delving into slave pasts because of fear of igniting criticism and debate; and (4) descendants of enslaved people and others knowledgeable of the oral history associated with slavery may be reluctant to talk about such painful subjects that could generate social discord.[5]

In Europe, the absence of an archaeology of the African diaspora appears to be related to the underdevelopment of the archaeology of the modern world (post 1500) within Europe.[6] Archaeology of the modern world began outside of Europe examining European settlers and the people and places Europeans colonized, not on how colonialism and modernity transformed Europe or affected the daily lives of people in Europe, including Afro-Europeans. Despite this trend, however, preliminary identification of sites and landscapes associated with African victims of the slave trade was undertaken in England to gather information for the installation of the transatlantic slave trade gallery that opened at the Merseyside Maritime Museum in Liverpool in 1994.[7] The exhibition, for example, featured photographic images of carved tombstones found on the graves of Africans and their descendants dating to the 1720s in Bristol, a port once thriving on the slave trade. Unfortunately, no program of archaeological research has developed from this beginning attempt to assemble information on potential Afro-British sites. Similar efforts to identify Afro-European sites should be encouraged elsewhere in Europe, particularly in port cities and towns once heavily engaged in the slave trade such as Nantes, Lisbon, and Amsterdam.

Archaeological research of the African diaspora in Africa and in the Americas originated independently and followed separate trajectories until the 1990s. In Africa, research on the recent past (last two millennia) emerged from late colonial and post-colonial interests in origins of specific states, development of trade and ethnic group relationships, continuities and changes of indigenous African economic and social institutions, and other topics that could foster national pride for newly independent African nations.[8] Limited excavations were also undertaken on West African castles and forts—European fortifications built along the Atlantic coast for trade and used to house trade goods, including human cargoes.[9] The purpose of these investigations, however, was to collect information for architectural studies of these buildings and ruins to aid in their preservation or restoration and reuse. Studies specifically directed toward understanding the transformations wrought by the transatlantic trade in general or specifically the slave trade in Africa were not conducted until the mid-1980s. These newer studies built upon earlier research on state formation, trade, and ethnic relations but also examined topics that were of potential interest to students of African diasporas such as studies of African lifeways at the time of transatlantic slave trade or the areas where enslaved people were extracted. Most of these investigations have been undertaken in West Africa and have focused on the transatlantic slave trade, but study of both trans-Saharan and the Indian Ocean slave trades are receiving increased archaeological attention.[10]

In the Americas, the United States is the site where the archaeology of African diaspora first developed into an academic research specialty. It is also where most of this research has been undertaken, and to date, archaeological study of African Americans has been conducted in thirty or more of the fifty states. Archaeological interest in African Americans arose from a number of social and intellectual movements in the 1960s and 1970s, with black activists playing a direct role in advocating for many initial investigations of specific sites in Massachusetts, New York, and California.[11] These activists saw in archaeology a means to document and preserve historic buildings, neighborhoods, and towns pertaining to African American life that had been forgotten or threatened with development and gentrification.

Outside the United States, African diaspora sites were investigated (and sometimes not investigated) for various reasons. In many cases, U.S. trained archaeologists introduced this research to several Caribbean islands and areas of mainland Latin America. A few countries developed this interest independent of U.S. influences. Cuba, for example, has a tradition of using archaeology to study plantations that dates from the 1950s and perhaps even earlier. Archaeological studies of slavery and of slave runaways in Cuba were first undertaken in the late 1960s and paralleled the first archaeological studies of slavery undertaken in the southern United States. The study of slavery and especially of slave runaways, known as Maroons, fits well within the nationalist agenda of Cuban archaeology in which struggle and resistance are important themes.[12]

Archaeological studies of the African diaspora have been slow to develop in parts of the Americas where archaeology of the modern world is not widely practiced, is deemphasized in favor of pre-Colombian archaeology (the study of indigenous peoples and cultures of the Americas), or is used primarily to study the "great white men" of independence movements. Moreover, the politics of "whitening" black populations—widely practiced in parts of Latin America—and historical amnesia of the African presence in predominately white communities today undermine the roles Africans played in the making of the Americas.[13] Such circumstances conspire against archaeological studies of the African diaspora throughout the Americas and perhaps as well in Asia and in Europe. Fortunately, this political landscape is changing with the work of a growing number of archaeologists. In Argentina, for example, Daniel Schávelzon uncovered evidence of African cultural life from nineteenth-century sites in Buenos Aries. He found pottery and pipes similar to those found at diaspora sites elsewhere in the Americas, artifacts suggestive of divination practices, and fragments of wooden swords described in written sources to have been worn by Afro-Argentineans in ceremonies. Given the prevailing popular image among Argentineans that Buenos Aires is and always was a white-only city, Schávelzon's findings are particularly significant, and they complement written evidence that the city's population was 30 percent black during the first half of the nineteenth century.[14] As more archaeologists challenge the silencing of the African past in parts of the Americas, Asia, and Europe, the archaeological study of the African diaspora will certainly expand beyond its current geographic limits.

Research Themes

African diaspora, from the perspectives of both Africanist and Diasporist archaeologists, is most often associated with African slave trade. Archaeology has been utilized in Africa primarily to examine the impact of slave trading on indigenous Africans, whereas studies of the diaspora focus on sites of resettlement yielding information on the lived experiences that diaspora communities found themselves. The discussion below describes major themes of archaeological research undertaken in Africa and in the Americas.

Archaeological studies in Africa related to African diaspora have examined three major themes: the rise of towns and polities, including Elmina, Allada, Savi, Whydah, and Dahomey, whose emergence or growth is associated with transatlantic trade; significant changes in trade, production, and consumption of certain commodities, particularly iron and pottery; and the effects of slave raiding and warfare on the African landscape as seen in site abandonment, depopulation, aggregation of disparate groups of people into new settlements, or the presence of fortified settlements.[15]

In regions such as Upper Senegal and southern Lake Chad Basin, archaeologists have studied the impacts of both the transatlantic and transSaharan slave trades by examining the transformations in these areas for the last 1,000 or more years.[16] Although some archaeologists think that it is impossible to identify which trade was the most devastating from archaeological perspectives, Alioune Dème and Ndèye Sokhna Guèye have tentatively identified differences in the impacts of the two trade networks in the Middle Senegal Valley from archaeological study. During the period of trans-Saharan trade (990–1500 AD), communities along the floodplain took advantage of the trade, converted to Islam, increased hierarchy, expanded the size of their settlements, and acquired copper, glass, and other exotic items from traders. Communities outside the floodplain experienced decreased population presumably due to floodplain groups raiding for slaves. The non-floodplain groups are believed to have been non-Muslim, based on the presence of non-Islamic burial practices found in non-floodplain areas. During the transatlantic trade (1500–1850), drastic changes in settlement occurred throughout the area with the proliferation of small, temporary hamlets and villages. Additionally, local craft production, technological innovations, and exchange declined. These conditions suggest the presence of intense mobility among communities due to sociopolitical instability. The archaeologists interpret the trans-Saharan trade as intersocietal conflict between Muslim entities who raided non-Muslim entities. The Atlantic trade, on the other hand, produced intrasocietal conflict because elites often sold members of their own polities into slavery, creating a situation whereby those vulnerable to being sold into slavery were constantly on the move, as seen in numerous temporary settlements.[17]

The Indian Ocean slave trade, although centuries older than transatlantic trade, has received little scholarly attention by archaeologists. Chapurukha M. Kusimba has undertaken investigations of fortified rockshelters—natural rock overhangs fortified with manmade stone walls in the Tsavo area of Kenya—a major stopping point of caravan trade located 150 kilometers inland from the coastal city of Mombasa. Coupling his investigations with oral histories and historical accounts, Kusimba infers that the rockshelter fortifications were built and used primarily for defensive purposes in response to slave raiding in the eighteenth and nineteenth centuries. Later, or perhaps in between slave raids, the enclosures also provided a place to safeguard livestock.[18] Located on steep cliffs, these structures allowed those within them to elude slave raiders because it shielded them, and at the same time, they provided a panoramic view of the surrounding landscape, making it possible to observe hostile groups entering the area. The use of hilltops naturally fortified with rocks to protect potential victims from slave raiders has been studied by archaeologists working in northern Ghana and in the Benue River Valley in Nigeria.[19]

Fortified settlements are ubiquitous in many parts of Africa and are often interpreted as signatures of slave raiding and warfare. In addition to the locations described above, they have also been studied in Cameroon, Sierra Leone, and several regions in Nigeria.[20] In northern Yorubaland in southwestern Nigeria, Aribidesi Usman observed that settlements were fortified in different ways using earthen ramparts, mud walls, ditches, and stone barriers. The head towns or capitals—where the royal elites lived—had the most extensive defensive systems and were surrounded by massive walls, some of which were 2.8 to 3.4 km in circumference. At the edges of hilltop settlements, stone barriers were arranged to considerable heights and extending to distances up to 1 km to slow down advancing intruders. Yet, despite these defensive measures, some of these settlements were taken and destroyed.[21]

Research themes in African Diaspora Studies cover a wide range of time (from seventeenth to twentieth centuries), settings, and social conditions under which people of African diasporas lived. Plantation slavery is a predominate focus, and various aspects of the lives of enslaved communities have been studied: everyday life, family formation, gender, household production and consumption, use of domestic space, religious beliefs and practices, identity formation, master/slave relations. As more former plantation areas are studied, we are beginning to see temporal and regional variations as well as similarities and differences among diverse colonial situations. Most work has taken place in English-speaking areas of the Americas, primarily in the United States, but research has been conducted and is ongoing in the Dutch-, French-, Spanish-, and Portuguese-speaking countries.

While plantation slavery is a major topic of research in United States, the study of slave runaways or Maroon communities is a major focus of diaspora research in many parts of the Americas, including Brazil, Cuba, Dominican Republic, Jamaica, and Suriname. In fact, the earliest known archaeological study of the African diaspora in the Americas was an excavation of burials found in caves of Serra Negra in southern Brazil and attributed to slave runaways during the 1930s.[22] Slave runaway sites range from long-term settlements with complex social structures such as the seventeenth-century runaway polity of Palmares in Brazil to short-term refuges in caves, overhangs, swamps, and other inaccessible terrains.[23] Cuban archaeologists distinguished between *Palenques*—substantial runaway settlements with evidence of agriculture and the sites of *cimarrones*, small groups of runaways who were frequently on the move, foraging wild foods and raiding nearby plantations for food and supplies. Archaeological sites of both types have been investigated in Cuba. Gabino La Rosa Corzo studied two *Palenques* in the mountains in eastern Cuba, where he observed clusters of dwellings laid out to form inner squares and inner paths leading from one cluster of dwellings to another.[24] These inner pathways may have facilitated communication and movement throughout the settlement without the knowledge of outsiders such as slave hunters who were in constant pursuit of runaways. In Jamaica and Suriname, where descendants of slave runaways still maintain autonomous communities, archaeologist Kofi Agorsah has collaborated with these present-day groups to locate, identity, and excavate historic Maroon sites linking their oral traditions and ethnography with their archaeological heritage. He has observed similarities in the settlement patterns between rural African communities and those of Maroon communities.[25] Exploratory studies of Maroon sites have been undertaken in southeastern United States, but such studies are fewer in number and at a very preliminary stage of research compared with those of Latin America and the Caribbean.[26]

Archaeological study of free persons of color, or simply free blacks— people of African descent who obtained their freedom from slavery legally during the time of slavery—and of post-emancipation sites has been limited to the studies in North America (both Canada and the United States), with a few notable exceptions.[27] Free black sites have been investigated in both southern and northern states dating as early as the eighteenth century, but most date to the first half of the nineteenth century. Studies of free black sites tend to be descriptive rather than analytical because excavations are usually undertaken for architectural restoration of a particular property or because the site was being threatened with development. In such studies, usually the recovered materials are described and limited interpretations are offered. Archaeologists are only beginning to analyze the precarious social position of free blacks as neither enslaved nor free with full rights of citizenship or their identity formation in relation to other communities.[28]

Studies of post-emancipation sites have shown how racial discrimination was manifested and how African American communities responded to those conditions in a variety of settings, including black towns, urban neighborhoods, tenant or wage labor plantations, and frontier settlements in the western United States.[29] Studies of post-emancipation provide opportunities to work directly with descendant communities who often have firsthand knowledge of the sites being investigated. Growing both in number and in importance, archaeological studies of post-emancipation hold great promise for putting into perspective the aftermath of slavery and the historical struggles of people of African descent for equal rights.

Research Area or Field of Study?

Given the immense geographical range—spanning five continents—and a time depth of 2,000 years or more, some archaeologists have suggested that archaeology of the African diaspora constitutes a separate field.[30] The African diaspora from an archaeological perspective is obviously more than an area study or regional specialization, as this research can conceivably involve archaeologists of diverse and disparate area specialties of Africa, South Asia, Middle East, Europe, North America, Latin America, and the Caribbean. At the same time, to propose that this research embraces a separate field would require advancing distinct methodologies, theories, or analytical frameworks. Traditional and arbitrary subdivisions in archaeology present significant barriers to uniting all archaeological research concerning African diasporas. For example, North Africa is often separated from sub-Saharan Africa in conferences and in publications. Egypt and African diasporas of the Classical World is a separate field of archaeology often taught in the classics or art history departments. Similarly, Near Eastern Archaeology (the Middle East) is sometimes taught in religion departments because it was the place of origin for several world religions. Additionally, other schisms can prevail that define specialties within archaeology (or any academic discipline) that tend to divide rather than unite researchers interested in similar themes but trained in different academic traditions and area specialties. That said, what would be achieved in uniting in one field of all archaeological research of African diasporas? What does a classical archaeologist interested in diasporas of African people who ended up in the Greco-Roman world or a specialist of Islamic archaeology who is studying slavery during the time of the Great Zanj slave revolt in AD 869–83 in Iraq have in common with an Americanist investigating eighteenth-century Afro-Caribbean communities? These examples illustrate the great diversity of African diasporas that are completely unrelated to each other both temporally and spatially and that may be of limited value to scholars interested in other African diasporas. The study of contemporaneous African diasporas, on the other hand, may offer some points for comparison and contrast in cases wherein the people involved originated from the same region or were taken from the same ports. For example, in the nineteenth-century slave trade on the southern Tanzanian coast, enslaved Africans ended up both in the Americas, primarily Brazil, as well as several designations in Asia, such as India.[31] Perhaps the best way to tie the disparate time periods and regions of African diasporas together is through theoretical and methodological approaches related to common themes: labor, everyday life, resistance, master/slave relations, identity formation, religious practices, and so forth. One of the greatest contributions of archaeology of the African diaspora to archaeology generally has been in raising issues on approaches to the investigation of subaltern peoples. In this sense, the archaeology of the African diaspora contributes to a post-colonial discourse that allows us to reevaluate colonialism and gain insights into the lives of those who suffered from it.

METHODOLOGIES FOR AFRICAN DIASPORA ARCHAEOLOGY

Until recently, the archaeology of the African diaspora did not have any special theories or methodologies. For the most part, research on the African diaspora is pursued in the same manner as research on any cultural or ethnic group utilizing archaeological concepts and methods. In the United States, for example, the archaeological study of African Americans partially developed out of a general interest in archaeological study of ethnicity, particularly racial minorities. The first edited volume containing archaeological case studies of African American communities paired the experiences of African Americans with those of Asian Americans.[32] Studies of ethnicity eventually gave way to analyses of the broader concept of identity. Though more broadly conceived than ethnicity, identity in African diaspora archaeology studies is equated often with ethnicity or race (as a social construction) or both. In studies of slavery, the analysis of identity almost always examines archaeological evidence suggestive of an African heritage.

A few archaeologists have proposed developing methodologies for the archaeology of the African diaspora that explicitly utilize the concept *diaspora* as a means to frame research questions.[33] Adoption of the term

"African diaspora" in archaeology has been used primarily as a label for this research and not as an analytical, conceptual, or methodological tool as in some other disciplines to investigate experiences of displacement, trace specific groups from the homeland to the new settings, or compare linkages with other groups of the African diaspora. Archaeology, however, is highly capable of addressing these and other issues pertaining to African diasporas. It has been most successful, to date, in the examination of displacement and re-genesis of people of African diasporas by providing direct evidence of their lived experiences. Analyses of archaeological materials recovered from the places where Africans and their descendants of diasporas lived, worked, sought refuge, or died provide information on their material world—housing, use of space, personal and household items, craft production, culinary practices, and so forth. Careful study of these material components of everyday life permits archaeologists to infer about nonmaterial aspects of diasporic peoples' lives, including their agency, group formations, survival strategies, religious beliefs, cultural practices, power struggles, and interactions with other peoples.

Archaeologists have also attempted to examine the relationship between the homeland (Africa) and settlement in host countries, but with mixed success. Research geared toward understanding the retention and transformation of African ideas and practices has figured prominently in African diaspora archaeology since its earliest inception. Knowledge of African archaeology would appear to be the place to begin the study of Africa diasporas, but this was not the case, because Americanist archaeologists were often unaware of archaeological research in Africa that might be relevant to the study of the diaspora or they were unable to evaluate research findings for use in analyzing problems in the study of diaspora.

Researchers in the Americas seeking to make connections between the material remains of people of African descent and African material culture, therefore, did so and continue to do so using ethnographic sources. Using such sources is problematical, however, as Africanist archaeologists have shown.[34] Ann Stahl makes the point that ethnographic sources of the first half of the twentieth century that culminated in George Peter Murdock's *Africa: Its People and Their Culture History*, published in 1959, were flawed because many of the "tribal groups" described by ethnographers often resulted from colonial constructions, thereby making historical analyses of these groups difficult.[35] Merrick Posnansky, on the other hand, criticizes the use of nineteenth-century African ethnographies and diaries, claiming that such sources were directed toward cultural groups whose ancestors were not, for the most part, victims of the slave trade. Instead, he recommends that Americanists study more recent ethnographies undertaken in African villages and, perhaps, collect their own ethnographic data where they can observe food procurement techniques, building technologies, culinary practices, household equipment, and spatial patterns firsthand.[36] Still others criticize the use of projecting the ethnographic present into the past. Despite these methodological drawbacks, many diasporist archaeologists have used ethnographic sources with caution to identify and interpret numerous ways in which African practices were incorporated in creating new cultural forms, particularly in housing, foodways, adornment, and so forth. Historian Philip Morgan has suggested that Africanist archaeologists should applaud "American archaeologists for beginning to strive to uncover certain African deep-level principles and fundamental ways of thinking."[37] Until more archaeology is undertaken on the African homelands of the victims of the slave trade, African ethnographic data will continue to be a primary source upon which to base interpretations of African culture in the diaspora.

Rather than see Africa and the diaspora as separate units of analysis, Akinwumi Ogundiran and Toyin Falola propose the use of the "continuous historical experience thesis"—the idea that African history is crucial to understanding Africa and that African history is incomplete without understanding the Atlantic diaspora—as a way to frame archaeological understandings of the African diaspora. In this thesis, Atlantic Africa and the diaspora are integrated into one unit of analysis, and scholarly investigation is restricted not to a landmass or racial category but to cultural expressions, ideas, and the historical spirit that linked Africa to the Americas through the Middle Passage. They justify the use of this approach on the basis that Africans in the Americas recognized themselves and lived their lives as Africans and in some cases perceived of themselves with specific African identities. They recommend that archaeological projects of the African diaspora should aim to be transatlantic in scope, such as those undertaken on iron technology and settlement patterns. Furthermore, they critique the one-way interest of archaeologists regarding how Africa influenced its diaspora. They suggest that archaeology could be productively used to examine cultural practices originating in Africa that survived in the Americas but are no longer practiced in Africa because of "multiple dislocations on the African continent over the past 500 years."[38] This use of diaspora archaeology would result in more of a two-way exchange of research questions, methodologies, findings, and interpretations between archaeologists of Africa and archaeologists of the African diaspora than currently exists.

Efforts directed toward comparing different diaspora groups from archaeological sites and assemblages of artifacts are in the beginning stages. The archaeology department of Thomas Jefferson Monticello Foundation created the Digital Archaeological Archive of Comparative Slavery (DAACS), a database of artifacts recovered from slave sites that utilizes the same classification scheme for all the sites included in it.[39] How an object is classified is directly related to how the archaeological findings are interpreted. Moreover, comparisons of findings also require that the artifacts are classified in the same way. Initially the database was developed for sites in the Chesapeake, but it has been expanded to include archaeological projects on slave sites found elsewhere in the United States and the Caribbean. It could also be expanded to include sites of free people of color and other diaspora communities. DAACS is the only analytical tool in widespread use that has been specifically developed for analyzing archaeological data recovered from African diaspora sites.

While the potential for comparing African diaspora sites is beginning, thereby making comparisons possible from archaeological data, the examination of links between African diaspora groups has not been pursued. The possibility exists, for example, of investigating secondary diasporas— subsequent migrations and relocations of diaspora communities. One of the largest secondary diasporas of the Atlantic world took place after the American Revolution. Thousands (some estimates run as high as 500,000) of black loyalists—enslaved and free people of African descent who sided with the British—were relocated to Canada, England, and British West Indies.[40] Archaeologists have investigated sites where black loyalists were relocated in the Bahamas and Nova Scotia, but the findings from these sites were not linked or compared with slave sites from areas where many black loyalists originated.[41] For example, many enslaved black loyalists who were relocated to the Bahamas originated from the coastal reaches of South Carolina and Georgia—areas where a great deal of archaeological research on slave sites has been undertaken. Moreover, there were close familial and business ties between Bahamian planters and those of the Georgia coast, increasing the possibility of links between slave communities in the two places that may be evident in archaeological remains. The trajectory of Bilali of Sapelo Island, Georgia, demonstrates that linkages between enslaved people of the Bahamas and coastal Georgia can be established. Bilali (also spelled Belali, Bu Allah, and Ben-Ali), born in Africa, appears to have been first enslaved in the Bahamas and then later sold to Thomas Spaulding, a planter on Sapelo Island. Bilali became a patriarch of the slave community on Sapelo and a legendary figure for the Gullah-Geechee people of the Georgia coast.[42] Perhaps future archaeological studies of black loyalists and other secondary diaspora sites will attempt to link the places of origin with the places of relocation and resettlement.

Walz and Brandt have proposed a methodology combining all three phases of a diaspora—extraction, transit, and new existence in host country—rather than focusing on archaeological sites associated with only one phase. Using the western Indian Ocean diaspora as an example— a diaspora spanning Africa, the Indian Ocean and its islands, and southern Asia—they outline an overall methodology for each of the three phases. In the extraction phase, sites like the fortified hilltops in Kenya, described earlier, and other sites or settlement patterns suggestive of slave raiding would be investigated. Transit sites would include caravan routes in Africa, ports of embarkation and disembarkation, water routes, and land routes in Asia. Many of the routes are locatable through aerial photography, digital satellite imagery, and ground surveys. The third component consists of themes that can be investigated at sites where enslaved individuals reached their final destinations and began rebuilding their lives. Potential sites of slave communities associated with the western Indian Ocean diaspora would be located in both Africa and Asia, including Ethiopia, India, Pakistan, Sri Lanka, Iraq, Yemen, Mauritius, and Madagascar.[43]

Implementing a research design of this magnitude obviously would require collaborative research with teams dedicated to working on each of the three components of the larger project. While the realities of undertaking such an ambitious project pose significant financial and political challenges, Walz and Brandt's methodological framework offers insights and possibilities of applying the concept of diaspora to archaeological investigation of the transatlantic diaspora. As some archaeological research has been undertaken on each of the three components of the Atlantic diaspora, it should be possible to begin evaluating the results from each component assessing what kinds of data are still needed. Archaeologists should aim to develop research strategies and methods that utilize the concept of diaspora in their research, rather than continuing to use it as merely a descriptive term.

ARCHAEOLOGY OF THE AFRICAN DIASPORA AND OTHER DISCIPLINES

Archaeology is an interdisciplinary pursuit that directly utilizes other disciplines in undertaking a research project. However, it has had an ambiguous relationship with other disciplines that study the African diaspora. On the one hand, it has been applauded by other disciplines that also study material culture, the tangible products of humankind that include architecture, decorative arts, folklore, and geography. Its contribution to these disciplines has been to provide new information on vernacular architecture, use of domestic space, craft production, and culinary practices, among other topics concerning African diaspora communities.

Archaeology, however, has had a contentious relationship in some cases with history in the study of the African diaspora. The conflict may stem, in part, from a lack of understanding on the part of both archaeologists and historians regarding the primary concerns of each other's discipline, when these concerns overlap and when they do not.[44] A historian of slavery once commented that archaeology is an expensive way to find out what we already know.[45] He was referring to the use of archaeology to investigate well-documented periods and sites. While it may appear that archaeology has little to contribute to our understanding of documented sites, an archaeological investigation rarely yields no new information. The relationship between archaeological data and historical sources can be complementary and interdependent or contradictory and independent.[46] In African Diaspora Studies, both situations occur. For example, at slavery sites archaeological findings frequently amplify written descriptions of slave housing, food allotments, or clothing, but they can also contradict written records.[47] Archaeological findings of items slaveholders provisioned to enslaved people have been found to be very different from what is described in written records. A now classic example is that of Thomas Jefferson, who indicated in his records that the slave houses and outbuildings along Mulberry Row matched the neo-classical architectural style of his mansion. But excavations revealed that the buildings along Mulberry Row were crude log cabins.[48] Slave personal items such as those indicating a degree of literacy, amulets, games, and recycling of metal, iron, or stone objects are not found on probate inventories or other slaveholders' records. Thus archaeological data and the interpretations they potentially offer contribute new and important information on slave life, agency, and survival strategies, the material basis of master/slave relationships, and other topics where material culture can provide a perspective on past life that written records, ethnography, or oral history alone cannot provide.

Scale of analysis and interpretation is another area of difference between history and archaeology. Most archaeological research is site specific. Some historical writing is also at this scale, but there is a greater tendency for historians to study a region, an island, or an entire nation. Archaeologists are also capable of synthesizing larger areas, but only after sufficient sites have been investigated. Archaeological study is a long, slow process, and regional syntheses take time. Certainly in some regions of North America, like the Chesapeake where numerous diaspora sites have been investigated, regional syntheses are long overdue.

A third problem may be related to the narrative styles of archaeology and history. Historians often present their interpretations as fact even when based on slim or questionable evidence. Archaeologists traditionally present their interpretations very cautiously, qualifying every statement because numerous factors such as site preservation, excavation methods, and recovery techniques used to collect artifacts and other physical materials all affect what kinds of data are collected and how the data are interpreted. Most archaeologists acknowledge that their interpretations are at best good guesses or works in progress. Some historians have commented to me on the tentative character of archaeological findings and expressed their skepticism about using such data in their interpretations.

In some cases, however, historians seem to choose the more speculative rather than more grounded interpretations when referencing archaeological research. This could be seen in the exhibition on slavery in New York City at the New York Historical Society in 2005 and 2006. Although the publication that accompanied the exhibition clearly acknowledged that the rediscovery of the African Burial Ground in the early 1990s brought to light the silenced history of slavery in New York City, the African Burial Ground was barely mentioned in the exhibition itself.[49] Moreover, the interpretation offered for the two graves chosen as examples to depict the burial ground are among the most speculative cases. A small photographic display, entitled "African Burial Ground: Encountering Black New York Directly," featured the graves and raised questions about the status and roles of the deceased individuals. One grave contained an older woman wearing waist beads and the exhibition text suggested that the woman was most likely a revered person in the slave community and possibly a religious specialist. The other grave contained a man whose clothing, presumably a jacket, had British naval buttons on it. The associated exhibition text asked whether the man served in the British navy or was a king at a Pinkster festival. (Pinkster was a religious holiday celebrated over several days by Dutch and African New Yorkers in the eighteenth century.) Archaeology alone cannot provide definite answers to questions concerning the occupations or social rankings of the people interred in the African Burial Ground because their identities are unknown. Yet there were numerous examples of other burials that could provide more definitive evidence of other aspects of slave life in New York. For example, the burial of a young woman who was beaten and shot to death illustrates the violence that enslaved people endured. There were also numerous examples of the physical toll that slave labor produced on human skeletons from carrying heavy loads or spending long hours kneeling or squatting.

It is unlikely that curators of the exhibition deliberately chose examples from the African Burial Ground to make archaeology appear to be a more speculative discipline than history. Yet this was the unfortunate result of their selection. The examples were most likely chosen because they had received a great deal of media attention when research on the African Burial Ground was taking place. Archaeology, unfortunately, often suffers from misrepresentation in public formats because popular images such as "Indiana Jones" portray archaeologists as treasure seekers, not as serious scholars. Such images may also explain why some other disciplines may not see the value of archeological work in the study of the African diaspora.

CONCLUSION

The archaeology of the African Diaspora began taking shape in the 1970s and 1980s. Although not referred to as such at the time, it has been expanding throughout the Americas, along with related research on the slave trade and its impact in Africa. The emphasis is primarily the Atlantic world, but work is beginning on the Indian Ocean slave trade and the Indian Ocean diaspora.

Where does archaeological research on the African diaspora appear to be headed? In the past ten years, research has become increasingly collaborative between Africanists and Americanists, as seen in recent publications that are also interdisciplinary.[50] We hope that such collaborations will result in more thorough analyses of diaspora populations. It may be possible to eventually trace specific communities from the homelands to a host country or to examine the return of diaspora communities to locations in Africa, including Sierra Leone, Liberia, Republic of Benin, Gabon, or Nigeria.

Most archaeological research on the African diaspora tends to be site specific, but more efforts toward the comparison of sites and assemblages of artifacts as well as between different groups of people have been initiated. In addition to the previously mentioned DAACS database, archaeologists in the Caribbean and elsewhere are comparing related sites. Kenneth Kelly has been conducting comparative research on plantations on the French islands of Guadalupe and Martinique.[51] In Cuba, Gabino La Rosa Corzo is attempting to link through archaeological investigations the sites where slave runaways sought refuge and the plantations that they left behind.[52] Douglas Armstrong's work at the Seville Plantation in Jamaica contained the occupation of not only enslaved people of African descent but also East Indian contract laborers, making it possible to compare households from two different diasporas.[53] African and East Indian laborers also resided on one of the excavated plantations located on Guadalupe.[54] Terrence Weik's research on African Seminole communities of Florida fills a neglected void—African interaction with indigenous peoples of the Americas.[55]

Archeological research of African Diaspora communities began with the investigation of sites once occupied by enslaved people. Slavery and the slave trade continue to be a major theme of this research, but many more sites, regions, and peoples are now being studied. Archaeology has and can make unique contributions to the study of African diasporas.

NOTES

1. Mitchell, *African Connections*, 206.

2. Fagan refers to the Out-of-Africa 2 as the Great Diaspora in *Ancient Lives*, 259–82.

3. Kusimba, "Archaeology of Slavery in East Africa," 60; Walz and Brandt, "Toward an Archaeology of the Other African Diaspora," 252.

4. Agorsah, "The Archaeology of the African Diaspora"; Orser, "The Archaeology of the African Diaspora"; Singleton and Bograd, "The Archaeology of the African Diaspora in the Americas."

5. Walz and Brandt, "Toward an Archaeology," 248–49.

6. Johnson, "The Tide Reversed."

7. Interview with Gary Morris, 13 June 1995. He was the public education specialist for the transatlantic slave trade gallery at that time.

8. Trigger, *A History of Archaeological Thought*, 184.

9. Lawrence, *Trade Castles and Forts of West Africa*; Posnansky and van Dantzig, "Fort Ruychaver Rediscovered"; van Dantzig, *Forts and Castles of Ghana*.

10. A few of these studies include DeCorse, *An Archaeology of Elmina*, and Stahl, *Making History in Banda*. See also case studies in DeCorse, ed., *West Africa during the Atlantic Slave Trade: Archaeological Perspectives*. See case studies in African archaeology in Ogundiran and Falola, eds., *Archaeology of Atlantic Africa and the African Diaspora*.

11. The origins of African diaspora archaeology in the United States are discussed in detail in Ferguson, *Uncommon Ground*, and Singleton and Bograd, "The Archaeology of the African Diaspora in the Americas," 14–15.

12. For discussion of archaeological studies of slavery in Cuba, see Domínguez, "Fuentes arqueológicas en el estudio de la esclavitud en Cuba." For discussion of the nationalist agenda of Cuban archaeology, see Berman, Febles, and Gnivecki, "The Organization of Cuban Archaeology."

13. Whitening refers here to a range of practices from government-sponsored European immigration to Latin America, particularly during the period of 1880–1930, for the purpose of increasing white populations, to the rejection of African-based culture by upwardly mobile black Latin Americans to gain acceptance by whites. See Reid, *Afro-Latin America, 1800–2000*, 117–31.

14. Schávelzon, "The Vanishing People." A more detailed discussion of this project is found in Schávelzon, *Buenos Aires Negra*.

15. Examples of archaeological studies of African polities include DeCorse, *An Archaeology of Elmina*; Kelly, "The Archaeology of African-European Interaction"; Monroe, "Dahomey and the Atlantic Slave Trade." For examples of the effects on ironworking, see Goucher, "Iron Is Iron 'til It Is Rust," and Barros, "The Effect of the Slave Trade on the Basar Ironworking Society, Togo." Changes in pottery are discussed in most studies, as pottery analysis is a mainstay of archaeological research. For examples of studies examining the effects of slave raiding and warfare, see Holl, "500 Years in the Cameroons: Making Sense of the Archaeological Record"; MacEachern, "State Formation and Enslavement in the Southern Lake Chad Basin"; Swanepoel, "Socio-Political Change on a Slave-Raiding Frontier."

16. For Upper Senegal, see McIntosh, "Tools for Understanding Transformation and Continuity in Senegambian Society, 1500–1900." For the southern Lake Chad Basin, see MacEachern, "State Formation and Enslavement."

17. Dème and Guèye, "Enslavement in the Middle Senegal Valley."

18. Kusimba, "Archaeology of Slavery in East Africa."

19. Fortified sites in northern Ghana, see Swanepoel, "Socio-Political Change," 275. Fortified sites in Benue River Valley, see Folorunso, "The Trans-Atlantic Slave Trade and Local Traditions of Slavery in the West African Hinterlands."

20. For fortified settlements in Cameroon, see MacEachern, "State Formation and Enslavement," 139–41. For Sierra Leone, see DeCorse, "Material Aspects of the Limba, Yalunka, and Kuranko Ethnicity."

21. Usman, "The Landscape and Society of Northern Yorubaland during the Era of the Atlantic Slave Trade," 153–54.

22. Singleton and De Souza, "Archaeologies of the African Diaspora in Brazil, Cuba, and the United States."

23. Archaeologists have investigated Palmares since the early 1990s and have produced numerous publications in English and Portuguese. Two of these are Funari, "The Archaeology of Palmares and Its Contribution to the Understanding of the History of African American Culture," and Orser and Funari, "Archaeology and Slave Resistance and Rebellion."

24. La Rosa Corzo, *Runaway Slave Settlements in Cuba*, 242–43.

25. Agorsah, "Ethnoarchaeological Consideration of Social Relationship and Settlement Patterning among Africans in the Caribbean Diaspora"; "The Other Site of Freedom"; "Scars of Brutality"; and *Maroon Heritage*.

26. Archaeological studies of slave runaways in the United States include Nichols, "No Easy Run to Freedom"; Deagan and Landers, "Fort Mosé"; Weik, "Allies, Adversaries, and Kin in African Seminole Communities of Florida."

27. Two examples post-emancipation sites outside of North America are Armstrong, *Creole Transformation from Slavery to Freedom*, and Haviser, "Identifying Post-Emancipation (1863–1940) African-Curaçaoan Material Assemblage."

28. Singleton, "Class, Race, and Identity among Free Blacks of the Antebellum South"; Beaudry and Berkland, "Archaeology of the African Meeting House on Nantucket."

29. For examples of post-emancipation sites including black towns, see Cox, "The Archaeology of the Allensworth Hotel"; for African American sites in urban communities, see Mullins, *Race*; for plantation tenant/wage laborers, see Wilkie, *Creating Freedom*; and for the western frontier, see Dixon, *Boomtown Saloons*.

30. Franklin and McKee, "Introduction African Diaspora Archaeologies."

31. Walz and Brandt, "Toward an Archaeology," 255–56

32. Schuyler, ed., *Archaeological Perspectives on Ethnicity in America*.

33. Franklin, "Archaeological Dimensions of Soul Food"; Weik, "Archaeology of the African Diaspora in Latin America"; Walz and Brandt, "Toward an Archaeology," 256–62.

34. DeCorse, "Oceans Apart"; Posnansky, "West Africanist Reflections on African American Archaeology."

35. Stahl, "Introduction: Changing Perspectives on Africa's Past," 10.

36. Posnansky, "West Africanist Reflections," 24, 37.

37. Morgan, "Archaeology and History in the Study of African Americans," 57.

38. Ogundiran and Falola, "Pathways in the Archaeology of the Transatlantic Africa," 6–7.

39. Thomas Jefferson Monticello Foundation, Digital Archaeological Archive of Comparative Slavery (DAACS), at www.daacs.org.

40. Pulis, "'Important Truths' and 'Pernicious Follies,'" 194.

41. MacLeod-Leslie, "Understanding the Use of Space in an Eighteenth-Century Black Loyalist Community: Birchtown, Nova Scotia"; Wilkie and Farnsworth, *Sampling Many Pots*.

42. Crook, "Bilali—The Old Man of Sapelo Island."

43. Walz and Brandt, "Toward an Archaeology," 256–62.

44. DeCorse and Chouin, "Trouble with Siblings."

45. Joyner, "Digging Common Ground: African American History and Historical Archaeology."
46. Little, *Text-aided Archaeology*, 4.
47. Singleton, "Using Written Records in the Archaeological Study of Slavery."
48. Gruber, "The Archaeology of Slave Life at Thomas Jefferson's Monticello:
Mulberry Row Slave Quarters 'r, s t.'"
49. Berlin and Harris, "Introduction: Uncovering, Discovering, and Recovering," 3.
50. Havsier and MacDonald, eds., *African Re-Genesis*; Ogundiran and Falola,
eds., *Archaeology of Atlantic Africa and the African Diaspora*.
51. Kelly, "From French West Africa to the French Caribbean."
52. La Rosa Corzo and Pérez Padrón, "La resistencia esclava en la Sierra de el
Grillo."
53. Armstrong and Hauser, "An East Indian Laborers' Household in Nineteenth-
Century Jamaica."
54. Gibson, "Daily Practice and Domestic Economics in Guadeloupe."
55. Weik, "Allies, Adversaries, and Kin in the African Seminole Communities
of Florida."

REFERENCES

Agorsah, E. Kofi. "The Archaeology of the African Diaspora." *African Archaeo-
    logical Review* 13, no. 4 (1996): 221–24.
——. "Ethnoarchaeological Consideration of Social Relationship and Settlement
    Patterning among Africans in the Caribbean Diaspora." In Haviser, *African
    Sites Archaeology in the Caribbean*, 38–64.
——, ed. *Maroon Heritage: Archaeological, Ethnographic, and Historical Perspec-
    tives*. Kingston, Jamaica: Canoe Press, 1994.
——. "The Other Site of Freedom: The Maroon Trail in Suriname." In Haviser
    and MacDonald, *African Re-Genesis*, 191–203.
——. "Scars of Brutality: Archaeology of the Maroons in the Caribbean." In
    Ogundiran and Falola, *Archaeology of Atlantic Africa and the African Di-
    aspora*, 277–91.
Armstrong, Douglas V. *Creole Transformation from Slavery to Freedom: Histori-
    cal Archaeology of the East End Community of St. Johns, Virgin Islands*.
    Gainesville: University Press of Florida, 2003.
Armstrong, Douglas, and Mark W. Hauser. "An East Indian Laborers' Household
    in Nineteenth-Century Jamaica: A Case for Understanding Cultural Diver-
    sity through Space, Chronology, and Material Analysis." *Historical Archae-
    ology* 38, no. 2 (2004): 9–21.
Barros, Philip Lynton de. "The Effect of the Slave Trade on the Basar Ironwork-
    ing Society, Togo." In DeCorse, *West Africa during the Atlantic Slave Trade*,
    59–80.
Beaudry, Mary C., and Ellen P. Berkland. "Archaeology of the African Meeting
    House on Nantucket." In Ogundiran and Falola, *Archaeology of Atlantic Af-
    rica and the African Diaspora*, 395–412.
Berlin, Ira, and Leslie M. Harris. "Introduction: Uncovering, Discovering, and

Recovering: Digging in New York's Slave Past Beyond the African Burial
Ground." In Berlin and Harris, *Slavery in New York*, ed. Ira Berlin and Leslie
M. Harris. New York: New Press, 2005.

Berman, Mary Jane, Jorge Febles, and Perry L. Gnivecki. "The Organization of Cuban Archaeology." In L. Antonio Curet, Shannon Lee Dawdy, and Gabino La
Rosa Crozo, eds., *Dialogues in Cuban Archaeology*, 47–59. Tuscaloosa: University of Alabama Press, 2005.

Cox, Beatrice. "The Archaeology of the Allensworth Hotel: Negotiating the System in Jim Crow America." Master's thesis, Cultural Management Resources
Program, Sonoma State University, 2007.

Crook, Morgan R. "Bilali—The Old Man of Sapelo Island: Between Africa and
Georgia." *Wadabagei: A Journal of the Caribbean and Its Diasporas* 10, no. 2
(2007): 40–55.

Deagan, Kathleen, and Jane Landers. "Fort Mosé: Earliest Free Black Town in the
United States." In Singleton, *"I, Too, Am America,"* 261–82.

DeCorse, Christopher R. *An Archaeology of Elmina: Africans and Europeans on
the Gold Coast, 1400–1900*. Washington: Smithsonian Institution Press,
2001.

———. "Material Aspects of the Limba, Yalunka, and Kuranko Ethnicity: Archaeological Research in Northeastern Sierra Leone." In S. J. Shennan, ed., *Archaeological Approaches to Cultural Identity*, 125–53. London: Unwin Hy-
man, 1989.

———. "Oceans Apart: Africanist Perspectives on Diaspora Archaeology." In
Singleton, *"I, Too, Am America,"* 132–49.

———, ed. *West Africa during the Atlantic Slave Trade: Archaeological Perspectives*. London: Leicester University Press, 2001.

DeCorse, Christopher R., and Gerard L. Chouin. "Trouble with Siblings: Archaeo-
logical and Historical Interpretation of the West African Past." In Toyin
Falola and Charles S. Jennings, ed., *Sources and Methods in African History:
Spoken, Written, Unearthed*, 7–15. Rochester, N.Y.: University of Rochester
Press, 2003.

Dème, Alioune, and Ndèye Sokhna Guèye. "Enslavement in the Middle Senegal
Valley: Historical and Archaeological Perspectives." In Ogundiran and Falola,
Archaeology of Atlantic Africa and the African Diaspora, 134–39.

Dixon, Kelly J. *Boomtown Saloons: Archaeology and History in Virginia City*.
Reno: University of Nevada Press, 2005.

Domínguez, Lourdes. "Fuentes arqueológicas en el estudio de la esclavitud en
Cuba." In *La Esclavitud en Cuba*, 267–79. Havana: Editorial Academia, 1986.

Fagan, Brian. *Ancient Lives: An Introduction to Archaeology and Prehistory*. 2nd
ed. Upper Saddle River, N.J.: Pearson Education, 2004.

Ferguson, Leland. *Uncommon Ground: Archaeology and Early African America,
1650–1800*. Washington, D.C.: Smithsonian Institution Press, 1992.

Folorunso, Caleb A. "The Trans-Atlantic Slave Trade and Local Traditions of
Slavery in the West African Hinterlands: The Tivland Example." In Haviser
and MacDonald, *African Re-Genesis*, 237–68.

Franklin, Maria. "Archaeological Dimensions of Soul Food: Interpreting Race,
Culture, and Afro-Virginian Identity." In Orser, *Race and the Archaeology
of Identity*, 88–107.

Franklin, Maria, and Larry McKee. "Introduction African Diaspora Archaeologies: Present Insights and Expanding Discourses." *Historical Archaeology* 38, no. 1 (2004): 1–9.

Funari, Pedro P. A. "The Archaeology of Palmares and Its Contribution to the Understanding of the History of African American Culture." *Historical Archaeology in Latin America* 7, no. 1 (1995): 1–41.

Gibson, Heather. "Daily Practice and Domestic Economics in Guadeloupe: An Archaeological and Historical Study." PhD diss., Department of Anthropology, Syracuse University, 2007.

Goucher, Candice. "Iron Is Iron 'til It Is Rust: Trade and Ecology in the Decline of West African Iron-Smelting." *Journal of African History* 22 (1981): 179–200.

Gruber, Anna. "The Archaeology of Slave Life at Thomas Jefferson's Monticello: Mulberry Row Slave Quarters 'r, s t.'" *Quarterly Bulletin of the Archaeological Society of Virginia* 46, no. 1 (1991): 2–9.

Haviser, Jay B., ed. *African Sites Archaeology in the Caribbean.* Princeton, N.J.: Marcus Wiener, 1999.

———. "Identifying Post-Emancipation (1863–1940) African-Curaçaoan Material Assemblage." In Haviser, *African Sites Archaeology in the Caribbean,* 221–63.

Haviser, Jay B., and Kevin C. MacDonald, eds. *African Re-Genesis: Confronting Social Issues in the Diaspora.* Walnut Creek, Calif.: Left Coast Press, 2006.

Holl, Augustin. "500 Years in the Cameroons: Making Sense of the Archaeological Record." In DeCorse, *West Africa during the Atlantic Slave Trade,* 52–178.

Johnson, Matthew. "The Tide Reversed: Prospects and Potentials for a Postcolonial Archaeology of Europe." In Martin Hall and Stephen W. Silliman, eds., *Historical Archaeology,* 311–16. Malden, Mass.: Blackwell, 2006.

Joyner, Charles. "Digging Common Ground: African American History and Historical Archaeology." Paper presented at the conference Digging the Afro-American Past: Archaeology and the Black Experience, University of Mississippi, Oxford, 18 May 1989.

Kelly, Kenneth G. "The Archaeology of African-European Interaction: Investigating the Social Roles of Trade, Traders, and the Use of Space in the Seventeenth- and Eighteenth-Century Hueda Kingdom, Republic of Benin." *World Archaeology* 28, no. 3 (1997): 77–95.

———. "From French West Africa to the French Caribbean: Archaeology, Slavery, and an Africanist Perspective." Paper presented at the conference Abolition 2007: Archaeology and Heritage of the African Diaspora in the New World, Institute of Archaeology, University College, London, 31 March 2007.

Kusimba, Chapurukha M. "Archaeology of Slavery in East Africa." *African Archaeological Review* 21, no. 2 (2004): 59–88.

La Rosa Corzo, Gabino. *Runaway Slave Settlements in Cuba: Resistance and Repression.* Trans. Mary Todd. Chapel Hill: University of North Carolina Press, 2003.

La Rosa Corzo, Gabino, and Joaquin Pérez Padrón. "La resistencia esclava en la Sierra de el Grillo: estudio arqueológico." In *Estudios Arqueológicos compilación de temas, 1990,* 101–27. Havana: Editorial Academica, 1994.

Lawrence, A. W. *Trade Castles and Forts of West Africa.* London: Jonathan Cape, 1963.

MacLeod-Leslie, Heather. "Understanding the Use of Space in an Eighteenth-

Century Black Loyalist Community: Birchtown, Nova Scotia." Master's thesis, Carleton University, Ottawa, 2002.

MacEachern, Scott. "State Formation and Enslavement in the Southern Lake Chad Basin." In DeCorse, *West Africa during the Atlantic Slave Trade*, 131–51.

McIntosh, Susan Keech. "Tools for Understanding Transformation and Continuity in Senegambian Society, 1500–1900." In DeCorse, *West Africa during the Atlantic Slave Trade*, 14–37.

Mitchell, Peter. *African Connections: Archaeological Perspectives on Africa and the Wider World.* Walnut Creek, Calif.: Altamira, 2006.

Monroe, J. Cameron. "Dahomey and the Atlantic Slave Trade: Archaeology and Political Order on the Bight of Benin." In Ogundiran and Falola, *Archaeology of Atlantic Africa and the African Diaspora*, 100–121.

Morgan, Philip D. "Archaeology and History in the Study of African Americans." In Haviser and MacDonald, *African Re-Genesis*, 53–61.

Mullins, Paul. *Race: An Archaeology of African America and Consumer Culture.* New York: Kluwer/Plenum, 1999.

Nichols, Elaine. "No Easy Run to Freedom: Maroons in the Great Dismal Swamp of North Carolina and Virginia, 1677–1850." Master's thesis, Department of Anthropology, University of South Carolina, Columbia, 1988.

Ogundiran, Akinwumi, and Toyin Falola, eds. *Archaeology of Atlantic Africa and the African Diaspora.* Bloomington: Indiana University Press, 2007.

———. "Pathways in the Archaeology of the Transatlantic Africa." In Ogundiran and Falola, *Archaeology of Atlantic Africa and the African Diaspora*, 3–45.

Orser, Charles E., Jr. "The Archaeology of the African Diaspora." *Annual Review of Anthropology* 27 (1998): 63–82.

———, ed. *Race and the Archaeology of Identity.* Salt Lake City: University of Utah Press, 2001.

Orser, Charles E., Jr., and Pedro P. A. Funari. "Archaeology and Slave Resistance and Rebellion." *World Archeology* 33, no. 1 (2001): 61–72.

Posnansky, Merrick. "West Africanist Reflections on African American Archaeology." In Singleton, *"I, Too, Am America,"* 21–37.

Posnansky, Merrick, and Albert van Dantzig. "Fort Ruychaver Rediscovered." *Sankofa* 2 (1976): 7–18.

Pulis, John W. "'Important Truths' and 'Pernicious Follies': Texts, Covenants, and the Anabaptist Church of Jamaica." In Kevin Yelvington, ed., *Afro-Atlantic Dialogues: Anthropology in the Diaspora*, 194–210. Santa Fe: School of American Research Press, 2006.

Reid, Andrew. *Afro-Latin America, 1800–2000.* New York: Oxford University Press, 2004.

Schávelzon, Daniel. *Buenos Aires Negra: Arqueología histórica de una ciudad silenciada.* Buenos Aires: Emecé, 2003.

———. "The Vanishing People: Archaeology of the African Population in Buenos Aires." In Ogundiran and Falola, *Archaeology of Atlantic Africa and the African Diaspora*, 373–82.

Schuyler, Robert, ed. *Archaeological Perspectives on Ethnicity in America: Afro-American and Asian American Culture History.* Farmingdale, N.Y.: Baywood, 1980.

Singleton, Theresa A. "Class, Race, and Identity among Free Blacks of the Antebellum South." In Orser, *Race and the Archaeology of Identity*, 196–207.
——, ed. *"I, Too, Am America": Studies in African American Archaeology*. Charlottesville: University Press of Virginia, 1999.
——. "Using Written Records in the Archaeological Study of Slavery: An Example
from the Butler Island Plantation." In Barbara Little, ed., *Text-Aided Archaeology*, 55–66. Boca Raton, Fla.: CRC Press, 1992.
Singleton, Theresa A., and Mark D. Bograd. *The Archaeology of the African Diaspora in the Americas*. Glassboro, N.J.: Society for Historical Archaeology,
1995.
Singleton, Theresa, and Marcos André Torres de Souza. "Archaeologies of the African Diaspora in Brazil, Cuba, and the United States." In Teresita Majewski
and David Gainster, eds., *International Handbook of Historical Archaeology*,
449–69. New York: Springer, 2009.
Stahl, Ann Brower. "Introduction: Changing Perspectives on Africa's Past." In
Stahl, ed., *African Archaeology: A Critical Introduction*, 1–23. Malden, Mass.:
Blackwell, 2005.
——. *Making History in Banda*. New York: Cambridge University Press, 2001.
Swanepoel, Natalie. "Socio-Political Change on a Slave-Raiding Frontier: War,
Trade, and 'Big Men'" in Nineteenth-Century Sisalaland, Northern Ghana."
In Tony Pollard and Iain Banks, eds., *Past Tense: Studies in the Archaeology
of Conflict*, 265–93. Leiden: Koninklijke Brill, 2006.
Trigger, Bruce. *A History of Archaeological Thought*. Cambridge: Cambridge Uni-
versity Press, 1989.
Usman, Aribidesi. "The Landscape and Society of Northern Yorubaland during
the Era of the Slave Trade." In Ogundiran and Falola, *Archaeology of Atlantic
Africa and the African Diaspora*, 140–59.
van Dantzig, Albert. *Forts and Castles of Ghana*. Accra: Sedco, 1980.
Walz, Jonathan R., and Steven A. Brandt. "Toward an Archaeology of the Other
African Diaspora: The Slave Trade and Dispersed Africans in the Western In-
dian Ocean." In Haviser and MacDonald, *African Re-Genesis*, 246–68.
Weik, Terrence. "Allies, Adversaries, and Kin in African Seminole Communities
of Florida: Archaeology of Pilaklikaha." *Archaeology of Atlantic Africa and
the Africa Diaspora*, 311–31.
——. "Archaeology of the African Diapora in Latin America." *Historical Archae-
ology* 33, no. 1 (2004): 31–49.
Wilkie, Laurie A. *Creating Freedom: Material Culture and African American
Identity at Oakley Plantation, Louisiana, 1840–1950*. Baton Rouge: Louisi-
ana State University Press, 2000.
Wilkie, Laurie A., and Paul Farnsworth. *Sampling Many Pots: An Archaeology
of Memory and Tradition at a Bahamian Plantation*. Gainesville: University
Press of Florida, 2005.

PART TWO
SOCIAL SCIENCES

6

CARIBBEAN SOCIOLOGY, AFRICA, AND THE AFRICAN DIASPORA

Paget Henry

If I were writing about sociology's representation of Africa and its diaspora in the 1960s or 1970s, I probably would write it from the perspective of American sociology in spite of being a person from and a sociologist of the Caribbean. This approach, which now sounds so peculiar, would probably have been the case because of my sociological training at Cornell University and also because of the very dependent relationship that existed between Caribbean and American sociology during those decades. However, with the turn to neo-Smithian models of market-oriented growth in the 1980s and the ending of the Cold War, the period of convergence between these two sociologies around Keynesian state-oriented models of development came to a rather abrupt end.[1] In the 1980s and 1990s, Caribbean and American sociology experienced very different patterns of adjustment and reorganization. This divergence has made it possible and even necessary for me to address this problem of African representation from an emerging Africana point within the terrain of Caribbean sociology. As the events of the current economic crisis—which has so far resulted in a trillion dollar bailout of the financial sector—continues to unfold, we can only wonder at the implications for the future of development theory and my emerging Africana point of view.

Nevertheless, from this perspective I will argue that even though the representation of Africa and its diaspora has improved in the second phase, it is still a major problem for Caribbean sociology. I will substantiate this claim in three basic steps: First, I will describe the two major phases in the history of Caribbean sociology. Second, I will point out some of the difficult cleavages and contradictions of this second phase that continue to compromise its ability to adequately represent Africa and its diaspora. Third, I will suggest an Africana solution to this representational problem.

THE FIRST PHASE OF CARIBBEAN SOCIOLOGY

In its early years, the practice of Caribbean sociology was primarily located at universities in Cuba, the Dominican Republic, and Haiti, as well as at the University of Puerto Rico and branches of the University of the West Indies in Jamaica and Trinidad. Beginning in the early 1960s, sociology in the English-speaking Caribbean experienced a period of dynamic growth and prominence that lasted until the early 1980s. This short but golden period was made possible by the coming together of a number of outstanding Caribbean, American, and British sociologists and anthropologists, including M. G. Smith, Lloyd Brathwaite, Vera Rubin, R. T. Smith, Fernando Ortiz, Leo Depres, Edith Clarke, George Roberts, and Orlando Patterson. This period gave us such classic works as M. G. Smith's *The Plural Society in the British West Indies*, Edith Clarke's *My Mother Who Fathered Me*, R. T. Smith's *Negro Family in British Guiana*, and Orlando Patterson's *Sociology of Slavery* as well as his novels *The Children of Sisyphus* and *An Absence of Ruins*.

However, the flowering of this golden period depended in large part on a close collaboration with American sociology. All of these Caribbean sociologists and anthropologists did their graduate training in American or British universities, and as a result they drew heavily on the intellectual traditions and resources of American and British sociology and anthropology. Among some of the more prominent American sociologists who were involved in these collaborations were E. Franklin Frazier, Leonard Broom, Edward Shills, Arthur Stinchcombe, Lewis Coser, and the anthropologists George Simpson and Sidney Mintz.

At the intellectual center of this collaboration was the tradition/modernity issue. The interests of both groups of sociologists and anthropologists converged around the Caribbean as an instance of a modernizing society. The centrality of this issue for the coming together of these two groups emerges very clearly from M. G. Smith's account of the field of Caribbean sociology. In his classic essay, "A Plural Framework for Caribbean Studies," Smith situates Caribbean sociology/anthropology within the larger context of the Caribbean and the American South (1974). As a result, the field of Caribbean sociology/anthropology is portrayed as the joint construction of primarily Caribbean and American sociologists and anthropologists. Smith dates the origin of the field to 1924 with the publication of Martha Beckwith's *Black Roadways*. From Beckwith, Smith moves to figures like Melville Herskovits, Robert Redfield, E. Franklin Frazier, Lloyd Warner, John Dollard, Leonard Broom, Hortense Powdermaker, Meyer Fortes, and Madeline Kerr. The primary interest of these scholars in the Caribbean was its traditional or premodern African cultures and their implications for middle-range theories and empirical studies of modernization processes. Similar, but in some respects different, views of the field emerged from other Caribbean sociologists and anthropologists such as Roberts, Brathwaite, Clarke, and Patterson. It was the interest that these scholars shared in the modernization of Caribbean societies that made this interdisciplinary and international cooperation possible.

Although the perspectives of Caribbean sociologists and American sociologists differed somewhat, on the whole the representations of Africa, its intellectual traditions, and its diaspora were inadequate in both. This shared inadequacy was largely the result of the extent to which Caribbean sociologists identified with and drew on the Western intellectual and sociological traditions. The latter was a tradition that dated its rise to the European figures of Karl Marx, Max Weber, and Emile Durkheim. It also linked its later American extensions to the work of figures like Robert Park, George Herbert Mead, Herbert Blumer, Talcott Parsons, and Robert Merton. It is important to note that this standard reconstruction of sociology's American extension completely overlooks the founding contributions of W. E. B. Du Bois and his Atlanta school of sociology. From the Africana perspective, this is a grave omission that Caribbean sociology has repeated and that both sociologies still need to correct.

In the American tradition, sociology employed two theories in the study of the African societies of the Caribbean: culture contact theory (Park, Frazier, Herskovits) and modernization theory (Parsons, Shills, Broom). In the former, the primary emphasis was on the degree to which non-European cultures were surviving the contact with imperial Europe. In contrast to the Asian countries, Park and Frazier argued that African cultures were experiencing very radical uprootings that were threatening their very existence as a result of their contact with Europe. In the case of Afro-America, they argued that there were no survivals of African culture among African Americans. Herskovits, although a culture contact theorist, argued very vigorously against this position.

In the case of modernization theory, Africa served as the *locus classicus* of tribal premodernity or the polar opposite of the now culturally rationalized and hence modern West. Its primary conceptual function was to be the prerational site from which Europeans could examine the "primitive" phase in the history of human development. Cast into this premodern role, African cultures, both continental and diasporic, were excessively frozen in prerational time by modernization theory. As a result, their capacities for growth and modern rational knowledge production were severely distorted and obscured. Western sociologists did not see premodern African cultures as sites of valid knowledge production in the way that they saw premodern Greek culture. Consequently, the former were not seen by modernization theorists as capable of making original and valuable contributions to the human stock of knowledge that would be of relevance in the modern period. This was one very important way in which Western sociology misrepresented Africa and its diaspora.

The distinct contribution that Caribbean sociologists and anthropologists brought to these discussions was the theory of cultural creolization. The primary emphasis of this theory was the phenomenon of cultural and racial mixing in colonial societies, rather than the problems of survival and rationalization stressed by the culture contact and modernization theorists. M. G. Smith's work on creolization is a very clear case in point. It rejected the rigid bipolar (black and white) construction of race in the United States as inappropriate for the more mixed constructions that could be observed in the Caribbean and Latin America (1974: 67). However, within this framework of racial and cultural mixing, there remained a privileging of whiteness and a devaluing of blackness. Thus, in spite of this distinctive emphasis on creolization, it was embedded within a broader framework that was shaped by the ongoing debates between culture contact and modernization theories. As a result, the theory of creolization absorbed many of the anti-African biases and assumptions of these two theories. Consequently, it too had difficulties adequately seeing and representing Africa and its intellectual contribution to the stock of human knowledge.

In addition to this external shaping of Caribbean sociology's perception of Africa and its own region, another peculiar feature of this first phase was the discipline's deep estrangement from both its own regional and the larger Africana intellectual tradition. During this period, Caribbean sociology did not systematically incorporate inputs from the indigenous Afro-Caribbean intellectual or the larger Africana intellectual tradition to which the former was connected. There was little or no consciousness of these two traditions of social thought, little or no sense of their presence or that their primary interests and texts could be of epistemic value to the production of sociological knowledge. It is important to note here that Smith's account of the field did not include Antenor Firmin's *Equality of the Human Races*, Edward Blyden's *Christianity, Islam, and the Negro Race*, W. E. B. Du Bois's *Philadelphia Negro*, or C. L. R. James's *Black Jacobins*. Consequently, there were no ongoing feedback relations with this local intellectual tradition with the result that the specifically Caribbean intertextual relations of Caribbean sociology were very weak. Thus, in spite of its impressive record of productivity and the theory of creolization, the first golden age of Caribbean sociology was marked by a peculiar paradox: systemic patterns of under-identifying with and excluding its own intellectual tradition while over-identifying with the Western intellectual tradition. It was this peculiar pattern of epistemic organization that was largely responsible for its inadequate representation of Africa and its diaspora, including the Caribbean.

THE BREAK

As noted earlier, one of the major differences between the first and the second phases of Caribbean sociology was the collapse of the collaborative effort with American sociologists. This break was brought on by a number of factors. First was the decline of culture contact and modernization theories. In the late 1970s, they were experiencing severe challenges from dependency and other Marxist oriented theories of development and change. Caribbean economists such as Lloyd Best and Kari Levitt (1975), George Beckford (1972), Norman Girvan (1976), and Clive Thomas (1974) were central to the rise of Caribbean dependency theory. With much of the old guard of American sociology remaining in the modernization tradition, the basis for the earlier collaboration was no longer there. Theoretical debates in Caribbean sociology came to be dominated by exchanges between M. G. Smith and other cultural pluralists on the one hand and the new dependency and other theorists on the other.

The separation initiated by this theoretical divergence was further widened by the rise of policies of neoliberal globalization in the West. It was the policy that resulted from the turn to neo-Smithian policies of market-oriented or private sector models of development. The latter challenged the state-led ones that had been dominant in the Caribbean. They were first articulated by the Caribbean Nobel Prize–winning economist Arthur Lewis (1950) and later reinforced by the dependency and Marxist theories. The major entrepreneurial roles that Caribbean states had assumed were now theoretically and politically incorrect according to neoliberal theory. These states were now under pressure to privatize and downsize in order to make room for a market-oriented but very mercantile and timid Caribbean private sector. These shifts in the Western political and economic outlook were reinforced by the dramatic collapse of state socialism in the Soviet Union and Eastern Europe. The effect of the latter was a deepening of the commitment to the market as the primary principle of socioeconomic organization. For American social scientists and policymakers, the interest in third world development was very closely related to the cold war and to Keynesian strategies of state intervention in the economy. With these gone, development could only mean private sector–led growth through competitive trading in globalized financial and commodity markets.

These dramatic shifts in both the theory and practice of socioeconomic development had significant implications for both Caribbean and American sociology. Both had to reorganize themselves in order to adjust to the new competition from neo-Smithian economic theory and a more conservative political environment. The latter was bent on reducing state interventions, many of which had been legitimated by sociological arguments and research. By the late 1980s, the outlines of the reorganization of American sociology were quite clear. Of particular note for us was the dramatic decline in the centrality of the sociology of development to the field as a whole and its replacement by economic sociology. One significant indicator of this shift was clearly registered in the mid-1980s reorganization of the major subfields of sociology used by the journal *Contemporary Sociology*. From a highly visible and explicitly recognized area of American sociology, development declined to an invisible and implicitly recognized area of the discipline. With this shift, American sociology became even more centered on the United States, with steep declines in the interest in Africa and its non-American diaspora.

THE SECOND PHASE OF CARIBBEAN SOCIOLOGY

As in the American case, the period after the break was one of epistemic and subfield reorganization for Caribbean sociology. In this second case of subfield reorganization, the sociology of development also registered a significant decline in status and visibility. This decline resulted from two factors. First, there was the absence of a strong Smithian or neo-Smithian tradition of thought in the region that could have seized the moment and retheorized in appropriate ways the regulatory and wealth-producing powers of the market. Consequently, no really outstanding theorists of the entrepreneurial capabilities of the Caribbean private sector emerged to fill this theoretical space. This rather stark vacuum was in itself a very telling instance of the failure of this new laissez-faire philosophy in both the academic and entrepreneurial marketplaces. In the concise words of Arthur Lewis, this philosophy claims that "if anything is worth doing, then someone will do it. If no one does it, then it cannot be worth doing, and the effort of a government to get it done must be contrary to the public interest" (29). Yet here were instances of activities that were clearly worth doing that simply did not get done in spite of the self-interested and profit-oriented motives of many individuals in the Caribbean private sector. In spite of both demand and opportunity, there were no dramatic increases in the entrepreneurial activities of the Caribbean private sector, and no economists arose who could either explain or remedy these crucial market failures. This could possibly have been an opening for a sociology of Caribbean markets leading to something like the rise of economic sociology in American sociology. But this also did not occur. Consequently, for those economists and sociologists who embraced the new laissez-faire philosophy, this void was filled with replays of the neoliberal ideas of the "Washington consensus" for which the Caribbean private sector was practically unprepared. This was clearly not a good foundation upon which to reformulate the sociology of development.

The second factor contributing to the decline of this subfield was the way in which this neo-Smithian turn clashed with the views and policies of the region's dependency theorists. For the most part, they remained committed to the view that governments must intervene in crucial instances where the current state or level of development of market institutions leave vital needs unmet. This particular configuration of Caribbean development theory and the changed policy contexts of its practice resulted in a rather unproductive environment that inhibited its output.

Corresponding to this decline in the sociology of development were expansions in other subfields of Caribbean sociology that resulted in the overall growth of the discipline. In addition to Cuba, the Dominican Republic, Haiti, Puerto Rico, Trinidad, and Jamaica, sociology was now being taught at universities in Barbados, Guyana, the Virgin Islands, Martinique, and St. Maarten. Along with these expansions, there were also significant shifts in the intertextual relations, theoretical orientations, areas of empirical study, personnel, and administration of the field. The nature of this reorganization is clearly indicated by the change in the department's name on the Mona campus of the University of the West Indies in Jamaica. From sociology, it became the department of sociology and social welfare. The strong anthropological ties of the earlier years were clearly not maintained, and that particular intertextual relationship has declined significantly.

On the St. Augustine campus of the University of the West Indies in Trinidad, the sociology department was incorporated into a department of behavioral sciences that included social work, psychology, and political science. On the Cave Hill campus of the University of the West Indies in Barbados, sociology is part of a department of government, sociology, and social work. At the University of Guyana, the sociology department was expanded to include social work and communications. These new linkages point to the new ways in which the assistance of Caribbean sociologists is being sought in the study and management of specific institutional areas such as social work and communications. Also an integral part of the formation of this second phase was the departure of many of these sociologists and anthropologists for positions in universities abroad expanding an already large expatriate community that now includes figures like Stuart Hall, Orlando Patterson, Paul Gilroy, George Danns, Don Robotham, Alex Dupuy, Linden Lewis, Heidi Mirza, Percy Hintzen, Michel Laguerre, David Scott, Brackette Williams, Althea Prince, Michel-Rolph Trouillot, and myself.

The impact of this reorganization on Caribbean sociology to date has been good extensively but not so good intensively. It has not produced a new period of dynamic growth with the production of books and articles to match the quality of the output of the earlier period. Some of the major texts of this second phase include Rhoda Reddock's *Women Labour*

and Politics in Trinidad and Tobago, Alex Dupuy's Haiti in the World
Economy, Paul Gilroy's Black Atlantic, Christine Barrow's Family in
the Caribbean, Frances Henry's Caribbean Diaspora in Toronto, Michel-
Rolph Trouillot's Haiti: State against Nation, David Scott's Refashioning
Futures, and my own Peripheral Capitalism and Underdevelopment in
Antigua. These works are important contributions and are very different
in their many theoretical orientations from the major works of the first
period.

However, in spite of the significance of this output, it has not restored
the visibility of the discipline to what it was before. The new interdisciplinary alliances and intertextual relations with social work, psychology,
and communications have not yet produced new creative syntheses that
would allow work in these areas to reinforce each other. This mutual reinforcing between the disciplines of sociology, anthropology, political science, and economics around questions related to development was a major
source of the strength and creativity of the golden period. The interdisciplinary cooperation was really quite significant. This is definitely going
to be more difficult with psychology and communications than was the
case with anthropology. Consequently, there have been marked tendencies for the various specializations in the departments to remain separate,
thereby creating new tendencies toward fragmentation. This fragmentation has also meant that there is less of a shared focus capable of bringing
these new subfields more into ongoing conversations and exchanges.

Two other factors must be taken into account when considering the
decline in intellectual vigor and productivity of this second period in the
history of Caribbean sociology. First, there was the impact of the rise
of poststructuralist theory. As a theory that explained social meanings,
identities, and social orders by mapping them onto the orders of linguistic structures, it constituted a major challenge to several areas of sociology and anthropology. In relation to sociology, the theory placed the
concept of semiolinguistic structures in direct competition with the concept of social structures. In this battle, particularly in the cultural areas
of identity and meaning construction, the semiotic approach of the post-
structuralist won sufficient converts to become the leading multidisciplinary theory in these areas.

Not only did post-structuralism become a leading theory; it also presented a cultural (semiotic) alternative to the survivalist, normative, and
politico-economic orientations of culture contact, modernization, and dependency theories. This alternative appeared in two forms: (1) a new cultural explanation of social domination and (2) a new cultural image of
freedom from social domination. The new cultural explanation of social
domination located it in the underlying hierarchical order of the binary
oppositions and founding categories presupposed by the discourses of the
speaking subject. As such, this hierarchical structure was an algebra of

positive and negative signs that privileged the contents of its positively marked categories over those in negatively marked ones. The key to social domination became the behavioral responses of the subject to the contents of his/her negatively marked categories—that is, whether they had to be destroyed, excluded, made invisible, punished, or dehumanized. Thus social domination was seen as the result of the behavioral consequences of the semiotic marking of one's discursive categories. This semiotic order was linguistically shaped and kept in place. The linguistic auto-instituting of this order gave it an a priori or always already presupposed status. In short, it semioticized Kant's transcendental analysis.

A result of this interpretation was that the overcoming of social domination, including its postcolonial, racial, and gendered forms, came to be seen as fundamentally a process of critiquing and disrupting the inherited semiotic orders of the discourses that envisioned and legitimated these orders of domination. These presupposed semiotic orders encoded domination by limiting the meanings or semiotic play available to particular concepts, images, or signs. The alternative to this semiotic concept of domination was an equally semiotic concept of freedom: that of the free-floating signifier. In other words, the speaking subject who would be free should strive to become a signifier that had somehow overcome the order of discourse in which it had been semiotically inscribed and was now able to mobilize all of the semiotic play that the order has either inhibited or appropriated for itself. The path to this new form of freedom was not political or mass organizing, but the practice of deconstructing a priori semiotic orders. This was the cultural alternative to the political practices of development that post-structuralism presented. Its impact on Caribbean sociology and anthropology can be seen most clearly in the work of Stuart Hall (1981), Paul Gilroy (1994), and David Scott (1999). In all three cases, the post-structural turn has left Caribbean sociology with new unsatisfactory relationships between culture and political economy.

The third factor contributing to the intellectual decline of the second period of Caribbean sociology has been its less direct relationships with the central problem of contemporary Caribbean societies: finding a way to renew economic growth and development within the context of the new global political economy. Without a more direct engagement with this crucial issue, the discipline will not regain the centrality it had when it was more deeply engaged with it. The failure of Caribbean economists to produce better answers to this problem has resulted in a weakening of intertextual ties between the two disciplines. This lack of buoyant and innovative input from Caribbean economists represents a significant change in the intertextual relations that define the second phase of Caribbean sociology, leaving the latter less able to engage as directly as before the problem of socioeconomic development. There is a deep sense of having been defeated and overwhelmed by this problem that I think is partly responsible for the current lack of dynamism in the field. Until we are once again able to bring culture and political economy together around questions of socioeconomic transformation, we will not overcome this current sense of being in retreat.

In short, the results of this period of reorganization have been mixed. The organizational growth of the field has been significant with increases in numbers of departments and interdisciplinary alliances. On the other hand, the intellectual output has not been able to match that of the first period in quality. The primary reason, I am suggesting, has been a much more complex local and global environment in which to be theoretically innovative and to link theory to transformative practices.

REORGANIZATION AND AFRICAN REPRESENTATION

The question to which we must now turn our attention is that of the representation of Africa and its diaspora in this second period of Caribbean sociology. Given the new pattern of subfield specializations, it should come as no surprise that the discipline, like American sociology, has become more inward looking. Its research activities are focused more intensely on solving specific social problems with an eye on improving the present and much less on the premodern past. In many ways, this more inward focus has improved the representation of the region and its problems in the discipline. In terms of its research, the field has indeed become more Caribbean centered when compared with the first period. Also very important here are the changed attitudes toward the African dimensions and contributions to the life of Caribbean societies. They have come out from under the spell of misrepresentation that had been cast over them by culture contact and modernization theories. These Afro-Caribbean contributions have now become important markers of Caribbean identity in the modern period. The contributions of the Rastafarians are probably the clearest example. The ideas of this group are no longer studied just from the perspective of what they can tell us about the premodern past or present of the Caribbean. In addition to revealing the group, these ideas are also studied for the contributions that they can make to the life of the inquiring scholar. This is indeed a significant shift that has brought the Afro-Caribbean contributions to Caribbean life into the mainstream of intellectual conversation and debate.

However, if the problem of representation is extended to Africa and the whole of its diaspora, then there is a lot of room for improvement. With the more inward focus, the comparative perspectives that culture contact, modernization, and to a lesser extent dependency theories gave to Caribbean sociology have been lost. In all of these comparative frameworks, Africa was included. In the case of dependency theory, the comparisons were more with Latin America, but nonetheless the comparisons with the African periphery were there primarily through the work of Samir Amin. Further, the rise of neoliberal and post-structural theories have helped to reinforce the shift away from the earlier comparative perspectives that systematically included Africa. Although the continent is no longer the quintessential site of premodernity, a clear role for Africa has not yet emerged from this period of reorganization. There are many competing positions on this issue. There are the anti-essentialist critiques of earlier notions of blackness or Africanness that can be found in the works of Scott (2004) and Gilroy (1994). On the other hand, there is the position of an Africana intellectual tradition that links the Caribbean to Africa that can be found in the works of scholars such as Lewis Gordon (2000), Anthony Bogues (2003), and myself (2000). However, the outcomes of these exchanges are still not clear. Thus it is fair to say that although the earlier misrepresentation of Africa is gone, a new and distinctive role for Africa has not yet emerged in this second phase of Caribbean sociology.

The same is also true for much of the non-Caribbean parts of the African diaspora. Thus relations with African communities in Canada, the United States, Latin America, Britain, and Europe are also in states of flux and underrepresentation in Caribbean sociology. Also contributing to this fluid state of affairs is the absence of a vibrant Caribbean sociological association or other institutional channels for collaborative work across these diasporas. In sum, as in the case of intellectual output, the problem of the representation of Africa and its diasporas still has a long way to go. Is it possible to remedy this situation? Is it possible to envision a second golden age of Caribbean sociology in which Africa and its diasporas are better represented? I think it is. In the remainder of this chapter, I will make the case for an Africana route to another dynamic and innovative period in Caribbean sociology. The basic challenge of this route is for Caribbean sociology to move much closer to the indigenous intellectual tradition that for so long it has failed to identify with and embrace.

CARIBBEAN SOCIOLOGY, REPRESENTATION, AND THE AFRICANA APPROACH

The Africana approach to the renewing of Caribbean sociology focuses on the relationship between this discipline and the intellectual traditions in which it is embedded. Disciplines do not exist in isolation. On the contrary, they are tributaries of larger intellectual streams from which they draw epistemic resources. During certain periods of intense focusing on particular problems, a discipline may lose sight of its connections to this larger intellectual stream of ideas and embrace the illusion that it is an autonomous center of knowledge production. However, the situations of disciplines are very different during times of crisis in which old paradigms have reached points of exhaustion for the doing of what Thomas Kuhn has called "normal science" (1970: 25). At times like these, it is the creative inputs of new ideas, images, metaphors, revolutionary movements, or policy shifts from larger intellectual traditions that must be engaged to produce new paradigms that will be able to motivate and renew activities of normal science or knowledge production.

In Caribbean sociology, the current crisis of normal knowledge production is unmistakable. It is a crisis that in part has been brought on by the disruptive manner in which paradigms that support normal knowledge are being displaced. The dynamism of these paradigm shifts has been largely externally driven, leaving Caribbean scholars with little control over the expiration dates of paradigms in use. This was the case with both culture contact and modernization theories. In the case of dependency theory, we played a more active role in determining the epistemic life of that paradigm. Thus the complex set of movements between paradigm shifts and the normal production of sociological knowledge points to the need for Caribbean sociologists to have greater creative control over the epistemic capital and resources that effect the formation and deformation of its paradigms. This epistemic capital resides primarily in intellectual traditions—stocks of knowledge and wisdom that a society or group has accumulated over centuries of living. These traditions feed specific disciplines and are in turn fed by them. This mutual reinforcing of each other results in what we can call processes of epistemic accumulation or the expansion of both disciplines and intellectual traditions.

As noted earlier, even in its second phase, Caribbean sociology has been functioning without deep ongoing feedback relations with the regional intellectual tradition. Although it has been better in this regard than the first phase, it is only now awakening to the full potential of this local tradition. Caribbean sociology is finally becoming aware of the distinct history, the record of achievements, and primary concerns of this tradition. The reliance on the Western intellectual tradition was still too strong for this regional one to emerge in all of its clarity, distinctiveness, coherence, and creativity. One consequence of this reliance on the West that is relevant here has been the tendency to see Caribbean and other Africana scholars in terms of the Western schools of thought by which they were influenced—in other words, to see someone like Fanon solely as an existentialist because of the Sartrean influence, James as a Marxist, or Edouard Glissant as a post-structuralist because of the Deleuzian influence. What very often does not get equally thematized is the influence of Africana thinkers on such Caribbean figures. Cases in point would be the influence of George Padmore, J. J. Thomas, and Marcus Garvey on James, or of Césaire on Fanon and Glissant. It has been in such moments of epistemic erasure or forgetting that the Caribbean and Africana intellectual traditions have experienced their disappearance.

Because of its deep roots in the larger Africana intellectual tradition, one of the distinctive marks of the Caribbean tradition is its interest in Africa and its definite abilities to adequately represent Africa and its diasporas. Consequently, the deepening of Caribbean sociology's links to this tradition can only help it with its problems of African representation. To see this, we must now take a closer look at what I've been calling the Caribbean intellectual tradition.

THE CARIBBEAN INTELLECTUAL TRADITION

The Caribbean intellectual tradition is the discursive framework of argument and counterargument that has shaped and thematized the origins and development of Caribbean society. It is the product of the intellectual quarrels that accompanied the building of colonial/plantation societies on the basis of indigenous Carib and later African slave labor. The legitimating by some and the delegitimating by others of this imperial and white supremacist social order were among the major intellectual challenges shaping the contours of this tradition. The long and angry dialogues between Prospero and Caliban over the former's domination have been the central problematic around which the major texts of the tradition have crystallized. The Prosperean texts of this tradition can be seen in the works of scholars such as Francisco de Vitoria, Gonzalo de Oviedo, Bartolomé de Las Casas, Richard Ligon, Bryan Edwards, and Edward Long. The counter voices of Caliban and Calherban (the black female) can be heard in slave narratives such as those of Mary Prince and Ottobah Cugoano, as well as in the antiracist and anticolonial critiques of Ann Hart, Jean Baptiste Phillipe, Michel Maxwell Phillip, Antenor Firmin, Robert Love, Edward Blyden, and others. Arriving from India as indentured servants between 1842 and 1917, Indo-Caribbeans joined this chorus of argument bringing their voices and unique contributions to the Caribbean intellectual tradition. Thus, to the Euro- and Afro-Caribbean voices mentioned above, we must add the writings of Joseph Ruhomon, Bechu, Cheddi Jagan, V. S. Naipaul, Sam Selvon, Ron Ramdin, Ramabai Espinet, and Clem Seecharan. The works of these three groups of authors must no longer be seen as isolated texts that exemplify various Western schools of thought, but as voices in ongoing exchanges that constitute the Caribbean intellectual tradition.

The failure of the golden period to connect with this tradition helps to explain the severity of the discipline's decline in the years following the break with American sociology. A similar failure also helps to explain why the current period has not been able to produce a second golden era. Since the break with American sociology, the discipline has been without the resources and inputs from a dynamic intellectual tradition with which to create new paradigms and reinvigorate normal sociological production. In my view, addressing this lack will go a long way toward solving both the productivity and African representation problems of Caribbean sociology. Thus a deeper convergence with this regional intellectual tradition is one of the major goals that the discipline must achieve.

This suggestion that Caribbean sociology needs to deepen its feedback relations with the regional intellectual tradition is now a much more accessible one than it was during the golden era. Since that period, the Caribbean intellectual tradition has gone through a process of categoric and conceptual decolonization that has dramatically increased its visibility, systematized its contents, and sharpened the outlines of its major contours. This ongoing process of intellectual decolonization can be seen from comparisons between current conceptions of the tradition and those of the golden period. The latter were given their classic formulation in Gordon K. Lewis's *Main Currents in Caribbean Thought*. The newer conceptions can be seen in works such as Denis Benn's *Caribbean: An Intellectual History*, Anthony Bogues's *Black Heretics, Black Prophets*, Silvio Torres-Saillant's *Intellectual History of the Caribbean*, and my own *Caliban's Reason*. These latter accounts all register dramatic increases in the recognition and epistemic evaluation of the contributions of Afro-Caribbean and Indo-Caribbean thinkers in relation to European and Euro-Caribbean thinkers. It is these shifts away from patterns of European normativity that are increasing the capacity of this tradition to adequately represent Africa and its diasporas. In short, this process of decolonization has succeeded in lifting the cloud of epistemic invisibility that had been cast over the tradition by the overvaluing of the European heritage. It is this more visible and vibrant state of the Caribbean intellectual tradition that makes it more accessible for deeper ties with Caribbean sociology.

In this increasingly vibrant state, the mutual benefits of deeper ties with sociology emerge more clearly. The Caribbean intellectual tradition has produced and continues to produce images and accounts of Caribbean societies that are of great sociological interest and value. Contributions of this type can be seen in the writings of many of its leading figures. As C. Wright Mills has observed, the sociological imagination is a three-dimensional epistemic formation that arises at the intersection of history, social structure, and biography. The historical and social structural dimensions of this imagination are subject to epistemic criteria that Weber called "causal adequacy." The biographical dimensions are subject to what he called "meaningful adequacy." All three of these dimensions and their related causal and meaningful logics must be present and working in dialectical concert if there is to be production of great sociological works in the Caribbean or elsewhere.

In terms of the historical and social structural dimensions of sociological production, the figures of the Caribbean intellectual who have spoken most directly to needs of Caribbean sociology are Antenor Firmin, Edward Blyden, W. E. B. Du Bois (of *The Philadelphia Negro*), Marcus Garvey, C. L. R. James, Frantz Fanon, and Oliver Cox. In terms of the meaningful or biographical dimensions of Caribbean sociological production, the most important figures are Sylvia Wynter, George Lamming, Wilson Harris, Gordon Rohlehr, Jamaica Kincaid, and W. E. B. Du Bois (of *Souls of Black Folk*). Of this group, Firmin, Du Bois, and Cox had formal training in either sociology or anthropology and thus truly have a lot to offer Caribbean sociology. However, the above group as a whole (and many others) has engaged and written about the problems of Caribbean societies in very profound ways. In short, we have here a body of sociological and presociological knowledge that not only mirrors ongoing trends in Caribbean societies but also has a strong interest in things African and a demonstrated capacity of representing them well. Given its current crisis of production, Caribbean sociology cannot continue to ignore this local intellectual stream, which most certainly can help to get it out of its crisis state.

NOTE

1. By neo-Smithian I am referring to policies of economic management that build on Adam Smith's idea of markets as self-regulating mechanisms that work best when kept free of state regulation. The reassertion of these arguments was in response to arguments by John Keynes that government management of the total income available for the purchase of goods and services (aggregate demand) was a positive and stabilizing contribution to economic performance.

REFERENCES

Barrow, Christine. 1996. *Family in the Caribbean*. Kingston: Ian Randle.

Beckford, George. 1972. *Persistent Poverty*. New York: Oxford University Press.

Beckwith, Martha. 1924. *Black Roadways*. Chapel Hill: University of North Carolina Press.

Best, Lloyd, and Kari Levitt. 1975. "The Character of Caribbean Economy." In George Beckford, ed., *Caribbean Economy: Dependence and Backwardness*. Mona, Jamaica: Institute of Social and Economic Research, University of the West Indies.

Benn, Denis. 2004. *The Caribbean: An Intellectual History*. Kingston: Ian Randle.

Blyden, Edward. 1994. *Christianity, Islam, and the Negro Race*. Baltimore: Black Classics Press.

Bogues, Anthony. 2003. *Black Heretics, Black Prophets*. New York: Routledge.

Clarke, Edith. 1957. *My Mother Who Fathered Me*. London: Allen and Unwin.

Du Bois, W. E. B. 1969. *Souls of Black Folk*. New York: Fawcett.

——. 1995. *The Philadelphia Negro.* Philadelphia: University of Pennsylvania Press.

Dupuy, Alex. 1989. *Haiti in the World Economy.* Boulder, Colo.: Westview Press.

Firmin, Antenor. 2000. *The Equality of the Human Races.* New York: Garland.

Girvan, Norman. 1976. *Corporate Capitalism.* New York: Monthly Review Press.

Gilroy, Paul. 1994. *The Black Atlantic.* Cambridge: Harvard University Press.

Gordon, Lewis R. 2000. *Existentia Africana.* New York: Routledge.

Hall, Stuart. 1981. "Notes on Deconstructing the 'Popular.'" In Raphael Samuel, ed., *People's History and Socialist Theory.* London: Routledge and Kegan Paul.

Henry, Frances. 1994. *The Caribbean Diaspora in Toronto.* Toronto: University of Toronto Press.

Henry, Paget. 1985. *Peripheral Capitalism and Underdevelopment in Antigua.* New Brunswick: Transaction Books.

——. 2000. *Caliban's Reason.* New York: Routledge.

James, C. L. R. 1989. *The Black Jacobins.* New York: Vintage Books.

Kuhn, Thomas. 1970. *The Structure of Scientific Revolutions.* Chicago: University of Chicago Press.

Lewis, Arthur. 1950. "Industrialization in the British West Indies." *Caribbean Economic Review*, May.

Lewis, Gordon K. 2004. *Main Currents in Caribbean Thought.* Lincoln: University of Nebraska Press.

Patterson, Orlando. 1967. *The Sociology of Slavery.* London: MacGibbon and Kee.

Reddock, Rhoda. 1994. *Women, Labour, and Politics in Trinidad and Tobago.* Atlantic Highlands, N.J. : Zed Books, 1994.

Scott, David. 1999. *Refashioning Futures.* Princeton, N.J.: Princeton University Press.

——. 2004. *Conscripts of Modernity.* Durham, N.C.: Duke University Press.

Smith, M. G. 1974. *The Plural Society in the British West Indies.* Berkeley: University of California Press.

Smith, Raymond T. 1956. *The Negro Family in British Guiana.* London: Routledge and Kegan Paul in association with Institute of Social and Economic Research, University College of the West Indies, Jamaica.

Thomas, Clive. 1974. *Dependence and Transformation.* New York: Monthly Review Press.

Torres-Saillant, Silvio. 2006. *An Intellectual History of the Caribbean.* New York: Palgrave Macmillan.

Trouillot, Michel-Rolph. 1990. *Haiti: State against Nation.* New York: Monthly Review Press.

7

AFRICAN DIASPORA AND POLITICAL SCIENCE

Robert Fatton Jr.

American Political Science—that is, political science as practiced in the United States—does not have a subdiscipline devoted to the study of the African diaspora. Subjects connected to the African diaspora are generally included in Race or Minority Studies within the field of American politics or in what has traditionally been called "Area Studies," which is itself part of what is known as "Comparative Politics." Area Studies is typically the study of particular regions of the world such as Africa or Latin America, and it is usually within these two geographical areas that one can find analytical explorations that have the most relevance for scholars interested in the African diaspora.

It seems to me that a political science devoted to the African diaspora should concentrate on the relations of power affecting the material, cultural, and moral conditions of people of African descent. This would imply the study of the worldwide dispersion of these people and thus of the modalities of that dispersion. This orientation, in turn, inevitably raises the issues of imperialism, colonialism, and racism and how these phenomena molded patterns of resistance, accommodation, and migration in Africa, Afro-America, or Europe. The conventional wisdom of American political science, however, has reflected a determined bias against inquiries related to these very subjects. It either downplays them, or ignores them as they are simply considered to be "out of bounds" in today's mainstream political science.

The cold war contributed greatly to this state of affairs in American political science. Area Studies and International Relations became intellectual fields at the service of what the powers that be in Washington deemed to be in the interest of the American state in its struggle against Soviet communism.[1] These fields were part of the larger project of enhancing the political, strategic, and military supremacy of the West in general and the United States in particular. The American goal was to maintain order in Third World countries and prevent the spread of communism.[2]

Depending on circumstances, this meant either supporting right-wing dictatorships or encouraging the liberal modernization of "traditional" polities. Not surprisingly, modernization became the dominant theory in Area Studies; it simply assumed that all countries went through the same sequence of developmental stages that had led to Western industrialization and liberal democracy. Any other path to development was either pathological or bound to fail. Success implied copying the West.[3] This belief in mimicking the West gained further strength with the collapse of the Soviet bloc in the late 1980s. The end of communism meant for many the "end of history."[4] In this view, there was no alternative to market capitalist modernity and liberal politics.

The impossibility of envisioning an alternative to the current global realities is not surprising. It reflects the early twentieth-century roots of American political science, which were implanted in the exclusive study of the Pan-European world. The United States, England, France, Italy, and Germany represented the "ideal types" of government. Polities departing from these ideal types were considered deviant and underdeveloped. As Immanuel Wallerstein put it:

> All four basic disciplines—history, economics, political science, and sociology—only analyzed the pan-European world, considered to be the world of modernity and of civilization. Their universalisms presupposed the hierarchies of the modern world-system. The analysis of the extra-European world was consigned to separate disciplines: Anthropology for the barbaric 'peoples without history," and Oriental Studies for the non-Western "high civilizations" that were, however, incapable of proceeding to modernity without European intrusion and reorganization of their social dynamics.[5]

To that extent, American political science has tended to remain silent on, or irrelevant to, African Diasporic Studies.[6] With rare exceptions, its dominant methodology, grounded in the so-called scientific persuasion of polling, regression analysis, and rational choice, is poorly equipped to make sense of the realities confronting the African diaspora. The discipline's claims of universalism are in fact provincial and they apply only to an unquestioning understanding of the status quo in advanced, industrial, liberal, capitalist societies. Questions of systemic power and change, of political exclusion and exploitation, of repression and resistance are seldom analyzed in any depth. Instead of "speaking truth to power," American political science operates within the constraining discursive parameters of the existing order. When it ventures beyond the safe borders of the United States it accepts the strictures of the major international financial institutions and imperial "think tanks" from which it obtains major portions of its funding and information.

It is true, however, that Robert Bates—one of the leading figures of both American Political Science and African Studies—has managed to use and creatively transform rational choice to uncover certain political realities that have contributed to Africa's predicament.[7] Whatever may be the pros and cons of Bates's theory of peasant behavior and urban coalitional formation, it elegantly colors the universalist claims of rational choice with a series of distinctively Africanist strokes. Moreover, Bates's emphasis on the critical role institutions play in allocating resources and in facilitating and constraining production illustrates the dialectical interaction between politics and markets and between norms and *homo economicus*. Like most accounts grounded in rational choice, however, Bates has difficulties explaining how the materialist calculus of individuals is ultimately transformed into collective purposeful action. How, for instance, has the "classness" of the Kenyan property-owning class crystallized, how have "its boundaries [been] delineated, and how [did] it define its collective identity and political coherence in the face of cross-cutting ties and identities?"[8]

In spite of these difficulties, Bates shows that it is possible to use a grand narrative—in his case, methodological individualism—and mold it with "local" knowledge to provide a subtle and elegant explanation of African systems of governance. As Bates argues:

> The combination of local knowledge and general modes of reasoning, of area studies and formal theory, represents a highly promising margin for our field. The blend will help to account for the power of forces that we know shape human behavior, in ways that we have hitherto been able to describe but not to explain.[9]

There is a danger, however, that the "scientific" pretensions of formal theory may be grossly exaggerated, especially in the African context where the robustness of any electoral or economic data is of highly dubious value. Moreover, it is not only that the models derived from such data are most questionable but that the whole modeling exercise may lead to very pedestrian conclusions. The full deployment of such mathematical arsenals is indeed intimidating, but it seldom illuminates fundamental questions of power, identity, and social transformation. Moreover, it is very unlikely that "hard" data can capture the particularities of predatory rule that have characterized African modes of governance. As Richard Sklar has put it:

> The force of traditional authority is far more difficult to render mathematically than that of modern governments which produce statistics. Most interactions between the two dimensions of government cannot be fathomed without the use of subjective methodologies.[10]

In fact, it is not clear at all that mathematical exercises are less "subjective" than the qualitative narrative stemming from "local" knowledge. But this is not the place to engage in such a complex debate. Suffice it to say that the export of "methods" to African politics reflects more the disciplinary hegemony of American political science than the revolutionary production of an allegedly "objective" form of knowledge. It symbolizes the growing influence of polling and electoral "counting," which, while not unimportant, are uncertain reflections of ephemeral and ever-changing moments of public opinion.

The obsession with polling public opinion is the single most pervasive phenomenon of American political science, and it is thoroughly consistent with the conservative adjustment and preservation of the given structures of power. American political science tends to study prevailing social and political systems and describes their workings, but it rarely challenges the harsh realities of imperialism, class power, and racial privilege, which it tends to take as inexistent or immutable. As Charles Lindblom has contended, if we were to regard social life as a game, political science would need to do more than merely "[assist] the game officials, and [study] the rules of the game, how it might be improved, and how to take care of game injuries." Our discipline would have to provide much more to the players. Players "need to know how the game came to be structured as they find it, how they were induced to take for granted that they should play, whether any other game exists, and how they might find and learn to play another game."[11]

The vocation of a truly liberating political science is to reject the benignity of existing arrangements of power and wealth, provide historical alternatives, and offer a transcending vision of the "good life" for which we would aim and with which we could measure the extent of current imperfections and injustices. This is the kind of political science that African Diasporic Studies require. To hold its promise, political science must be gripped by what Edward Said called "a spirit in opposition," because, as he pointed out, "the romance, the interest, the challenge of intellectual life is to be found in dissent against the status quo at a time when the struggle on behalf of underrepresented and disadvantaged groups seems so unfairly weighted against them."[12]

The problem with the study of the African diaspora, however, is that it confronts the same marginal status that Africanist Political Science suffers in the discipline. Such marginality is not merely a reflection of Africa's rather powerless role in international relations; it is also that Americanists tend to perceive the theoretical contributions of Africanists as the weakest among practitioners of the other subfields of Area Studies. Richard Sklar, one of the leading Africanists in the United States, acknowledged the very low esteem enjoyed by his own subfield among his colleagues in the discipline:

I cannot think of a widely recognized problem or theory, of concern to political scientists generally, that requires African area expertise to either explore scientifically or explain to students. . . . On balance, however, Africa's own marginality to the mainstream of global exchanges is a professional liability. For Africanists to capitalize on that liability and convert it into a professional asset, they must adduce fresh empirical evidence for new propositions about political life. Under existing conditions, nothing else is likely to enhance their market value relative to other regional specialists.[13]

Sklar's claim that little of great value comes from the Africanist study of politics is a gross exaggeration; in fact, it is a provocation. The intellectual contribution of Goran Hyden, René Lemarchand, Mahmood Mamdani, Ali Mazrui, and Crawford Young, to name only a few of a much longer list of prominent Africanist scholars, is at the very least of equal if not superior quality than anything produced by Americanists.[14] This contribution is simply of a different genre which until recently has tended to reject the mathematical models as well as the polling obsessions dominating much of American Political Science. Africanists have emphasized the exploitative and racist nature of Western imperialism as well as the authoritarian and paternalistic legacies of colonialism. They have condemned the impact of both international trade and the worldwide expansion of the capitalist market; rather than embracing them as vehicles of development, Africanists have generally analyzed these forces as portent of either polarized and unequal growth or accelerated underdevelopment. These ideas are not the monopoly of Africanists, but they evoke in America a sense of whining victimhood that smacks of simplistic propaganda and unscientific methodology.

That American Political Science interprets the contributions of Africanists in this way may in fact be the product of its own "exceptionalism," which at times betrays the arrogant provincialism of imperial power. Americanists tend to look with suspicion and sometimes contempt at works rejecting or criticizing their core belief in the universalizing nature of an idealized capitalist modernity stemming from the Western liberal experience. They are likely to develop the same reaction toward African diasporic study in so far as the latter will inevitably gravitate around radical and critical traditions of left-wing scholarship. In fact, I would contend that the ideas of Karl Marx, Antonio Gramsci, and Rosa Luxemburg cannot be ignored and that they must be revived and reinterpreted in the context of the experiences of the African diaspora. This obviously was a task that occupied the major intellectual figures of this diaspora. By contextualizing the broad currents of Marxism, W. E. B. Du Bois, Oliver Cox, Frantz Fanon, C. L. R. James, Samir Amin, Clive Thomas, Amilcar Cabral, and Walter Rodney,[15] to mention only a few, made decisive interventions in the study of the social origins and conditions of the African diaspora. They generated a powerful interpretation of how imperialism

shaped the interactions between class and race to produce patterns of resistance and accommodation to the worldwide spread of capitalism. They
explained how the utterly constraining economic dependence of postcolonial societies confined them to enduring poverty, inequality, and authori-
tarianism. It was not a matter of tradition overwhelming would-be modernizers, as conventional political science would have it. Rather, it was
the structure of the world economy constructed in the period of colonial
expansion that blocked the development of Africa and the diaspora.

As Fanon argued, however, imperialism is not the only cause of the
African diaspora's plight; processes of class formation within newly independent states produced the "pitfalls of national consciousness" whereby
a pseudo-bourgeoisie could acquire its material grounding only through
its illegal monopolization of state resources.[16] Such monopolization invited the corruption and repression of what is known among Africanists
as *la politique du ventre*—the politics of the belly. This phenomenon, fu-
eled by acute material scarcity, has made control of the government apparatus a violent and deadly business. Politics tends to be an exercise in
acquiring public resources for individual gains. For those not born into
privilege, it has been the principal vehicle for the private accumulation of
wealth. Not surprisingly, those holding state power have used fraud and
violence to keep it from potential challengers.[17]

Cabral's belief that the struggle for independence would create the
conditions for the "class suicide" of the top cadres of the revolutionary
movement proved illusory. Once in power, these cadres developed an un-
controllable appetite and devoured the nation's limited resources. Their
aggressive "eating" was not just a matter of immediate gratification but
of grabbing power, keeping it, and monopolizing it for the *longue durée*.
With or without a revolution, the result seemed to be the same: those in
power became what Haitians called the *"gro manjers,"* the big eaters, and
what East Africans dubbed the *"wabenzi,"* the people driving the Mer-
cedes.

The intersection of the domestic and international political economy
led to the underdeveloped peripheral capitalism and authoritarian governance characterizing most diasporic societies. Not surprisingly, these realities have generated systematic patterns of "exit" as diasporic citizens
seek to escape from the squalor and deprivations of their own territorial
entities. This is no longer the brutalizing and despicable forced departure
of free people into slavery but the legal or illegal migration of diasporic
people to the advanced centers of capitalism. This new "passage" into
the developed industrial areas of the world can be dangerous and trau-
matizing, but it reflects a desire and indeed a necessity for improving life
chances. As René Préval, the president of Haiti, put it in a moment of extreme bluntness and desperation, *"Cé najé poun soti,"* "You must swim
to exit." You have to swim away from Haiti to American shores to have

the opportunity to "make it." In the process, the meeting of the so-called "other" with Westerners on the latter's soil is fraught with contradictions, tensions, and apprehension. It invites the recrudescence of old forms of racism and xenophobia.

These global phenomena of dependence and migration, as well as the persistent salience of race and class, can be studied with a retooled version of the radical Western tradition in the social sciences. To elucidate fully the specificities of diasporan political life, we must, however, draw on local knowledge. By local knowledge I mean the particular and contextual expressions and interpretations of power. In other words, how do local people exercise, apprehend, and experience their own realities? Local knowledge, however, is not just domestic distinctiveness and specificities; it exhibits striking similarities in its various manifestations in both Africa and the diasporic nations. For instance, strong parallels exist in the systemic effects of *la politique du ventre* on patterns of governance and on popular understandings of power in the continent and in the Caribbean. In my own work I have discovered that many of the concepts I applied to apprehend Senegalese, Kenyan, or Congolese regimes could be usefully deployed to decipher Haiti's political modalities; in the same vein, popular perceptions of power in these countries share striking similarities.[18]

Such popular perceptions can be comprehended through an exhaustive study of both "public" and "hidden transcripts," to use James Scott's terminology.[19] While the former embodies the open airing of the common wisdom of rulers and subordinate classes, the latter expresses the secret discourse of the victims of power—the opaque and "unobtrusive realm of infrapolitics." This kind of exploration requires an investigation of the very visible signs and language of power, on the one hand, as well as of the underground counter-projects of subaltern groups on the other. This implies, for instance, taking seriously the metaphors of the ruler as "father" and society as a "family," of the common folk as "children" having failed to achieve mature adulthood, and of power as a prize that can be won and manipulated through magic. Diasporic politics operate under similar sorts of hegemonies, and its actors explain their world with a distinctive logic that cannot be captured or analyzed by standard political science approaches.[20]

For example, the conventional assumptions of American political scientists about the separation of religion and state, and state and civil society do not hold up well in advanced capitalist countries like the United States itself, let alone in the diasporic milieu. There, the parameters of politics derived from an idealized Western experience are only partially, if at all, duplicated. It is exceedingly difficult to draw neat analytical boundaries between politics, religion, and civil society because the dominant patterns of beliefs and association of the homeland remain ubiquitous in the new settings of the diaspora. In fact, these patterns of beliefs and association are reinforced because they tend to be reproduced by diasporans as a means of coping with the vicissitudes of an alien environment. In their new location, diasporans inevitably regroup along the lines of family, region, ethnicity, and class. The old is reproduced in new but familiar forms.

People of African descent use their own specific means of understanding and shaping their existential conditions. Like any other people, they avail themselves of multiple methods to influence events and may ultimately believe in different and indeed contradictory modes of causality. Depending on circumstances and objectives, they may resort to modern "rational" science while simultaneously appealing to the powers of the occult, witchcraft, and sorcery.[21] Diasporic people are certainly not the only ones making use of these multiple and often inconsistent forms of explaining and shaping social reality. As Michael Schatzberg pointed out correctly, "Reliance on alternative understandings of causality may be quite universal."[22] After all, under Ronald Reagan's presidency, astrology played a decisive role in the day-to-day running of the White House. Millions of Americans believe in the agency of angels, while millions more pursue alternative healing therapies and embrace psychic and mystical explanations for events that are not borne out by Western science.[23]

To uncover these different logics, it is crucial to study the pervasive role of rumors in the making and unmaking of homeland politics. What is called *teledyol* in Haiti—the spreading of unconfirmed and invented news—is not merely the legacy of living under dictatorial censorship. It is also the fabrication of information to influence reality itself. Such *teledyol* is practiced in the homeland and exported to the Haitian diaspora in the United States, Canada, and Europe, where it takes new forms through the new technologies of the internet. In a boomerang effect, the diaspora is now becoming the digital hub disseminating back home an electronic *teledyol* reflecting its ever-increasing power. The diaspora's influence is not limited to the dissemination of information; it extends to the financial sphere because of its critical remittances to the homeland. In certain cases, particularly in the Caribbean and West Africa, these remittances represent a critical contribution to the economic survival of the country of origin. Not surprisingly, the growing economic power of the diaspora has been accompanied by a concomitant rise in its political influence. It is an influence that comes also from the role that some diasporic figures play in their new environment and in international organizations.

The diaspora is a strategic "reserve army of talent" for the homeland that can be used to serve foreign as well as national interests. In many cases, diasporic cadres are "parachuted" into their mother country to fulfill "special assignments" on behalf of major powers and international financial institutions. They become police chiefs, cabinet members, prime ministers, and even presidents. Haiti offers an interesting case in point whereby the homeland politician can turn into a diasporan private individual and the diasporan private individual can turn into a homeland politician. As Michel Laguerre put it:

> The former president, Jean-Bertrand Aristide, became a diasporan, while the diasporan, Gérard Latortue, who was living in Florida, was offered and accepted the job of prime minister. . . . The dynamics of this transnational version of local politics . . . are best understood and captured by the metaphor of "circulation" rather than of "exit" and by the metaphor of "repositioning" rather than of "exile."[24]

This transnational version of local politics is, however, deeply implanted in imperial soil. Had it not been for the hegemonic influence of the United States and to a lesser degree France and Canada, the diasporan Latortue would have remained a diasporan. To that extent, while diasporic politics has its own rhythm and logic, its autonomy is still very limited by the realities of global power. Only those strategic diasporans operating within imperial circles can hope to exploit their position to become important political actors in the homeland.

While such strategic diasporans represent the upper echelons of an international class of organic functionaries of imperialism, other diasporans from different class backgrounds can become vehicles of social disintegration. Indeed, the harsh and brutalizing conditions of American urban ghettoes experienced by segments of an alienated immigrant youth generate high levels of dysfunctionality. Such youth can easily lose their homeland traditions and come to espouse the violent life of gangs. The phenomenon is significant because many immigrant youth lacking legal residence are repatriated to their countries of origin with criminal skills acquired in the diaspora. The diaspora is thus a contradictory space. For some it represents heaven away from a heartless homeland—a source of material advancement, social climbing, and political "positioning." For others it represents simply a descent into criminality en route to a forced return to the mother country.

For people of African descent, the diaspora embodies the opportunities, inequalities, and violence of the world system itself. In that perspective, any understanding of diasporan politics is a mandatory invitation to analyze the historical development of the world system. Indeed, the "local" cannot be apprehended without a comprehensive examination of the "national," and any understanding of the "national" cannot be separated from an exploration of the "global." Thus the study of the African diaspora transcends the narrow confines of American political science—or any political science, for that matter. It must destroy the artificial walls separating the major disciplines. It calls for thinking about rethinking an unthinking political science.[25] To that extent, Diasporic Studies demands that the major disciplines be unbounded and freed from their constraining academic straitjacket. The diasporic intellectual must therefore celebrate the freedom of an "undisciplined" pursuit of knowledge.

NOTES

1. Frank, *Latin America.*
2. Huntington, *Political Order in Changing Societies.*
3. Almond and Verba, *The Civic Culture;* Inkeles and Smith, *Becoming Modern;* Lerner, *The Passing of Traditional Society;* McClelland, *The Achieving Society.*
4. Fukuyama, *The End of History and the Last Man.*
5. Wallerstein, *The Decline of American Power,* 91–92.
6. A recent and important exception to this tendency is Anthony Marx's comparative analysis of race in Brazil, the United States, and South Africa in *Making Race and Nation.*
7. Bates, *Markets and States in Tropical Africa; Essays on the Political Economy of Rural Africa; Beyond the Miracle of the Market.*
8. Cooper, review of Bates's *Beyond the Miracle of the Market.*
9. Bates, "Area Studies and the Discipline: A Useful Controversy?"
10. Sklar, "The African Frontier for Political Science," 104.
11. Lindblom, *Inquiry and Change,* 279.
12. Said, *Representations of the Intellectual,* xvii.
13. Sklar, "The African Frontier for Political Science," 84–85.
14. See Hyden, *Beyond Ujamaa in Tanzania; No Shortcuts to Progress; African Politics in Comparative Perspective;* See also Lemarchand, "Political Clientelism and Ethnicity in Tropical Africa"; *Burundi: Ethnocide as Discourse and Practice;* Mamdani, *Citizen and Subject; When Victims Become Killers;* Mazrui, *Towards a Pax Africana; The Africans;* Young, *The Politics of Cultural Pluralism; The African Colonial State in Comparative Perspective.*
15. See Amin, *Accumulation on a World Scale;* Cabral, *Revolution in Guinea;* Cox, *Caste, Class, and Race;* Du Bois, *W.E.B. Du Bois Speaks;* Fanon, *The Wretched of the Earth;* James, *C. L. R. James Reader;* Rodney, *How Europe Underdeveloped Africa;* Thomas, *Dependence and Transformation.*
16. Fanon, *The Wretched of the Earth,* 148–205.
17. Bayart, *The State in Africa;* Fatton, *Haiti's Predatory Republic.*
18. Fatton, *Haiti's Predatory Republic* and *Predatory Rule.*
19. Scott, *Domination and the Arts of Resistance.*
20. Schatzberg, *Political Legitimacy in Middle Africa.*
21. See, for instance, the superb work of Adam Ashforth on the power of witchcraft in the increasingly violent environment of scarcity and disease characterizing urban life in post-apartheid South Africa. *Witchcraft, Violence, and Democracy in South Africa.*
22. Schatzberg, *Political Legitimacy in Middle Africa,* 205.
23. Phillips, *American Theocracy,* 99–104.
24. Laguerre, "Homeland Political Crisis," 206. Another recent case is that of

former World Bank economist Ellen Johnson-Sirleaf, who was elected president of Liberia.

25. Wallerstein, *Unthinking Social Science.*

REFERENCES

Almond, Gabriel A., and Sidney Verba. *The Civic Culture.* Boston: Little, Brown, 1965.

Amin, Samir. *Accumulation on a World Scale.* 2 vols. New York Monthly Review Press, 1974.

Ashforth, Adam. *Witchcraft, Violence, and Democracy in South Africa.* Chicago: University of Chicago Press, 2005.

Bates, Robert H. "Area Studies and the Discipline: A Useful Controversy?" *PS: Political Science and Politics* 30, no. 2 (June 1997): 169.

———. *Beyond the Miracle of the Market: The Political Economy of Agrarian Development in Kenya.* Cambridge: Cambridge University Press, 1989.

———. *Essays on the Political Economy of Rural Africa.* Cambridge: Cambridge University Press, 1983.

———. *Markets and States in Tropical Africa.* Berkeley: University of California Press, 1981.

Bayart, Jean-François. *The State in Africa: The Politics of the Belly.* New York: Longman, 1993.

Cabral, Amilcar. *Revolution in Guinea, an African People's Struggle: Selected Texts.* New York Monthly Review Press, 1969.

Cooper, Frederick. Review of Robert Bates's *Beyond the Miracle of the Market. American Historical Review* 96, no. 4 (October 1991): 1255.

Cox, Oliver. *Caste, Class, and Race.* New York Monthly Review Press, 1970.

Du Bois, W. E. B. *W. E. B. Du Bois Speaks.* Ed. Philip S. Foner. New York: Pathfinder, 1970.

Fanon, Frantz. *The Wretched of the Earth.* New York: Grove Press, 1968.

Fatton, Robert, Jr. *Haiti's Predatory Republic.* Boulder, Colo.: Lynne Rienner, 2002.

———. *Predatory Rule: State and Civil Society in Africa.* Boulder, Colo.: Lynne Rienner, 1992.

Frank, Andre Gunder. *Latin America: Underdevelopment or Revolution.* New York: Monthly Review Press, 1969.

Fukuyama, Francis. *The End of History and the Last Man.* New York: Free Press, 1992.

Huntington, Samuel. *Political Order in Changing Societies.* New Haven, Conn.: Yale University Press, 1968.

Hyden, Goran. *African Politics in Comparative Perspective.* Cambridge: Cambridge University Press, 2006.

———. *Beyond Ujamaa in Tanzania.* Berkeley: University of California Press, 1979.

———. *No Shortcuts to Progress.* Berkeley: University of California Press, 1983.

Inkeles, Alex, and David H. Smith. *Becoming Modern: Individual Change in Six Developing Countries.* Cambridge: Harvard University Press, 1974.

James, C. L. R. *The C.L.R. James Reader.* Ed. Anna Grimshaw. Oxford: Blackwell, 1992.

Laguerre, Michel. "Homeland Political Crisis, the Virtual Diasporic Public Sphere, and Diasporic Politics." *Journal of Latin American Anthropology* 10, no. 1 (April 2005): 206–25.

Lemarchand, René. *Burundi: Ethnocide as Discourse and Practice.* New York: Cambridge University Press, 1994.

———. "Political Clientelism and Ethnicity in Tropical Africa: Competing Solidarities in Nation-Building." *American Political Science Review* 66, no. 1 (1972): 91–112.

Lerner, David. *The Passing of Traditional Society: Modernizing the Middle East.* New York: Free Press, 1958.

Lindblom, Charles E. *Inquiry and Change.* New Haven, Conn.: Yale University Press, 1990.

Mamdani, Mahmood. *Citizen and Subject: Contemporary Africa and the Legacy of Late Colonialism.* Princeton, N.J.: Princeton University Press, 1996.

———. *When Victims Become Killers: Colonialism, Nativism, and the Genocide in Rwanda.* Princeton, N.J.: Princeton University Press, 2001.

Marx, Anthony. *Making Race and Nation.* Cambridge: Cambridge University Press, 1998.

Mazrui, Ali. *The Africans: A Triple Heritage.* Boston: Little, Brown, 1986.

———. *Towards a Pax Africana.* Chicago: University of Chicago Press, 1967.

McClelland, David C. *The Achieving Society.* Princeton, N.J.: Van Nostrand, 1961.

Phillips, Kevin. *American Theocracy.* New York: Viking, 2006.

Rodney, Walter. *How Europe Underdeveloped Africa.* London: Bogle-l'Ouverture, 1972.

Said, Edward W. *Representations of the Intellectual.* New York: Pantheon Books, 1994.

Schatzberg, Michael G. *Political Legitimacy in Middle Africa: Father, Family, Food.* Bloomington: Indiana University Press, 2001.

Scott, James C. *Domination and the Arts of Resistance.* New Haven, Conn.: Yale University Press, 1990.

Sklar, Richard. "The African Frontier for Political Science." In *Africa and the Disciplines,* ed. Robert Bates, V. Y. Mudimbe, and Jean O'Barr, 83–110. Chicago: University of Chicago Press, 1993.

Thomas, Clive Y. *Dependence and Transformation.* New York Monthly Review Press, 1974.

Wallerstein, Immanuel. *The Decline of American Power.* New York: New Press, 2003.

———. *Unthinking Social Science.* Cambridge: Polity Press, 1991.

Young, Crawford. *The Politics of Cultural Pluralism.* Madison: University of Wisconsin Press, 1976.

———. *The African Colonial State in Comparative Perspective.* New Haven, Conn.: Yale University Press, 1994.

8

THE AFRICAN DIASPORA AND PHILOSOPHY

Olúfémi Táíwò

What could be difficult about writing on the subject of African diaspora and philosophy? The African diaspora[1] has increasingly become the object of scholarly exertions. What is more, given my awareness that the United States is one of the fastest growing markets for the subdiscipline of African philosophy, and the closing decades of the last century saw the emergence of a few titles from respectable publishers on the theme of diasporic Africans' exertions in philosophy, especially those by African Americans, there can be no doubt that the conjunction of philosophy and the diaspora has considerable significance attached to it. Add to these the growing expansion of divisions within universities and colleges devoted to differing degrees of concentration in African American, Africalogical, Pan-African, Global African, Diasporic, and the ever-present Black Studies, and one would be hard put to justify any pessimism regarding some discursus on the diaspora and philosophy. However, to my chagrin, the more I reflected on the theme,[2] the clearer it became that I may have been too sanguine in my initial reaction. There has been considerable output in philosophical works respecting the diaspora, and I don't think I exaggerate when I say that there has been little or no exploration of the conundrums that are thrown up by a discipline-focused discussion of philosophy and the diaspora. This could have been a more daunting task but for the suggestion that the current engagement is "devoted to meta-level conceptual examinations of the practice of African diaspora studies within and at the intersections of the disciplines."[3]

Any invitation to indulge in a "meta-level conceptual examination" of any subject matter must gladden a philosopher's heart. After all, whatever divergences philosophers may share regarding the contours, boundaries, and content of their discipline, they usually are convergent on some of its basic characteristics: (1) that philosophy asks questions and (2) it does so at the most general level with the ultimate aim of unearthing the logos of being, *sans* differentiation. The *"sans* differentiation" is what sets philosophy's way of proceeding apart from all the other disciplines. While this claim usually rubs other disciplines the wrong way, we must see beyond its appropriation by some arrogant practitioners to discern its kernel of truth: it is not an accident that when a discipline turns its searchlight on its own craft we do not call the outcome by the name of the discipline concerned. We say simply in those situations that we are doing "the philosophy of the discipline" concerned. It would seem easy enough to dilate on our theme. But, in reality, it is not. Why this is so I will point out in some detail in a moment. For now, let me focus on the easy part of the task.

The concept of "the African diaspora" is very problematic in philosophy, and this is quite unlike the situation in other disciplines. Ordinarily, one understands the concept to conclude those inhabitants of the world outside of Africa whose origins can be or are traced to the African continent. It wouldn't matter where they are found in the world; what matters is that at some point in the distant past, their forebears emigrated from Africa—voluntarily and involuntarily—and became part of an African-descended community in exile. Meanwhile, in exile, even as they retain some memory—dim or acute, pleasant or unpleasant, conscious or unconscious—of their African origins, African-descended peoples have gone on to create new cultural matrices in their new non-African abodes. The African presence in such abodes from trace to substantive legitimizes any talk of "the African diaspora." Absent this common genealogy I am not sure that there can be any talk of a diaspora in the first place. But there has to be much more than this to constitute and typify the diaspora. I take it that any talk of diaspora scholarship refers, in part at least, to scholarship about the African inflection in *this* diaspora as opposed to other diasporas in our world.

For a very long time the idea of this diaspora was easily understood. It referred in the main to the communities created and nurtured by generations of African peoples descended from those forebears who were forcefully removed from various parts of the African continent and brought as slaves to the New World of the Western Hemisphere. Although it was always understood that not all Africans who came at that time were slaves, the slavery experience and its aftermath have continued to be the hallmark of the African diaspora. And when scholars talk of the diaspora or of diaspora scholarship, they always have in mind something that will *ultimately* touch on this experience, however tangentially. But it is one thing spatially to locate the African diaspora—assuming this is the case.[4] It is an entirely different matter to conceptualize it as an object of study.

Although I do not do so in this essay, I think that our understanding of the diaspora needs to be expanded to include other groups of African-descended peoples especially in Asia and Europe. After all, even before the discovery of the New World, there had been commerce between Africa and the lands due north and northeast of the continent. That commerce witnessed at various times conquest and migrations in both directions, highlighting the salience of African participation in some of the signal events of world history even before the fifteenth century. A vital element of that commerce was the export of Africans as both slaves and emigrants across the Sahara and Nubian deserts to Europe, Asia Minor, and the Arabian Peninsula. Nor should one ignore the movement, in immemorial times, of African-derived peoples all along the East African littoral to the Indian subcontinent and points farther east in Asia. Expanding the boundaries of the diaspora in this way is bound to bring us closer to the truth of the global distribution of African peoples and, simultaneously, remind us of the complexity of the diaspora. Unless otherwise indicated, my attention in the rest of this discussion is riveted only on the New World segment of the diaspora.[5]

Even when we limit our purview as stated above, our task is not any bit lightened. As long as we understood the African diaspora in terms of the exilic community peopled preponderantly by the descendants of slaves in the New World and their secondary dispersal to points in Europe, especially the United Kingdom, France, and the Netherlands, as difficult as it might seem, we at least had a compact body of artifacts—material and ideological—to sate our scholarly hunger. Things have become a lot more complicated in recent decades, though. The recent past has witnessed the influx into the African diaspora of a fresh cohort of African immigrants. Certainly, there always have been continental Africans in the diaspora. The difference is that in the past many such continental Africans lived only temporarily in this diaspora and treated it with some detachment. Even when some of them became, by default, immigrants, their presence there was always characterized by some ambivalence: while it looked unlikely that they would repatriate to the continent, they never failed to impress on their fellows and others their desire to return "home" at some future date. Again, I do not mean to suggest that the phenomenon I have just described is a simple one. Continental Africans who regarded themselves as temporary sojourners did not exhaust the range of responses to be found among their cohort in the diaspora. There have always been African immigrants who either came intending to stay or stayed by default and have evinced similar sensibilities to those of diasporic Africans even though it would be a stretch to think of them as sharing the specific historical experience that denominates the identity of African-descended peoples in the diaspora. There is a sense in which this much-neglected potential for fissure in the diaspora may have come to the fore at the present time marked by the arrival in the last twenty years or so of a new wave of continental African immigrants. I would like to suggest that this represents the first genuine mass movement of free Africans to the diaspora, and this has some severe implications for our study of it.

Therefore, when we speak of African diaspora and philosophy at the present time, we need to sort out the many components of this diaspora prior to establishing what the relationship is or should be between it and philosophy as a discipline. If we limit ourselves to the intellectual output of the original diaspora, we will acknowledge a particular relationship to philosophy. And if we expand our purview to include the intellectual exertions of the diaspora's new arrivals, we will describe another relationship to our discipline. I shall explain these divergences momentarily. However difficult these relationships may seem, they are nothing compared to what difficulties we encounter when we try to make sense of philosophy's relationship to the African diaspora.

The theme of the relationship between the African diaspora and philosophy can be understood in different ways. One way is to look at the place of philosophy in the African diaspora, however understood. Do the cultures of the African diaspora generate any philosophical traditions to speak of? Is there philosophy in the African diaspora? If so, what is it? Who are its practitioners? What are its principal themes? What does its history look like? How does that history relate to the history of other philosophical traditions? What role does it play in the culture of the African diaspora? For illustration, the philosophical exertions of African Americans will be prime examples of diasporic philosophy. Yet the fact that a fair amount of it partakes of domestic American philosophy and helped to constitute the latter means that questions can legitimately be raised concerning its membership in the African diaspora. This only means that we cannot always be certain of the boundaries of the relevant qualifier—African, American, African American, black, diasporic, etc.—and mindfulness of this limitation will always contribute to a more complex but more accurate description of our subject matter.

But the question may turn on the issue of what relationship philosophy, as a discipline, has to the African diaspora. Does the discipline of philosophy recognize the African diaspora and its study as a legitimate field within it? The short answer to this question is no. But this short answer is misleading in some respects. Whereas one could have said no and left it at that, let's say, thirty years ago, today one has to qualify the answer even if one does not feel at ease answering in the affirmative. In recent years, as part of the burgeoning field of Black Studies and African American Studies, the philosophical exertions of thinkers from among the communities of the African diaspora have furnished doctoral dissertations, books, and anthologies,[6] not to mention well-established and long-running workshops and conferences,[7] such that many now speak distinctly of black or African American philosophy as a subdiscipline of philosophy.[8] I must not omit to mention that it is no longer a rare occurrence to find articles and reviews on themes in African American philosophy in the dominant journals of the discipline.

Does it mean that if one now uses any of the conventional search terms based on the Library of Congress classification system one is likely to be put in touch with the richness of the output of which I speak? The answer is an unqualified no.[9] Quite often many of the works are not cataloged under philosophy. Many are simply put in history or area studies and other such categories. What this means is that by the canons of what we might call "mainstream philosophy," the products of the philosophical imaginary of the diasporic Africans do not have a place in philosophy's tent. There are numerous indicia of philosophy's refusal to accommodate the philosophical denizens of the African diaspora. For the most part, dominant sections of the discipline do not adjudge philosophical the themes arising from the peculiar historical experience of African-descended peoples, regardless of the sophistication with which thinkers from within the tradition present their ideas. Moreover, even those African-descended philosophers who work with the dominant idiom and hew strictly to the debates of the mainstream on themes ranging from Plato to Rawls or profess membership of various schools are hardly referenced by their non-African fellow practitioners of the dominant philosophical tradition.

At one remove, the refusal to accommodate the philosophical denizens of the African diaspora by the "mainstream" is an extension to the diasporic Africans of the contempt with which Western-inflected academic philosophy treated the philosophical exertions of the African intellect for so long until African scholars recovered their voice and domesticated their master's voice toward the re-creation of African philosophy in the closing quarter of the last century. So, in similar vein, the efforts of diasporic Africans, too, at domesticating their master's voice and re-creating philosophy in their own idiom, focused on their history and struggles for both their own edification and the improvement of our world, are beginning to force recognition from the "mainstream." This, in turn, is inspiring more and more younger diasporic African scholars to bet their futures on contributing to the philosophical heritage of humanity in voices distinctly their own even as the questions they seek to answer remain perennial. If what I have just said is true, then it follows that the subsidiary question of how philosophy defines the African diaspora, too, must be answered in the negative, even if it is qualified.

It is one thing for the "mainstream" to fail to embrace African, Africana, or African American philosophy. It is a completely different thing for African-descended scholars to accept such a rejection and in so doing yield to those who, that is, in the so-called mainstream, arrogate to themselves the role of lawgivers to the world and whose say-so suffices to delimit the contours of whatever humanities discipline is at stake. We must resist this temptation. In fact, part of the challenge for a discussion like this one is, on one hand, to acknowledge the current situation in which Africa and its diaspora remain significant absences in professional philosophy and, when present, are relegated to the margins. On the other hand, we are called upon simultaneously to restore a part of the original vocation of philosophy—speculation—by focusing on what a discipline of philosophy will look like that recognizes the complexity of the world and the multiversity of its cultural forms. That is, speculate on what philosophy will look like if it permits itself to embrace the African diaspora as both an object of study and a locus of insights into the human condition; if it engages with the issue of understanding and debating the boundaries of the African diaspora; if it dares to consider that those who gave their lives for the vote, who had lived the dread of unfreedom and for whom freedom was something they had to remain willing to die to keep may actually be better singers of freedom's song than they for whom being free has always been a banal element of their quotidian existence. It is on this speculative note that I wish to proceed in the rest of this discussion.

One final note of clarification on the theme is warranted. I said earlier that the influx of recent African immigrants has altered the landscape of the African diaspora. I also pointed out that this new influx of African immigrants comes with a potential for fissure in the ranks of African-descended peoples in the diaspora. For one thing, there is the challenge of figuring out where these immigrants belong in the historical imaginary of the diaspora. Demographically, they are listed with the native diasporic Africans. The problem, though, is that in terms of their specific historical experiences, only in a marginal sense could one justifiably say that they share the same historical experience as the native diasporic Africans. There is a wide range of responses on both sides of the divide to this divergence in the historical experiences of the respective groups.

For a very long time, the philosophical output of native diasporic Africans and of some of the immigrant Africans was mediated by their ideational responses to that singular experience constituted by slavery and their struggle with it. No one doubts that the transatlantic slave trade and New World slavery jointly constitute the *differentia specifica* in the historical experience of that division of the African diaspora that continues to dominate our general understanding. Nor do I think that one should quibble about the centrality of these twin phenomena to the constitution of the identity as well as the intellectual heritage of African-descended peoples in the New World, especially in the United States. This centrality explains the current dominance of two different but related themes in the philosophical discourse of diasporic Africans: (1) race and identity and (2) freedom.

The issue of race and identity always lurks in the philosophical exertions of diasporic Africans. This is easy to explain. Slavery worked by denuding its victims, as soon as possible after their arrival, of every shred of memory that they might possess of their previous lives, most notably those elements pertaining to who they were, their identity, and all that attached to it, from their languages to their names, both personal and familial. Members of ethnic groups were separated; those who spoke mutually intelligible languages were dispersed across vast distances, and whatever seemed to survive the severe transaction costs associated with remembering past associations, kinship relations, and linguistic affinities had to go underground. Much was lost over the centuries of widespread violence and unimaginable suffering. What is more, the slavers were hardly eager to allow their slaves to become one with them through acculturation and the sharing of the same identity. Worse still, given the peculiar nature of the slavery that predominated in the United States—chattel slavery—the very humanity of the slaves was continually in question.

When emancipation did come to various regions of the New World, it did not mean that their erstwhile owners admitted the ex-slaves to human status. It was one thing for slave owners to deny the humanity of their slaves. It was an entirely different thing for the slaves themselves to concede such a defect to their owners. On the contrary, even in the darkest days of enslavement, African slaves refused to accept their nonmembership of humanity. Rather they claimed and celebrated their humanity in ways that were often instructive to their owners. And it is this struggle to claim and sustain their humanity that led to their ongoing philosophical disquisitions on issues of identity. Such disquisitions could not take place without a serious engagement with the idea of race, given that it is in the name of racial difference that their humanity has, in the main, been and continues to be denied or denigrated.

The idea of freedom played an even more important role in the philosophical engagements of diasporic Africans. When the United States was founded, the fundamental principle in the name of which its founding fathers repudiated the authority and suzerainty of the British was the freedom of the human individual, regardless of birth, family inheritance, and other ascriptive characteristics, to be and to have his or her own concept of the good life as well as to seek to realize such without interference from others, insofar as he or she does not preempt the right of others to have the same latitude in their lives. The ultimate irony of the transatlantic slave trade and the slavery that it spawned was that both flourished in a period in which the sovereignty of the individual and the impermissibility of rule that the individual has not consented to made their appearance and became the dominant principle of social living and political governance. The New World was rightly celebrated as the source of these epochal developments. We then must not be surprised that African slaves appropriated this fundamental attribute of their being—freedom—and fought their slavers in the name of this same principle. In affirming and celebrating their subjectivity, diasporic Africans not only lived freedom but created some of the shiniest examples of human achievement in the culture that they have fashioned from the depredations of slavery and the denial of their freedom that has continued in its wake to the present. What is more, as I have argued elsewhere,[10] given that diasporic Africans have lived with the dread of unfreedom and have had to lay down their lives to have their freedom recognized, it may be the case that they indeed are more proficient singers of freedom's song than their erstwhile owners and their descendants.

What is scandalous is that so-called mainstream philosophy has been slow, if not recalcitrant, in taking seriously and incorporating in its freedom discourse the contributions from diasporic African philosophers. On a more problematic note, however, the focus on identity and freedom explains in part some of the contradictions and tensions in contemporary diasporic African philosophy. Few would deny that one of the commonalities that denominate the identity of African-descended peoples across the globe and is the glue that supposedly holds together the ideal of Pan-Africanism is a shared history of oppression poignantly symbolized in the denial of our common humanity in the diaspora—slavery—and in the continent itself—colonialism. For a while in the past, Africans, wherever they happened to be, shared a common engagement in the twin philosophical themes of race and identity and freedom. Not only did Africans struggle together but they also were on the same page regarding what identity and freedom meant for their common world. They shared those ideas, and it was not rare to find African nationalists freely quoting one another across their many divides in their common struggle against racism and colonialism. Such was the convergence that when African countries began scoring victories in their anticolonial struggles, they claimed such victories for *all* black peoples everywhere, and one of them, Kwame Nkrumah, invited diasporic Africans to come to Ghana and make a home there. Simultaneously, the victories in the anticolonial struggle as well as the intellectual discourse that informed them—theories of national liberation, as they were then styled—and the theories of identity that they formulated—especially those regarding "the African personality"—all served as inspiration for African Americans in their bitter struggle against racism, in particular the inhumanity of Jim Crow laws and social practices in the United States.[11]

But then things changed. The attainment of independence by African countries meant that, at least at the formal level, the struggle for freedom was definitely won. Although continental African thinkers and their allies across the globe reflected on and wrote extensively on the phenomenon of neocolonialism and its deleterious consequences on Africa's formal freedom as well as its implications for the well-being of Africa's peoples, to all intents and purposes, freedom, as an organizing principle and focus of sociopolitical struggle, stopped being a central theme in African philosophy. In the diaspora, too, similar changes affected the role of freedom as a theme of struggles in the Caribbean. And in the United States, the struggle for freedom which was prosecuted for the better part of the twentieth century under the banner of civil rights also met with notable successes, especially in the last half of the century. Formal rights were secured for African Americans and the pressure for integration, rather than the previous focus on separatism or, at least, national identity was intense. As was the case with the fortunes of freedom in Africa and the Caribbean in the aftermath of independence, so did its fortunes also decline in the United States.

As things changed in Africa and the Caribbean and the focus turned in those places on developing the constituent countries, decreasing attention was paid to exploring the shared identity—racial and sociohistorical—between the different segments of the global African world. As things changed in the United States and the integrationist ramifications of contemporary American civil rights movement took roots, the place of Africa and other areas of the diaspora in the African American imaginary began to decrease. The consequence is that the twin themes of race and identity and freedom that had served as a rallying point for social, political, and philosophical interchanges between Africa and its diaspora declined in importance, and the cross-fertilization of ideas that used to mark their common relations almost ceased.

Meanwhile, the declining salience of issues related to race and identity in Africa and the Caribbean was not matched by a similar decline in the United States. Indeed, the irony enfolded in the pressure for integration manifested itself in the continuing problematization of African American identity in the larger context of U.S. citizenship. In light of the continuing dominance of white supremacist tendencies, African Americans have been forced continually to rue the ideas of race and identity in the contemporary period. This is where our earlier reference to the importance of the crucial changes represented by the recent influx of continental African immigrants can be seen in bolder relief. The current politics of racial identity—in a sense, a product of the backlash against integration-inflected civil rights—is that to or against which new African arrivals react. African immigrants are coming from majoritarian backgrounds in which questions of identity are more likely to be *national* or *ethnic* rather than *racial*. Of course, exceptions will include black South Africans, Asian East Africans, and black North Africans. So it is unlikely that African immigrants would be exercised in any but the most perfunctory degree by the specificities of racial politics in the United States, at least not immediately upon their arrival.[12]

The new arrivals are not ignorant of racism. Indeed, depending on what part of Africa they come from and the degree of penetration of neocolonial rule in their countries of origin, they themselves may have experienced racism. However, they are often ambivalent about racism in their country of sojourn. They usually exhibit much faith in meritocracy and expect that if they work hard in their host country they will make it. In this they are not different from what is generally recognized as immigrant consciousness that drives immigrant groups to seek to realize better lives for themselves and their progeny than what their erstwhile home countries offered. Add to this the fact that, in philosophy, many immigrant African scholars have received their training elsewhere and have grown up doing philosophy, *simpliciter*, rather than as a piece in ideological struggle. They have definitely not done philosophy as a racially inflected enterprise even when they have, as part of the debate about African philosophy as a subdiscipline, had cause to confront the racially exclusionary nature of Western philosophy in which they have been trained. Of course, it is always possible that some among this group may be victims of colonial mentality and adopt an uncritical attitude toward their colonial inheritance.

The discourse of freedom that bound Africa and its diaspora receded in importance as more and more African Americans came to take their freedom for granted and Africans, also got used to being free, however that term is understood. But the fact that freedom declined in significance in the daily concerns of the global African world did not mean that it stopped being a core theme in African American philosophy. The difference is that the texts and expostulations that used to dominate the universe of discourse shared by the different segments of the global African world disappeared almost completely from the writings of the leading thinkers in current African American philosophy. This explains, in part, the absence of serious references to African thinkers and scholars in the narratives of some of the more prominent voices of diasporic philosophy in the United States—Cornel West, Bernard Boxill, Howard McGarry, Frank Kirkland, Michelle Moody-Adams, and so on. Exceptions will include Lucius Outlaw, Leonard Harris, Lewis Gordon, and Albert Mosley. What I say here should not be read as a critical comment on the state of African American philosophy. I am merely describing a context that I think will enable us to make sense of some of the new elements that are added by recent African immigrants in order to locate some of the tensions that demographic changes in the constitution of the diaspora do occasion. How those tensions are processed has implications for the evolution of the relationship between philosophy and the diaspora.

Into the above mix we throw the new African arrivals. Many in this group are more hewn to the demands of the dominant Western inflection of the discipline, even when they do African philosophy, which, after all, was forged in debate with the so-called mainstream. For reasons already adumbrated above, they are less attracted to the issues of race and are engaged with the issue of freedom more as an ethico-metaphysical issue and only secondarily as a theme in political philosophy. They instead are more likely to focus on the traditional divisions of philosophy even when they are doing African Philosophy. In this respect, they have contributed some seminal ideas in epistemology, metaphysics, and ethics. Nevertheless, anyone who is familiar with philosophy in Africa knows that it will be a very long time indeed before contributions in the areas I just listed will match the breadth and profundity of African contributions in social and political philosophy. Thus, in spite of the current divergences between continental and diasporic African philosophers, philosophy in Africa and in its diaspora is notable for its high achievements in social and political philosophy. Again, this should come as no surprise.

We have seen that the fact that "mainstream philosophy" relates to the philosophical productions of the African diaspora with measured obliviousness is no reason not to take very seriously the philosophizing that goes on in the global African world. What will philosophy look like if it takes the complexity of the world and the multiversity of its cultural forms seriously? What if it permits itself to embrace the African diaspora as both an object of study and a locus of insights into the human condition? Once we pose this question, one thing becomes very clear: it is not only "mainstream philosophy" that needs to expand its vista to encompass the philosophical contributions of the global African world. Diasporic African philosophers, too, will have to take seriously and engage with the contributions of continental Africans, both those who remain in the continent and those who have taken up residence in the diaspora.

Let us illustrate with the idea of liberalism at the present time and what its discourse might look like if its theorists were to take seriously the contributions of global African peoples to the constitution, evolution, and worth of liberal philosophy. In the past several years, I have been concerned to understand liberalism—as a political movement, a form of government, a strand in the complex intellectual history of the so-called West, and so on. The immediate motivation must be traced to my experience of the failure of liberalism to take root in other parts of the world, including many putatively Western countries. This has since been reinforced by my relocation to North America and the subsequent deepening of my understanding of the fractured history and fractious appropriations of liberalism in these climes.

Let me be more specific about the twin inspirations for my project. I start with the second one. Over the years I have had the privilege of teaching, at two different institutions, advanced seminars in political philosophy. In them I decided to focus on liberalism. Of course, all of the registrants in the courses knew "liberal" to be a term of political abuse. In their minds, "liberal" refers to a politician who is a spendthrift with other people's money—"liberal spender"; is eager to cuddle criminals because of some misplaced faith in human perfectibility; is an unreasoning enthusiast of big government and an idolatrous worshipper of government omnipotence at solving every problem. You can take any recent election-eering period in the United States and find the paradoxical status of liberalism in the political imaginary of the ruling classes in the country. At the same time as the ruling class is busy savaging liberalism at home, it is busy selling it abroad as the panacea to all that is wrong with and in the world. The ongoing debacle in Iraq is merely the latest in a string of misadventures in the name of procuring freedom for people abroad. And, among its ideologists, there is a resurgent triumphalism whose pace has been quickened by the well-deserved demise of Eastern Europe's misbegotten socialisms. So what explains this disjuncture?

Then there is the issue of the veracity and adequacy of the dominant discourse of modernity. Triumphalists and other ideologists of liberalism are wont to omit from their narratives of the career of liberalism, or of the larger movement of which it was a part, modernity, the contributions of Africans—diasporic and continental—to the evolution of modernity and liberalism. That is, one does not obtain from a reading of John Rawls, Robert Nozick, William Galston, Ronald Dworkin, Bruce Ackermann, Richard Flathman, Stephen Macedo, Robert D'Amico, Jean-Bethke Elshtain, Michael Sandel, Robert Dahl, Seymour Lipset, Carole Pateman, Alan Gilbert, etc., any serious attempt to reach beyond the borders of the United States or, occasionally, the United Kingdom and Germany and recognize, if they cannot accommodate, the not-so-happy, decidedly unfortunate experiences of millions of others in Africa, Asia, and South America who have been used as fodder for liberal cannons in wars fought to make the world safe for democracy—liberal democracy, that is. Their refusal has become even more scandalous in the last two decades in which the world has witnessed widespread transitions to democracy of differing degrees of completeness.[13] When challenged, they usually have very simple, I daresay simplistic, answers for why such issues are not worth their theoretical attention: those are all areas of "low political culture," inured to autocratic rule, bereft of the liberal democratic temper, etc.

Now, here is the problem: the Western hand has touched almost all these areas. In the case of the ex-colonies, they were not merely touched. Western agents sought to remake their destinies supposedly guided by ideas whose provenance is to be traced to modernity and its political spin-off, liberal democracy. Given that this is so, we are right to ask why serious efforts are not made to understand this unhappy history. And I would like to suggest that in understanding the unhappy relationship between liberalism (modernity) and those that were imperialized in its name, we might come to a better understanding of why it is so problematic even in the lands of its birth and in soils most hospitable. The works of Frantz Fanon, Albert Memmi, Aimé Césaire, Julius Nyerere, and C. L. R. James have a lot to impart in this respect. And in saying this, I am not just looking at what happens in the strictly colonial situations in Africa and Asia.

One can also look at those populations that are the equivalents of colonized peoples elsewhere within countries such as the United States and Canada: Native peoples and peoples of African descent in them. For these peoples, historically, the highfalutin expostulations of the theorists of liberalism have, for the most part, been constructed in complete obliviousness, intended or not, of the real experiences of Native peoples and African Americans. We saw above that the theme of freedom has always permeated African American philosophy, and much of that turns on the unredeemed promise of liberalism and modernity for African Americans. The metaphysical template on which liberalism is founded, the principle of subjectivity, was elaborated in such a way that African Americans were excluded. The open future that promised careers open to talent was shut to African Americans by the operations of myriad forms of racism. African Americans needed special amendments to the Constitution for them to benefit from universal provisions that ought to have included them all along, and the primacy of process over outcome has always needed additional legislation to ensure that African Americans would benefit from the triumph of rules. African American thinkers have always known and theorized these peculiar experiences. The works of W. E. B. Du Bois, Frederick Douglass, Martin R. Delany, Sojourner Truth, and Anna Julia Cooper have a lot to impart in this respect.

I am arguing that when discussions of freedom and liberalism by "mainstream philosophers" unfold without their evincing any awareness of the ways in which the liberal legacy has been affected by its migration across borders—physical and cultural—they do violence to what ought to be the true history and complexity of the liberal idea. By the same token, when diasporic philosophers working in the same tradition criticize the "mainstream" for its exclusionary tendencies even as they prosecute their own exclusions of what their continental African compatriots have offered from their nook of their shared experience of being shafted by the "mainstream," they, too, do violence. And when African philosophers behave or write as if the reflections of diasporic philosophers have little relevance to their contemporary situation, they do not do any less violence to their subject matter. Insofar as freedom and the yearning for it are not the exclusive preserve of any one people in the world, once the necessary allowances have been made for pragmatic difficulties on the path to knowledge, it behooves those who are desirous of expanding the frontiers of knowledge to present their ideas in their most historically accurate and complex form.

I would like to conclude this section by considering one other example of what philosophy will look like if it takes seriously the experiences and philosophical reflections on them of Africans, both continental and diasporic. This time, it is the idea of the person. No doubt, the concept of personhood is a preeminently philosophical problem. As things stand, the dominant tradition inaugurated by René Descartes continues to process the problem in terms of the conundrums generated by the nature of and relations between *mind* and *body*. Even the latest forays into cognitive science do not manage to elude the centrality of the mind-body problem. All they do is issue new variations on the theme.

Now given what we said earlier about the twin issues of freedom and identity, one cannot overemphasize the importance of the *subject* whose identity and freedom exercise philosophers both in Africa and its diaspora. This is where we begin to see the overweening influence of the modern idea of the person on the dominant discussions of the issue of freedom in the African diaspora. Simultaneously, the dominant discussions of the idea of personhood among continental Africans have veered away from the Cartesian-inflected project to source in indigenous African traditions alternative conceptions of the person which take the focus away from the *subject* to the *community*. In reaction, sometimes warranted, at other times needless, to the ravages of colonialism and what many regard as the colonization of the African mind, continental African philosophers and a cadre of their diasporic counterparts denigrate the Cartesian idea and its successors. Instead they have isolated some strains of what they call African *communalism* undergirded by a philosophical anthropology in which the individual privileged by Descartes would be a nonentity. Here the works of John Mbiti, Segun Gbadegesin, Dismas Masolo, Julius Nyerere, Ifeanyi Menkiti, Kwame Gyekye, Barry Hallen, and William Abraham come to mind.[14] On their view, the individual *cannot* be conceived in any significant sense as being anything outside of her intimate connection with the community that spawned her. They argue that personhood is earned, not automatic, and may admit of development.

Not unlike the debate over the relationship between the mind and the body, the individual-community dialectic generates its own share of philosophical conundrums. What is of moment here is that few diasporic African philosophers recognize this strand of philosophical exertion as legitimate candidates for inclusion in their own discourse and even fewer engage or make it an integral part of their own work. The one who, using the tropes of academic "mainstream" philosophy to fashion a metaphysics of the person that creatively combines the best insights available from continental African and diasporic African philosophies is Paget Henry in his *Caliban's Reason*. The irony, though, is that he comes to us as an academic sociologist. Lucius Outlaw, Albert Mosley, and Leonard Harris incorporate elements from both sources, and Mosley has been almost singular in working on and disputing with continental African philosophers and themes in epistemology and metaphysics. Nevertheless, most don't fashion an integrated whole from continental African philosophy like Henry does. And, of course, one must recognize that the ones who have done the most at using continental African philosophical materials to fashion a diasporic African philosophical anthropology are the Afrocentrists at the top of which group one must place the philosophical exertions of Molefi Kete Asante and Maulana Karenga. Again, most of those who fall into this group are not professional academic philosophers.

Just like what we said respecting the discussion of freedom and identity, a mainstream philosophy that recognizes and incorporates insights from both divisions of African-inflected philosophy is one that might give itself a chance to break free from some of the sterility and solipsism that some of us now believe afflict the traditional mind-body problem. Diasporic Africans who engage and incorporate wisdom derived from their remote ancestry in continental Africa might give us more original syntheses to challenge our accepted wisdom regarding what it is to be a person. Continental Africans who embrace the novel emergence that diasporic philosophy represents might come away with a more profound understanding of their heritage provided by the creative accretions brought about by their diasporic cousins.

In this essay, I have traced the relationship between the African diaspora and the discipline of philosophy as well as between diasporic (principally the United States and the Anglo-French Caribbean) and continental Africans and their philosophical exertions. I have argued that the recent influx of continental Africans into the diaspora occasions new tensions but also spawns new opportunities for rethinking both the dimensions of the diaspora and its intellectual inheritance and those of the discipline of philosophy itself. When we shall have responded to the challenges and exploited the opportunities on offer, we will have brand-new insights into and novel responses to the perennial questions of philosophy, not to mention the development of genuinely comparative philosophy that bridges the gulf between the world's multifarious philosophical traditions. One cannot overstress the possible impact of these developments on the discipline of philosophy itself. But the ultimate beneficiaries of these multiple embraces are the students who, for a change, will be put at the crossroads of some important human experiences and can then luxuriate in the intellectual wealth so made available. At the same time, I hope that the reader comes away with considerable optimism regarding the bounty that awaits the willing and intrepid explorer.

NOTES

The final revision of this paper was done during the sabbatical term that I was privileged to spend at the Department of Philosophy and Scranton College of Ewha Womans University, Seoul, Korea, in the fall term of 2008. I would like to register my gratitude to Professor Heisook Kim, the dean of Scranton College, who arranged my appointment. She and her associates provided me with optimal conditions for very serious research and writing.

1. Unless otherwise stated, subsequent references will be to the diaspora, for short.

2. And the deeper I delved into the questions posed by the organizers of the original workshop on which the current discussion is based.

3. A description supplied by the organizers.

4. I have cause to believe that this is not the case. Think of the export of Africans as both slaves and emigrants across the Sahara Desert to Europe, Asia Minor, and the Arabian Peninsula as well as Asia itself and you have an idea of the complexity that I have in mind. In this respect one must welcome Michael A. Gomez's *Reversing Sail*.

5. My choice is purely pragmatic based only on location. If I were writing this essay for a European primary audience, my choice would shift accordingly.

6. See, for examples, Pittman, ed., *African-American Perspectives and Philosophical Traditions*; Harris, ed., *Philosophy Born of Struggle*; Outlaw, *On Race and Philosophy*; Boxill, *Blacks and Social Justice*; Mills, *The Racial Contract*; Gordon, *Existence in Black* and *Bad Faith and Antiblack Racism*; Asante and Abarry, eds., *African Intellectual Heritage: A Book of Sources*; Brotz, ed., *African-American Social and Political Thought, 1850–1920*.

7. These include Philosophy Born of Struggle, the Alain Locke Conference, the New York Society for Africana Philosophy, the International Society for African Philosophy and Studies (ISAPS), and the Caribbean Philosophical Association.

8. Lott and Pittman, eds., *A Companion to African-American Philosophy* is a good indicator of this development.

9. For a similar complaint see Outlaw, *On Race and Philosophy*, 188.

10. Táíwò, "'The Love of Freedom Brought Us Here.'"

11. For representative samples of the tendencies represented in this paragraph, see Kilson and Hill, eds., *Apropos of Africa*; Cartey and Kilson, eds., *The Africa Reader: Independent Africa*; Langley, ed., *Ideologies of Liberation in Black Africa, 1856–1970*; Mutiso and Rohio, eds., *Readings in African Political Thought*.

12. See the essays in Hintzen and Rahier, eds., *Problematizing Blackness*.

13. Jürgen Habermas is a popular figure with some Iranian scholars who have hosted numerous conferences in Tehran on his and related ideas. Chinese youth during their brief but heroic pro-democracy march in Tiananmen Square in 1994 held aloft a replica of the Statue of Liberty. South Africans were laying down their lives for the right to have the vote and be determiners of their own destinies. Filipinos braved tanks in 1986 to safeguard a nascent liberal democracy from the jackboots of a dictator.

14. See, in general, Nyerere, *Ujamaa: Essays on Socialism*; Menkiti, "On the Normative Conception of a Person"; Masolo, "The Concept of the Person in Luo Modes of Thought" and "African Communalism and Western Communitarianism"; Gbadegesin, *African Philosophy*; Abraham, *The Mind of Africa*; Gyekye, *An Essay on African Philosophical Thought*; Wiredu and Gyekye, eds., *Person and Community*.

REFERENCES

Abraham, William E. *The Mind of Africa*. Chicago: University of Chicago Press, 1966.

Boxill, Bernard R. *Blacks and Social Justice*. Totowa: Rowman and Littlefield, 1984.

Brotz, Howard, ed. *African-American Social and Political Thought, 1850–1920.* New Brunswick: Transaction, 1999.

Cartey, Wilfred, and Martin Kilson, eds. *The Africa Reader: Independent Africa.* New York: Vintage, 1970.

Gbadegesin, Segun. *African Philosophy: Traditional Yoruba Philosophy and Contemporary African Realities.* New York: Peter Lang, 1991.

Gomez, Michael A. *Reversing Sail: A History of the African Diaspora.* Cambridge: Cambridge University Press, 2005.

Gordon, Lewis R. *Bad Faith and Antiblack Racism.* Atlantic Highlands, N.J.: Humanities, 1995.

———, ed. *Existence in Black: An Anthology of Black Existential Philosophy.* New York: Routledge, 1997.

Gyekye, Kwame. *An Essay on African Philosophical Thought: the Akan Conceptual Scheme.* Philadelphia: Temple University Press, 1995.

Harris, Leonard, ed. *Philosophy Born of Struggle: Anthology of Afro-American Philosophy from 1917,* 2nd ed. Dubuque: Kendall/Hunt, 1983, 2000.

Henry, Paget. *Caliban's Reason: Introducing Afro-Caribbean Philosophy.* New York: Routledge, 2000.

Hintzen, Percy C., and Jean Muteba Rahier, eds. *Problematizing Blackness: Self-Ethnographies by Black Immigrants to the United States.* New York: Routledge, 2002.

Kilson, Martin, and Adelaide Hill, eds. *Apropos of Africa: Afro-American Leaders and the Romance of Africa.* New York: Anchor, 1971.

Langley, J. Ayo, ed. *Ideologies of Liberation in Black Africa, 1856–1970.* London: Rex Collings, 1979.

Lott, Tommy L., and John P. Pittman, eds. *A Companion to African-American Philosophy.* Malden, Mass.: Blackwell, 2003.

Masolo, Dismas A. "The Concept of the Person in Luo Modes of Thought." In Lee M. Brown, ed., *African Philosophy: New and Traditional Perspectives,* chap. 6. New York: Oxford University Press, 2004.

———. "African Communalism and Western Communitarianism: A Comparison." In Kwasi Wiredu, ed., *A Companion to African Philosophy,* chap. 40. Malden: Blackwell, 2004.

Menkiti, Ifeanyi. "On the Normative Conception of a Person." In Kwasi Wiredu, ed., *A Companion to African Philosophy,* chap. 24. Malden: Blackwell, 2004.

Mills, Charles W. *The Racial Contract.* Ithaca, N.Y.: Cornell University Press, 1997.

Molefi Kete Asante, and Abu S. Abarry, eds. *African Intellectual Heritage: A Book of Sources.* Philadelphia: Temple University Press, 1996.

Mutiso, Gideon-Cyrus M., and S. W. Rohio, eds. *Readings in African Political Thought.* London: Heinemann, 1975.

Nyerere, Julius. *Ujamaa: Essays on Socialism.* Dar es Salaam: Oxford University Press, 1968.

Outlaw, Lucius. *On Race and Philosophy.* New York: Routledge, 1996.

Pittman, John P., ed. *African-American Perspectives and Philosophical Traditions.* New York: Routledge, 1997.

Táíwò, Olúfémi. "'The Love of Freedom Brought Us Here': An Introduction to Modern African Political Philosophy." Paper presented to the 10th Annual Conference of the International Society for African Philosophy and Studies

(ISAPS), University of the West Indies, Mona, Kingston, Jamaica, April 10–11, 2004.

Wiredu, Kwasi, and Kwame Gyekye, eds. *Person and Community: Ghanaian Philosophical Studies*. Washington, D.C.: Council for Research in Values and Philosophy, 1992.

PART THREE
ARTS AND CULTURE

9

"FUNCTION AT THE JUNCTION"? AFRICAN DIASPORA STUDIES AND THEATER STUDIES

Sandra L. Richards

To specify a relationship between African Diaspora Studies and Theater Studies is in one sense to draw a map, but it soon becomes apparent that one can not get there from here, for African Diaspora Studies has, at present, little connection to or visibility within Theater Studies. Unable to pinpoint the place or official site of conjuncture, I offer instead an itinerary by which we may arrive at a space where the practice of diaspora and theater meet in their pursuit of the cherished objective of enacting community.[1] Given the consistent conflation of Performance Studies with Theater Studies, the essay first reviews disciplinary distinctions that determine the object of study and status of evidence. As will become apparent, the dominance of the written text in Theater Studies has negatively predisposed the discipline toward African Diaspora Studies, a fact that the subsequent review of doctoral dissertations and recent publications confirms. The essay then turns its focus outside the academy in order to offer a brief survey of the emergence within the arts of an Afrocentric perspective that necessarily assumed diaspora, understood as cultural continuity between an original source culture and descendant societies produced by forced migration and adaptation to hostile new environments. This Black Arts movement of the 1960s and 1970s would provide infrastructural resources for contemporary Black Theater and Black Performance Studies in the United States. But because its definition of diaspora tended in practice to be oriented toward ritual and/or the past, the essay then turns to a brief reading of texts, selected so as to highlight questions of memory and bodily archives, circulation, translation, imagination, and reinvention that are central to how diaspora is currently understood. Finally, it proposes routes that African Diaspora Studies scholars may opt to travel in further shaping an interdisciplinary field that through its rigorous self-reflexivity, conceptualizes itself not as the colonizing center of the map of scholarship on African peoples but rather as one dynamic itinerary of how humans institute community and struggle for a better life.

A STARTING POINT

Because a cartographer's perspective at least partially determines the map she draws, I wish to indicate the location from which I am surveying the terrain, a space shared, I believe, by the relatively few scholars trained during the 1960s and 1970s in dramatic literature in American academies and specializing in black theater. Responsive to the sociopolitical ferment of the times, this cohort was committed to thinking about black cultural production in terms that did not reduce it to a poor derivative of Euro-American achievements. We entered the academy at a time of struggle for the introduction of Black and Ethnic Studies, such that if we encountered the scholarship of W. E. B. Du Bois, Melville Herskovits, Janheinz Jahn, or Lorenzo Dow Turner, our likely route to these pioneers in African Diaspora Studies was through informal study groups and self-directed reading. Although some of us may also have been involved in making theater as actors, directors, or costumers, as PhD graduate students (and then later, as doctoral holders) we largely adhered to the textual dominance in Theater Studies, discussed below, even while trying to revise, expand, or introduce new categories of what constituted theater. Although much has changed in the intervening three or four decades, the emphasis on theater scripts remains strong. And because written scripts circulate more easily than people, I will use the former as the space from which to chart an itinerary or relationship between Theater Studies and African Diaspora Studies.

THEATER STUDIES, PERFORMANCE STUDIES

Though many academic colleagues use the terms "theater studies" and "performance studies" interchangeably, and scholars trained in one area sometimes publish in the other, these two disciplines have distinct yet interdependent histories that differently determine their study of black cultural production. Within the history of Western theatrical practice, the scriptural has come to dominate other languages of the theater, such as music, dance, and gesture, so that even though the study of theater encompasses attention to how reenactment is made, the written text is at the center, providing the raison d'être for performance decisions (McAuley 4–7). Linked to the assumption of the dramatic text as having an essential stability, which is modified rather than substantially disrupted in any given production, was the development of perspectival painting and the proscenium or picture-book stage that focused spectatorial attention squarely on the action onstage, with the consequence that audiences learned to behave as silent voyeurs, passively consuming actors/characters who were conceptualized as being totally unaware of their presence. Even though twentieth-century practitioners like the German Bertolt Brecht or the Brazilian Augusto Boal articulated strategies whereby audiences were encouraged to critically intervene in events onstage, most modernist Western drama and theater practice continues to assume minimal spectatorial contribution to meaning; that is, meaning is thought to inhere in the individually authored drama that a hierarchically organized group of artists-technicians then realize in the theater before a silent (and hopefully appreciative) audience whose responses to the event are largely determined within the hermeneutically closed parameters set forth by the production. The cultural work achieved by these practices all too often is the "reification of socially dominant, normative values" (Knowles 65). Furthermore, the overall divide within American universities between theory and research, on the one hand, and practice or applied knowledge, on the other, often is reproduced within theater departments themselves, such that those who study the written—dramatic texts, theater histories, design methodologies—enjoy higher status than those who teach embodied practices—acting, voice, dance, costume construction (Jackson, chapter 2).

This emphasis on the written text created by an individual artist locates the cultural production of Africa-descended peoples as outside the norm on several accounts. Given histories of enslavement, imposed illiteracy, and impoverishment throughout the Americas, the majority of black people have eschewed the production of drama or verbal, text-based theater. Rather, they have used the body itself and its ability to create music, song, and dance as an archive (Taylor) into which knowledge and value systems could be embedded, remembered, and passed down intergenerationally. One need only think of carnival, second-line parades, or *candomble* ceremonies as examples of spectacular, polyfocal enactments of a community's history, aspirations, and creativity. Even when black authors have chosen to utilize Western forms of playwriting, their audiences have not necessarily opted to act like polite, middle-class spectators, for there are numerous historical accounts of audience members talking back to actors onstage or engaging among themselves in audible critique of events onstage. Indeed, this behavior when juxtaposed to other examples of black orature, such as the dilemma tale genre popular throughout Africa, high-spirited barbershop discussions, or testimonial protocols in black Christian churches, argues for a conception of theater that insists upon multigenre, dialogical interactions, with fluid distinctions between performer and audience, as the preferred mode of meaning-making and potential transformation.

While Theater as a mode of academic inquiry in the United States is relatively young, having been established in the early years of the twentieth century, Performance Studies is even younger, having emerged only in the mid-1980s (Jackson; Madison and Hamera). Starting, like its older sibling, with an interest in the oral interpretation of literature, Performance Studies defines its object of study as larger than Theater's preoccupation with "putting on a show." Performance is understood

> in the expanded sense that subsumes aesthetic performances, ritual and religious observance, secular ceremonies, carnival, games, play, sports, and many other cultural forms as its object of inquiry and unites the tradition of theater studies with techniques and approaches from anthropology, sociology, critical theory, cultural studies, art history, and other disciplines. (Auslander 99–100)

Conceptualized as a way of knowing, an embodied process through which human beings come to construct and understand their world, negotiate relationships to others, and represent their realities to themselves and others (Madison and Hamera), it stands as a counter to "the anti-theatrical prejudice that, since Plato, has aligned performance with fakery and falsehood" (Conquergood, "Caravans" 138).

Though black people figure prominently in the prehistory of the field, their involvement has only recently been recognized with articles like Dwight Conquergood's essay on nineteenth-century elocution.[2] Moreover, a generation of scholar-artists like Njoki McElroy at Northwestern and Wallace Ray Peppers at University of North Carolina, Chapel Hill had to struggle in the early 1970s to win recognition for a redefinition of "literature" that would include black artists and for the adoption of curricula that would inspire and train today's young Black Performance Studies faculty (Johnson 448). While its institutional origins in the aftermath of the sociopolitical turmoil of the 1960s, coupled with its focus on the body as a site of knowledge, have made Performance Studies more receptive to black cultural production, it has not managed to escape completely from the racism of the larger American society. Further, its academic youth has meant that the discipline remains relatively unrecognized in universities outside the United States. The consequence of these disciplinary formations is that whether one pursues a Theater Studies or Performance Studies route, one is unlikely to encounter African Diaspora Studies along the way.

IN THE LIBRARY

A trip to the written archives offers corroborating detail to my claims. A review of *Theater Journal*, one of the premier journals in the field, attests to the relative invisibility of the category. During the period of 1996–2005, for which information is easily accessible online, no Theater Studies doctoral candidate wrote on "diaspora." Rather, students researched various national dramas, individual playwrights, gender studies, educational theater, architecture, costume and makeup, and performance studies.[3] Not surprisingly, most dissertations completed in American universities focused on English-language drama, and the most elaboration of categories occurred within the study of American and English drama, where these sub-areas were further divided by centuries. Approximately eighteen dissertations focused on "Africa," while fewer than five concentrated on the "West Indies."

A survey of prominent, U.S.-based journals with a focus on black cultural production confirms the impression that few scholars are writing specifically on theater and performance from the framework of the African diaspora, rather than as an instance of national culture. *Callaloo*, which describes itself as "the premier African diaspora literary journal," focuses more on poetry, fiction, nondramatic literary analysis, and the visual arts. An online perusing of titles for the period from Winter 2001 to Fall 2005 (approximately 188 scholarly articles) suggests that approximately 15 essays considered drama, performance, and diasporic artists.[4] While *Diaspora: A Journal of Transnational Studies* seems to have published, between 2000 and 2003, some 9 articles on the African diaspora, none of them were performance or theater-related. *Small Axe: A Journal of Criticism*, devoted to "the renewal of practices of intellectual criticism . . . in and about regional/diasporic Caribbean," distinguishes itself with some ten scholarly articles, other than book reviews, published between September 2001 and September 2006 (total of 75 essays), in addition to proffering two special issues, one on popular culture in the Caribbean and a second on "Crossing Borders of Language and Culture."

In the realm of book-length manuscripts, the category of African diaspora theater is, again, relatively invisible, even though plays and productions that might fit under such a designation are being discussed. For example, Femi Euba's *Archetypes, Imprecators, and Victims of Fate: Origins and Developments of Satire in Black Drama*, though it argues for connections between Yoruba values and black American satire, is not categorized as "diaspora," according to the Library of Congress subject headings. Similarly, Tejumola Olaniyan's *Scars of Conquest/Masks of Resistance: The Invention of Cultural Identities in African, African-American, and Caribbean Drama* is not designated "diaspora," even though the dust jacket description and reviewers' comments refer to the category.[5] Under the rubric of *Theater for Development*, one will find scholarship on African or Caribbean theater that is oriented toward social change as well as comparative research on practices in the global South (Boon and Plastow). Theater texts and criticism from various sites in the African diaspora are occasionally brought together under the category of the *postcolonial*, but by definition this field focuses more on relations of the colonized peripheries to the colonial metropole, and black people in the United States, though having been subjected to conditions that approximate colonialism, are most often omitted from consideration.[6] The category of *intercultural theater*, with its attention to cultural exchange between different geographic regions and performance traditions, is another area in which one would hope to find African diaspora scholarship, but dominated by high profile, well-funded projects of European artists like Peter Brook, Eugenio Barba, and Ariane Mnouchkine, this line of endeavor has faltered, as these stars have been justly criticized for engaging in a form of Orientalism that functions so as to (re)invigorate Euro-American theaters. Largely missing from the practice and critical reviews of this movement is serious reflection on issues relevant to African Diaspora Studies, namely, "the temporality and context of borrowings" (Bharucha, *Politics* 32) that necessarily account for and confront asymmetrical power relations operative among participants, source, and target cultures (Bharucha, *Theater*; Jeyifo).

If one widens the lens from theater to performance, the African diaspora becomes more discernible in a number of relatively recent, interdisciplinary anthologies that encompass some of the themes and approaches found in the "anti-discipline" discipline of Performance Studies (Johnson, personal communication). Here, we may think of collections such as Holloway's *Africanisms in American Culture* (1990), Okpewho, Davies, and Mazrui's *The African Diaspora: African Origins and New World Identities* (1999), Rahier's *Representations of Blackness and the Performance of Identities* (1999), or Walker's *African Roots/American Cultures: Africa in the Creation of the Americas* (2001). Yet as the subtitles of several of these books suggest, an older definition of diaspora as forced migration to a new home and cultural continuity prevails.

AN ALTERNATIVE ROUTE? AFROCENTRIC AND AFRICAN DIASPORA THEATER

But if one begins outside the American academy in the mid-1960s, she can travel a route that by the early twenty-first century formally connects theater to African Diaspora Studies. Coalescing as the "sister" to the Black Power movement (Neal), the Black Arts movement in the United States instigated a vigorous exploration of the saliency of Africa for black cultural production; adding fuel to these struggles for self-representation were examples of liberation and decolonization movements on the African continent and in Cuba and the Anglophone Caribbean. Artists and theoreticians like Amiri Baraka, Larry Neal, Ed Bullins, Addison Gayle, Harold Cruse, Robert Macbeth, Haki Madhubuti, Sonia Sanchez, Barbara Ann Teer, Glenda Dickerson, and Woodie King sought to fashion forms that would instill black self-esteem and located their aesthetics in a black folk, whose ethos was allegedly untouched by the American mainstream and bore traces of a continuity with African cultures. Although scholars such as Neal, Gayle, Barbara and Carlton Molette, and Kariamu Welsh-Asante have analyzed performance from an African-centered perspective, Paul Carter Harrison has dominated the field by virtue of his prolific output.

Starting in 1972 with his *Drama of Nommo*, Harrison has, over a thirty-four-year period, authored or edited some eleven plays, two critical works, and two anthologies of plays by men and women from the United States, Martinique, South Africa, Trinidad, Nigeria, and Cuba. He rejected what he disparaged as a 1960s kitchen sink realism that froze life into "limited frames of reference such as black poverty, black power, and black is beautiful" (*Kuntu Drama* 5). In place of Western drama with its exposition, middle-scene conflicts, and final act resolution that assumes a linear, cause-and-effect relationship and mimetic fidelity to a contained, visible world outside the theater, Harrison proposed a modal drama with a fluid matrix, akin to that of the black church.[7] While the black church has some of its origin in African religious practices, Harrison has this to say about the place of Africa in his theory:

> Yet while race memory cannot be denied its progenitive place of value, it is not necessary to regard Africa as the primary source of expressive inclination. To do so would encourage a gross and erroneous self-mockery of ancestral traditions. (*Kuntu Drama* 23)

Thus, in a 1974 collection of plays entitled *Kuntu Drama*, Harrison would use the term "plays of the African continuum," a descriptor repeated some fifteen years later in a second anthology, *Totem Voices: Plays from the Black World Repertory*. The term "African diaspora" would appear in his 2002 anthology of critical essays, *Black Theater and Ritual Performance in the African Diaspora*, co-edited with Victor Walker and Gus Edwards. As indicated by the title, ritual continues to dominate Harrison's conception of black theater. Yet the collection also marks how much black theater scholarship has developed over the past thirty years. Responding perhaps to interventions of scholars like Paul Gilroy who have questioned formulations of cultural authenticity and proposed attention to the creative circulation of ideas, people, and artifacts throughout the (Black) Atlantic, this anthology may be said to probe *roots* with essays exploring the African foundations of black theater and to attend to *routes* or dialogic appropriation and circulation with works on carnival, Yoruba-based Brazilian and Cuban ritual practices, and black theater in Britain. Further, the inclusion of essays on women-centered dramas and on the masculinist construction of the community or the nation, typical of the Black Arts/Black Power movements and decolonization struggles, indicates the revisionary impact that black feminism has exerted on cultural production. In addition, this collection bridges another divide common in Theater Studies, namely, the distinction between theorists and historians, on the one hand, and theater practitioners, on the other, for it includes essays on dramaturgical practice and performance.

Despite all the anthology's strengths, a challenge remains: Can we imagine African diaspora theater in terms other than ritual? A reading of a set of texts that theorize diaspora in their structures and circulation offers not only a response to this question but also a sense of the complexity of issues involved.

PERFORMING DIASPORA

Because cultural alienation, desire for community, will toward justice, and restoration to wholeness loom large in diaspora aspirations and practice, performance, with its appeals to imagination and identification, is a particularly apt venue through which to think the mechanisms by which diaspora communities construct a sense of themselves as part of an ethno-national group (Butler). Given my disciplinary training, I turn to a set of exemplary dramatic texts: Dennis Scott's *An Echo in the Bone*, Ama Ata Aidoo's *Dilemma of a Ghost*, and Wole Soyinka's *The Beatification of Area Boy*. Chosen in part in order to disrupt the American-centered genealogy offered earlier, these plays require a critical methodology familiar to the field of Theater Studies, for a scholar, director, or designer would conduct biographical, historical, political, social, and anthropological research as part of an attempt to specify and make palpable the world of the play. But as will become apparent in the discussion, ethnographic research, in particular, will introduce a different worldview and conception of theater beyond the ocular-centrism, linearity, and narrative closure characteristic of much of Western drama. These dramas theorize diaspora through their very construction. In their rehearsal, production, and performance, they possibly enact a diaspora consciousness for actors, production teams, and spectators. In their circulation to other locations in the African diaspora, they also engage issues of cultural translation and (mis)recognition, raising in a different register issues central to a diaspora sensibility.

Set in 1930s Jamaica and premiered in 1974, Dennis Scott's *An Echo in the Bone* revolves around remembrance of the dead. Through the enactment of a wake or nine-nights ceremony, rooted in Afro-Christian religions like Kumina and myalism, Scott takes what might otherwise be a sordid tale of a drunk peasant killing an influential community member and transforms it into a larger universe extending back to the slave trade. Through drumming, song, and "magical" transformation, the play performs memory such that the histories of an individual, a village community, and a larger collective of West Africans and English are made palpable. In reenacting history, these characters also have the opportunity to restructure their relationships to each other, to remember differently, so that the dead can be settled or buried properly and the community can move forward with a greater appreciation not only of its tensions but also of its possibilities for healing. Significantly, the fictive community of the written drama moves toward a better understanding of itself and resolves some of its animosities. But I suspect that in performance, the text may remain more open; that is, depending on the actors' skill in rendering nuance, audience members may be struck by the struggle and fragility with which this move toward a "blessing" is achieved.

Openness of the question performed is also characteristic of Ama Ata Aidoo's *Dilemma of a Ghost*. Written in 1965, the play centers around the return of Ato Yawson from the United States, where he has gone for a university education. Accompanying him home to the Cape Coast area of Ghana is Eulalie Rush, an African American woman whom Ato has married without his family's knowledge. Here the diaspora has returned making claims for inclusion. In the shadow of the slave castles, the Yawson clan and, by extension, Ghana as one of the first newly independent African nations must discern relationships between past, present, and future; it must ascertain how disparate histories and forgotten memories can be molded to forge Nkrumah's Pan-Africanism.[8] Aidoo signals her answer in labeling and structuring the play as a dilemma tale, a traditional African genre in which discussion of problems—enacting a public sphere—is more important than conclusions arrived at (Odamtten 18–21). Obviously, the conclusions that any audience may proffer are contingent, for with another performance, another group of spectators may settle upon a different set of conclusions—or fail to come to consensus—regarding who is the ghost or how claims from the past are to be resolved in the present. What is enacted, then, both onstage and in the auditorium is the labor through which a group of people may come to experience themselves as community. As tourism between Ghana and the United States has increased, *The Dilemma of a Ghost* has achieved some measure of visibility on American college campuses, suggesting that in reading and performing the text, students are working through some of the central questions of diaspora, namely, how to build affective bonds within the context of historical differences.

The circulation of Soyinka's *Beatification of Area Boy* brings to the fore another salient issue related to diaspora, namely, the potential for misrecognition (as well as for identification) among various diaspora communities. In addition, its production history raises questions concerning the possible insignificance of race as a point of identification. Targeted for a Nigerian audience, *Beatification* rehearsals began in Nigeria in 1994. But when military dictator Sani Abacha ordered Soyinka detained, the project was aborted, and Soyinka fled into exile. The play premiered as part of the Africa '95 Festival in Leeds, England, where Soyinka and a number of other prominent African theater scholars and practitioners schooled. In

October 1996, the play received a one-week performance run at the Majestic Theater in Brooklyn's Academy of Music, and between the 1996/97 and 1997/98 seasons, it was produced in Kingston, Jamaica, by a community theater group known as The Company Ltd, for which Sheila Graham is artistic director.

When this play about the corruption and moral depravity of the Nigerian elite opened in England, the Nigerian government had, only hours earlier, issued a death sentence against writer-activist Ken Saro-Wiwa and his colleagues, the Ogoni 9, who were protesting the exploitation of oil resources in their area by the Royal Dutch/Shell Company and the Nigerian government. During the run of the play, the Ogoni 9 were executed. For a sympathetic English audience the performance had the feel of eavesdropping on a passionate political conversation among Nigerians (Gibbs).[9] Because of their own social realities, the English audience remained at a distance, unable to properly calibrate certain textual elements. For example, in constructing Sanda as an articulate university drop-out who has learned that he can earn more as security guard, extorting money from the rich to "protect" them from his thievery, Soyinka is critiquing a society that can offer its young no meaningful future. Sanda's function as a vocal critic of a blighted nation read loudly in Leeds, but in Nigeria (and in Jamaica, too) audiences would have filtered that interpretation through an embodied social lens. They have experienced area boys who must be paid to provide safe passage from the car to the shop or to guard one's car from vandalism. A history of thuggery and manipulation, projected onto the bodies of actors playing these characters, would in Lagos or Kingston have remained visible throughout, thereby complicating audience sympathy with Sanda's social critique.

Production reviews document the potential for misrecognition that obtains with the circulation of cultural texts. The New York production received two reviews, one in *Slate.com*, an online newspaper, the other in the academically oriented *Theatre Journal* (Malcolmson; Halm). Significantly, the black-oriented *Amsterdam News* did not review the production.[10] The online reviewer saw Brooklyn as an awkward venue for the production, because in his mind, the play was clearly intended for a Nigerian audience. Apparently, issues of economic deprivation, or a continuum of thievery from the small criminal to the richest and most powerful, were not issues of perceived relevance to an American audience. For both reviewers, the production became more of a comedy whose theatrical mix of music, dance, spectacle, and supernatural stories about missing organs was "infectious" and entertaining.

In Jamaica, the play's "meaning" changed yet again; that is, audiences read performances through their particular cultural realities. Given a populace terrorized by heavily armed neighborhood garrisons of youth who control residents' movements, distribute resources such as schooling opportunities, medical care, or jobs, and sell neighborhood allegiance to competing political parties, artistic director Sheila Graham and her production team saw the Nigerian text as dramatizing state-sponsored violence and its invidious impact on young people (Amkpa). Collaborating with Soyinka, Graham's The Company Ltd. produced not only *Beatification* but also a Theater for Development project in which teens expressed their views about violence and began to build connections between warring neighborhoods.[11] Clearly, in this setting, diasporans understood themselves as sharing with continental Africans similar, diminished life chances, inherited from slavery and colonialism, and maintained by the alienation and corruptibility of their national elites and their nations' dependant status within a world economic order. Theater artists and audiences may have enacted a consciousness of themselves as an ethno-transnational group, thereby satisfying one of the criteria most scholars identify as central to the concept of a diaspora (Butler 192). But they may have additionally—or primarily—identified around their post/neo-colonial status as hard pressed residents of the Third World. This latter reading, where race does and does not matter, where it is present, operative, and superseded by capitalist forces, offers a significant challenge to those of us conditioned by racialized minority status to insist upon the saliency of "blackness" (Zeleza 63). It recalls Stuart Hall's analysis of the concept of articulation and demands that rather than taking comfort in some ideal of essential sameness, we confront instead relations of "difference within unity" (Hall qtd in Edwards 59). And it challenges us to think "beyond diaspora toward black globality" constituted by embeddedness in processes and movements, like industrialization or Marxism, that are not exclusively black (Patterson and Kelley 24–28).

These three dramatic texts challenge audiences to confront questions central to diaspora and, indeed, to human sociality more generally, namely, to examine the bases upon which a sense of community is built. In their appeals for identification, these texts demand that spectators/readers scrutinize similarity/difference, recognize mediation and reinvention inherent in representation, and develop "diaspora literacy" (Clark). The paradox of performance offers instruction in how to make sense of the world. Performance is fleeting: no gesture can ever be repeated exactly; our actions and responses are always contingent, determined by specific conditions operative at a given point in time and subject to revision at some later point. Yet performance is enduring: "people learn through participation" (J. Jones), and performance produces knowledge sedimented in the body and passed intergenerationally, such that the performer's body becomes an archive of history and memory (Taylor). As a site of mnemonic reserves, performance has been the mechanism of countermemories, through which African diaspora peoples have nurtured a sense of themselves in the face of dominant practices bent on dehumanizing them (Roach 26).

But performance also carries with it the risk of misrecognitions. A skillful or artistic performer offers an invitation to experience this ar-

chive in a compelling manner that affectively diminishes the distance
between past and present or between on- and offstage realities. We as
spectators may be so moved by the performer's technique and aura, along
with the other semiotic systems of lighting, sound, costuming, and sets,
that for the duration of the event, we identify with the characters or emo-
tionally enter the fictive world engaging our senses to the extent that we
forget to question how this representation has been constructed, how it is
both similar and different from the world we know.[12] Although the ma-
teriality of the actors' bodies in space may preclude complete identification, performance nonetheless—whether on the formal stage, in the museum, or on a tourist visit to another diaspora location—often adopts a
"you are there" approach (J. Jones 8) that occludes the fact that representation is always already mediated and in service to a particular agenda.
Away from the visual "interference" of the actors' bodies and reflecting
upon the collective affect of the performance event, we may produce a discourse in which we consume the narrative, projecting our own concerns
onto the performance text (Boler).[13] We have forgotten that interpretation
insinuates the necessity of acknowledging and calibrating the various,
meaning-producing locations—of the text itself, its onstage interpreters,
institutional venue, other spectators, and ourselves—converging in the
performance event and shaping understanding (Knowles).

In order to locate the text, its onstage interpreters, and often other
spectators, we must deploy what Vèvè Clark terms a "diaspora literacy"
but what can also be considered simply cultural literacy, for it is an interpretive strategy cultivated through "a knowledge of historical, social, cultural, and political development generated by lived and textual experience" (42). Using this literacy, we reflect upon how this representation
may be like and not like what we already know and feel. Ideally, we undertake the "discomfort" of naming and working through our own emotional,
intellectual, political, or social investments that cause us to identify with
(or resist) what we have experienced in performance.[14] Megan Boler's comments about the identificatory demands of written texts are equally pertinent to performance, as experienced in artistic materials and/or everyday
encounters:

> I must learn to question the genealogy of any particular emotional response.
> My scorn, my evaluation of others' behavior as good or bad, my irritation—
> each provides a site for interrogation of how the text challenges my invest-
> ments in familiar cultural values. As I examine the history of a particular
> emotion, I can identify the taken-for-granted social values and structures
> of my own historical moment which mirror those encountered by the pro-
> tagonist. Testimonial reading pushes us to recognize that a novel or biog-
> raphy reflects not only a distant other, but analogous social relations in our
> own environment, in which our economic and social positions are impli-
> cated. (170)

Having performed this homework, so to speak, we come face to face with questions such as: How with a changing sense of self and other can we perceive affinity? What obligations does that perception impose upon us for action in the world in which we and the other live?

The very titles of two of these exemplary texts, *Echo in the Bone* and *Dilemma of a Ghost*, suggest productive stances we may adopt in practicing diaspora. Although culture is transmitted intergenerationally, often within familial and other tightly knit circles, and thus may feel natural or biological and pleasurable, an echo is a distortion of the original sound, and bone is a dense medium that further changes what is passed to a younger generation. Hence the importance of a diaspora literacy that can locate the object of study and ourselves in the proper material contexts and account for the re-inventions of history and memory that may have transpired. As Avery Gordon has argued, the ghost is a social figure that haunts, demanding that what was forgotten, dismissed, or erased be reckoned with (8). It disrupts and makes impossible the life we have known. The ghost presses its insistent claims and poses a question from which it will not allow retreat: How do we as individuals, inextricably linked to social networks, act responsibly to a past, present, and future? In answering the ghost, we practice *sankofa*. A visual symbol used by the Asante people to represent the injunction "go back and fetch it" (Agbo 4; Quarcoo 17), sankofa is most often drawn as a bird whose body is poised in one direction, while its head is facing the opposite direction. Presumably this bird, momentarily arrested from flight, is surveying its past and deciding what it will need for the impending journey. Similar to Jonathan Arac's "critical genealogy," which "aims to excavate the past that is necessary to account for how we got here and the past that is useful for conceiving alternatives to our present condition" (qtd in Roach 25), the sankofa principle challenges us to critical self-reflection: Where are we standing? How did we come to be there? How has this "we" been constituted? Toward what future does this "we" or a newly (re)constituted collectivity want to move? How does, or should, that future articulate with our past(s)?

ROADS TOWARD THE FUTURE?

In our varied passages into what has become the African diaspora, so much has had to be silenced or suppressed, so many ghosts demand our attention. How are we to respond? The obvious and general answer is that we approach our task with an intellectual rigor and commitment to a diaspora literacy that is steeped in the histories, languages, and literatures of the circuitry of encounter and exchange. While considerable scholarship has focused on the diaspora in the circum-Atlantic, researchers like Joseph Harris, Paul Zeleza, Edward Alpers, John Hunwick, Tiffany Patterson, and Robin Kelley remind us that this diaspora also includes encounters with people around the Indian Ocean, in Asia, and throughout the Middle East. In terms of its geographical and historical spread, certainly the African diaspora as an object of study is huge. Students and administrators worried about course enrollments are likely to object that other areas of study do not demand such breadth of focus or mastery from its majors.

The response to these concerns is twofold. First, it should be noted that because we live in a world where the pace and consequences of global interconnections have intensified tremendously, no matter what our disciplinary backgrounds, we are all under the imperative to "think globally and act locally." While we must know the histories of the locales in which we reside and from which we partially draw a sense of identity, we must also recognize that this small collectivity is inextricably embedded in larger networks of signification and exchange. To our students and colleagues in other fields, we must argue the value of global, transnational, interdisciplinary perspectives because the negative consequences of proceeding along the old, insulated roadways are prohibitive.

Second, we must advocate the importance of collaborative research and comparative scholarship, wherein scholars expert in a specific area— region, gender, historical period, ideological movement, or theoretical approach, for example—share their findings, interrogate each other, and produce interdisciplinary, co-authored texts that, while rich and capacious, acknowledge the necessarily partial and contingent nature of their research. These texts might be thought of as the intellectual equivalent of black women's multiply patterned quilts with diverse, competitive, and sometimes contradictory energies juxtaposed and fashioned into one piece that provides sustenance and comfort for persons who must rise and enact a new day (Wahlman). African diaspora research units and academic departments could institute interdisciplinary workshops or projects where this collaborative research can be pursued and modeled as an appropriate methodology for the field.

For us in African Diaspora Studies especially, Africa must be re-inserted into our practices, not as an undifferentiated, mythologized point of origin confined to some temporality markedly distinct from our global North present and future. Rather, we need regard Africa as a continent of historical as well as contemporary specificities that link to our fates. As scholars and/or as people of African descent, we are inheritors of racialized discourses that continue to enable exploitation and dehumanization; we are also inheritors of the unfinished projects of Pan-Africanism, a paradigm that envisioned agency and livability for transnational communities suffering from slavery, colonialism, and imperialism. We do not escape our dual inheritance by concentrating solely on the circulation of cultural artifacts, people, and ideas outside continental Africa. In fact, by studying Africa in its linguistic, cultural, political, social, and historical diversity, we practice better sankofa. We will know more about what is circulating, both historically and at present, we will know more about what peoples have chosen to bring along—or discard—on their journeys, and we will be better equipped to recognize multiple and sometimes overlapping diasporas existing, historically as well as contemporarily, under the umbrella term "the African diaspora."

The space where Theater Studies and African Diaspora Studies meet can be particularly productive for performers, researchers, and members of the general public. "If people are genuinely interested in understanding culture, they must put aspects of that culture on and into their bodies," says performance artist-scholar Joni Jones (7). Certainly, that is the task of the actor, to "tireless[ly] strive for the physical details that make up cultures" (J. Jones 14), understanding that culture is not geographically bound but circulates and changes in the course of its travel. As stated earlier, in so doing, the performer's body becomes an archive of history and memory. But, of course, not all aspects of an event—particularly the subjectivities embedded in that occurrence—will be captured in the written record or kinesthetic archive and repertoires of the body that the theater practitioner studies. Here, theater-makers will need memory's powerful, imaginative capacity to fashion what might have been and what can now be, all the while listening attentively to their own responses, scrupulously tracking their sense of the I/not I dynamic central to the assumption of character and performance. They will need to note in that discrepancy between self and other the destabilizing gift or "counsel" (Walter Benjamin qtd in Simon) that the social figure of the ghost extends about the world we, theater practitioners and audiences, inhabit. Obviously, the formal performance will not aim for closure. Rather, as with texts discussed above or with Jones's own performance piece *Searching for Osun*, it will seek critical reflexivity, thereby inviting audience members to move from a passive spectatorship to a responsive/able witnessing. In seeking to offer audiences questions rather than answers, performance practitioners may seem to be denying people, who are the marked inheritors of race-based oppressions, the very impulse that has prompted their construction of a diaspora sensibility, namely, the pleasures of psychic fulfillment of desires for home. Our production work and research need to be respectful of these desires (J. Jones 12) while nonetheless striving to offer a compelling but different concept of "home": no longer the idealized site of familial unity and stability, but a space of love and of struggle, a space of change (like all of life), a space of committed reflexiveness and responsibility where our perceptions and apprehensions of identity/difference may enable us to imagine and practice a more expansive and just sense of home or community that is necessarily embedded in networks of other cultural homes. In fact, models of such "homes" are already before us, for as Patterson and Kelley argue, "Africa—real or imagined—is not the only source of 'black' internationalism, even for those movements that embrace a nationalist or pan-Africanist rhetoric" (32). International socialism, Third World solidarity, or women's peace movements, for example, have all been locations from which black peoples pursued freedom and justice.

As is evident from these comments, African Diaspora Studies is just one paradigm through which to confront the larger questions of social justice and livability that "we" want for our future. The junction or crossroads have typically been a site of possibilities: of arrivals and departures, endings and beginnings, anxiety and adventure, commerce and conviviality, separation and union. The 1960s Motown hit tune "Function at the Junction," while bearing the painful imprint of racial stereotyping and cold war imperialism, also conjured up a dynamic spot in which various cultural practices came together in seemingly inconceivable combinations to party and enjoy each other's company.[15] Certainly, the function at the junction of African Diaspora Studies and Theater Studies is also marked by a history of exclusions and conflicts. Nonetheless, it is a potent space in and from which to practice, research, play, and labor for conditions that allow us to experience ourselves most fully as members of distinct and inextricably linked human communities.

NOTES

1. Here I am relying upon Michel de Certeau's distinctions between place as the site of the official or proper, and space as produced by the operations upon it from multiple sectors, interventions, or agents; similarly, while a map provides a "plane projection totalizing operations," an itinerary offers stories concerning conditions of possibilities (117–22).

2. Not only does Conquergood analyze the prominence of black abolitionists on the lecture circuit in "Rethinking Elocution," but he also argues provocatively for a dialectical tension between the contemporaneous performance genres of elocution and minstrelsy.

3. It's important to note that departments and individuals must self-report, so that these statistics are an approximate representation of research now underway.

4. This total does not include the sixty short essays on the American flag in the Winter 2001 issue. *Callaloo*'s twenty-fifth anniversary issue (24.4, Fall 2001) included not a single article on drama or performance; furthermore, the previous two issues of that year focused on the "best" poetry and prose published by the journal, but seemingly it had not accumulated a sufficient number of "best" essays to warrant a special section on performance.

5. Although Olaniyan discusses Afrocentricity (see the next section of this essay) and its post, a check of the index reveals that he himself does not deploy the term "diaspora."

6. See, for example, Helen Gilbert and Joanne Tompkins, who examine cultural production in such settler colonies as Canada and Australia but decline to adopt an analogous conceptualization of the United States.

7. Note that Harrison launches his critique specifically against realism, the genre most favored by American playwrights. In so doing, he ignores twentieth-century European avant-garde artists like Antonin Artaud, who also conceptual-

ized theater in affective, semispiritual terms (*Theater and Its Double*). The omission of Artaud is indicative of the discourse of racial purity typical of the period, for inspired by Balinese theater, Artaud articulated theater as a plague that would cleanse audiences, an idea that Amiri Baraka (then LeRoi Jones) would virtually repeat—without acknowledgment—in calling for a theater of victims in his "Revolutionary Theater" essay.

8. My use of the seeming oxymoron "forgotten memories" is deliberate because I want to signal how forgetting—conscious or unconscious—is constitutive of what is remembered. See Kirmayer; Simon.

9. See also Larson. Nigeria would, in fact, be suspended from the Commonwealth.

10. The newspaper had published, however, an article about Soyinka's Harvard University lecture series, which would culminate in his book *The Burden of Memory, the Muse of Forgiveness*. See "Soyinka, Exiled Nigerian Nobel Laureate."

11. Soyinka, in writing about his experiences working on this play in Jamaica, comments that the youth's passionate embrace of the arts as a vehicle of social critique and self-creation recalled for him the heady period in which he established his first theater, Orisun in Nigeria ("Ghetto"; "Letter").

12. Indeed, performance's ability to seduce spectators into accepting an illusion as equally, if not more, compelling than their actual reality is at the heart of the West's centuries-long distrust of theater and drama. See, for example, Barish.

13. Such displacement often occurs during the performance of tourism to slave sites. See Richards ("Who," 495–96).

14. On discomfort, see Boler. On the question of our own investments, see Simon's discussion in *The Touch of the Past* of the "double attentiveness" that listening requires.

15. With lyrics by Eddie Holland and Shorty Long, "Function at the Junction" imagined a raucous party: "We got Ling Ting Tong from China / Long Tall Sally from Carolina / We got 007, the private eye, / And he's bringin' all the guys from *I Spy*. . . / We serving egg foo yung and barbecue / We got chicken dumplings and kidney stew / We gonna make big fun till the break of dawn."

REFERENCES

Agbo, Agbo. *Values of Adrinka Symbols*. Kumasi: Ebony Designs and Publications, 1999.

Aidoo, Ama Ata. *Dilemma of a Ghost and Anowa*. Longman African Writers. New York: Longman, 1995.

Alpers, Edward A. "Recollecting Africa: Diasporic Memory in the Indian Ocean." *African Studies Review* 43.1 (April 2000): 83–99.

Amkpa, Awam, dir. *It's All About Downtown*. Five Colleges Incorporated/Mt. Holyoke College, 1997. Video.

Artaud, Antonin. *The Theater and Its Double*. Trans. Victor Corti. London: Calder and Boyars, 1974.

Auslander, Philip. "Postmodernism and Performance." In Steven Connor, ed., *Cambridge Companion to Postmodernism*. Cambridge: Cambridge University Press, 2004.

Barish, Jonas A. *The Antitheatrical Prejudice*. Berkeley: University of California Press, 1981.

Bharucha, Rustom. *The Politics of Cultural Practice: Thinking through Theater in an Age of Globalization.* Hanover, N.H.: Wesleyan University Press, University Press of New England, 2000.

———. *Theater and the World: Essays on Performance and the Politics of Culture.* New Delhi: Manohar, 1992.

Boler, Megan. *Feeling Power: Emotions and Education.* New York: Routledge, 1999.

Boon, Richard, and Jane Plastow, eds. *Theater and Empowerment: Community Drama on the World Stage.* London: Routledge, 1996.

Butler, Kim D. "Defining Diaspora, Refining a Discourse." *Diaspora* 10.2 (2001): 189–219.

Clark, Vèvè. "Developing Diaspora Literacy and *Marasa* Consciousness." In Hortense Spillers, ed., *Comparative American Identities: Race, Sex, and Nationality in the Modern Text,* 40–61. New York: Routledge, 1991.

Conquergood, Dwight. "Rethinking Elocution: The Trope of the Talking Book and Other Figures of Speech." In Judith Hamera, ed., *Opening Acts: Performance in/as Communication and Cultural Studies,* 141–62. Thousand Oaks: Sage Publications, 2006.

———. "Of Caravans and Carnivals: Performance Studies in Motion." *TDR* 39.4 (Winter 1995): 137–42.

de Certeau, Michel. *The Practice of Everyday Life.* Trans. Steven Rendell. Berkeley: University of California Press, 1984.

Edwards, Brent Hayes. "The Uses of Diaspora." *Social Text* 19.1 (2001): 45–73. Rpt. in Genevieve Fabre and Klaus Benesch, eds., *African Diasporas in the New and Old Worlds: Consciousness and Imagination,* 3–38. Amsterdam: Rodopi, 2004.

Euba, Femi. *Archetypes, Imprecators, and Victims of Fate: Origins and Developments of Satire in Black Drama.* New York: Greenwood Press, 1989.

Gayle, Addison, comp. *The Black Aesthetic.* Garden City, N.J.: Doubleday, 1971.

Gibbs, James. "Not Lagos but Leeds." *African Quarterly on the Arts* 1.4 (1996): 50–54.

Gilbert, Helen, and Joanne Tompkins. *Post-colonial Drama: Theory, Practice, Politics.* London: Routledge, 1996.

Gilroy, Paul. *The Black Atlantic: Modernity and Double Consciousness.* Cambridge: Harvard University Press, 1993.

Gordon, Avery. *Ghostly Matters: Haunting and the Sociological Imagination.* Minneapolis: University of Minnesota Press, 1997.

Halm, Ben B. Review of *The Beatification of Area Boy,* by Wole Soyinka. West Yorkshire Playhouse. Brooklyn Academy of Music. 9 October 1996.

Harris, Joseph E. *The African Presence in Asia: Consequences of the East African Slave Trade.* Evanston, Ill.: Northwestern University Press, 1971.

Harrison, Paul Carter. *Drama of Nommo.* New York: Grove Press, 1972.

———, ed. *Kuntu Drama: Plays of the African Continuum.* New York: Grove Press, 1974.

———, ed. *Totem Voices: Plays from the Black World Repertory.* New York: Grove Press, 1989.

Harrison, Paul Carter, Victor Leo Walker II, and Gus Edwards, eds. *Black Theatre: Ritual Performance in the African Diaspora.* Philadelphia: Temple University Press, 2002.

Holland, Eddie, and Frederick "Shorty" Long. "Function at the Junction." *Motown Hitsville USA*. Vol. 1, disc 2. Accessed at http://lyricsplayground.com/alpha/songs/f/functionatthejunction.shtml.

Holloway, Joseph E. *Africanisms in American Culture*. Bloomington: Indiana University Press, 1990.

Hunwick, John. "Black Africans in the Islamic World: An Understudied Dimension of the Black Diaspora." In Howard University Black Diaspora Committee, eds., *The African Diaspora: Africans and Their Descendants in the Wider World to 1800*, 63–77. Needham Heights, Mass.: Ginn Press, 1989.

Hunwick, John, and Eve Troutt Powell. *The African Diaspora in the Mediterranean Lands of Islam*. Princeton, N.J.: Markus Wiener, 2002.

Jackson, Shannon. *Professing Performance: Theater in the Academy, from Philology to Performativity*. Cambridge: Cambridge University Press, 2004.

Jeyifo, Biodun. "The Reinvention of Theatrical Tradition: Critical Discourses on Interculturalism in the African Theater." In Patrice Pavis, ed., *The Intercultural Performance Reader*, 149–61. London: Routledge, 1996.

Johnson, E. Patrick. "Black Performance Studies: Genealogies, Politics, Futures." In Soyini Madison and Judith Hamera, eds., *The Sage Handbook of Performance Studies*, 446–63. Thousand Oaks: Sage Publications, 2006.

Jones, Joni L. "Performance Ethnography: The Role of Embodiment in Cultural Authenticity." *Theater Topics* 12.1 (2002): 1–15.

Jones, LeRoi. "The Revolutionary Theater." In *Home: Social Essays*, 210–15. New York: William Morrow, 1966.

Jones, LeRoi, and Larry Neal, eds. *Black Fire: An Anthology of Afro-American Writing*. New York: William Morrow, 1968.

Kirmayer, Laurence J. "Landscapes of Memory: Trauma, Narrative, and Dissociation." In Paul Antze and Michael Lambek, eds., *Tense Past: Cultural Essays in Trauma and Memory*, 173–98. New York: Routledge, 1996.

Knowles, Ric. *Reading the Material Theater*. Cambridge: Cambridge University Press, 2004.

Larson, Charles R. Review of *The Beatification of Area Boy* by Wole Soyinka. *Nation*, 27 May 1996, 31–34.

Madison, D. Soyini, and Judith Hamera, eds. *The Sage Handbook of Performance Studies*. Thousand Oaks: Sage Publications, 2006.

Malcolmson, Scott L. "State of the Bully." Posted on *Slate* 23 October 1996. http://slate.msn.com/id/3316.

McAuley, Gay. *Space in Performance: Making Meaning in Theater*. Ann Arbor: University of Michigan Press, 1999.

Molette, Carlton W., and Barbara J. Molette. *Black Theater: Premise and Presentation*. Bristol, Ind.: Wyndham Hall Press, 1986.

Neal, Larry. *Visions of a Liberated Future: Black Arts Movement Writings*. New York: Thunder's Mouth Press, 1989.

Odamtten, Vincent. *The Art of Ama Ata Aidoo: Polylectics and Reading against Colonialism*. Gainesville: University Press of Florida, 1994.

Okpewho, Isidore, Carole Boyce Davies, and Ali A. Mazrui, eds. *The African Diaspora: African Origins and New World Identities*. Bloomington: Indiana University Press, 1999.

Olaniyan, Tejumola. *Scars of Conquest/Masks of Resistance: The Invention of*

Cultural Identities in African, African-American, and Caribbean Drama. New York: Oxford University Press, 1995.

Patterson, Tiffany Ruby, and Robin D. G. Kelley. "Unfinished Migrations: Reflections on the African Diaspora and the Making of the Modern World." *African Studies Review* 43.1 (April 2000): 11–45.

Quarcoo, Alfred. *The Language of Adrinka Symbols.* Legon: Sebewie Ventures, 1994.

Rahier, Jean Muteba, ed. *Representations of Blackness and the Performance of Identities.* Westport, Conn.: Bergin and Garvey, 1999.

Richards, Sandra L. "Who Is This Ancestor? Performing Memory in Ghana's Slave Castle-Dungeons (A Multimedia Performance Meditation)." In Soyini Madison and Judith Hamera, eds., *The Sage Handbook of Performance Studies,* 489–507. Thousand Oaks: Sage Publications, 2006.

Roach, Joseph. "Deep Skin: Reconstructing Congo Square." In Harry J. Elam Jr. and David Krasner, eds., *African American Performance and Theater History,* 101–13. New York: Oxford University Press, 2001.

Scott, Dennis. *An Echo in the Bone.* In Errol Hill, ed., *Plays for Today,* 73–137. Harlow: Longman, 1985.

"Shorty Long." http://www.answers.com/topic/shorty-long.

Simon, Roger I. *The Touch of the Past: Remembrance, Learning, and Ethics.* New York: Macmillan Palgrave, 2005.

"Soyinka, Exiled Nigerian Nobel Laureate, to Deliver Lecture." *Amsterdam News,* 19 April 1997, 2.

Soyinka, Wole. *The Beatification of Area Boy, a Lagosian Kaleidoscope.* London: Methuen Drama, 1995.

———. *The Burden of Memory, the Muse of Forgiveness.* New York: Oxford University Press, 1999.

———. "Foreword: A Letter from Kingston." In Richard Boon and Jane Plastow, eds., *Theater Matters: Performance and Culture on the World Stage,* xi–xviii. Cambridge: Cambridge University Press, 1998.

———. "From Ghetto to Garrison: A Chronic Case of *Orisunitis.*" *Research in African Literatures* 30.4 (Winter 1999): 6–23.

Taylor, Diana. *The Archive and the Repertoire: Performing Cultural Memory in the Americas.* Durham, N.C.: Duke University Press, 2003.

Wahlman, Maude Southwell. *Signs and Symbols: African Images in African-American Quilts.* New York: Studio Books in association with Museum of American Folk Art, 1993.

Walker, Sheila S., ed. *African Roots/American Cultures: Africa in the Creation of the Americas.* Lanham, Md.: Rowman and Littlefield, 2001.

Welsh-Asante, Kariamu. *The African Aesthetic: Keeper of Traditions.* Westport, Conn.: Greenwood Press, 1993.

Zeleza, Paul Tiyambe. "Rewriting the African Diaspora: Beyond the Black Atlantic." *African Affairs* 104.414 (2005): 35–68.

10 ETHNOMUSICOLOGY AND THE AFRICAN DIASPORA

Melvin L. Butler

E thnomusicologists seldom fit comfortably within disciplinary boxes. Like music making in the African diaspora, the practice of ethnomusicology seems always to push beyond academic boundaries almost as soon as they are constructed. While it is true that departments of Music are the principal academic homes for those who study music as cultural practice, many scholars choose to borrow heavily from, or even work within, Anthropology, Media Studies, Performance Studies, and other areas. Even those operating under the same disciplinary label debate some deceptively complicated questions: What is the proper definition of "music"? What methods and approaches are best suited to the study of music in Africa and its diaspora? And to what extent, if at all, can musical texts be analyzed apart from the contexts of their performance? Since John Blacking's (1973) influential assertion that music is "humanly organized sound," there have been countless attempts to rethink this definition and the ways in which music should best be described, analyzed, and represented in scholarly texts. The gerund *musicking* (Small 1998), a term that demolishes conceptions of music as a "thing" to be analyzed on a score, is particularly helpful to ethnomusicologists who study African and African diasporic communities in which music and dance are inextricably linked to a broad constellation of social practices and values. Indeed, the inseparability of music making and everyday life lends ethnomusicology a particular salience in the study of African-derived peoples.

In the pages that follow, I survey some of the major issues and themes in ethnomusicology as they relate specifically to research on Africa and its diaspora. My goal is to convey a sense of how ethnomusicologists have conceptualized the African diaspora, explain some of the major theories and paradigms that have shaped their work, and provide a sampling of work by some influential Africanist, African Americanist, and Caribbeanist music scholars. My conclusion offers some lingering questions and concerns, as I discuss some of the challenges awaiting new ethnomusicological research on the African diaspora. I recognize that one of ethnomusicology's distinguishing features is, as Neuman suggests, the "constant challenging of canons" resulting in a "heterogeneity of tales" (Neuman 1991, 272). This heterogeneity is no doubt related to the vastness of the African diaspora and the richness of its musical products. As this essay suggests, creative musical differences within the African diaspora may parallel the diverse subject positions of ethnomusicologists. Scholars who increasingly write from home bases outside of North America and Europe bring a variety of cultural perspectives to bear on our field.[1]

ETHNOMUSICOLOGICAL FOUNDATIONS

When the Society for Ethnomusicology was launched in 1955 "to promote the research, study, and performance of music in all historical periods and cultural contexts,"[2] its founders clearly envisioned research on Africa and its diaspora as one of the organization's most important endeavors. Just two years prior, a trio of scholars—Willard Rhodes, David McAllester, and Alan Merriam—had gathered at the meeting of the American Anthropological Association in Philadelphia to brainstorm about a newsletter that would keep likeminded scholars abreast of happenings in the new field of ethnomusicology. Describing Merriam as "a spirited young man who had just returned from his first field trip in Africa," Rhodes reflects on the influential role this trio would have on the development of ethnomusicology into a full-fledged discipline. Of the three, only Rhodes was a professor of Music; McAllester and Merriam taught in the Anthropology departments of Wesleyan University and Northwestern University, respectively.[3] This interdisciplinary foundation, especially an affinity toward anthropological theories and methods, undoubtedly shaped the approach subsequent researchers would take to studying musical practices of the African diaspora.

Bruno Nettl, one of ethnomusicology's iconic figures, has provided three definitions of ethnomusicology: "the comparative study of musical systems and cultures; the study of music in or as culture; the study of a musical culture from an outsider's perspective." Nettl adds that despite his own relatively flexible definition of the field, few "ethnomusicological" studies have actually focused on music from the Western classical tradition (Nettl 1989, 1). Rather, ethnomusicologists have tended to conduct fieldwork in the more "exotic" locales outside of Western Europe, where "world music" styles are found. The term *world music* has been a common source of criticism (e.g., Feld 1994); its nagging presence in the Western academy is perhaps due to the ease with which it connotes otherness, particularly for some undergraduates thirsting for exposure to "different" genres of music. But this practical division of "the West" from "the rest" is also understood to be deeply troubling. Over the past few decades, music scholars have grown increasingly suspicious of the notion that African derived music is intellectually relevant only as the cultural expression of a monolithic, ethnic Other.

Major research universities often structure ethnomusicological curricula in remarkably different ways. A growing number of North American universities are offering less traditional approaches to the study of musical practice. At the University of Virginia, where I taught from 2005 to 2008, the Music Department's program in Critical and Comparative Studies encourages graduate students "to develop interdisciplinary perspectives on music and musical culture." Unlike schools or departments of Music in which graduate students choose a course of study corresponding to either an ethnomusicology or musicology track, the University of Virginia's Music Department seeks "to transcend boundaries between 'musicology' and 'ethnomusicology,' looking toward a transdisciplinary study of musical life." Several universities maintain disciplinary labels but require students to engage an assortment of theoretical viewpoints from outside of ethnomusicology. Such is the case at my current institution, the University of Chicago, where two of the four full-time ethnomusicology professors specialize in African diasporic musics. Graduate students and faculty embrace theory as a vital thread that connects scholars and inspires conversations within the Music Department and across the University. The University of Pennsylvania offers its ethnomusicology curricula through an Anthropology of Music program that "reflects the interdisciplinary nature of ethnomusicology, combining approaches from anthropology, musicology, folklore, literary theory, religious studies, linguistics, critical theory, and gender studies in order to interrogate the cultural webs of meaning within which music resonates."[4] While ethnomusicology's boundaries are fluid, many contend that it persists as a distinct area of study with its own set of approaches to understanding the diversity of the world's musics. UCLA even boasts a Department of Ethnomusicology, unlike most institutions in which a relatively small graduate program in ethnomusicology is offered only under the auspices of a larger Department or School of Music. Nevertheless, I believe that text-based approaches to music scholarship are hegemonic in the vast majority of European and North American universities. Moreover, a musicology-ethnomusicology dichotomy continues to inform the thinking of most Western-educated music scholars, particularly given that most receive training in universities where graduate study in music is divided into these two discrete subdisciplines. In the twenty-first century's first decade, most "musicologists" are still expected to conduct archival research on some aspect of Western European art music. Ethnomusicologists still pick from a wider palette of geographical regions and embrace fieldwork as the *sine qua non* of their subdiscipline. Notwithstanding some significant exceptions (e.g., Agawu 2003), the musics of Africa and its diaspora, along with other forms of "world music," fall predictably under ethnomusicology's purview.

A number of major research journals provide space for music-centered research on Africa and its diaspora. The journal now known as the *Yearbook for Traditional Music* appeared in 1949, when it was originally titled *Journal of the International Folk Music Council*.[5] *Ethnomusicology* is considered the flagship publication of the discipline for which it is named, and other important publications have emerged in recent decades. For example, *Popular Music and Society* was established in 1971,[6] followed by the *Black Music Research Journal*, which first appeared in 1980.[7] While approaches to the study of the world's music cultures may vary according to the type of publication in which research is presented and in terms of the structure of programs and departments of music, there is a broad institutional consensus that ethnomusicological training must involve study across academic disciplines.

REFLECTIONS, RETENTIONS, AND REPRESENTATIONS OF AFRICA

Given the profound link between musical expression and cultural values in societies around the world, it is no surprise that music scholars have made invaluable contributions to our understandings of African and African diasporic communities. Despite the considerable amount of scholarly attention given to these communities, it is also not surprising that scholars of African descent have been noticeably underrepresented in music-centered studies and at annual meetings of the Society for Ethnomusicology. But following anthropology's lead, critical examinations of ethnomusicological work have at least called for greater reflexivity and spawned an ongoing interest in how a writer's positionality affects his or her ethnographic descriptions and analyses. Michelle Kisliuk's provocative work (1998) is particularly noteworthy in this regard, as it highlights "the interpersonal negotiations of power dynamics and epistemological grappling involved in research and writing" (13). Jean Ngoya Kidula (2006), who provides a thorough review of African music research by African-born music writers, sheds much needed light on how the latter have dealt with a legacy of music scholarship that has been transmitted largely by Europeans and North Americans. She even advocates a distinctly African brand of musicology that gives voice to musicians and scholars who have too often been ignored or underappreciated by those educated in the West.

Ghanaian music scholar and composer J. H. Kwabena Nketia is another of the numerous "native" ethnomusicologists whose perspectives on African and African diasporic music often differ from those of their

North American and European counterparts. It seems certain that his cultural background played a role in his approach to the study of the African diaspora. Reflecting on his formative experiences with ethnomusicology in the 1950s, he writes that as a young student of ethnomusicology, he was disheartened by its "narrow and somewhat ethnocentric definitions" (2005, 4). Seeking to study his own country's music from an ethnomusicological perspective, he naturally found problematic the notion of ethnomusicology as a discipline composed of scholars in the West studying music makers in the non-West. He laments that it took until at least the 1960s for ethnomusicologists to fully appreciate an African capacity to produce "simultaneous occurrences of otherwise unrelated sounds made purposely to heighten dramatic tension, to animate a performance, to add to the texture of a piece of music, or to provide signals" (Nketia 1967, 88). However, Nketia eventually discovered some redeeming qualities in ethnomusicology, and he is particularly pleased that while "other branches of musical scholarship . . . are narrowly focused on one tradition of music, ethnomusicology accepts the diverse musical cultures of the world as its subject matter" (Nketia 2005, 8). Above all, he states, it was ethnomusicology's "humanistic goals and interdisciplinary orientation that bonded [him] to it" (9). Having already completed six years of studying African music as a research fellow in the University of Ghana's Sociology Department, Nketia found himself compelled to implement a multifaceted approach to musical scholarship, and ethnomusicology was well suited to this goal. He came to see ethnomusicology as "a way of thinking about music that enables the perceptive scholar or creative individual to respond in a particular way to the challenges of his/her field context or to data presented by others" (2). Nketia's Ghanaian heritage, along with his many experiences studying and teaching ethnomusicology around the world, may very well have afforded him a certain sensitivity toward the interconnectedness of one's fieldwork site and the effective means of collecting, interpreting, and analyzing field "data." In Ghana, he met Melville Herskovits, who mentored Nketia as he engaged in his first bit of African diasporic ethnographic research. Through his contact with African Americans, particularly his Sunday visits to Chicago's storefront churches, Nketia gained a thorough understanding of "the ethnomusicological task of the African scholar" and valuable experience that would prepare him for subsequent field trips to South America and the Caribbean (15).

The first half of the twentieth century saw some significant developments in the study of African-derived music. Ethnomusicologists born in late nineteenth-century Europe deserve much credit for putting in place theoretical and methodological paradigms that would inform subsequent research. By the 1920s, these early ethnomusicologists found that "the musics of Africa and their transformations in the New World proved to be difficult subjects of inquiry," particularly as they (mis)applied European musical terminology to African genres (Blum 1991a, 3). Often defined as the study of "people making music" (Titon 1997, 91), ethnomusicology did not clearly emerge as a distinct branch of musical scholarship until after World War II (Neuman 1991, 270). In the sociopolitical climate of the pre–World War II era, Africans and their descendents were most often deemed incapable of developing complex musical systems. The work of pioneer ethnomusicologists such as Erich Moritz von Hornbostel and George Herzog was not immune from the racist stereotypes and fantasies concerning black music making. Born in Austria, Hornbostel often drew distinctions between European and African music making. In a discussion of African rhythmic conceptions, he famously asserted, "We [Europeans] proceed from hearing, they [Africans] from motion" (1928, 53). As Blum explains, Hornbostel believed that the "primordial unity between impulses to motion and the sounds that result had in large measure vanished from the experience of Europeans, as aural and tactile perception had become separate domains" (1991a, 20). The Hungarian-born ethnomusicologist George Herzog was strongly influenced by Hornbostel's work. Herzog stressed the need to view music in relation to specific sociocultural contexts, but he believed that blacks in the United States owed little, if any, of their musical traits to an African cultural heritage (Herzog 1936, 52; McAllester 1985, 86).

Melville Herskovits's work, particularly his *Myth of the Negro Past* (1941), has influenced generations of scholars, some of whom have refined his arguments. A good example of such refinement lies in *The Birth of African-American Culture: An Anthropological Perspective*, by Sidney Mintz and Richard Price. These authors suggest that Herskovits's linking of African and Afro-American cultural traits is too direct. The African inheritance, they argue, is more accurately identified at the level of underlying structures and orientations that shape outward manifestations of musical and spiritual practice. Mintz and Price (1976, 62–65) summarize the well-known "debate" between E. Franklin Frazier and Melville Herskovits over the issue of African retentions in the Americas. Frazier (1939) saw blacks in the United States as culturally bankrupt as a result of their enslavement in the New World. A history of brutal oppression had, in his view, stripped African Americans of any realistic connection to an African past. Herskovits (1941) strongly disagreed with this view, positing instead that blacks in the Americas possessed a distinct cultural heritage and that their social institutions (e.g., marriage practices, family structures) could be linked to an identifiable African past. Responding to this debate in the 1970s, Mintz and Price settled on a more nuanced assessment of an African cultural inheritance characterized by a set of "common basic assumptions about social relations or the workings of the universe" (11).

While anthropologists have debated the issue of African retentions, the musical link between Africa and its diaspora has been one of the most prevalent themes throughout the history of ethnomusicological thought. Ethnomusicologists have now come to accept the view that "Africa has had much to do with the ways that New World Blacks have chosen to address the realities before them from the moment they emerged from the ships" (Okpewho 1999, xv). Samuel Floyd (1995) likewise asserts the relevance of African retentions, which exist insofar as "the musical *tendencies*, the mythological beliefs and assumptions, and the interpretive strategies of African Americans . . . continue to exist as African cultural memory [and] inform the continuity and elaboration of African-American music" (5). A similar assessment is made by Christopher Small (1987), who asserts that for over 500 years, black musical and bodily expressions have served as "tools by means of which [black] people . . . have struggled, and continue to struggle, to assert their own definition of themselves" (10) He adds that while African diasporic music is by no means monolithic, it is clearly distinguished by an African-derived capacity to adapt to changing circumstances and draw from new sources of creative energy. While not focused directly on musical practice per se, Joseph Murphy's work (1994) fuels ethnomusicological speculation into musical evocations of the supernatural among various diasporic spiritual communities that cohere around an African-based conception of "working the spirit."

Gerard Béhague's volume, *Music and Black Ethnicity* (1992), addresses the issue of black ethnicity in Caribbean and South American locales in which "black" ethnic groups are quite frequently in the minority. The editor points out that since there is such tremendous diversity—both of people and the terminology they use to racially self-identify—the notion of black ethnicity, along with a supposed link to Africa, can be problematic. Béhague therefore urges scholars "to reflect in a more sophisticated manner on the relationship of music expressions and black ethnicity in the Caribbean and South America" (vi). The influence of Melville Herskovits and the historical processes specific to various locales have often led to speculation as to which, if any, Africanisms have been retained. Nevertheless, Béhague contends that "the search for Africanisms and the very concepts of syncretism and acculturation are to a great extent symptomatic of colonialist thought," primarily because they "privilege the notions of socio-cultural assimilation . . . to the dominant segments of society" (vii). Certainly, an exclusive focus on "blackness" in the Caribbean and South America may underestimate the importance of musical expressions of indigenized or creolized cultural. After all, Béhague asserts, "Some aspects of cultural expression in contemporary Afro-American communities in the Caribbean and South America may not be of historic African derivation at all, but fulfill an equally vital purpose and sense of heritage" (vii). In *Caribbean Currents* (2006), Peter Manuel argues that "the scholarly pendulum may have swung a bit too far in the direction of emphasizing the ability of slaves to retain and construct their own cultures" (6). Not surprisingly, then, Manuel emphasizes intra-Caribbean diversity, even devoting a chapter to the Caribbean's East Indian musical heritage, which is especially noticeable in Guyana and Trinidad.[8] One of the most frequently cited criticisms of African retention theory has come from English scholar Paul Gilroy. In *The Black Atlantic*, Gilroy scolds North American scholars for failing to acknowledge African America's debt to the much broader African diaspora and especially to the African Caribbean. Heidi Feldman's *Black Rhythms of Peru* (2006) is particularly refreshing in that it highlights a "Black Pacific" musical tradition and reminds us that even as Gilroy's work has been embraced, scores of African continental and diasporic musics remain marginalized.

The criticisms launched against ethnomusicologists who supposedly err on the side of emphasizing African retentions have never wholly discouraged scholars from positing a vibrant cultural link between African and African American musical traditions. In an article that first appeared in 1979 and was reprinted in a 1985 edited volume, Portia Maultsby argued that "the Black musical tradition will continue to evolve and mirror new values, attitudes, philosophies, and lifestyles, but it will never lose its West African essence" (1985, 51). She steers clear of Herskovits's notion of direct retentions, aligning herself more closely with the more moderate school of thought espoused by Mintz and Price (1976). "It is really West African concepts," Maultsby asserts, "more so than elements, that have been retained in U.S. Black music" (43). More recently, Gerard Kubik's *Africa and the Blues* (1999) posits that many of the fiddling traditions espoused by early New World blacks have direct antecedents in West and Central Africa.

FROM AFRICA TO AFRICAN AMERICA

Studies of "black" musical genres have contributed much to ethnomusicological literature on music in the United States. But scholars have been less successful at analyzing, or even recognizing, intradiasporic musical practices occurring within this nation's boundaries. In the United States, these types of practices, which include Caribbean and African inflections of popular music genres, are particularly prominent in urban areas populated by an array of African-descended peoples from around the globe. Most research on black musical genres in the United States has highlighted the distinctly African *American* characteristics of particular genres such as blues, jazz, gospel, or hip-hop. The failure to deconstruct reified notions of blackness feels self-perpetuating, as this academic void goes hand in hand with the tendency for Malians, Ghanaians, Kenyans,

Jamaicans, Haitians, St. Lucians, and many others to be lumped into an assumedly monolithic racial category. With the continuing migrations of African diasporic peoples to the United States, and with the intermingling of black ethnicities in urban musical settings, there are dynamic communities of cultural interaction ripe for ethnomusicological analysis. And ethnomusicologists are finally rising to the challenge. Best known for her 2006 work on African American hip-hop and girls' musical games, Kyra Gaunt (2005) has explored intradiasporic interactions at St. Nick's Pub in Harlem. She notes that scholars of black music have generally failed to acknowledge the ways in which traditionally African American musical spaces are often inflected with "black" expressions that emanate from outside U.S. borders. Through her fieldwork at St. Nick's Pub, Gaunt was able to interact—and to watch herself interacting—closely with a diversity of "black" voices and bodies. In so doing, she gained precious insight into the "conflicting performances of diaspora" (3) that typically go unacknowledged in the academy.

Scholars in disciplines outside of music have greatly influenced music-centered discourses on the nature of African American music. Samuel Floyd was among the first ethnomusicologists to expound on Henry Louis Gates's (1988) well-known analysis of "Signifyin(g)" practices. Examining the West African trickster figure, Esu-Elegbara, and his "Afro-American relative, the Signifying Monkey" (44), Gates makes a compelling case that "[t]he black [literary] tradition has inscribed within it the very principles by which it can be read" (xxiii–xxiv). Applied to music, Signifyin(g) describes the multiple types of indirect referencing that musicians and listeners experience in a variety of contexts. As Floyd states, "It has been through the repetition and revision of texts, through the interplay of black language and black music in a long chain of Signifyin(g) tropes, that African-American peasants became and continue to be poets in a land that initially denied them the right to be called artists of any stripe" (1995, 225).

In *Saying Something* (1996), Ingrid Monson also draws on Gates's work to illustrate the "intermusicality" of jazz performance. Through analysis of solo improvisations by artists such as John Coltrane and Rahsaan Roland Kirk, Monson reveals an African American propensity to allude to previous renditions and performances and refashion musical material in a way that promotes individuality and creative expression. Monson's influential edited volume, *The African Diaspora: A Musical Perspective* (2000), probably represents the most theoretically rigorous attempt to explore the African diaspora from an ethnomusicological point of view. Various topics and locales are held together not only by the volume's title, but also by the authors' attempts to situate their work within an African diasporic contextual framework of analysis. Organized in three parts, the volume contains chapters on Caribbean and African American musics, but also looks carefully at "the redefinition of tradition and modernity through music in contemporary Africa, with particular emphasis on gender, urban popular theatre, and the selling of 'traditional experience' on the international market" (2). The material on Africa is well exemplified by Lucy Duran's chapter, which focuses on the valorization of the "hunter" in Malian popular music. Duran discusses the ways in which traditional hunters' songs serve to evoke a non-ethnic based identity in contradistinction to the dominant Mande musical and political voices. She also illustrates that the hunter theme has been evident in Malian popular music since at least the 1970s, when dance bands and solo artists incorporated hunters' songs in their performances. One of Mali's most famous musicians, Salif Keita, frequently donned hunter apparel and featured the "hunter's harp" in his recordings and album covers of the 1980s. Furthermore, Duran emphasizes that women singers have been major contributors to the "mystique" that continues to surround hunters in Mali. When appropriated by women singers, the hunter's mystique provides "a springboard from which [women] can claim their place within Mali's great historical past and renegotiate their own social status" (178).

Travis Jackson's chapter (2000) on jazz ritual makes important reference to the use of ritual forms whose specific manifestations clearly derive from an African spiritual orientation. Jackson also summarizes how blues music has been described by writers such as Amiri Baraka, Ralph Ellison, and Albert Murray as a vital element in African American culture and performance. Drawing strongly on Herskovits, Baraka saw blues as "the parent of all legitimate jazz" (Baraka 1963, 17, qtd. in Jackson 2000, 26). According to this line of thought, blues and jazz must remain closely intertwined in order for jazz to retain its authenticity as an African American expression. Whites, Baraka argued, have tended to dilute authentic jazz by performing and recording material that lacks an identifiable blues component. Jackson contrasts the theoretical premise of Baraka's *Blues People* (1963) with the views of author Ralph Ellison, who critiqued Baraka's "facile linking of social status and racial purity with forms of musical expression" (Jackson 27). Ellison felt that "[t]he tremendous burden of sociology which [Baraka] would place upon this body of music is enough to give even the blues the blues" (Ellison 1964, 249, qtd. in Jackson 27). To a much greater extent than Baraka, Ellison highlighted the blues' ritual dimensions, positing that this form of music allows individuals and groups to self-identify within American society through musical sound, lyrics, and a spiritual component that is often overlooked by the dominant segments of society.

Albert Murray refined Ellison's ideas in his well-known book, *Stomping the Blues* (1976). Murray argued that blues music functions to "drive the blues away and hold them at bay at least for the time being" and to evoke "an ambiance of Dionysian revelry in the process" (Murray 1976, 17, qtd. in Jackson 30). Jackson's work suggests that jazz's vitality as a ritual form is felt through its inextricable link to the blues and other forms of African diasporic expressive culture. This emphasis on African American music as a ritual form is not without precedent. For example, an essay by Morton Marks (1974) posits a link between African American musical genres and West African ritual drumming. In contrast to Jackson's work, Marks's primary interest is on Protestant and Pentecostal Christianity and the role of music in facilitating "trance" experiences on both sides of the Atlantic.

Burnim (1980a), Jackson-Brown (1990), and Ramsey (2003) offer useful overviews of black religious music scholarship has have emerged since 1960, when George Ricks completed his highly influential doctoral dissertation. Ramsey's *Race Music: Black Music from Bebop to Hip-hop* is largely a personal memoir of his upbringing in Chicago and exposure to a wide variety of black musical styles. However, the author interweaves literature reviews of some major works of black music scholarship produced by African Americans. Indiana University professors Mellonee Burnim and Portia Maultsby edited a much-anticipated volume (2006) that takes a comprehensive look at African American music. The volume features chapters by an all-star cast of music scholars and is designed to build on Eileen Southern's 1971 classic work, while "advancing the discussion of African American music to include topics that have risen to the forefront in contemporary discourse" (1). Burnim and Maultsby have done other highly significant work: Through thick descriptive ethnography of African American congregational singing, Burnim (1980b) has identified musical and cultural elements of gospel music that comprise a "black aesthetic." Maultsby (1992) has looked broadly at African American musical genres and specifically at gospel music's impact in "secular" arenas. Both have followed in the footsteps of Horace Boyer (1973; 1995), a well-respected pioneer in black gospel music research and the compositional and vocal traditions of African American church worship.

Historically minded scholars have made huge contributions to research on African American musical traditions. Eileen Southern's landmark book, *The Music of Black Americans* (1971), is widely considered a classic scholarly work. Musicologist Sandra Graham (2001) has much more recently written an award-winning dissertation on the concert spiritual tradition.[9] With respect to jazz scholarship, Thomas Owens's *Bebop: The Music and Its Players* (1995) and DeVeaux's *The Birth of Bebop* (1997) are primarily historical in scope, while Monson's *Saying Something: Jazz Improvisation and Interaction* (1996) draws on the author's ethnographic research to provide insights into the phenomenology of jazz performance. With the increased global spread and popularity of hip-hop came a keen scholarly interest in the subject (e.g., Mitchell 2002). Monographs by Tricia

Rose (1994), Joe Schloss (2004), Felicia Miyakawa (2005), and Kyra Gaunt (2006) are but a few of the works that have become emblematic of an on-going ethnomusicological fascination. The contributors to Anthony Pinn's volume (2003) comment on the spiritual dimensions of rap in a way that draws on the theomusicological speculations of Jon Michael Spencer (1991). Spencer is persuasive in his suggestion that African American culture in the United States is infused with a spiritual component that renders traditional sacred-secular dichotomies ineffective as frameworks for understanding the popular vitality of black musical expressions. Likewise, Teresa Reed's discussion (2002) of blues artists demonstrates that "their lyrics suggest the centrality of their belief in God and a deeply religious understanding of themselves and the world around them" (60).

CARIBBEAN PERFORMANCE, POWER, AND IDENTITY

In recent years some of the most fascinating contributions to the study of music in the African diaspora have centered on Caribbean locales. Caribbean-born scholars have done significant work on local musical traditions. Olive Lewin's rich (2000) analysis of Jamaican folk music and Gerdes Fleurant's detailed exploration (1987) of music in Haitian Vodou ritual are two noteworthy examples. However, nonnative researchers have penned most of the in-depth studies of Caribbean music cultures. Jocelyne Guilbault's important work (1993) discusses the popular dance genre known as *zouk* in the Francophone Caribbean as a transnational expression of Antillean identity. Her work is emblematic of Caribbeanist ethnomusicology of the 1990s, much of which accentuates the role of music as a transnationally mediated form of popular culture that provides subaltern groups a vehicle for identity assertion in the face of local and global hegemonies. Gage Averill (1997) provides a window into the tumultuous history of power negotiations within Haitian popular music. Contending that "the urban elite never achieved anything like hegemony in rural Haiti" (7), he offers both a historical survey of Haiti's musicopolitical scene and a contemporary (1980s and 1990s) fieldwork-based ethnography of Haitian popular music genres. Averill was one of the first ethnomusicologists to explore the role of music as a transnational tool of resistance to state and global hegemony. At events such as the annual Carnival, music becomes a means of creative resistance, as the masses are able to launch indirect critiques of the rich and powerful. Elizabeth McAlister's groundbreaking ethnography (2002) furthers this discussion by underscoring the often neglected political, spiritual, and gendered dimensions of Haitian *rara*. Averill's work has also influenced ethnomusicologists such as Timothy Rommen, Norman Stolzoff, and Robin Moore, who explore similar issues in Trinidad, Jamaica, and Cuba, respectively.

Although members of Jamaica's wealthy elite typically view the island's dancehall music with disdain, ethnomusicologist Norman Stolzoff provides a refreshingly nuanced perspective toward this musical genre in connection with the sociomoral values of Jamaica's poorer class of people. In Stolzoff's book, *Wake the Town and Tell the People: Dancehall Culture in Jamaica* (2000), dancehall is described as a highly complex "field of cultural production" in which negotiations of power and status take place.[10] The author explains the historical processes that gave rise to this musical practice, and he also follows Averill's lead by merging historical data with a rich ethnographic portrayal of contemporary dancehall life. Most significantly, the author contends that the current sociopolitical struggles that unfold in Jamaica, along with their historical antecedents, can be understood through the country's popular music genres. "Dancehall" is presented not simply as a modern form of mass-mediated club music but rather as a dynamic expressive genres that has existed in various forms since the slavery era. In different musical manifestations, Stolzoff argues, dancehall musics and spaces have "been an important medium for the black masses to create an alternative social universe of performance, production, and politics" (227). Like Averill, Stolzoff draws on what some cultural theorists refer to as "neo-Gramscian hegemony theory" (e.g., Storey 1993, 13), insisting that the music of subaltern groups represents a highly significant expression of popular agency and empowerment in the face of oppression.

In *Nationalizing Blackness* (1997), Robin Moore takes a historical approach to Afro-Cuban popular music, focusing on the 1920s and 1930s. Moore sets out to show that contemporary imaginings of Cuba have been strongly shaped by national sentiments that were brewing in the decades before Fidel Castro's rise to power. Moore sees his research into Cuba's past as a useful means of exploring racial tensions and biases that continue to plague the Caribbean island. The 1920s and 1930s represent a relatively progressive era in Cuba's history, as the country's artists and intellectuals engaged in a broader reexamination of inherited colonial prejudice and a tentative acceptance of black working-class culture." The author finds that "a qualified acceptance of black expression was the only recourse of intellectuals and performers desirous of creating ideological unity in a country so heavily influenced by Africa" (220). Expressions of African heritage in Cuba ultimately became limited to socially "respectable" performances that often featured whites in blackface or involved gross caricatures of blacks. These displays bore little resemblance to working-class Cuban culture, yet solidified negative stereotypes of Afrocuban life. Moore concludes that "the entire history of Cuban popular music since the early nineteenth century can be viewed as a debate over the relative prominence of Afrocuban forms in a country dominated by Eurohispanic culture" (221).

LINGERING QUESTIONS,
ONGOING CONCERNS

Clearly, there is much more to say about ethnomusicological approaches to Africa and its diaspora. This essay has really only scratched the surface of inquiry into the contributions of music scholars to an enhanced understanding of black expressive cultures around the globe. In ethnomusicological fieldwork and writing, there remain many unresolved issues. Perhaps some of the longest-standing debates among those who endeavor to study the world's musical traditions revolve around the issues of epistemology, fieldwork, and representation, which I have only touched on. What is required for a scholar to "know" a piece of music? To what extent can ethnomusicologists gain an "insider's" understanding of a musical tradition? In what ways does a scholar's national, racial, and/or gender identity impact how African diasporic musical forms are represented visually and ethnographically?

Another persistent concern in African diasporic ethnomusicological research is the relation between local and global music cultures. Ethnomusicologists have long realized the intellectual senselessness of trying to explore single, geographically bounded locales as though they were sterile Petri dishes of uncontaminated "data"; and new technologies link people and places like never before. Although books and articles on the African diaspora still tend to focus on individual locales, recent decades have witnessed louder calls for scholars to acknowledge the transnational migrations of black diasporic peoples and their expressive cultures. In fact, a central theme in ethnomusicological research at least since the 1990s has been the intradiasporic connections between various musical communities and styles. Washburne (1997) examines the Caribbean contributions to the development of African American jazz. In other cases, scholars have moved from one diasporic locale to another. For example, Paul Berliner (1978; 1994) and Jacqueline DjeDje (1978; 1985) have each done research projects on both African American and African musical genres. I imagine that throughout the twenty-first century, ethnomusicologists will continue to struggle with the transmigration of music and what George Lipsitz refers to as its "peculiar relationship to the poetics and the politics of place" (1994, 3). With the explosive popularity of digital technologies and media, Lipsitz's comments from the mid-1990s ring all the more true more than a decade later. He states,

> Music that originally emerged from concrete historical experiences in places with clearly identifiable geographic boundaries now circulates as an interchangeable commodity marketed to consumers all over the globe. . . . Jamaican music secures spectacular sales in Germany and Japan. Rap music from inner-city ghettos in the U.S.A. attracts the allegiance of

teenagers from Amsterdam to Auckland. Juke boxes and elaborate "sound systems" in Colombia employ dance music from West Africa as the constitutive element of a dynamic local subculture, while Congolese entertainers draw upon Cuban traditions for the core vocabulary of their popular music. (4)

What does it mean, then, to research music of the African diaspora? How should ethnomusicologists locate the Who, What, and Where of our chosen topics? As "virtual" music communities continue to heighten the sense of disconnect between physical places and digital spaces, scholars of musical practice will have to continually rethink their modes of conducting fieldwork and writing about music in the African diaspora.

NOTES

1. Commenting on the role of a scholar's positionality in disciplinary critiques, Stephen Blum (1991b) points out,

> Some of the most telling criticism of academic dichotomies between "text" and "context," between the "musical" and the "social," has come from African musicologists . . . who have correctly identified the bad faith with which too many Western ethnomusicologists have emphasized "social function" over "artistic value." It is superfluous as well as condescending for scholars to find "redeeming sociological significance" in musical practices they treat as undeveloped or as products of "restricted" rather than "elaborated" codes.

2. Society for Ethnomusicology Mission Statement, http://webdb.iu.edu/sem/scripts/aboutus/aboutsem/sem_mission.cfm (accessed 6/24/07).
3. http://webdb.iu.edu/sem/scripts/aboutus/aboutsem/sem_history_founding.cfm (accessed 6/24/07).
4. Quotes regarding the Departments of Music at the Universities of Virginia and Pennsylvania are taken from the section "Guide to Programs in Ethnomusicology" on the Society for Ethnomusicology's website. See http://webdb.iu.edu/sem/scripts/guidetoprograms/guidelist.cfm (accessed 6/26/07).
5. http://www.ictmusic.org/ICTM/about.php.
6. http://www.tandf.co.uk/journals/titles/03007766.html.
7. http://www.cbmr.org/pubs/bmrj.htm.
8. Revised and expanded in 2006, Peter Manuel's *Caribbean Currents* first appeared in 1995. Supplemented by material from Ken Bilby and Michael Largey, who contributed significant material on Jamaica and Haiti, respectively, the book is intended as a critical survey of musical genres native to particular New World locales, and it has appealed to students and professors of Caribbean popular music for use in undergraduate courses.
9. Graham's book, *From Slave Song to America's Music: The Popularization of Negro Spirituals*, is forthcoming from University of Illinois Press.
10. An important prior work on Jamaican dancehall is Carolyn J. Cooper's pro-

vocative *Noises in the Blood*. Stolzoff shares Cooper's view that dancehall has been underappreciated as a valid cultural expression of the masses, and he views her as "representative of an intellectual class which opposes the uptown snobbery that categorically condemns dancehall" (245). However, he is generally less enthusiastic than Cooper toward the view that dancehall participants, especially women, have the potential to resist misogynistic oppression and cultivate subaltern agency within dancehall spaces.

REFERENCES

Agawu, Kofi. 2003. *Representing African Music: Postcolonial Notes, Queries, Positions*. New York: Routledge.

Averill, Gage. 1997. *A Day for the Hunter, a Day for the Prey: Popular Music and Power in Haiti*. Chicago: University of Chicago Press.

Baraka, Amiri (LeRoi Jones). 1963. *Blues People: Negro Music in White America*. New York: Morrow.

Béhague, Gerard H., ed. 1994. *Music and Black Ethnicity: The Caribbean and South America*. New Brunswick, N.J.: Transaction.

Berliner, Paul F. 1978. *The Soul of Mbira: Music and Tradition of the Shona People of Zimbabwe*. Berkeley: University of California Press.

———. 1994. *Thinking in Jazz: The Infinite Art of Improvisation*. Chicago: University of Chicago Press.

Blacking, John. 1973. *How Musical Is Man?* Seattle: University of Washington Press.

Blum, Stephen. 1991a. "European Musical Terminology and the Music of Africa." In Bruno Nettl and Philip V. Bohlman, eds., *Comparative Musicology and Anthropology of Music: Essays on the History of Ethnomusicology*, 3–36. Chicago: University of Chicago Press.

———. 1991b. "Prologue: Ethnomusicologists and Modern Music History." In Stephen Blum, Philip V. Bohlman, and Daniel M. Neuman, eds., *Ethnomusicology and Modern Music History*, 1–20. Urbana: University of Illinois Press.

Boyer, Horace Clarence. 1973. "An Analysis of Black Church Music with Examples Drawn from Services in Rochester." PhD diss., Eastman School of Music, University of Rochester.

———. 1995. *How Sweet the Sound: The Golden Age of Gospel*. Washington, D.C.: Elliott and Clark.

Burnim, Mellonee V. 1980a. "Gospel Music Research." *Black Music Research Journal* 1: 63–70.

———. 1980b. "The Black Music Gospel Tradition: Symbol of Ethnicity." PhD diss., Indiana University.

Burnim, Mellonee V., and Portia K. Maultsby, eds. 2006. *African American Music: An Introduction*. New York: Taylor and Francis.

Cooper, Carolyn J. 1993. *Noises in the Blood: Orality, Gender, and the "Vulgar" Body of Jamaican Popular Culture*. London: Macmillan.

DeVeaux, Scott. 1997. *The Birth of Bebop: A Social and Musical History*. Berkeley: University of California Press.

DjeDje, Jacqueline Cogdell. 1978. *American Black Spirituals and Gospel Songs from Southeast Georgia: A Comparative Study.* Los Angeles: University of California Center for Afro-American Studies.

———. 1985. "Women and Music in Sudanic Africa." In Irene Jackson, ed., *More than Drumming: Essays on African and Afro-Latin Music and Musicians,* 67–89. Westport, Conn.: Greenwood Press.

Duran, Lucy. 2000. "Women, Music, and the 'Mystique' of Hunters in Mali." In Ingrid Monson, *The African Diaspora: A Musical Perspective,* 137–86. New York: Garland.

Ellison, Ralph. 1964. *Shadow and Act.* New York: Random House.

Feld, Steven. 1994. "From Schizophrenia to Schismogenesis: On the Discourses and Commodification Practices of 'World Music' and 'World Beat.'" In Charles Keil and Steven Feld, eds., *Music Grooves: Essays and Dialogues,* 257–89. Chicago: University of Chicago Press.

Feldman, Heidi Carolyn. 2006. *Black Rhythms of Peru: Reviving African Musical Heritage in the Black Pacific.* Middletown, Conn.: Wesleyan University Press.

Fleurant, Gerdes. 1987. "The Ethnomusicology of Yanvalou: A Study of the Rada Rite of Haiti." PhD diss., Tufts University.

Floyd, Samuel A. 1995. *The Power of Black Music: Interpreting Its History from Africa to the United States.* New York: Oxford University Press.

Frazier, E. Franklin. 1939. *The Negro Family in the United States.* Chicago: University of Chicago Press.

Gates, Henry Louis, Jr. 1988. *The Signifying Monkey: A Theory of Afro-American Literary Criticism.* New York: Oxford University Press.

Gaunt, Kyra. 2005. "'African Night' at St. Nick's Pub: Music and the Unfinished Migrations of Diaspora in a Harlem Nightclub." Paper presented at the Society for Ethnomusicology conference, Atlanta, November 16.

———. 2006. *The Games Black Girls Play: Learning the Ropes from Double-dutch to Hip-hop.* New York: New York University Press.

Graham, Sandra Jean. 2001. "The Fisk Jubilee Singers and the Concert Spiritual: The Beginnings of an American Tradition." PhD diss., New York University.

Guilbault, Jocelyne. 1993. *Zouk: World Music in the West Indies.* Chicago: University of Chicago Press.

Herskovits, Melville. 1941. *The Myth of the Negro Past.* Boston: Beacon Press [1990].

Herzog, George. 1936. *Research in Primitive and Folk Music in the United States.* Bulletin 24. Washington, D.C.: American Council of Learned Societies.

Hornbostel, Erich Moritz von. 1928. "African Negro Music." *Africa: Journal of the International African Institute* 1: 30–62.

Jackson, Irene, ed. 1985. *More than Dancing: Essays on Afro-American Music and Musicians.* Westport, Conn.: Greenwood Press.

Jackson, Travis. 2000. "Jazz Performance as Ritual: The Blues Aesthetic and the African Diaspora." In Ingrid Monson, *The African Diaspora: A Musical Perspective,* 23–82. New York: Garland.

Jackson-Brown, Irene. 1990. "Developments in Black Gospel Performance and Scholarship." *Black Music Research Journal* 10, no. 1: 36–42.

Kidula, Jean Ngoya. 2006. "Ethnomusicology, the Music Canon, and African Music: Positions, Tensions, and Resolutions in the African Academy." *Africa Today* 52, no. 3: 99–113.

Kisliuk, Michelle. 1998. *Seize the Dance! BaAka Musical Life and the Ethnography of Performance*. New York: Oxford University Press.

Kubik, Gerhard. 1999. *Africa and the Blues*. Jackson: University Press of Mississippi.

Lewin, Olive. 2000. *Rock It Come Over: The Folk Music of Jamaica*. Kingston: University of West Indies Press.

Lipsitz, George. 2006. *Dangerous Crossroads: Popular Music, Post-modernism, and the Poetics of Place*. New York: Verso.

Manuel, Peter, with Kenneth Bilby and Michael Largey. 2006. *Caribbean Currents: From Rumba to Reggae*. Rev. ed. Philadelphia: Temple University Press.

Marks, Morton. 1974. "Uncovering Ritual Structures in Afro-American Music." In Irving Zaretsky and Mark Leone, eds., *Religious Movements in Contemporary America*, 60–134. Princeton, N.J.: Princeton University Press.

Maultsby, Portia K. 1992. "The Impact of Gospel Music in the Secular Music Industry." In Bernice Johnson Reagon, ed., *We'll Understand It Better By and By: Pioneering African American Gospel Composers*, 19–36. Washington, D.C.: Smithsonian Institution.

———. 1985. "West African Influences and Retentions in U.S. Black Music: A Sociocultural Study." In Jackson, *More than Dancing*, 25–55.

McAlister, Elizabeth. 2002. *Rara: Vodou, Power, and Performance in Haiti and Its Diaspora*. Berkeley: University of California Press.

McAllester, David P. 1985. "In Memoriam: George Herzog (1901–1984)." *Ethnomusicology* 29 (Winter): 86–87.

Mintz, Sidney, and Richard Price. 1976. *The Birth of African-American Culture: An Anthropological Perspective*. Boston: Beacon Press.

Mitchell, Tony. 2002. *Global Noise: Rap and Hip-hop outside the USA*. Middletown, Conn.: Wesleyan University Press.

Miyakawa, Felicia. 2005. *Five Percenter Rap: God Hop's Music, Message, and Black Muslim Mission*. Bloomington: Indiana University Press.

Monson, Ingrid, ed. 2000. *The African Diaspora: A Musical Perspective*. New York: Garland.

———. 1996. *Saying Something: Jazz Improvisation and Interaction*. Chicago: University of Chicago Press.

Moore, Robin. 1997. *Nationalizing Blackness: Afrocubanismo and Artistic Revolution in Havana, 1920–1940*. Pittsburgh: University of Pittsburgh Press.

Murphy, Joseph M. 1994. *Working the Spirit: Ceremonies of the African Diaspora*. Boston: Beacon Press.

Murray, Albert. 1976. *Stomping the Blues*. New York: Da Capo.

Nettl, Bruno. 1989. "Mozart and the Ethnomusicological Study of Western Culture (An Essay in Four Movements)." *Yearbook for Traditional Music* 21: 1–16.

Neuman, Daniel. 1991. "Epilogue: Paradigms and Stories." In Stephen Blum, Philip V. Bohlman, and Daniel M. Neuman, eds., *Ethnomusicology and Modern Music History*, 268–77. Urbana: University of Illinois Press.

Nketia, J. H. Kwabena. 2005. *Ethnomusicology and African Music (Collected Papers): Volume 1: Models of Inquiry and Interpretation*. Accra, Ghana: Afram Publications.

——. 1967. "Multi-part Organization in the Music of the Gogo of Tanzania." *Journal of the International Folk Music Council* 19: 79–88.

Okpewho, Isidore. 1999. Introduction to Isidore Okpewho, Carole Boyce Davies, and Ali A. Mazrui, eds., *The African Diaspora: African Origins and New World Identities*, xi–xxviii. Bloomington: Indiana University Press.

Owens, Thomas. 1995. *Bebop: The Music and Its Players*. New York: Oxford University Press.

Pinn, Anthony, ed. 2003. *Noise and Spirit: The Religious and Spiritual Sensibilities of Rap Music*. New York: New York University Press.

Ramsey, Guthrie P. 2003. *Race Music: Black Cultures from Bebop to Hip-hop*. Berkeley: University of California Press.

Reed, Teresa L. 2002. *The Holy Profane: Religion in Black Popular Music*. Lexington: University Press of Kentucky.

Rhodes, Willard. "A Short History of the Founding of SEM." http://webdb.iu.edu/sem/scripts/aboutus/aboutsem/sem_history_founding.cfm.

Ricks, George Robinson. 1977. *Some Aspects of the Religious Music of the United States Negro: An Ethnomusicological Study with Special Emphasis on the Gospel Tradition*. New York: Da Capo, [1960].

Rommen, Timothy. 2007. *"Mek Some Noise": Gospel Music and the Ethics of Style in Trinidad*. Berkeley: University of California Press.

Rose, Tricia. 1994. *Black Noise! Rap Music and Black Culture in Contemporary America*. Middletown, Conn.: Wesleyan University Press.

Schloss, Joe. 2004. *Making Beats: The Art of Sample-Based Hip-Hop*. Middletown, Conn.: Wesleyan University Press.

Small, Christopher. 1987. *Music of the Common Tongue*. New York: River Run Press.

——. 1998. *Musicking: The Meanings of Performing and Listening*. Hanover, N.H.: Wesleyan University Press.

Southern, Eileen. 1971. *The Music of Black Americans: A History*. New York: W. W. Norton.

Spencer, Jon Michael. 1991. *Theological Music: Introduction to Theomusicology*. Westport, Conn.: Greenwood Press.

Stolzoff, Norman C. 2000. *Wake the Town and Tell the People: Dancehall Culture in Jamaica*. Durham, N.C.: Duke University Press.

Storey, John. 1993. *An Introductory Guide to Cultural Theory and Popular Culture*. London: Harvester/Wheatsheaf.

Titon, Jeff Todd. 1997. "Knowing Fieldwork." In Gregory F. Barz and Timothy J. Cooley, eds., *Shadows in the Field*, 87–100. New York: Oxford University Press.

Washburne, Christopher. 1997. "The Clave of Jazz: A Caribbean Contribution to the Rhythmic Foundation of an African-American Music." *Black Music Research Journal* 17, no. 1 (Spring): 59–80.

Suggestions for Further Reading

Agawu, Kofi. 1995. *African Rhythm: A Northern Ewe Perspective*. Cambridge: Cambridge University Press.

Burnim, Mellonee V. 1985. "The Black Gospel Music Tradition: A Complex of Ideology, Aesthetic, and Behavior." In Jackson, *More than Dancing*, 147–67. Westport, Conn.: Greenwood Press.

Butler, Melvin L. 2000. "Musical Style and Experience in a Brooklyn Pentecostal Church: An 'Insider's Perspective.'" *Current Musicology* 70: 33–50.

Charry, Eric. 2000. *Mande Music: Traditional and Modern Music of the Maninka and Mandinka of Western Africa*. Chicago: University of Chicago Press.

Chernoff, John Miller. 1979. *African Rhythm and African Sensibility*. Chicago: University of Chicago Press.

Collins, John. 1992. *West African Pop Roots*. Philadelphia: Temple University Press.

Darden, Robert. 2004. *People Get Ready! A New History of Black Gospel Music*. New York: Continuum.

Erlmann, Veit. 1991. *African Stars: Studies in Black South African Performance*. Chicago: University of Chicago Press.

Ekwueme, Laz E. N. 1975. "African Musicological Investigation in a Culture Conscious Era." *African Music* 5 (4): 4–5.

Euba, Akin. 1990. *Yoruba Drumming: The Dùndún Tradition*. Bayreuth: E. Breitinger, Bayreuth University.

Friedson, Steven. 1996. *Dancing Prophets: Musical Experience in Tumbuka Healing*. Chicago: University of Chicago Press.

Graham, Sandra J. 2010. *From Slave Song to America's Music: The Popularization of Negro Spirituals*. Urbana: University of Illinois Press.

Guilbault, Jocelyne. 1997. "Interpreting World Music: A Challenge in Theory and Practice." *Popular Music* 16 (1): 31–44.

Harris, Michael W. 1992. *The Rise of Gospel Blues: The Music of Thomas Andrew Dorsey in the Urban Church*. New York: Oxford University Press.

Heilbut, Tony. 1975. *The Gospel Sound: Good News and Bad Times*. Garden City, N.J.: Anchor Books.

Jones, A. M. 1959. *Studies in African Music*. 2 vols. Oxford: Oxford University Press.

Meintjes, Louise. 2003. *Sound of Africa! Making Music Zulu in a South African Studio*. Durham, N.C.: Duke University Press.

Nketia, J. H. Kwabena. 1963. *African Music in Ghana*. Evanston, Ill.: Northwestern University Press.

———. 1974. *The Music of Africa*. New York: Norton.

Olaniyan, Tejumola. 2004. *Arrest the Music! Fela and His Rebel Art and Politics*. Bloomington: Indiana University Press.

Reagon, Bernice Johnson. 1992. *We'll Understand It Better By and By: Pioneering African American Gospel Composers*. Washington, D.C.: Smithsonian Institution.

Roberts, John Storm. 1998. *Black Music of Two Worlds: African, Caribbean, Latin, and African American Traditions*. 2nd ed. New York: Schirmer Books, 1998.

Stone, Ruth M. 1982. *Let the Inside Be Sweet: The Interpretation of Music Event among the Kpelle of Liberia*. Bloomington: Indiana University Press.

Trouillot, Michel-Rolph. 1992. "The Caribbean Region: An Open Frontier in Anthropological Theory." *Annual Review of Anthropology* 21: 19–42.

Veal, Michael E. 2000. *Fela: The Life and Times of an African Musical Icon.* Philadelphia: Temple University Press.

Waterman, Christopher. 1990. *Juju: A Social History and Ethnography of an African Popular Music.* Chicago: University of Chicago Press.

Waterman, Richard Alan. 1952. *African Influence on the Music of the Americas.* Chicago: University of Chicago Press.

Wilcken, Lois E., with Frisner Augustin. 1992. *The Drums of Vodou.* Crown Point, Ind.: White Cliffs Media.

Wilson, Olly. 1992. "The Heterogeneous Sound Ideal in African American Music." In Josephine Wright, ed., *New Perspectives on Music,* 326–37. Harmonie Park, Mich.: Harmonie Park Press.

———. 1974. "The Significance of the Relationship between Afro-American Music and West African Music." *Black Perspective in Music* 2 (1): 3–22.

Zemp, Hugo. 1971. *Musique Dan: La Musique dans la pensée et la vie sociale d'une sociéte africaine.* Paris: La Haye.

11 SEMIOPTICS OF AFRICANA ART HISTORY

Moyo Okediji

For every successful Michael Jordan, Mohammed Ali, or O. J. Simpson, there are hordes of young black men whose lives have been negatively impacted by the popularity of basketball and other contact sports in the United States. This reality is shown in the work of several African American artists, notably David Hammons, John Yancey, and Jean-Michel Basquiat, who convey the contradictions of athleticism that have made multimillionaires and celebrities of a few black people. But African American art historians and critics lag far behind and have not kept pace with artists who have constantly examined the place of professional athleticism as a star maker and a systematic killer in black American popular culture. A paradigmatic distance separates artists and art historians in African American visual cultures.

A similar statement could be made about African art scholarship, which seems to have failed to draw the brightest minds in analytical and conceptual criticism. Historical evidence has demonstrated that a large number of African art objects in museums and private collections in the West were produced between the sixteenth and nineteenth centuries, marking a period coinciding with transatlantic slavery, one of the mammoth black holes of human history.[1] An institution based on asymmetry, slavery is not congruent with balance. In an emergent diasporic visual culture that originated within this asymmetrical system, will the traditional structures that evolve from this state of imbalance produce a symmetrical story? Will the standard master metaphors fully interpret the art and vision of the tradition that suffered slavery?

As Audre Lorde couched it, "The master's tools won't dismantle the master's house." In this context, "master" is race-blind, because there were slaves and masters in Africa as much as in America and Europe.[2] The asymmetry of historical traditions therefore extends beyond the West to embrace indigenous African sources primed to present the master's stories only.

Do we therefore need new symmetrical theoretical approaches, or can we safely investigate meaning in the visual cultures of Africa and its diasporas with the asymmetrical tools of relativist traditional art history? Given the context of slavery, colonization, and immigration within which art history has developed, and given the partiality to hegemonic master values of traditional art history, are the methodologies of art history adequate for the evaluation of art that is not Eurocentric? More specifically, can the traditions that suffered from transatlantic slave trade also gain understanding, fairness, symmetry, and balance from the art history emanating from the methodologies of the traditions that profited from slave trading?

And to what extent does the present art historical approach to Africana arts continue to drive the postslavery motors of justifications and concealments that benefit and sustain hegemonic master narratives? Are asymmetrical Western values and interests historically embedded in the practice of African and diasporic art historical narratives? How symmetrical is Western art history in its engagement of the art of Africa as Other?

The art history of Africans and their overseas descendants, kin, cousins, affiliations, and diasporas, which is often de-scribed as Africana art history, is a terrain of imagistic complexities that remains largely insufficiently investigated. It constitutes a history fractured by heterogeneous and pathological contentions of race, gender, class, and religion among other polarizing and fraternal agents. Most of these denominations have not received the intellectual attention that they deserve, particularly as they affect the collection, curatorship, and conservation of Africana art.

Although remarkably and tactically ignored, pigments of race have always been known to color and inform the present practice in academia that divides Africana art into three overlapping disciplinary categories: historical (also known as traditional) African art history, contemporary African art history, and diaspora art history.[3] The last of these categories is often limited to the study of African American art history. The triadic categories have become so separated that individuals specialize in one specific category, but we do have scholars, curators, and private collectors interested in more than one area. It is becoming more practical in recent years to provide students with a broad training in Africana art, although no single text exits to link the fragments. Memory, which links the three Africana art categories, is also what separates them into the three distinct disciplines that they are today.

Memory is the mirror of amnesia, where anamnesia, the natural blend of memory and amnesia in actual life and recollections, is the mediating webbed site and the spider that weaves temporal threads across the three passages. Because we are re-viewing *visual* art historiography, we are also viewing a specialized form of anamnesia, a visual form of memory, which I call photic memory and which is different from phonetic memory. The photic memory, which Yoruba people call *aworan*, is the ability to remember visually and weave together visual and other aspects of experience. For instance, the photic memory enables the viewer to weave visual experiences with phonetic memory, to remember things clearly both visually and verbally. The photic memory is about seeing and remembering things in the context of what is seen, weaving together various things, like the spider weaves together the different sightings of its various eyes into one cohesive vision. Re-membering and re-collecting are active efforts at composing and of voluntary and involuntary choice making, of arranging and rearranging events into anamnesic narratives that best suit the purposes and agents of recollection.

It seems easy enough to see things and remember them. But sometimes certain historical contradictions form layers of veils that separate the viewer from what is viewed and dismembers the object on view from the subject that is viewing it. For the so-called traditional African art history, the veil that dismembers object from viewer is slavery; for contemporary African art, the veil is colonization; for African American art, the veil is immigration. But you could also move these veils around in multiple layers and see how they form layers of veils, in order to dislocate each of these categories. For instance, one could layer veils of slavery, colonization, and immigration as palimpsests that conceal and distort each of these categories, uniting them rather than dividing them.

In a complementary manner, one may project these veils to separate and dismember the study of Africana visual cultural history into the three categories of traditional, contemporary and diaspora. All of these veils make it difficult to see art objects for what they truly are. Rather, the veils deflect experiences through cultural prisms, which transform the body of Africana art history into a dismembered and decapitated subject in search of re-membering. One of the tasks of metacriticism in Africana art history, therefore, is to re-member the various parts of the subject into one symmetrical body, using photic memory. Let us start with the so-called traditional African art history and its dismembering veils of slavery, which I will introduce here with the concept of Ibadan *Konkobility*.

People outside the southwestern Nigeria are often not familiar with the concept of Ibadan *konkobility*.[4] It is an unscripted street opera that openly and wantonly transpires in the women's spaces at the Oja Oba, Beere, Aleekuso, Inalende, Gbagi, Dugbe, and other traditional markets of the volatile city of Ibadan, Nigeria. This operatic drama is often shocking at first and, upon further reflection, instructive and comic. When a particularly aggressive customer, often male, crosses the boundaries of civility in the rituals of bargaining for a commodity, he often initiates the process of Ibadan *konkobility*. The male customer has apparently named a price for a desired commodity, a particularly low price that the market woman considers ridiculous and inconsiderate. But if she is angered by his aggressiveness or cheapness, her countenance or tone does not betray her feelings. She simply says, "*E wa a gbe e,*" meaning, "Why bother to pay? Why not simply shoplift it?"

To a savvy bargainer, the discussion is just about to collapse into the leveling gravity of the black hole: this is the amber light before the red. When the Ibadan market woman coldly says, "*E wa a gbe e,*" he simply apologizes and departs or raises his bargaining price to a reasonable sum that brings a friendly smile to her face. But to the unwary bargainer, this is the prelude to the full balance of the Ibadan *konkobility*. The customer is shocked that she has addressed him with such a foul and insulting language and lets her know his mind. That is when she begins to balance the two halves of the laws of Ibadan simultaneous equation on his unsuspecting head.

As a small crowd of onlookers begins to gather, including street urchins, vagrant dogs, and free-range chickens, she unleashes a systematic admonition of this gentleman. But what is fascinating is that she does not immediately touch her opponent verbally. She starts by painting a vivid self-portrait that seems like a castigation of her own physical body. After finishing her self-rebuke, she then performs a thorough oral dismantling of her antagonist—combining narratives with poetry and songs[5] in such a systematic, scrupulous, and meticulous manner that may leave the customer speechless and gasping for air. She is happy, and the onlookers, as well as the object of ridicule, go home entertained and a little wiser for the street opera.

What is so fascinating about Ibadan *konkobility* is that it offers a semblance of symmetry: the market woman begins with her own critical self-portrayal before deconstructing the errant other. But one may call her critical self-portrait a mockery, more of a stage performance than a reality show, and even somewhat opportunistic and vindictive. Nevertheless, one cannot dismiss the fact that she realizes that you need to take a hard look at yourself before you begin to engage the world.

Art historians may find the *principle* of Ibadan *konkobility* useful and enlightening, although the style may seem unorthodox. Art historiography, especially concerning the dogging debate on primitivism and modernity in art, demonstrates that Western art history may benefit from a symmetrical methodology that is first self-critical before pouncing so relentlessly and mercilessly on the other. As Yoruba people say, the *dùndún* talking drum has two mouths: one praises the king, the other admonishes him. But the master drummer knows which mouth to use, depending on the occasion. For instance, in Benin art historiography, Western scholarship would like to pretend that the plunder by the British of Benin art is not an issue, and what matters are the aesthetic and iconographic aspects of the images.[6] On the other hand, some prominent African nationalists, scholars, and politicians want to turn attention away from the aesthetics of Benin art, and focus only on the 1897 plunders.[7]

The Parliament in Nigeria recently passed a motion for the repatriation of all the Benin art objects abroad.[8] Some Africanist art historians want to insist that Benin art objects have no independent formalist significance and cannot function outside the kingdom of Benin. Others, mostly Western art historians and critics, think that the objects contain universal formal qualities that transcend cultural limitations. The objects, as containers of global aesthetic values, are therefore totally fine where they reside in various Western collections. In African art generally, there are those artists, curators, and writers who want to focus on the aesthetic aspects only. One may call them the formalists. There are also those iconoclasts who do not acknowledge or discuss the aesthetics as much as they focus on issues of art repatriation along with ethnic considerations. I call them iconoclasts because of their insistence on disregarding the universal significances of the forms of African images, beyond strictly cultural and ethnic contents. They would terminate the new life or functions of Benin and other African art objects wherever these objects may now be located outside of the African continent. Both the formalists and the iconoclasts tacitly and tactically avoid the issue of slavery as pertinent to the photic memory that the indigenous art objects preserve. Yet it is clear that Benin and other art objects from Africa are often inseparably tied to slavery both in subject matter and in form.

Before Europeans arrived in Benin in 1486, Benin artists did not have any local sources for procuring brass. The minerals that constitute brass, namely copper and zinc, are not native to Benin soil. Scholars have long debated about the sources of the brass cast into objects by these artists and have speculated that they were most probably derived from the benefits of the trans-Sahara trade routes.[9] One of the ways by which scholars have dated Benin art is in terms of the use of materials. But the quantity of these pre-European sources of brass must have been paltry, judging by the relatively thinly cast wall of the naturalistic forms produced during the so-called Early Period.

The advent of the Portuguese to the Bight of Benin brought an incredible transformation to slavery as the Benin people knew it, but it also brought substantial transformation to Benin art. The arrival of the Portuguese with a plentiful supply of manila, which Benin sculptors melted down as raw materials for brass casting, launched Benin art into what the British scholar William Fagg has described as the Middle and Late periods. The brass heads that Benin sculptors cast became far more elaborate, with thicker walls on which intricately carved elephant tusks were mounted.

The Late Period sculptures are far more elaborate than the Middle Period works. Although other slave-procuring markets opened up, especially in the Bights of Biafra—and the markets from west central and southeast Africa, especially in the Kongo, intensified dramatically—there were still enough slave-marketing opportunities at Benin to facilitate access to European sources of brass. Late Period sculptures demonstrate more lavish representations of beaded works, with elaborate beaded wings— ornately cast in brass—projecting above the summit of the heads, from both sides, almost like elongated ears or feathered ornaments. Flat bases also extended beyond the circumference of the neck, creating a protuberance that enabled artists to display metaphoric and mythological characters such as dwarfs, sacrificial animals, and decorative assortments that further provide a more monumental presence to the heads.

Without the investment in slavery, Benin art might not have taken the formal directions that it took following the arrival of European traders, which opened up a new source of raw materials and another world of imagination. All of these historical developments have not escaped the content of Benin art, which is replete with the images of the rulers, their slaves, and the various European merchants, sailors, and soldiers who participated in the complex exchange in humans for goods. Without understanding slavery as an iconographic meter and cultural catalyst—albeit one that led to catastrophic consequences—it is impossible to understand Benin or almost any artistic tradition in Africa. In other words, slavery touched most parts of Africa and impacted the making of art in most cultures. The interpretations of the art of Benin must be located in the specificity of the culture of slavery. No scholar seems prepared to undertake such deconstructive analysis, beyond surface-level formal analysis to explore slavery as side bars, rather than the central iconological argument for making formal interpretations.

The Yoruba neighbors of the Benin are no better. A huge part of Yoruba art may be de-signed and de-scribed as slavery art, although discussions of these objects in art history has hardly elaborated on this issue. It is clear that scholars from Africa are avoiding the interpretation of their culture with the meters of slavery. Two books recently edited by the prolific historian Toyin Falola on Yoruba culture, one focusing on the diaspora and the other on the *in situ* culture, demonstrate the blindness of African scholars to the contingencies of slavery in the sculpting of African culture. The book, containing essays written mostly by African scholars, *Yoruba Creativity: Fiction, Language, Life, and Songs*, has no discussion of slavery in any shape or form. Almost as a taboo, slavery is hardly mentioned in the entire book, which, in its avoidance of the subject, only brings attention to its absence. In the only piece on Yoruba art in this book, Chris Adejumo, a prominent artist and art educator, writes, "Yoruba artisans have produced exquisite works in brass, textiles, terracotta, stone, and bronze. Aspects of Yoruba culture and traditional practices, such as folklores, myths, legends, and religious ceremonies, mostly inspire the contents of their works." Important and illuminating as his essay stands in the content of Yoruba art history, he does not mention that giant Yoruba gates and doors are replete with images of enslaved people, as well as representations of the rulers who benefited from the trade, the soldiers who committed the atrocities and caused so much grief, the European merchants who traded in slaves with the elites, and the women and children who grieved as a result of the trade.

In the corpus of Yoruba art, on shrine figurations, decorative icons, and secular designs, many of these women are shown with their babies on their backs or in their arms, supplicating and begging the divinities to deliver them from their insecure lives and times. I find Adejumo's writing to be refreshing and educative. Nevertheless what remains missing from his analysis is that he is like most writers who see these objects outside of the catastrophic historical context in which they are produced. His writing, following the pattern before him, presents the picture of a culture that is frozen in time, irresponsive to the travails of the terrible fate of enslavement within which the artists work. A detailed de-signing and de-scribing of these objects will show that the veil of slavery hangs heavily over the entire body of Yoruba art, just as it hangs over Benin art, and casts a shadow across the landscape of African art and its visual cultural historiography.[10]

Slavery has also contributed to the anonymity of African art, in the form of a curious dismembering that separates the body of the artist from the body of his or her work. This separation of signature from style causes identity alienations that deliver reverberations in the realm of gender and class. The consequence obscures issues of gender in African art, because there is no reference to the individual artist in the writings and exhibitions addressing African art. Separating artist from work is part of the history of the decimation of the continent caught in the middle of the triangular trade.

The collection of African art by private and public organizations began largely in the heyday of slavery, although these collection activities intensified considerably during the colonial era. Anthropology, the discipline responsible at that time for the documentation and analysis of the collected works, did not focus on the contributions of individual hands and styles. Rather, anthropology has explored what may be called an ethnic stylization, which attempted to identify iconographic distinctions along ethnic lines, rather than along the lines of individualism and specifically named artists. This ethnic stylization is a major motif in the "barbarian narratives" cooked to justify slavery and colonization as part of the European burden in the historical epic to Christianize, civilize and modernize. Yet this approach remains the methodology of choice in the study of historical African art.

Only a few Africanist art historians, notably Robert Farris Thompson, Henry Drewal, and Rowland Abiodun, have been interested in exploring the hands of the individual artist. Very few curators, namely Rosalyn Walker and Alisa Lagama, have explored the work of the individual artist within the indigenous artistic traditions. Because all of these historians and curators have invested mostly in Yoruba art, it is not an accident that most of the known individual artists in African art are Yoruba sculptors.

Pioneers such as William Fagg, Frank Willett, and Phillip Dark had visions that envisaged the study of individual hands in African art. But their anthropological and archaeological orientations seduced them and others to essentialist cultural interests. Susan Vogel, brilliant and important as her work has become in the dissemination of interpretations of African art, still fails to find validity in the individuality of the African artist. These scholars, curators, and critics of African art often fail to separate scholarly visions from ethnic or local interests. Vogel often argues that issues of individuality are a Western notion in which African societies are not often interested. She is unable to separate disciplinary interests from ethnic or societal limitations. If the regular person on the street of Houston, Texas, is unable to distinguish between Picasso and Braque in the Cubist period, does this mean that such distinctions are not crucial to the study of Cubism? More recently, young scholars such as Wole Famule are trying to locate the aesthetics of African art in the responses by ordinary folks participating in local festivals. The limitation is that ordinary folks in *any* society cannot participate in aesthetic discussions beyond the ordinary level. To obtain critical aesthetic perspectives in any society, scholars must delve more discriminately into layers of articulations that include folk responses as well as more rigorous views from more specialized members of the society. But all of these articulations must remain raw materials for the mediation of art historical and critical analysis, at the most intense levels of rigorous interventions.

It took an intellectual torrent such as Thompson to move the debate on African art to the theme of individual artistry and the verve of Drewal to refine and project the voice of the individual artist. Drewal's video on Ebosegbe, a Yoruba sculptor, defines in practical and audio-visual terms what Thompson and Willett have documented in their work on the creative process in Yoruba art. A sad and sobering note to young graduate students in this discipline: forget it. Because if you think you have a new and brilliant idea, R. F. Thompson has already done a book on it. Thompson's work on Jean-Michel Basquiat is one of the most enlightening and eloquent statements ever phrased about the impetuous Africana artist. Does it, therefore, mean that Thompson does not recognize the contemporary African artist as a viable category, or why has he held his tongue on this topic? Many African artists have remarked that if only Thompson, Abiodun, Cole, and others would write about contemporary African art, they would transform the discipline.

Babatunde Lawal used to balance his interest in historical art with contemporary works. His insight into the works of contemporary Nigerian artists including Bruce Onobrakpeya and Jimoh Buraimoh has been illuminating. But like many other African art historians, he has abandoned the contemporary art of Africa, and he seems to be more drawn into diasporic connections between African American artists and historical African art. Lawal's training and background began in contemporary design before he went to the United States to study art history. When he returned to Nigeria in the early seventies, he was the first chairman of the art department at the University of Ife, which combined art history and art training at the undergraduate level. He singlehandedly wrote the entire program of the art department, but he no longer seemed interested in contemporary African art after he moved to the United States in the eighties.

Rowland Abiodun's relationship with contemporary African art is more complicated because he actually was a painting teacher, as well as an art historian, from the late sixties to the late eighties. Although he curated several shows of contemporary African art when he was in Nigeria, he has refrained from committing himself in writing on that category of Africana art, a category whose validity some art historians and curators, including Yale's Fred Lamp, question as a viable "field" of study.

Abiodun has been busy with providing theoretical frameworks for the analysis of historical African art. His insistence on the importance of oral traditions in the study of African art marks a turning point in the discipline because it provides the opportunity to scrutinize the ancient canons as a dynamic process that continues to unfold. This scrutiny provides a scope for separating texts and designs into what Wande Abimbola calls malevolent and benevolent forces, which re-draws the constantly obliterated lines between the master narratives versus popular voices, power versus powerlessness, the oppressor versus the oppressed, in a postcolonial formulation. Abiodun's paradigmatic shift puts the pressure on the master narratives and reminds one of Bob Marley's counter-colonial Africana admonitions that "We are tired of the teachings of His Majesty. What we now want is a rebel philosophy." Marley renders in lyrical language what Abiodun couches in doctoral garbs.

The majesties on both sides of the Atlantic have in-scribed masternarratives into the bodies of many royal and popular art objects, and Abiodun's insistence on examining the details of traditional sources separates popular from master narratives. First, he suggests tiredness for a majestic and imperial Eurocentric art historicism that seeks to obliterate the legitimate indigenous voices in-scribed into the bodies of African art via traditional Western theories. Second, he suggests impatience with ahistorical viewings of African art that do not understand the different genres of oral traditions and cannot separate the voices of the men from the women, the masters from the rulers, the benevolent from the malevolent, and the royal from the popular cultures. It is from this perspective that Abiodun has provided tremendous insights into the understanding of gender in Africana art.

Gender is the understatement in historic African art studies, a category that is still in full denial of gender issues. The focus on sculpture by curators and art historians who succeeded the anthropologists in the study of African art, however, has gender implications. It is significant for the study of African art to note that men sculpt and women paint in most traditions in Africa. The inundation of private and public collections with sculpture and the typical absence of indigenous painting in most collections insinuate that the collection of African art, which is seemingly gender-neutral, is in fact fraught with gender partiality for men's works, to the exclusion of women's work. Although Thompson, one of the pioneers in African art history, painstakingly studied the work of Abatan, a female potter from the Niger-Benue region, museums and collectors have been a little reluctant to embrace women's work—usually painting, ceramics, and textiles—as art. But sometimes they show these women's works as examples of inspired crafts.

The separation of images into art and craft has been imported from European canons and imposed on African art, resulting in gender and class implications for the collection, display, preservation, documentation, and analysis of works from Africa. The hegemonic imbalance caused by the ravages of enslaving Africans by the West has stood in the way of analyzing African art with concepts that illuminate the shadows of anonymity and gender neutrality exogenously cast on the indigenous traditions of art making. Although a few art historians, notably Abiodun from Africa and Susanne Blier from the West, have interpreted the imaging of women in African art, little work has been done to rectify the gender imbalance in the study of African art.

Oyeronke Oyewunmi's discovery that the Yoruba language is silent on gender must not be misinterpreted and misapplied to the visual arts to suggest that there is no gender basis for the making of art in most parts of Yoruba culture or that gender is invisible in the making and consumption of Yoruba art.[11] As the indigenous traditions of art making enjoy a more multidisciplinary approach, the fragmentation of the discipline by issues of gender and class continues to diminish. The present resistance of Africanist art historians to theory makes it difficult to move the discipline forward beyond the cult of primitivism that continues to govern the collections and publications of indigenous African art. Residues from the days of slavery—in the form of condescending essays such as those authored by Gene Blocker—also condition the historiography generated from the perspectives of the master narratives.

Beyond slavery, the veil of colonization hangs over contemporary African art history, which separates artists, writers, and curators into three categories, namely, the "Bridges," "Progressives," and the "Generalists." The Bridges, regarded as ethnic essentialists, are contemporary artists, writers, and curators who seek connections between—as well as departures from—contemporary African image and the indigenous traditions of African. They see the work of the contemporary artist as a bridge between old and new cultures. The Bridges assert and focus on the desire by African artists to associate their art and identities with indigenous African traditions. These are people who do not see the colonization of Africa as the end of the old and the beginning of the new. They regard the culture as one integrated and organic flow, marked by the tides of time that relate to the daily lives of the people. The Bridges tend to ignore artists who do not make the iconographic connections between their works and their ancestral heritage as Africans.

In contrast and reaction to the Bridges is the assumption of the Progressives for the need to "move forward" from a traditional or ethnic culture, and embrace the modern or postmodern world without any ethnic baggage. The Progressives celebrate, promote, and encourage artists whose careers hinge on developing conceptual frameworks that deny the importance of bridging the old and the new aspects of African cultures, but whose works seek a clean break with the old. The artists, curators, and writers in this category prefer images that abruptly terminate the indigenous past of Africa and represent a freedom to be part of a larger, flat world. Moyo Ogundipe's paintings demonstrate the art of the Bridges, and the photographs of Zanele Muholi illustrate the work of the Progressives.

Ulli Beier, Dennis Duerden, Uche Okeke, Babatunde Lawal, and other critics and art historians associated with the Bridges assert and focus on the desire by African artists to identify their art with indigenous Africa, however ill-defined or romantic their concept of indigenous Africa remains. Such critics tend to disregard as naïve, reactionary, or colonized all contemporary artists who ignore connections between the old and new aspects of African culture.

The second group defined as the "Progressives" focus on the denial by African artists of any crucial connection between their works and their identities as Africans.

In reaction to the first group, the Progressives coalition, associated with artists and critics such as Okwui Enwezor, Olu Oguibe, and Orlando Jinorio, celebrate, promote, and encourage artists whose careers hinge on developing conceptual frameworks that deny the importance of indigenous African culture in the making and interpretation of contemporary art works. The artists and critics in this category doggedly ignore those artists who do make indigenous Africa art the cornerstone of their creative experience.

The voice of the Progressives became increasingly prominent toward the last decade of the twentieth century. It is a curiously aggressive voice that was not part of the pioneering discussions of African art, but now seeks to hijack, define, and manipulate the growth of contemporary African art in their conceptual directions. In their pronouncements in symposia, conferences, and essays, a number of these scholars and critics attempt to give the impression that there was no important debate before them or that what transpired before them was theoretically weak. The Progressives are often young writers and curators whose resonant voices usually sound impatient, self-promoting, and eloquent. With one or two exceptions, the Progressives have no formal training in African art history or criticism. But with strong convictions mediated by a paucity of exposure tinged with a large dosage of literary theory, these Progressive have bashfully stomped on iconographic grounds that more prudent scholars tread most softly.

Backed by Western critics, curators and collectors who sometimes privilege the ringing voices of the Progressives over and above the works of more subtle, experienced, historically grounded, and painstaking scholars, the Progressives have become the dominant group in the curating and analysis of contemporary African art. The Progressives collaborate with their Western promoters to curate elaborate art exhibitions and produce grandiose publications with generous public, independent, and corporate funding. The Progressives, as a result of their aggressive self-promoting, have displaced other important voices in the discussion of African art and have positioned themselves to their Western sources of funding as the only relevant scholars, curators, and artists in Africa. These Progressives, as they discard or taint everything that came before them, have succeeded in promoting a narrow concept of African art, focused on the production of images that mirror radical developments in contemporary Western art. They have also succeeded in marginalizing and alienating contemporary African artists who produce images that these critics do not consider "conceptual" or sufficiently "Modernist."

It is noteworthy that Okwui Enwezor has apparently not needed any formal training as an artist or art historian to build a deserved reputation as an international and imaginative curator. His curatorial style sometimes follows the international approach that uses works to illustrate prescribed themes. This illustrative curatorial approach almost assumes that art criticism and curatorship are not a secondary-level vocation that succeeds the primary level of art making. Almost like a collector, the illustrative curator may commission artists to fulfill their visions, rather than explore what artists actually do, and work with these studio products as raw curatorial materials. The curator now plays the artist. Needless to say, the increasing international visibility of illustrative curators such as En-wezor promotes their taste for making a break with the indigenous ances-try and looking to the West for inspirations, themes, and grants to sus-tain that taste.

Mediating between the Bridges and Progressives are the works of the Generalists such as Kojo Fosu, Marshall Ward, Nkiru Nzegwu, Jean Ken-nedy, Bolaji Campbell, and Sidney Kasfir. They equally address artists who deny or desire the importance of their identities as Africans. These critics do not openly join any side of the debate, but align themselves with all artists from Africa, irrespective of the conceptual positions—or lack thereof—of the artists. Bolaji Campbell, an artist, art historian, and curator, exemplifies the Generalists from Africa, who often are broadly trained, as opposed to the more narrow training of the art historian from the west. Trained in both the old and new art traditions of Africa, Camp-bell is comfortable with discussions of contemporary and historical art objects, as well as diasporic visual culture. He has written mostly on the Yoruba art in which he specializes, and because of his broad training, he is able to draw on his understanding of the old materials to reflect on contemporary art, as well as on diasporic arts. But this does not limit his writing and curating to the Bridges artists who explore their African roots. Although he was trained as an artist—he earned an MFA from Ile-Ife before his doctorate in art history from Madison—he has not allowed his own stylistic tastes to close his understanding and empathy for artists working in styles totally different from his own.

In a distinctive space that she has created for herself is Nkiru Nzegwu, whose work on gender in contemporary art remains matchless. She is one of the first Africanist art historians to recognize the potentials of the in-ternet as a tool for promoting debates of gender in African art. Nzegwu is also one of the few art historians of African art trained in aesthetics within an essentially philosophy discipline—which provides her with a rigorous background in the history and language of analytical thinking. The fear of theory that permeates the study of African art suggests that the discipline requires urgent doses of discourse from philosophy, espe-cially in the training of graduate students. Nzegwu trained as a painter before she became a philosophy crossover to art history. She has given up the making of art to become an art historian, following in the footsteps of her painting teacher, Rowland Abiodun. Nzegwu was a brilliant colorist and wonderful draftsperson. Her creative insight into composition is now evident in her detailed and inventive analysis of the works of contempo-rary African female artists on whom she has almost exclusively focused.

Sidney Kasfir exemplifies the rare Generalists from the West, because her training has enabled her to span both the historical and contemporary African art categories with ease and erudition. She is interested in all art-ists from Africa irrespective of race, gender, medium, religion, or style, as her far-ranging publications show. Her book on contemporary African art is remarkable in its encyclopedic coverage and analytical insight. Beyond her writing and curating work, her influence in the classroom has been tremendous because she has trained and continues to train young African art historians to imbibe widely from an offering that balances the historical, the contemporary, and the diasporic Africana visual cultures. Perhaps because of her Commonwealth origin, her interest in diasporic Africana art is exceptional because it includes black British as well as African American art.

*　*　*

In African American art history, a schism resulting from the crises of immigration is dividing the visual culture into conceptual camps between the "Integrationists" and the "Returnees." Some African American artists, curators, and writers who may be labeled the Integrationists profess that Africa is redundant or irrelevant in the discussion of African American art. The artist Kara Walker may represent this group. Others, the Returnees, represented by Jeff Donaldson, may insist that African American art must only be interpreted using African aesthetic parameters. Both sides could benefit from the symmetry of the *dùndún* talking drum and the symmetrical street language of Ibadan *konkobility* to create a more balanced discourse around the images.

One of the African American curators and writers providing a more balanced voice is Michael Harris, who says, "Connection to ancestral presences and memories by its very nature links the artist to larger aspects of his or her identity without threatening diversity or individuality. . . . Art with ancestral and individual qualities can have a powerful impact on people."[12] Harris understands the need for individuality in creative expressions and impressions, even in a collective vision that grounds itself in the present by connecting with its past. In his discussion of the work of Aaron Douglas, an African American artist, Michael Harris says, "One important aspect of Aaron Douglas's murals was his continual traversal of the period of black slavery back to an African past in his imagination of African Americans."[13]

But not all African American artists are eager to make a connection with Africa. Kara Walker said, "I don't know if I really have an Africa."[14] Although declared with nonchalant bravado, her statement is phrased as a lack in terms of what she does not have, rather than what she does have or even knows.

Kara Walker's position at the beginning of the twenty-first century somewhat reminds one of the debate of the early twentieth century between the Africanist Allain Locke and the universalist James Porter. But desegregation laws have officially removed the color line that W. E. B. Du Bois highlighted in the relationship between African Americans and

Anglo-Americans. This does not mean that the color line is no longer
there. It simply means that the line is now officially permeable, fragmented, and subject to willful transgression—from class, religion, gender,
and sexual transgressors, among other interests that previously remained
in the ethnic closet. The ancestral images and references to Africa in
feminist-related art by African American women are considerable and remarkable. The famous lesbian poet Audre Lorde grounded her lyrical and
performance imageries in African metaphors, colors, and phrasings. However, recent writings that have focused on gender and African American
women artists, whether as exhibition catalogs or as books, have not done
justice to the depth of transatlantic connections in visual and performance works by African American women.

In her parting of ways with Afro-centric essentialism, Frieda High
W. Tesfagiorgis has withdrawn her concept of Afro-femcentrism from the
metalanguage of African American art history, although the reverberations and applications of the term remain resonant and valid. In the company of female African American artist/scholars including Adrian Piper
and Howardena Pindell, Tesfagiorgis shows the possibility of combining
a transatlantic vision with a black feminist resolution, while in-scribing
an individualistic head, heart, and hand into the writing. The details and
illuminations of Tesfagiorgis's work are matched only by the brilliance
of Adrian Piper, whose meta-artistic assays bridge the boundaries of philosophy, art making, and activism. Piper's voluminous writings are part of
her art making, and the art often levitates into writing, making her one of
the most fascinating creative minds in contemporary art and art history.
Although she teaches philosophy and not art or art history, her influence
radiates across the three disciplines of philosophy, providing her with an
invaluable insight that she brings into Africana studies. So far she has not
asserted an interest in Africa in her writing or art. But she thinks she has
an Igbo ancestry that she drops into a personal conversation. Because she
blends the boundaries of life and performance art, the mode of personal
conversations is an important medium of in-scribing and de-scribing for
her. Her work de-signs and de-scribes patriarchal modes of de-scribing
others.

Ten years ago, one could count all the books on African American
art history on the fingers of one hand. There was mostly the timeless
textbook, Samella Lewis's *African American Art*, and a couple of volumes, mostly catalogs associated with the energy of James Porter, David
Driskell, and Romare Bearden. In the last ten years, many new and exciting publications have emerged, focusing on African American art and
artists and associated with the works of curators, writers, and art historians, including Richard Powell, Thelma Golden, and Lowery Simms.
Although the bibliographic size is still thin relative to publications on
contemporary Western art, the quality of discussion gets increasingly nu-

anced, and it has remained relevant toward the projection of the African American culture as a dynamic humanistic collective that has no physical or psychological boundaries, yet remains within and transgresses beyond conceivable conceptual frameworks of stereotypes and prototypes. One could make a similar statement about the thinness of published volumes on contemporary African art, which some international curators have described as the new frontier in artistic experience. The question of the theoretical perspectives of the writers remains pertinent in the metacritical analysis of the debate.

The tendency to regard black art in America as essentially diasporic without further analytical complication is in itself highly problematic. Beyond the text, psychology, and analogy of double consciousness defined by W. E. B. Du Bois in his classic book, *The Souls of Black People*, repeating patterns of contradictory dualism fragment the artistic visions, psyches, and physiologies of black artists in the United States. These contradictory fragmentation patterns ironically coalesce and become a unifying characteristic element of this black culture. Nobody defines these patterns of contradictory fragmentation better than the prominent and quite controversial African American painter Michael Ray Charles, who declares:

> When I began making art several years ago, I was defined as an African American artist. As time went on, those who marketed my work in New York began to redefine me as an American artist, to broaden my audience, and make my work appeal beyond the limitations and walls of race and racial stereotypes. Much later, as I reflected on this renovation and redefinition of my identity, I realized that as much as the market promotes me beyond the stigma of race, the dominant culture continues to see me as an angry black man wherever I step, and there is no escape from that ethnic label. The reality is inevitable, because as long as race matters, as long as people must define you in a specific way, there is no running away from the double bind. It is a sort of double-edged sword. I now describe myself as an African American artist. It's a contradiction that one cannot resolve. One lives it up, and it shows up in the work that one does.

Using his own painting as a metaphoric reference as well as an illustration of this ongoing complex identity dilemma that he says was a cause of bother to him, Ray says:

> There is this painting that I did titled *Disappearing Self*, in which I depict a black man standing before a white background, painting himself white to fit in within the picture. This is the drama of the black culture in America. One cannot go back to Africa because this is the only home we know. One must continue to stay here within the contradictions and definitions of the dominant society.[15]

In explaining works by artists such as Michael Ray Charles, many studies of African American art have staked too much claim on Double Consciousness as the most abiding truth for analyzing diasporic creative productions. But as I argued in the preface of *Colored Pictures* by Michael Harris, the theories of Double Consciousness are metaphoric assumptions beyond which one must reach for meaning to understand late twentieth-century and early twenty-first-century contradictory fragmentations within which the black body is located. It is pertinent to draw on the body of Michael Jackson, the silhouettes of Kara Walker, the paintings of Michael Ray Charles, the early performance art of Adrian Piper, the photographs of Michael Harris, and the mixed-medias of Jeff Donaldson as venues for exploring the contradictions and fragmentations of race in black diasporic bodies.

Second, it is important to complicate the thesis of contradiction and fragmentation by theorizing psychological issues of masquerading, using visual integration and alignment of home and exile. Scholars may elaborate on themes of "cleaning" as healing and masking, in terms of revelation and concealment. The work of Bing Davis and other artists who explore similar paths of appropriating African images becomes an equation for balancing and interrogating the contradictions and fragmentations of African American experiences, where home is perceived as a land of exile. Scholars have not sufficiently investigated the psychoanalytical and biographical journey tracked on theoretical paths of mask making. It is totally appropriate to use the Greek god Janus as the embodiment of the gatekeeper in Western cultures to explore metaphors of crossing borders and transgressing beyond boundaries and conventions of homelands, while expanding on Freudian strategies of concealment and revelation. As allusions and illustrations, one may reference the productions of similar diasporic workers, including John Coltrane, Lawson Oyekan, and Michael Harris, who could be categorized as the Black Argonaut, for whom returning home has contradictory implications both of psychic introspection and physical excursions into foreign places, relocated as home.

Studies of rape in the African American culture are dirty linen that was well hidden until relatively recently when writers including Ntozake Shange and Alice Walker began to illuminate the problem in ways that have focused on and fragmented black struggles and solidarity. In Africana art history, writers have yet to investigate this problem with a psychoanalytic twist in African American visual culture, elaborating on inordinate and hypersexual consumption in the works of artists including Renee Cox and Kara Walker. Using Freudian ideas of male decapitation enables scholars to study such works as a reversal of the Oedipus and Electra complex, where the black female Amazon warrior, alienated from the father figure, not only symbolically emasculates the black male but also joins forces with his perceived tormenters to decapitate him, mostly as a purgative act of self-humiliation.

Several prominent writers including Walter Dean Myers, Eric Dyson, and Peter Goldman have examined and debated the portrayals of Martin Luther King and Malcolm X as opposites, complements, and contrasts. Portraits of both black leaders, as symbolic figures, abound in high and low places including museums and street graffiti. It is, however, crucial to examine the psychosomatic amalgamation of both figures and their visual fragmentation into caricatures as *dreamer* versus *fighter* in a land of nightmares. The location and displays of sculptures of Martin Luther King in public places, including college campuses, civic centers, and public parks, suggests a cultural statement about public perception of this civil rights leader as dreamer. The gestures and body language of his representations are equally semantic as acts of dreaming. The silent restrictions placed on the display of Malcom X's portraits in public places suggests a general political attitude toward the perceived life and death of this black leader as fighter. Both representations, nonetheless, collapse into the myth of angry black men in conceptual reworkings by Michael Ray Charles. Writers who continue to focus on racial stereotyping have not yet explored the explosion of black macho-male mythologies in Charles's work, mostly as a psychoanalytical study in self-portrayal.

Using the work of Jean-Michel Basquiat as visual points of reference, writers including bell hooks are elaborating on the prodigious contribution of his work to visual cultures. But no one situates his work within the larger definition of pathological consumption and consequent creativity of black artists and celebrities including John Coltrane, Oprah Winfred, Biggie Smalls, and Star Jones. The evolution of jazz and hip-hop cultures produces contradictions of engorgement and dissipation, including "up is down," "singing is crying," and "violence is peace." Consumptions of drugs and guns complicate these contradictions that manifest themselves in the creative surges of blues, jazz, R&B, and hip-hop cultures. To contextualize this phenomenon, it is illuminating to explore the productions of John Coltrane and Marvin Gaye, together with the works of older rap artists including Grandmaster Flash, Kool Moe Dee, and Public Enemy. These artists are inversely comparable with recent rap artists such as Snoop Doggy Dog, Biggie Smalls, and others produced by Marion "Suge" Knight, founder and former CEO of Death Row Records. While highlighting Basquiat, scholars may draw on the visual culture of representing musicians by artists as far back as Henry Tanner (*Banjo Player*), but also as recent as Romare Bearden, Louis Delsartes, and Jeff Donaldson, to explore the contradictions of popular culture in the fragmentation of black American society with addiction and creativity, hope and despair, as well as alienation and redemption.

No important writing in African American visual culture has visited the sexually and racially charged work of Glen Ligon. Perhaps it is possible to invent a concept of "tripled consciousness" and draw on fragmental issues of *sexuality* and *pathology* that have driven Ligon's work outside of the confines of *race*. Deflected into the margins and ghettos of the most technologically and scientifically experimental nation of the late twentieth and early twenty-first centuries, blacks have crossed substantial cultural barriers with their bodies, contributing to the international domination in sports and entertainment by America. Perhaps less popular has been the heightened sexual experiments in black diasporic cultures where boundaries are crossed and envelopes pushed in areas often regarded as strictly taboo, especially in diasporic gay communities. Already marginalized, black artists of gay dispensation often become permanent dwellers in the closet, whereas white artists have felt bolder to publicly assert themselves. The consequences are dire, including the explosion of HIV infections and complications into full-blown AIDS within diasporic cultures. Largely uninvestigated, the work of Ligon is perhaps the most prominent diasporic venue that has brought the plight of HIV infections into the open.

A story that is hardly told is the process through which the systematic subversion of Christian values contributed tremendously to liberation struggles in black diasporic culture, despite the popular association of civil rights activities almost exclusively with black churches. The work of John Biggers, in its diasporic theological pluralism, looks at the contributions of diversity in religious worship in African American communities. Biggers visually argues that the campaigns and struggles for equality and civil rights in diasporic cultures transcend the confines of Christianity. His work elaborates on the re-presentation of African Americans to explore African myths, symbols, and religions. He further articulates the historical presence of a poly-theological praxis that sometimes regards Christian orthodoxy as part of the black diasporic problem. The transition from theological faith to political skepticism, as shown in writings and paintings by African Americans including Ralph Ellison, Amiri Baraka, Charles White, Harriet Powers, Aaron Douglas, and Jean-Michel Basquiat, reveals a systematic polarization of theological activities that mirrors the multiple political history of struggles against subordinating values imposed by the dominant culture, within which blacks are (dis)located.

With its symmetrical structure, *konkobility* sets up a critical value system that, in spite of its street crudeness, recognizes how justice or equity operates on symmetry and balance. *Konkobility* also highlights how the story may be totally asymmetrical when represented from the "one-point-perspective" (of the market woman, in this case), despite the underlying purpose of presenting a balanced view. The market woman ends up presenting her own values, even as she purports to present the whole story, from a symmetrical perspective. This may also be regarded as coloring. Everything is colored, not just in a literal way but also figuratively.[16] The question is how to discover the complementary form of the colors to create symmetry. In its representation of Africana arts, does art history totally ignore the complementary values of indigenous others, thus ending up presenting Africana art with colored, asymmetrical hegemonic structural values and interpretations from the perspective of slave ownership?

Values, subsequently, are pivotal visual cultural experiences in metaphorical terms. Value, in its reference to light and dark experiences in visual culture, is primarily a photic and secondarily a phonetic experience, although both do not so easily separate in ordinary anamnestic recollections of daily experience. Semioptics, coined from semeion+optics (sign and seeing), is the semiological system of art historical de-scribing and de-signing that is positioned to highlight the photic and phonetic importance of *values* and illuminate the place of *symmetry* and *balance* in the search for meaning in art history. Semioptics therefore emphasizes the value of *equilibrium* and *justice* in the *equation* for interpretation in visual cultural speculations. Evolving as the Manichean balance to semiotic de-scribing, semioptic de-signing addresses speculations that are visual in the context of recollection or anamnesia.

To strike a critical balance, semioptics equates the outer or contextual content of an artwork with its inner or subtexual content. This is what I call *de-signing*, a *balanced de-scribing*. The value of semioptics in the de-signing of Africana art is remarkable partly because semioptics focuses its balanced semantic light on the subtextual or in-scribed content behind the content, and not solely on the direct contextual, ascribed, or immediate cultural content of the art object. For example, because the Benin culture has been active from the earliest contact between Africa and the West, the semioptic content of Benin art will contain and transcend the ascribed immediate functional Benin court iconography, to include a hidden inscribed content that highlights the history of European encounter, interaction, and subjugation. That history, for example, must highlight the role of slavery in the production of the art works and balance the weight and pains of enslavement with the clamor for repatriation. Semioptic equations are illuminating only to the extent to which they evaluate Africana images as cultural linkages between Africa and the Diasporas, including photic or visual memories and retinal recollections of the activities of the triangular trade. In Africana art, semioptics explores the in-scribed content of a-scribed visual content and the in-scribed form of a-scribed visual form through de-signing and de-scribing.

Semioptics, as visual culture, is therefore applied art history resulting from the need to balance the semiotic master narratives emanating from the West about Africana culture since the arrival of the Portuguese ships.

As a consequence of its birth in the horrendous maternities of the Middle Passage, semioptics is specifically de-signed to emphasize the functional aspects of visual cultural studies and to highlight the value of art history as a humanistic tool—to illuminate and evaluate with geophysical, biological, psychological, and historical perspectives that de-signs designs and de-scribes descriptions. Because of the insidious presence of trauma in the art and art historiography of Africana visual culture, the place of ethical and aesthetic balance is paramount in semioptics, to balance the semiotic inclination for mere representation. The judicious and critical application of the semioptic values of balance is therefore most revealing and compelling, as we re-member the fragments and shards of traditional African art, contemporary African art, and diasporic African art into an integral Africana visual culture. We await the hour of a thoroughly de-mastered semioptic narrative re-membering the three fragments into one unified historical form with humanistic anamnesia.

NOTES

1. The dating in this paper relies mostly on the work of William Fagg, whose contribution has been controversial in some respect. Because of his seeming defense of the British Punitive Expedition to Benin, he is sometimes regarded as a colonial agent. His dating of the Nok culture is disputed by Cheikh Anta Diop in *Notes Africaines*, no 152, October 1976, IFAN, Dakar. I'm indebted to Babarcar M'bow for offering me an illuminating if radical and speculative African nationalist perspective on the history of metallurgy in Africa.

2. This is not a debate on whether African slave owners treated their slaves better than Anglo slave owners, or whether slavery was better or worse in Africa or the Americas. Semioptics seeks to de-sign and de-scribe the in-scribed master narratives, signs, and designs a-scribed to the dominant cultures on both sides of the Atlantic.

3. Babatunde Lawal, "Aworan: Representing Self and Metaphorical Other in Yoruba Art," *Art Bulletin*, September 2001.

4. This is a pidgin form of *culpability*.

5. The beginning of one of the chanted poetry goes: *Yo biladi fuulu / Konkobility / Bo ba di kootu / Ma gbe o ta / Ma fi o sanwo ile.* Translation: You bloody fool / Culpability / I'll take you to court / And get you sold / Your proceeds will pay for the suit.

6. About a decade ago, there was a heated exchange between William Fagg, one of the Western pioneers in Benin art studies, and Ekpo Eyo, one of the pioneering Africans to study Benin art. Fagg defended the British attack of Benin City and the plunder of the art works. Eyo took a contrary position, advocating the immediate repatriation of the works. Western scholars have played a prominent role in the study of Benin art and history, but hardly do they tackle the issue of the repatriation that is usually raised by the indigenes.

7. The British attacked the kingdom of Benin in 1897, sacked the capital city of Benin, exiled the king, and removed hundreds of art objects from the kingdom.

8. See Heather Holloway, "African Royalties Demand Return of Ancient Stolen Treasures," in *Blink: Black Information Link*, www.blink.org.uk, March 26, 2004.

9. Timothy Garrard, "Benin Metal-casting Technology," in *The Art of Power / The Power of Art: Studies in Benin Iconography*, ed. Paula Ben-Amos and Arnold Rubin (Los Angeles: Museum of Cultural History, UCLA, 1983), 18.

10. Harvard's Abiola Irele cautions me, "Moyo, frankly, you exaggerate here. Let's take a pot, any pot, from the old tradition. How does that reflect slavery?" Impossible, I think, to know whether the pot embodies slavery or not, but the shadow of slavery hangs over it, as long as it has been decontextualized and dismembered from the name of the artist, date of manufacture, original patronage, and place of manufacture. Without this information, the pot cannot be cleared of its potentiality as a slave paraphernalium.

11. The brilliance of Oyewunmi's work is most manifest in her discussions of language and less focused on images.

12. Michael D. Harris, *Colored Pictures: Race and Visual Representation* (Chapel Hill: University of North Carolina Press, 2003), 250.

13. Ibid., 219.

14. Jerry Salt, "Kara Walker: Ill Will and Desire," *Flash Art*, November/December 1996, 86.

15. Michael Ray Charles, interview conducted in his office, August 2008, Austin, Texas.

16. Harris, *Colored Pictures*.

REFERENCES

Eyo, Ekpo. 1986. "A Threat to National Art Treasures: The Illicit Traffic in Stolen Art." In Yudhishtir Raj Isar, ed., *The Challenge of Our Cultural Heritage: Why Preserve the Past?* Washington, D.C.: The Smithsonian Institution Press.

Diop, Cheikh Anta. 1976. *Notes Africaines*, no. 152. Dakar: IFAN.

Fagg, William. 1967. *The Art of Western Africa: Tribal Masks and Sculptures*. London: Collins/UNESCO.

Garrard, Timothy. 1983. "Benin Metal-casing Technology." In Paula Ben Amos and Arnold Rubin, eds., *The Art of Power/The Power of Art: Studies in Benin Iconography*. Los Angeles: Museum of Cultural History, UCLA.

Harris, Michael D. 2003. *Colored Pictures: Race and Visual Representation*. Chapel Hill: University of North Carolina Press.

Holloway, Heather. "African Royalties Demand Return of Ancient Stolen Treasures. March 26, 2004. http://www.blink.org.uk. Accessed 2007.

Lawal, Babatunde. 2001. "Àwòrán: Representing Self and Metaphorical Other in Yoruba Art." *Art Bulletin* 83, no. 3: 498–526.

Oyewumi, Oyeronke. 1997. *The Invention of Women: Making an African Sense of Western Gender Discourses*. Minneapolis: University of Minnesota Press.

Saltz, Jerry. 1996. "Kara Walker: Ill Will and Desire," *Flash Art* 29, no. 191: 82–86.

12 OUT OF CONTEXT: THINKING CULTURAL STUDIES DIASPORICALLY

Grant Farred

> By itself, out of context—but a context, always, remains open, thus
> fallible and insufficient.
> —*Jacques Derrida, Specters of Marx*

The singular claim of Cultural Studies is that there can be no project of the political, no thinking of the political, without culture,
without the study of culture at its core.[1] As a discipline inherently resis-
tant to definition, Cultural Studies can be broadly understood as a field
of study (founded in the mid-1950s) attentive to historical conjuncture. It
is marked as a field that has, from its inception, taken seriously the intersection amongst politics, various popular cultures (as well as cultures
of resistance, subversion, and subaltern innovation), and the possibility of
culture as a mode of thinking that critically engages all articulations of
power—state, institutional, personal, and so on. For precisely this reason,
there can be no thinking of the political without the serious consideration
of that confluence between the political and the popular. Cultural Studies
articulates the complicated relationship that always exists amongst politics, "Culture," and popular culture. So central is culture and popular culture to the thinking of the political, in fact, that several Cultural Studies scholars—many of whom have turned to the business of intervening
in the process of state policymaking—have suggested that the preoccupation with popular culture has displaced politics as the discipline's primary project. Nowhere has the turn to Policy Studies been more evident,
of course, than among Australian Cultural Studies thinkers such as Tony
Bennett, Ien Ang, Ian Hunter, and Stuart Cunningham.[2] These scholars
have argued against the "abstraction" of Cultural Studies, against the
literary-based analysis that has long held sway. They have insisted that

the only way to do Cultural Studies with any kind of political efficacy is to intervene at the level of the state: at the level of the political where bureaucratic decisions are made; in those political offices from which the state administers power. Policy Studies is, in Foucaultian terms (that resonate, intriguingly and discordantly, with that of Carl Schmitt's), the recognition that Cultural Studies can only impress itself upon the political by articulating itself as a critique of "governmentality."

However, because the history of Cultural Studies is—and has been since its founding in the ideological, intellectual and ethical crises of the mid-1950s[3]—the history of intervention in the particularities of successive political moments, Cultural Studies is perforce the discipline of necessary and generative insufficiency. Because it has no one methodology—in fact, it can be said to have either several methodologies or none at all—Cultural Studies cannot address every political event in the same way; one mode of intervention is, in all likelihood, insufficient for another. Paradoxically, it is precisely this disciplinary insufficiency that has created the space for those scholars who favor policy advocacy, to do their political work within the broad Church of Cultural Studies. This "inherent insufficiency," the political and disciplinary response to the specificity of the event, has created in Cultural Studies not only the possibility for thinking particularity but also the imperative to think "out of context": to think outside (if we can conceive of the outside as antonymic to orthodoxy; which is to say, not unrelated to the "object" itself), outside a discipline that has no history of orthodoxy.

Cultural Studies has established itself through thinking outside the available paradigms with which it has long been associated (literature, history, and sociology, to name but three), through a disregard for disciplinary boundaries and purity (even as it retains strong links to Literary Studies, a connection that remains too strong for many within Cultural Studies). Cultural Studies derives its critical force from its ability to think both within and outside the immediate conjuncture, inside, outside, and beyond the demands of the particular moment. Cultural Studies compels a thinking of the political despite the potential for fallibility—for being wrong—and despite the insufficiencies at hand—conceptual, political, practical—that are constitutive of any event. Cultural Studies demands, in that most difficult of negotiations, the simultaneity of dis-articulation and re-articulation of context. It engenders a thinking "out of context," against the prevailing logic, and an imagining of how that context might be differently named, politically. We might then say that Cultural Studies represents a perpetually dislocated or diasporic thinking. This is not the same as suggesting that Cultural Studies, especially in the United States, always addresses the issue of the diaspora. There are, however, traditions, amongst which the Centre for Contemporary Cultural Studies (CCCS) at the University of Birmingham is preeminent, where the diaspora can be said to have been pivotal in politically reorienting Cultural Studies. Both these tendencies will be engaged more fully later.

Writing about the experience of an author entering a language from the outside, Kafka as a "Czech writing in German, and Beckett an Irishman (often) writing in French," Gilles Deleuze argues that this signals an approach to the use of a language that is not the author's own: "What they do . . . is invent a *minor use* of the major language within which they express themselves entirely; they *minorize* this language, much as in music, where the minor mode refers to dynamic combinations in perpetual disequilibrium" (Deleuze, 109, original emphasis). The experience of the diaspora, following Deleuze's thinking, could be represented as the "minorizing" constitutive of human dislocation and deracination. The diaspora "minorizes" the experience of the political subject: relocated to the metropolitan center, the political subject is disenfranchised and desubjectivated by the event of occupying the time and space of the other (while being identified as Other); the other who (fully or even partially) acknowledge the time, culture, language, and history of the Other. This is the condition of the diaspora: to struggle with, against, in spite of the event of being "minorized." It is to stake a claim for the right to "write"—think, speak, imagine in a language that is "outside" of the "major" language. To be diasporic is to think "minorization" while acquiring fluency in the major language that can never be either fully owned—inhabited—or dismissed.

Because Cultural Studies, which exemplifies the complicated experience of disciplinary "minorization," is premised on the recognition that every historical moment is founded on its own political, that every historical moment produces its own particular articulation of the popular, and that every historical moment demands that Cultural Studies think itself in relation to the specific relations between the political and the popular, every Cultural Studies conjuncture is a "context" unto itself, outside of the context of the event before or after; out of context in relation to every other context. The crises (Suez, Nikita Khrushchev's denunciation of Stalin's violence and the Soviet invasion of Hungary) that produced Cultural Studies in the mid-1950s are distinct from the conditions that enabled its institutional location in Britain and the United States in the 1960s and '70s—institutions such as CCCS and the University of Warwick.

Consequently, the only way to think about Cultural Studies is as a series of dislocations, a series of "diasporas." That is, to think of Cultural Studies as analogous to movement, often the consequence of economically, politically, ethnically, and/or ideologically inspired deracination—the forced migration of black African (or Asian or Caribbean) bodies to places outside of their originary locale. While acknowledging the value of the long-standing Cultural Studies tradition of always thinking contextually, from its origins with the deeply rooted work of Raymond Williams (from his groundbreaking essay "Culture is Ordinary" to his autobiographical novel *Border Country*) to Richard Hoggart's *Uses of Literacy* and Fredric Jameson's famous opening injunction in *The Political Unconscious*, "Always historicize," the argument here is for a different, countervailing recognition: to think out of context, to complicate the understanding of how context might work, to think the insufficiencies of "context." Cultural Studies, it could be argued, cannot presume that it needs only to repeat itself in order to do its political work. In fact, the discipline has always been politically singular but contextually "sovereign," simultaneously composed of contiguous events and practices but also political sites and moments outside of and particular to itself.

Thinking the African diaspora from outside can produce, as in the work of diasporic South African author J. M. Coetzee, a connection—a thinking—with other diasporas and indigeneities—as in the work of diasporic Australian writer David Malouf (who writes about his native Australia, sometimes from Italy)—that reveals the political necessity of maintaining not only the locality of the "outside" but retaining in any such reading the tension inherent in producing a "minorized" political subject.

THE SINGULAR AND THE REPETITION OF THE SINGULAR

> The fact remains that any mode of thinking that is the least bit singular reveals itself in saying basically the same thing, which it cannot but hazard every time in the colorful prism of circumstances.
> —Jacques Rancière, *The Philosopher and His Poor*

Thought as a constitutive outside, Cultural Studies is, following Rancière, "singular." It is a particular way of reading the political and yet, even as it refuses repetition, it retains a commitment to intervention. Every event of Cultural Studies thus "says the same thing" without "saying the same thing." Every articulation of the African diaspora is unthinkable without the recognition that saying the "same thing" is never saying the same thing. It is not simply that every experience of the Africa diaspora is particular, specific to itself, as much as it shares key phenomena with other experiences of the diaspora, but that every account of the African diaspora is "out of context." It belongs to another place, in another place, a place that is not the place where it is, a place for which the diasporic subject may or may not yearn, a place where the diasporic subject may or may not want to return, if such a return were at all possible. To be diasporized is to be articulated to, disarticulated from, and rearticulated through a context that is outside of the place from where the subject speaks. The fallibilities and insufficiencies inherent to the diaspora emerge out of context beyond the place of speaking. The African diaspora must be thought as a multiple and variegated articulation, as that precarious, and precariously dis-advantaged, position of the outside (that is problematically related to the "inside"). The outside, which is of course simultaneously its own kind of inside, is the only place from which to speak the diaspora.

Because of its Rancièrean "singularity," Cultural Studies has always been a venerable poacher's practice. It is a "discipline" that borrows from other forms of thought in order to think itself precisely because it cannot "say the same thing," even when the political appears to be the "same." In order to produce its critiques and interventions, Cultural Studies has drawn from, and continues to draw from, a range of disciplines. These include, but are not limited to, Literary Studies, Sociology, Political Theory, Policy Studies, Philosophy, and Anthropology. Cultural Studies has been and remains, in Derrida's *Specters of Marx* sense, "open" to other disciplines because of its fallibilities and insufficiencies. It is "open" to other disciplines precisely because it is at once less than its "disciplinary host" and, by virtue of its political practice, more than that discipline. Critically attentive to its lacks, Cultural Studies understands the imperative to address—and redress—its "disciplinary" insufficiencies. It is, in this regard, a "discipline" that cannot be "closed": it must always be open to that which it is not. Cultural Studies cannot do its work without a singular commitment to—an openness to—the contingencies of the moment; it cannot do its conceptual work without the tools it has culled from those disciplines with which it is dialogically linked. However, the effects of disciplinary openness work both ways. Cultural Studies is both, in Shakespeare's terms, a "borrower and a lender": it enriches and problematizes those other disciplines as much as it utilizes them. It has, among other things, infused Literary Studies with a critical means for incorporating into its orbit strategies for reading the popular; it has lent sociology a keener, more contested notion of how culture functions; and it has made available to anthropologists a more difficult articulation of the role of culture in society.

It is in its dislocation, its disarticulation and rearticulation of itself, that Cultural Studies reveals itself to be, both paradigmatically and philosophically, a diasporic practice. The diaspora is, like Cultural Studies, out of sheer psychic and political necessity, a poacher's modality. This is in large measure because Cultural Studies has, with rare exceptions, never had the benefit of a permanent institutional location.[4] Like a diasporic subject, at once in search of a space of respite and insurgent, at once tolerated and made to feel unwelcome, simultaneously aggressive and unsure about this new place in which it finds itself, Cultural Studies has had to rely on the kindness of institutional—well, if not strangers, then— "reluctant relatives" in order to do its work. Following Derrida, we might think Cultural Studies and the diaspora as an "autoimmunity."[5] There can be no diaspora without the preparedness to risk death (the literal, psychic, and social death of the deracinated subject), and yet it is the very "inhospitality" of home (politically, economically, and socially induced inhospitality) that makes the taking of that risk absolutely necessary.

To extend this autoimmune logic, there is always a double risk of in/hospitality: the metropolis could result in the repetition of the very inhospitality that is being fled—such as the hostility experienced by African migrants in Europe or the persecution visited upon that paradigmatic diaspora, the Roma, in places such as Italy, Slovenia, Bulgaria, and Slovakia. Of course, the metropolis could also prove "hospitable," inhabitable in ways that "home" is precisely not. It is in this way that in/hospitality is always, by dint of historical force, central to any discussion of the diaspora. It is for this reason that questions are asked: How in/hospitable are conditions in the place of arrival? What form does in/hospitability take? Are all diasporas equal? (How, for example, to think the relationship between African Americans—the "political subjects" of the Middle Passage—and late twentieth and early twenty-first-century African migrants to the United States? How much, if any, "racial solidarity" can be presumed? In fact, who has the historic right to be named "African American?" Should there not be a place for the term "American Africans" in the lexicon of the diaspora?) What series of political events or what political climate shapes the discourse of in/hospitability? Are all pivotal to the diasporic experience? In/hospitality, risk, death ("suicide" is Derrida's more trenchant term), and the language of profound uncertainty are fundamental to writing the diaspora, to writing the encounter of the other with the Other.

Cultural Studies has operated, sometimes furtively, always with a greater or lesser sense of in/hospitality, sometimes with the consent of the institutional authorities, from within language departments, especially English, anthropology, and sometimes sociology, political science, or comparative literature—or, to use the more precise architectural metaphor, Cultural Studies has had to function under the in/hospitable auspices of these departments. As a consequence, Cultural Studies has been relieved of the burden of institutional maintenance or institution building and is without a base within the academy: without a secure place from which it could do its work so that the possibility of doing work, to say nothing of the conditions of labor, is always understood as a contingent possibility.

As a result, Cultural Studies has "wandered," if not like a Wordsworthian "cloud" then certainly like the displaced subject of the diaspora, from one institutional site to another, making institutional accommodations here, concessions there, staking claims, in order to continue its work. If there is no one Cultural Studies methodology, an aspect of the "discipline" many of its practitioners value rather than express any concern about, then it is because it has for more than half a century operated as a diasporic subject of the university—a (barely) acknowledged presence, a sometimes ghostly presence, haunting "pure" disciplines, spectrally present, but a presence, nevertheless, and almost invariably a political one. Cultural Studies' propensity for innovative, creative thinking, for working across and often in disregard for disciplinary boundaries, is a consequence of it never being "disciplined" into a methodology, into a singular way of thinking, into political or cultural one-ness. Cultural Studies, we might say at the risk of romanticizing diasporic existence, has made a virtue out of institutional in/hospitable homelessness—or semi-homelessness, at the very least.

It is in the process of living out of context that Cultural Studies has, like the diasporic subject, perfected the Marxist art of necessity, of making—as Marx says in "The Eighteenth Brumaire of Louis Bonaparte"— history under conditions not of its own choosing. Cultural Studies has, like the diasporic subject, constructed an institutional viability for itself by borrowing from the "host" culture, determining what can be adapted, retooled, and modified from the place of origin and what cannot; it is the act of making do, of experimenting, of sometimes acknowledging the borrowing and sometimes not. It is about recognizing that to be out of context occasionally means having access, simultaneously, unequally, to more than one context; conceptually and politically, it is to make poaching a way of life. To be "out of context" is to ontologize the diaspora: to think from the place of dislocation. To think the diaspora is to open up into the condition of autoimmunity—the vulnerability of the displaced subject within the political and therefore the possibility of enfranchisement that will inscribe it differently, less vulnerably, within the political; its out of placeness within the (new) political; its uncertainness before and in relationship to the Law, the epistemological insufficiency which means that, because the subject can never fully "know," the subject can only speculate about what it knows it does not know and therefore does not always know what it is speculating about.

It is the autoimmunity, fallibility, and insufficiency of the place of origin that produces the violence of deracination: epistemological, affective, and psychic violence, a violence that recalls for many diasporic subjects the "origin" and the raison d'être of the diasporic experience—the flight from the dictatorship, the gulag, genocide, or, more "mundanely," the desperate departure from economic hopelessness, increasingly the narrative of raced diasporic subjects in Europe and the United States. That is the narrative of vengeance, the violence that attends to the out of placeness, that is inherent to the experience of the diaspora. The diaspora is the narrative of love: the ineradicable memory: the ineradicability of attachment to that place (we might call it "home") of deepest attachment and affiliation. The diaspora represents the psychic costs of negation, a cost that not even the logic of autoimmunity can always ameliorate: the costs of not staying, of having left, of leaving behind—because it a process that is always in process—the place of origin, the place of love. The diaspora is, reductively phrased, not that which was. It is not the Maghreb for North Africans in Spain, not West Africa for those black traders selling cheap imitation designer goods in New York or Buenos Aires.

The diaspora is always the narrative of the insufficient, that which in itself is never enough to, for, and in and of itself (like autoimmunity, the subject can never protect itself from itself): there can never be an equivalence between the place of origin and the place of contemporary habitation, living permanently, sometimes more uneasily than others, with the condition of in/hospitality so that there is always the recognition that there can never be a diaspora with the greatest risk—life or death, life and death, life in death, death in (deracinated) life. Above all else, the diaspora articulates the narrative of being out of context: of being historically fallible and insufficient in relation to the psychic and affective logic of place. In taking this un/imaginable risk, there is always the task of political measuring: of "evaluating" the risk, its effects, its consequences, producing the ontological question: is the risk worth the risk? In the stark, almost Darwinian (which also, strikingly enough, evokes the fiercely "survivalist" rhetoric of Malcolm X) terms of David Malouf's protagonist Gemmy, from the novel *Remembering Babylon,* "Since he had somehow found his way into the world, his object, like any creature's, was to stay in it and by any means he could" (Malouf, 25). It is always a violent, autoimmune struggle to "stay in it," this place that is not the site of origin, and yet it is now inhabited precisely because it is not that original place; the place of origin is always autoimmunely related to the place in the diaspora.

The diaspora, the desire to "stay in it," demands nothing so much as a thinking "out of context": the historical thinking of the dislocated subject in relation to its out of placeness, its removal from "itself"; the diaspora demands a thinking beyond immediate and historic contexts. The diaspora constitutes a necessary affective, political, and psychic insufficiency in that it requires the holding together of the contradiction: the "disarticulation," like the Deleuzian "disequilibrium," of the place of origin and its re-articulation in the place of habitation; and the re-articulation of the place of inhabitation in the difficult (to translate) terms of the place of origin. The diaspora is not simply a matter of contextual translation—the act of making affective and historical sense of the processes of dislocation and relocation—but the constitutive site of autoimmunity: to live diasporically is to recognize the condition of living without the possibility of a singular context. It is to live with the fallibility of history, the violence that constitutes love and memory, and the insufficiency of place. Not just the place of habitation or the place of origin, but any place. Not simply, say, the poverty of Morocco but the precarious temporary inhabitation of Andalusia by the "boat people" who cross the straits in the twenty-first century in search of work. Andalusia is, moreover, a region of Spain haunted by La Reconquista,[6] the history of Moorish conquest and Catholic Spain's reconquest of the region of centuries gone by; for this reason, the contemporary diaspora is indissolubly linked to the bloody violence of colonization and the "liberation" era of the Crusades, of the aggressive march of Islam and the determined resurgence of an imperial, militaristic Castilian Catholicism.

To live diasporically is to live "out of context," beyond the place of physical occupation or affective imagining. Bound by their mutual "out of contextness," Cultural Studies and the African diaspora can do more than learn from each other, and they can do more than animate each other. Thinking them together demonstrates how these two modes of critical thinking, this poacher's discipline and this political condition that is increasingly crucial to the lives of innumerable people throughout the world, are conceptually constitutive of each other. There can be no thinking of Cultural Studies without thinking of the diaspora; there can be no articulation of the diasporic experience without the recognition of the constitutive, supportive, and critically symbiotic and symbolic role that the popular—and culture more generally—plays in the insufficient process of dis- and re-articulation of the deracinated subject. There can be no thinking of the popular and the diasporic without an accounting for race. Located at the core of the history of Cultural Studies in Britain is the narrative of metropolitan dis-articulation and re-articulation by the resilient experience of migration.

The *Empire Windrush* docked on the English coast port of Southampton in 1947, filled to the gills with colonials from the Anglophone Caribbean. Cultural Studies was founded less than a decade later. No sooner had the Ugandan and Kenyan governments expelled their Asian nationals in 1972 than Hall and his colleagues at the CCCS were confronted with the violence of metropolitan racism. They produced *Policing the Crisis* (*PTC*), a study of the "moral crisis" that arose in response to the "epidemic" of "muggings" in the racially mixed Birmingham neighborhood of Handsworth. All of the "muggers" in the Handsworth event had diasporic backgrounds—Irish, Caribbean, or Turkish. This was a "crisis," not simply for diasporic subjects and the British state but also—in the most dynamic sense—within Cultural Studies. The local and (global) post-imperial conjunctures of 1972 compelled Cultural Studies to think race in its locally diasporic formation. Through their work in *PTC*, the Birmingham scholars recognized how the dissolution of Britain's imperial past was taking place right before their eyes. The now dilapidated, racially diverse neighborhood of Handsworth, where the infamous "mugging" of an older white man by three youths from the area took place, was only a stone's throw from the University of Birmingham's campus where CCCS was housed and directed by the Jamaican-born Hall, himself a product of this postwar diaspora. (Hall came to England in the early-1950s on a Rhodes scholarship to Oxford's Merton College.) Out of that historic 1972 conjuncture, out of the critiques developed in *PTC*, out of that "crisis," a Cultural Studies was born that attended more closely to the politics of race. For the very first time, *PTC* made race a political category that had to be thought alongside class and sometimes before it. Before this Handsworth-centered work, the white English working-class experience predominated Cultural Studies, studied as it was across a broad sweep of the discipline's history—from the nineteenth-century dissenters in E. P. Thompson's magisterial writing in *The Making of the English Working Class* to Paul Willis's study of contemporary biker culture.

The history of Cultural Studies can thus be said to coincide with the massive postwar migration of black populations from Africa, the Caribbean, and the Asian Subcontinent to Europe and the United States. The *Empire Windrush* was merely metonymic of the diaspora and the politics of the diaspora to come: it was simply the first postwar ship to bring black bodies in such large, and mainly masculine, numbers. Coming firstly as gastarbeiters required by a metropolitan economy desperately in need of workers, and then later on as workers fleeing either their own devastated economies or simply in search of better financial prospects, these successive waves of black migration substantively remade metropolitan sites through their culture; after Third World independence, events such as the African expulsion of already once-diasporized Asians (the "kala pani"—"dark waters"—voyage that displaced nineteenth-century Asians from their native subcontinent to Africa, the islands of the Pacific Ocean, Caribbean, and elsewhere), 1972 produced a new wave and type of diasporic subject—the diasporized subject dislocated by colonization now again deracinated by the excesses of Kenyan and Ugandan postcolonial rule. It is precisely this experience and articulation of the violence of dislocation that distinguishes British from North American Cultural Studies.

The diaspora has never been constitutive of Cultural Studies in the United States, where the discipline arrived later and in a very different political form. In North America, it could be said, Diasporic Studies was less disjoined from Cultural Studies than it was never really constitutive of the discipline. The politics of the diaspora, in the North American academy, was accommodated within language departments, especially those hospitable to the study of postcolonial literature and culture, those institutional redoubts where the novels of V. S. Naipaul, Assia Djebar, and Monica Ali, the fiction and drama of Wole Soyinka, and the poetic verse and drama of Derrick Walcott are read. The literature, culture, and critical theory of the postcolonial found a home, sometimes with the politics of Cultural Studies, often shorn of it, in English, Romance Studies, and Spanish or Portuguese departments. What did not go unremarked upon from the mid-1980s, however, by both Cultural Studies and postcolonial scholars, and on both sides of the Atlantic and in places beyond such as Australia and Taiwan, was how new forms of dress, physical self-representation, and artistic expression emerged through the presence of this "influx" of migrants—sometimes labeled "diasporic" or "postcolonials," occasionally understood as constitutively similar political subjects.

The jazz music that had marked the diasporization of African Americans fleeing the racism of the United States during the interwar years and afterward (as the essays and fiction of James Baldwin so poignantly and painfully recounts for us) was supplemented—not displaced—in the 1970s and '80s by the reggae and Rastafarianism of the Caribbean, the haunting melodies of an Ali Farka Touré. Through the music of Bob Marley, the narratives of grand return to Africa (from the Caribbean and the United States) voiced in such stentorian tones in the early decades of the twentieth century by his countryman Marcus Garvey were recast, made relevant for the Babylonian experience of the late twentieth century; in the ghostly but seductive tunes of Salif Keita and Angelique Kidjo, there is the recall—and return to popularity—of Baaba Maal, Ali Farka Touré, and Fela Kuti. For later generations there would be the anger, social critiques, and bling-bling romance of American hip-hop filtered through the experiences of Brixton, London, and the ghettoes named "suburbs" on the outskirts of Paris, those diasporic locales where the "Trinadadians," "West Africans," and the "Arabs"—from North Africa—live; hip-hop, it should be said, "gone native" and sometimes augmented by a jazz itself long rooted in these re-diasporized spaces; or those metropolitan locales subjected to a fresh dose of diasporic cultural creativity and economic desperation; those metropolitan spaces made, for the first or the umpteenth time, "out of place" to themselves in order to accommodate diasporized subjects, that movement of black and brown bodies that made the "natives" out of place in "their" place by an array of sociopolitical forces that was both global and local in origin. The colonial project, after all, began in newly industrialized metropolitan sites such as the port city of Liverpool and the factories of Manchester, so that the locals were intimately involved in—and, to a large extent, benefited from—the economy of colonialism.

Out of these diasporic and rediasporized cultures, out of the history of poaching and the imprints made by the black subjects of the diaspora on the metropolis, new political identities emerged. These identities, it should be said, mobilized diasporic communities because they addressed issues of race, black alienation from the political, gender, sexuality, and ethnicity. In remaking the metropolis, diasporic communities from Africa to Asia can also be said to be partly responsible for disarticulating the political pieties of the metropolitan Left and reconfiguring the political landscape of Europe and North America. Recognizing that the new claims that diasporic communities, as well as women, gays, lesbians, and environmentalists, were making on the metropolitan political were creating not only a new language for politics, "identity," but an entirely new way of doing politics, Cultural Studies—ever attentive, especially in the work of theorists such as Hall, to transformed conditions of politics—helped to address this new configuration. Identity politics became, in its very formulation and reformation of the Left political, a critique of grand political narratives that had long excluded people of color and those from the diaspora; identity politics did not so much make room or accommodate those who had once been "Lonely Londoners," those who drifted, almost every one of them at the very edge of poverty, in Sam Selvon's 1950s novel (*The Lonely Londoners*), from one lumpenproletariat mode of existence to another. Rather, it was from the politics of identity produced by constituencies such as the grandchildren of Selvon's black Londoners, now cast as the diasporic "yardies" of Victor Headley's early 1990s black pulp fiction,[7] that the metropolitan Left and Cultural Studies took its political cue.

Located on the outside of the traditional metropolitan Left, working from a position of historic vulnerability, it was through the act of demanding that their material, political, and cultural insufficiencies be addressed, be redressed, that the experience of the diaspora proved crucial to providing both Cultural Studies and diasporic communities themselves with the critical tools to conduct a different kind of politics: a politics that opened from the position of the diasporized. Having to think their politics from outside of the context of the traditional Left, diasporized communities demonstrated the political value of insufficiency. Or, as *Slow Man's* Paul Rayment would have it, it is about the "out-side." Reflecting on his own complicated diasporic trajectory, Paul says, "I can pass among Australians. I cannot pass among the French. That, as far as I am concerned, is all there is to it, to the national-identity business: where one passes and where on the contrary one stands out" (Coetzee, 197). It is precisely because diasporic subjects "stand out" that they reveal their inability to "pass" as or among the French, Australians, or British to be a generative position, a position from which the political could be reconceived, recalibrated, and reimagined. To "stand out" is to make Left politics unrecognizable to itself, to make this "national-identity business" matter in ways that Paul will have no truck with, requires the act of wrenching the class-based, white, masculinist (with which Paul aligns himself) purveyors of a deeply racist unconscious and sometimes not so unconscious Left out of its own historic context. The "non-Pauline" diasporic subject[8] represents the voice of Deleuzian "disequilibrium": the inability, like Paul among the French, to pass, to signify a visceral out of contextness, makes outsiderness an identity, the centrifugal force of a "minorized" political speaking against a majoritarian political language. If, that is, only for the brief historical moment that has been the two decades or so of the identity politics movement. For this instant, the discourse of what I have named "fallibility and insufficiency" has been displaced from the diasporic communities to the historically dominant ones. Through its insurgent discourses, Cultural Studies and the political ingenuity of the diaspora have—if only briefly—demonstrated how disarticulation can be made to work against dominant constituencies and their narratives.

To speak that place named "out of context" can occasionally disarticulate an entire context—can make it fallible in ways previously unimagined as the violent articulations of the politically enfranchised but culturally and ideologically dispossessed subjects of France's Arab suburbs demonstrated in October 2005. The riots that began in Clichy-Dubois, after the murder of two Arab teenagers by the French police, showed how an "out of place" raced and denigrated constituency in republican France could make an entire country seem momentarily "out of place" to itself. Those Arab and Berber communities were displaced from North Africa decades earlier to serve the needs of the French economy in menial capacities (or, as in the case of Berber footballer Zinedine Zidane, to lead the nation to World Cup triumph in 1998 and to "infamy" in 2006, thereby making the Algerian diasporic subject the cultural incarnation of an "inclusive" French republicanism). These "Arab" subjects returned, in the political persons of the children and grandchildren, to disarticulate an entire European nation into a political and psychic out of placeness—if only for a traumatic few weeks.

THE AFRICAN DIASPORA IN THE ANTIPODES

Unconditional hospitality exceeds juridical, political, or economic calculation. But no thing and no one happens or arrives without it.
—Jacques Derrida, *Rogues*

The traces of this unexpected disarticulation, this displacement of the discourse of dislocation from the familiar, the subaltern black body, to the unfamiliar, this rendering of the diaspora as "out of context," is encountered most saliently in the fiction of white, diasporic African novelist J. M. Coetzee. Dislocated to Adelaide, Australia, the same city in which his protagonist, Paul Rayment of the novel *Slow Man*, lives, Coetzee has created in this novel the "out of contextness" that marks diasporic life.

Coetzee's Paul Rayment openly admits to the problematic of diasporic existence. As he tells Elizabeth Costello, "I had three doses of the immigrant experience, not just one, so it imprinted itself quite deeply. First when I was uprooted as a child and brought to Australia; then when I declared my independence and returned to France; then when I gave up France and came back to Australia. *Is this where I belong?* I asked with each move. *Is this my true home?*" (192, original emphasis).

The deracinations, each movement between North and South, each voyage between France and Australia, reveal the "out of contextness" that is constitutive of diasporic life. The experiences that mark the diaspora preclude an easy, "permanent" answer to the inquiry about "home" and "belonging," so Paul is "condemned" to live fallibly, insufficiently. He is perpetually out of context, out of place, neither fully Australian nor fully French, at home in neither the old world nor the new. *Slow Man* does not only engage the issue of Western European diasporas. Coetzee's novel also foregrounds the Central European experience—via the Baltic origins of his Croatian nurse Marijana ("Marijana of the Balkans, giver of care, compelled even more than he to conduct her life in a foreign tongue")— and the diasporic constitution of Australia, a nation-state inconceivable without the history of several white (and later, Middle Eastern and Asian) diasporas, some of whom, of course, were not originally presumed to belong categorically to Australian whiteness (Coetzee, 165).

It is in this way that Paul is forced to recognize that his struggle with the diasporic experience, the disconcerting autoimmunity of his condition, is not singular but prevalent. The facts of the Australian diaspora are brought home to him by his interactions with the women who "interrogate" (Elizabeth Costello) and care for him (Marijana), the Irish Catholic and the Croatian Catholic women who simultaneously enable and disrupt Paul's world after he is hit by a car and his leg is amputated. It is Elizabeth, the more historically established of the "immigrants," who is the more easily given to mocking Paul: "A pukkah little Catholic boy. I can see that, Paul. . . . Don't forget, I am a proper Irish Catholic girl myself, a Costello from Northcote in Melbourne" (Coetzee, 156). However, if it is the linguistic intensity and cheek of Elizabeth's questions that unsettle Paul, it is the shared linguistic discomfiture with Marijana that enables Paul, the "notional Frenchman," to recognize how the diaspora operates to separate the dislocated subject from her or his language (161).

Elizabeth bluntly declares: "'Does it all come down to the English language, to your not being confident enough to act in a language that is not your own?'" (Coetzee, 230). Paul understands that he and Marijana are both "minorized" by the language they (cannot but) need to, are compelled to, speak: "she speaks a rapid, approximate Australian English with Slavic liquids and an uncertain command of *a* and *the*, coloured by slang she must pick up from her children, who must pick it up from their classmates. It is a variety of the language he is not familiar with; he rather likes it" (27).

The diaspora demands that the deracinated learn to speak a language that is not their own. They are, as Deleuze argues, made to inhabit a language in which they patently lack facility. Paul and Marijana, more so than Elizabeth, are "foreigners in the language" (Deleuze, 109). However, it is precisely their foreignness that enables them to "make the language itself scream, stutter, stammer, or murmur" (110). The language they inhabit so complexly is, as it were, diasporized against itself, disarticulated into a different, strange, French-inflected, Ireland-intonated "murmur"; with the "uncertain [Croatian] command" of the definite and the indefinite articles, the very grammatical structure of the language is put under diasporic pressure by a dislocated speaker learning a language thirdhand: indirectly from her children, who "pick it up" directly "from their classmates."

Of course, what troubles Coetzee's "newly diasporic writing" are the colonial, racially overburdened ghosts that haunt the Australian psyche in much the same way that Paul Rayment is autoimmunely bonded forever to the different Europes of his past (France, the Netherlands, England, and even Elizabeth Costello's Ireland): "Not just bush. . . . Not just black-fellows either. Not zero history. Look, that is where we come from: from the cold and damp and smoke of that wretched cabin, from those women with their helpless black eyes, from that poverty and that grinding labour on hollow stomachs. A people with a story of their own, a past. *Our* story, *our* past" (Coetzee, 52, original emphasis). In this way, *Slow Man* reveals the traces of an Australia historically haunted by a racialized "oldness," an Aboriginal culture older than Paul Rayment's French one. *Slow Man* insists that it is not only Paul who is always burdened with the sense that absolute belonging is inaccessible to him and denied its singularity. Even Paul insists, sometimes desperately, upon his singularity. In fact, any sense of place is always prefaced by the interrogative, "Is this where I belong?" a question that is pluralized so that it motivates against anything but a contingent understanding of place that rests uneasily, uncannily, upon autoimmunity. The specter of out of placeness haunts Australia, the Balkans, Europe, and the Africa that Elizabeth visited so indiscriminately in a previous Coetzee novel, *Elizabeth Costello*. It is precisely because Cultural Studies engenders an "out of context" thinking that it becomes possible to understand how the African diaspora might be rearticulated— might rearticulate itself—as and in the experience of a white diasporic African writer grappling with the several diasporas Coetzee has encountered since his relocation from South Africa. Read "out of context," read against both his place of origin and his place of "resettlement," Coetzee's novel comes to reveal how it becomes possible to locate the diaspora outside of itself, outside of its historical visage.

Coetzee's invocation of the Aboriginal experience, the "history of the past," which in so many ways recalls the experience of indigenous black South(ern) Africans, the "chtonic, the ones who stand with their feet planted in their native earth,"[9] sets his work in conversation with an Australian writer such as David Malouf in *Remembering Babylon*, in part because of their shared preoccupation with language (Coetzee, 198). Coming upon the white settlement, the "white" survivor (of the shipwreck, of parental neglect, of adult abandonment and abuse) Gemmy ("saved," in part through initial indifference, by the Aborigines), is silently and not so subtly ridiculed: "He was a parody of a white man. If you gave him a word for a thing, he could, after a good deal of huffing and blowing, repeat it, but the next time round you had to teach it to him all over again. He was imitation gone wrong, and the mere sight of it put you wrong, too, made the whole business somehow foolish and open to doubt" (Malouf, 39).

While Paul never comes fully to grips with English, and Marijana mangles her use of "a" and "the," Gemmy Fairley has to relearn the use of a language that he can now never inhabit fully or comfortably again after acquiring not only an Aboriginal tongue but the silent and "other worldly" form of communication that the indigenous people count as critical to their engagement with each other and the universe. This is why the white settlers are so afraid of him, so "open to doubt" not only about Gemmy but about themselves: "It was the mixture of the monstrous strangeness and unwelcome likeness that made Gemmy Fairley so disturbing to them, since at any moment he could show either one face or the other; as if he were always standing there at one of those meetings, but in his case willingly, and the encounter was an embrace" (Malouf, 43). An "embrace" with the Other, that is also an embrace with the Self. Gemmy is the incarnation of the "stutterer," of the once-monolingually fluent but now bilingual (if the Aboriginal tongue can be reduced to a singular linguistic facility) and, as Deleuze says, *"When a language is so strained that it starts to stutter, or to murmur or stammer . . . then language in its entirety reaches the limit* that marks the outside and makes it confront silence" (Deleuze, 113, original emphasis).

Gemmy takes the language of the settler, once his own and only language, and stretches its possibilities to its very limits: to that point, for the settlers (so familiar to Coetzee's Southern Africa), where they are haunted by their own outsiderness to the land, to Australia (or South Africa) itself. They are definitively not the "chtonic." It is because of Gemmy's return, which is also a "first" turning to (the settlers, their language, culture, "civilization," their very way of life) that is simultaneously a turning away from (putatively, the Aboriginals, always, potentially, the settlers as well), that the settlers of Malouf's *Remembering Babylon* have to confront their out of contextness, their own (now indisputable) status as diasporic subjects.

Each of them, children, adults, those long settled, those newly arrived, the "educated" and the unlettered, is haunted by the specter of outsiderness: outside their place of origin (Ireland, Britain), outsiders in land where they (the notional landowners), unlike the Aboriginally conversant Gemmy, do not understand the language of the country in which they live. Gemmy's "return" was psychically deracinating to the settlers, so much so that it infantilized the settlers: "It brought you slap up against a terror you thought you had learned, years back, to treat as childish: the Bogey, the Coal Man, Absolute Night" (Malouf, 42). Like children afraid of the Dark, afraid in the Dark, afraid because of the Dark, they resort to a language frightful in its simplicity: "the Bogey, the Coal Man, Absolute Night." Malouf becomes, in this moment, a great Deleuzian author because "He makes the language as such stutter: an affective and intensive language, and no longer an affectation of the one who speaks" (Malouf, 107). The language of the outside is the language produced in and by fear (the "Bogey" man's language, so to speak): To "stutter" is not only to demonstrate uncertainty or lack of facility in a language. It also marks the struggle against fear toward another command of language. Both Gemmy and the settlers are, in this way, engaged in the same project: they are "stuttering" their way to language, to linguistically marking their "minorized" status. Malouf, like Coetzee, makes the "language as such" diasporic, not the author or Gemmy's own, and yet, autoimmunely, inveterately their own.

Through the theoretical openness of Cultural Studies, the diaspora can be located "out of context": it can be dislocated to, or located in, the personage of the white European speaking for the white African author, struggling with the condition of out of placeness in Australia, surely one of the most extreme racially charged sites within the diasporic imaginary. Australia is, moreover, a country in which the history of violence done to the native peoples by successive white diasporas—colonialists, "settlers," prisoners who later founded a nation in which they, and not the natives, were the dominant subjects of the political, Central and Eastern European immigrants fleeing from their own deracinations; Australia, a nation in which the history of violence turned on the issue of racism, on the issue of the identity and culture—or the supposed lack thereof—of the native peoples. It is only through the critical lens of Cultural Studies' "out of contextness" that the complexities, the unexpected incarnations and mediations of the African diaspora, suggest how the African diaspora is secretly—or not so secretly, given the difficult political conditions under which Coetzee was "compelled" into the diaspora—articulated in locales well beyond those one would ordinarily suspect.

Even, that is, in the very heart of South African and Australian whiteness that is conceived by the diasporic white South African novelist recently removed to the Antipodes or the Australian author who writes (sometimes) Australia from Southern Europe. In *Slow Man* (a project in various degrees shared by Malouf, albeit with a very different literary and political sensibility), Australia is figured as the last bastion of the white imperial imaginary that can be thought out of context: as the singular articulation of the African diasporic subject speaking the diaspora in its most "universal" conception: as stretching from Western Europe to Eastern Europe, from Europe to Australia, written from within—and, arguably, against—the ghostly presence of an Africa that is not named but cannot, will not, be escaped because this mapping emerges from the South African novelist who traces this series of relentless, haphazard, diasporic movement that, despite his best efforts, and because of Elizabeth Costello's presence and the haunting evocative in Malouf's work, will not allow the facticity of black Africa or Aboriginal Australia to be erased.

NOTES

I would like to thank Tejumola Olaniyan and James Sweet for their invitation to participate in the conference on the African diaspora and the disciplines. It was an event remarkable in its ability to bring together such a focused group of participants who were serious in their commitment to thinking the problematic at hand. And, no less an achievement, it was significant in its ability to forge friendships amongst the diasporized.

1. I am using "the political" in Carl Schmitt's sense of the term: the concentration of power in the figures of the "state" (so that the distinction between one political party and another is, at best, minimal) and the sovereign (the figure that at once absorbs all of the state into itself and, of course, exceeds the populace through its position as sovereign) so that everything outside of this formation has, according to Schmitt, very little to do with the political. Cultural Studies, of course, presents itself as a challenge to Schmitt's notion of the political. What I am interested in, for this reason, is the relation—if such a relation can indeed be imagined—between the political and Cultural Studies as a critique of the formation of power, state power, or any other such articulation. See, in this regard, Schmitt's *The Concept of the Political*.

2. See, for example, Tony Bennett's essay, "Putting Policy into Cultural Studies," and Ien Ang's "Who Needs Cultural Research?"

3. See Michael Kenny's *The First New Left* and Dennis Dworkin's *Cultural Marxism in Postwar Britain* for accounts of the critical events of 1956 that produced the New Left and Cultural Studies: Nikita Khrushchev's denunciation of Stalin, the Suez Crisis, and the Soviet Union's invasion of Hungary.

4. The "practicality" of the Policy Studies critique is, arguably, most evident here: the need to not only build sustainable institutions but to attend to issues such as jobs, both within and outside of the academy, for those who graduate, with the necessary skills, from Cultural Studies programs is a concern that has only been addressed directly by Policy Studies advocates. It is not an issue that has occupied the "theoretical" and "literary" wings of Cultural Studies with the same urgency.

5. Derrida offers his fullest delineation of "autoimmunity" in *Rogues: Two Essays on Reason:* "For what I call the autoimmune consists not only in harming or ruining oneself, indeed destroying one's own protections, and in doing so oneself, committing suicide or threatening to do so, but, more seriously still, and through this, in threatening the I [*moi*] or the self [*soi*], the *ego* or the *autos*, ipseity itself, compromising the immunity of the *autos* itself: it consists not only in compromising oneself [*s'auto-entaner*] but in compromising the self, the *autos*— and thus ipseity. It consists not only in committing suicide but in compromising

sui- or *self*-referentiality, the *self* or *sui* of suicide itself. Autoimmunity is more or less suicidal, but, more seriously still, it threatens always to rob suicide itself of its meaning and supposed integrity" (45).

6. See Hooper, *The New Spaniards,* and Williams, *The Story of Spain,* for an account of La Reconquista.

7. See Victor Headley's novel, *Yardie,* which inaugurated a new genre of black pulp fiction that directly addressed the condition of black diasporic life in the postcolonial metropolis. See also my critique of "yardie fiction," "When Postcolonial Chickens Come Home to Roost."

8. I am referring here to the return of St. Paul as a figure for thinking the politics of diaspora (the emblematic new "cosmopolitanism" or "universalism"), for articulating the movement of subjects between the Orient (places such as Jerusalem or Damascus) and the Occident (especially Rome, the capital of early Christianity). St. Paul is now, again, a political conundrum for our times, courtesy of the work of Giorgio Agamben (*The Time That Remains: A Letter to the Romans*), Alain Badiou (*Saint Paul: The Foundation of Universalism*), and Slavoj Žižek (*The Puppet and the Dwarf: The Perverse Core of Christianity* and *The Universal Exception*).

9. There is in much of Malouf's work a deep sense of (white) Australia being haunted by the "chtonic." Even in his work on the exiled poet Ovid in imperial Rome, *An Imaginary Life,* there are echoes of the "chtonic." In this regard, in addition to *Remembering Babylon, The Conversations at Curlow Creek* is especially noteworthy.

REFERENCES

Agamben, Giorgio. *The Time That Remains: A Letter to the Romans.* Trans. Patricia Dailey. Stanford, Calif.: Stanford University Press, 2005.

Ang, Ien. "Who Needs Cultural Research?" Working paper, Consortium of Humanities Centers and Institutes, University of Western Sydney, www .chcinetwork.org/angfv.htm.

Badiou, Alain. *Saint Paul: The Foundation of Universalism.* Trans. Ray Brassier. Stanford, Calif.: Stanford University Press, 2003.

Bennett, Tony. "Putting Policy into Cultural Studies." In *Cultural Studies,* ed. Lawrence Grossberg, Cary Nelson, Paula Treichler. New York: Routledge, 1992.

Coetzee, J. M. *Slow Man.* New York: Viking, 2005.

Deleuze, Gilles. "He Stuttered." In *Essays Critical and Clinical,* trans. Daniel W. Smith and Michael A. Greco. Minneapolis: University of Minnesota Press, 1997.

Derrida, Jacques. *Rogues: Two Essays on Reason.* Trans. Pascale-Anne Brault and Michael Naas. Stanford, Calif.: Stanford University Press, 2005.

Dworkin, Dennis. *Cultural Marxism in Postwar Britain: History, the New Left, and the Origins of Cultural Studies.* Durham, N.C.: Duke University Press, 1997.

Farred, Grant. "When Postcolonial Chickens Come Home to Roost: How Yardie Fiction Has Created a New Postcolonial Subject." *South Atlantic Quarterly* 100 (Winter 2001).

Hall, Stuart, Chas Critcher, Tony Jefferson, John Clarke, and Brian Roberts. *Policing the Crisis: Mugging, the State, and Law and Order*. London: Macmillan, 1978.

Headley, Victor. *Yardie*. New York: Atlantic Monthly Press, 1993.

Hooper, John. *The New Spaniards*. London: Penguin Books, 1995.

Kenny, Michael. *The First New Left: British Intellectuals after Stalin*. London: Lawrence and Wishart, 1995.

Malouf, David. *An Imaginary Life*. New York: G. Braziller, 1978.

——. *Remembering Babylon*. New York: Vintage Books, 1994.

——. *The Conversations at Curlow Creek*. Toronto: Random House of Canada Limited, 1996.

Schmitt, Carl. *The Concept of the Political*. New Brunswick, N.J.: Rutgers University Press, 1976.

Williams, Mark R. *The Story of Spain*. San Mateo, Calif.: Golden Era Books, 2004.

Žižek, Slavoj. *The Puppet and the Dwarf: The Perverse Core of Christianity*. Cambridge: MIT Press, 2003.

——. *The Universal Exception*. Edited by Rex Butler and Scott Stephens. London: Continuum, 2007.

PART FOUR
DIASPORA CONTEXTS

13 AFRICAN DIASPORA STUDIES IN THE CREOLE-ANGLOPHONE CARIBBEAN: A PERSPECTIVE FROM THE UNIVERSITY OF THE WEST INDIES, MONA, JAMAICA

Carolyn Cooper

The topography I delineate here is, of necessity, well-traveled terrain. I rehearse arguments I have elaborated in my own work on Jamaican popular culture in order to demonstrate the scope of African diasporic praxis in a Caribbean context. I certainly do not claim "exemplary" status for my culture-specific readings of African diasporic cultural texts. Rather, I carefully delimit the boundaries of my project, drawing attention to a corpus of critical texts produced in Jamaica that, for me, exemplify the global/local dialectic in African diaspora studies. First, I deploy language as an important borderline: I focus on the Creole-Anglophone Caribbean. Second, I privilege the Jamaican cultural landscape, developing both "popular" and "academic" conceptions of African diaspora studies. Finally, from the perspective of literary/cultural studies, I examine a cluster of oral texts in which African diasporic discourse is articulated.

The African diaspora is a long-established concept in Jamaican popular culture. Marcus Garvey, the preeminent Pan-Africanist, energized Africans at home and abroad to reclaim an originary, continental identity. Garveyism, that grand ideological movement of the twentieth century, spectacularly engendered a liberatory African diasporic consciousness in Jamaica and across the globe. Garvey's philosophy of "African Redemption" mobilized both continental and diasporan Africans to envision full emancipation from dehumanizing colonialist discourses and disempowering sociopolitical institutions.

In a 1913 newspaper article, "The British West Indies in the Mirror of Civilisation," which was published in the *Africa Times and Orient Review*, Marcus Garvey declared with characteristic panache: "I make no apology for prophesying that there will soon be a turning point in the history of the West Indies; and that people who inhabit that portion of the

Western Hemisphere will be the instruments of uniting a scattered race who, before the close of many centuries, will found an Empire on which the sun shall shine as ceaselessly as it shines on the empire of the North today." Conceding that he would be derided for that proclamation, Garvey preempted his detractors: "Laugh then you may, at what I have been bold enough to prophesy, but as surely as there is an evolution in the natural growth of man and nations, so surely will there be a change in the history of these subjected regions."[1]

The Rastafari movement, which lays rightful claim to the legacy of Garveyism, is a classic example of the authority of African diasporic discourse in the Jamaican popular imagination. Garvey's reaffirmation of the biblical prophecy that "[p]rinces shall come out of Egypt; Ethiopia shall soon stretch out her hands unto God" heralded the coronation in November 1930 of Emperor Haile Selassie I, King of Kings, Lord of Lords, and Conquering Lion of Judah, whom Rastafari thereafter claimed as God incarnate. The fashioning of God in the image of Africa was a fundamental ideological revolution that signified emancipation from mental slavery.

Furthermore, the pervasive sense of estrangement in the West and the perennial desire to return to ancestral homelands are recurring motifs in Rastafari philosophy and *livity*.[2] Indeed, Rastafari cosmology is a potent manifestation of the multivalent conception of the African diaspora elaborated on by Joseph Harris at the historic Howard University conference convened in 1979:

> For FADSI [First African Diaspora Studies Institute] and this volume, the African diaspora embodies the following: the voluntary and forced dispersion of Africans at different periods in history and in several directions; the emergence of a cultural identity abroad without losing the African base, either spiritually or physically; the psychological or physical return to the homeland, Africa. Thus viewed, the African diaspora assumes the character of a dynamic, ongoing and complex phenomenon stretching across time and geography.[3]

The cultural production of Africans scattered across the globe decidedly functions as a potent means of celebrating a shared heritage and a common history of struggle against multiple isms and schisms—racism, colonialism, and imperialism. We Africans, transferred as property to the Americas, rehumanized ourselves in ecstatic acts of artistic creativity. One of the most engaging sites of African diasporic knowledge and the practice of African diaspora studies in Jamaica is popular music—both foundation reggae and contemporary dancehall. Like Rastafari praxis, Jamaican popular music manifests a global African consciousness that transcends insularity; it is an inclusivist aesthetic that embraces both the continental and the diasporan.

Bob Andy's poignant 1966 reggae lament, "I've Got to Go Back Home," is a haunting evocation of the myths of transport that recur throughout

the African diaspora, articulating a primal sense of loss and the desire
to return to ancestral homelands. Though "home" here may primarily
signify Jamaica—there are, indeed, concentric circles of identity and
alienation—the word also evokes continental Africa, particularly given
the politics of the time in which the song was written:

> I've got to go back home
> This couldn't be my home
> It must be somewhere else
> Or I would kill myself
> Cause
> I can't get no clothes to wear
> I can't get no food to eat
> I can't get a job to get bread
> That's why I've got to
> I've got to got to go back home
> If I've got to walk
> If I've got to swim
>
> There is no gladness
> Nothing but sadness
> Nothing like a future here
> I've got to I've got to leave this life
> I just can't stand this life I'm living

Bob Andy's constrictive island of exile cannot constrain his psyche.
He must walk, swim, fly, even beyond its confining shores.[4] The sea here
functions not so much as a constricting boundary but as a waterway connecting the island to distant lands. As dancehall DJ Shabba Ranks puts
it so poetically in "Back and Bellyrat," it is his talent as a performer that
makes him "fly offa Jamaica map" [fly off the map of Jamaica]. There is a
large corpus of reggae and dancehall song texts produced in Jamaica and
the diaspora that fly off the map, articulating the Pan-Africanist, continental identity of island peoples: the Mystic Revelation of Rastafari with
their "Tales of Mozambique"; Buju Banton's "African Pride"; Steel Pulse
rallying round Rasta, Garvey, and the red, gold, black, and green flags of
cultural independence; and Third World's "Lagos Jump," which mischie-
vously celebrates Pan-Africanism as an erotic/cultural connection with a
bewitching African woman.

Peter Tosh's anthemic "African" is the most lucid articulation of African diasporic consciousness in Jamaican popular music:

> Don't care where you come from
> As long as you're a black man
> You're an African
>
> No mind your nationality
> You have got the identity of an African

Tosh uses "African" as a marker of racial identity, thus subverting conventional representations of racial/national politics in Jamaica. It is only
people of African descent who do *not* define their racial/cultural identity
in terms that denote ancestral homelands. Europeans, Chinese, Syrians,
and Indians are all routinely raced and placed in their very naming. It is
only displaced Africans in Jamaica who are unequivocally "local."

Africa has been so dehumanized in the colonial imaginary that relatively few Jamaicans, even today, want to identify themselves as African. Many obviously "pure" black Jamaicans routinely claim ancestors of
other races—usually distant great-great-great-grandfathers who have left
no visible traces of their greatness on the body of their putative progeny.
Even in cases where some racial admixture is evident, the African element in the mix is always the half that has never been told. Mixed-race
Jamaicans are half-Indian, half-Chinese, half-Syrian, half-white, but never
half-African.

This un-naming of the black half may signify that "African" is grudg-
ingly recognized as the norm. But, much more likely, this silence may
speak eloquently of the unresolved question of race and the contested status of African people in Jamaican society. Consider, for example, the Jamaican names for two mixed-race categories: "chiney royal" and "coolie
royal." The *Dictionary of Jamaican English* defines chiney royal as the
"offspring of a Chinese and (usually) a negro, or (sometimes) a white or
East Indian." Similarly, coolie royal is defined as "a person of mixed East-
Indian and negro stock."

The unnamed African appears to be the "royal" in both hybrids. But
this is no cause for celebration. A more cynical reading suggests that it
is only in admixture that the royalty of African stock can be recognized;
or worse, "royal" neutrally signifies admixture and is thus a valorization
of the "mixed-race" ideal of Caribbean acculturation in which "pure" African stock is devalued. Indeed, the African majority in Jamaica has been
subjected to a fictive definition of national identity that is essentially
multiracial. This national myth is inscribed in the national motto, "Out
of many, one people."

The homogenizing impulse effectively delegitimizes the commonsense claim that, on the face of it, Jamaica very much looks like an African society. The mixed-race motto does speak to the economic imbalance in the society that concentrates wealth in the hands of a few who are
mostly the out-of-many-one type, that is, not African. I will never forget
the way in which the contradictions encoded in the national motto were
deftly exposed by one of my high school English teachers, an English-
woman who could clearly see the self-deception enshrined in "Out of
many, one people." Which one?"

Furthermore, in Jamaican society the discourse of race is usually articulated only in reference to black people. Other people are not "raced"

in quite the same way. In a witty article entitled "Perkins and Black History," the late Eric "Macko" McNish, then editor of the newspaper *Jamaica Beat*, relates an amusing anecdote illustrating the way in which some Jamaicans refuse to acknowledge race as a marker of their own identity, although they can see it in others. McNish reports:

> When Chinese Jamaicans and East Indian Jamaicans used to organise annual cricket matches between an All-Indian XI and All-Chinese XI at the Chinese Cricket Club (now owned by Melbourne), all Jamaicans applauded it.
>
> However, when two Black Jamaicans (which included this writer) asked the captain of the East Indian XI, who was a former Boys' Town player, if an All-African XI of Black Jamaicans could play the winner of his match against the Chinese XI, his answer was, "Bwoy wi doan waan get inna di race ting" [Man, we don't want to get into this race thing].[5]

Tosh's assertion of an "African" identity for black Jamaicans immediately contests the divisive, racist devaluation of continental Africa in Jamaica. Having established "African" as a racial category, Tosh proceeds to affirm a quintessential "African" racial identity that is not exclusively bound to the particular geographical location of national origin: "No mind yu nationality / You have got the identity / Of an African." Global African identity manifests itself in a variety of local settings. Somewhat paradoxically, Tosh asserts both the coterminality of "race" and "place" and contests that very identification. All black people come from Africa originally. So to be black is to be African. But to be African is not necessarily a function of having been physically born on the continent. Africa is a continent of black consciousness from which some "Europeans" who are born there voluntarily exile themselves.[6]

Conversely, there is a sense of home that compels Africans born outside the continent to valorize repatriation of the mind, especially when the body does not have the economic resources to follow the spirit. At one of DJ Sizzla's free concerts at August Town Open Land in Kingston, one of the performers on the bill, Sandokan, I think it was, used a brilliant metaphor to describe the sense of primal connection that scattered Africans feel for the continent: "Africa is a[n] emotional magnet." Tosh invokes the magnetic concept of the African Diaspora, or "scattered Africa," as the Trinidadian Garvey scholar Tony Martin would prefer.

In the essay, "Garvey and Scattered African," Martin interrogates the word *diaspora* and the politics of mimicry it embeds:

> Before I begin my discussion of Garvey I would like to make a simple suggestion that the term *diaspora* be deleted from our vocabulary, because the term *African diaspora* reinforces a tendency among those of us writing our history to see the history of African people always in terms of parallels in

white history. On this model of thinking Garvey is called a "black Zionist"; George Padmore, a "black revolutionary"; and Du Bois, a "black titan." There are parallels between black history and white history, of course, but it is unfortunate that blacks do not see our history primarily in its own right. We always seem to be looking for parallels in the experience of other peoples to shape our history. In the old days, other peoples told us we had no history at all; now they acknowledge that we have a history, but only in terms of other people's history. So, we should do away with the expression African diaspora, because we are not Jews. Let us use some other terminology. Let us speak of the African dispersion, or uprooted Africa as somebody suggested, or scattered Africa.[7]

"Uprooted" Africa signifies catastrophe, the toppling of an ancient tree of life that sheltered countless generations on the continent. And, indeed, the wrenching Middle Passage that violently dislocated so many of us Africans is a genocidal disaster of oceanic proportions. I prefer the metaphor "scattered Africa," which denotes disruption and dislocation but also connotes regeneration. "Scattering" encodes an agricultural image of germination—seeds sown to the wind that eventually bear fruit. The dispersal of African peoples across the globe engenders cultural cross-fertilization. Hybrid strains and hardy new varieties of Africanness emerge from the sowing.

Tosh establishes ever-widening concentric circles of racial/cultural affiliation. Beginning at the center, Jamaica, he sings:

> Cause if yu come from Clarendon
> Or if yu come from Portland
> Or if yu come from Westmoreland
> You're an African

These three parishes are selected, I believe, because they represent different points on the compass: Portland to the east, Westmoreland to the west, and Clarendon somewhat central.

The waves of racial/cultural/transnational affiliation expand to the wider Caribbean:

> If yu come from Trinidad
> If yu come Nassau
> If yu come from Cuba
> You're an African

By the final refrain of "African," Tosh, following the routes of Caribbean migration to North America, Britain, and beyond, invokes many of the cities/countries of the world in which scattered Africans have reestablished home: Brixton in the United Kingdom, the Bronx, Brooklyn, and

Miami in the United States, parts of Canada, as well as an ever-widening circle containing Switzerland, Germany, and Taiwan.[8]

Moving from the politics of location, Tosh addresses phenotypic differences between Africans across the globe:

> No mind yu [your] complexion
> There is no rejection
> You're an African
> Cause if yu plexion high, high
> If yu plexion low, low
> If yu plexion in between
> You're an African

The "complexion"/"rejection" rhyme contrasts the exclusionary racial politics of white racists with the inclusionary discourse of many Africanists. In addition, though Tosh seems to establish a hierarchy of high, low, and in-between complexions, it is the very notion of hierarchy that is being contested. Whatever the physical manifestation of "Africanness" in terms of skin color, there is a rooted cultural identity that transcends the physical.

On this score I must confess that I feel very little sympathy for those "in-between" racial types who refuse to claim what is perceived as a limiting, unitary "African" identity. These new tragic mulattoes, victims of an old-fashioned Euro-American racism that masquerades as newly fashioned cultural theory, derace and erase themselves. They fail to acknowledge the complexity of complexion that Peter Tosh so effortlessly celebrates: "There is no rejection" of mixed-race people from the category "African." Whosoever will may come. Furthermore, in affirming the equal value of high, low, and in-between complexions, Tosh contests the neocolonial racial politics in Jamaica that conventionally defines melanin-rich skin as "low color" and melanin-deficient skin as "high-color."

Religion is as effective an instrument of alienation as are color and class. So Tosh asserts in "African":

> No mind denomination
> That is only segregation
> You're an African
> Cause if yu go to the Catholic
> If yu go to the Methodist
> If yu go to the Church of God
> You're an African

The primary point of Tosh's allusion to these Christian denominations is not to valorize them so much as to affirm the shared African identity of their devotees.

Like popular music, the media is another powerful site of dispersal of African diasporic knowledge in Jamaica. For example, the very popular radio program *Running African*, first aired in October 1990 on the all-reggae radio station IRIE FM, plays a vibrant role in consolidating a global African identity for many Jamaicans across class lines. Conceived and hosted by the visionary Andrea Williams-Green, the program, which is broadcast on Sunday mornings between 6 and 10 a.m., functions somewhat like a church service and engages a faithful congregation of listeners. There is often a call-in component that evokes the call-and-response structure of African rhetorical styles.

The mission statement of the program, "Reuniting the African family for development," honors the spirit of Garveyism. Williams-Green conceives the interactive radio program as a virtual classroom in which the curriculum focuses on political and social issues of immediate relevance to African peoples and which are not always highlighted in the mainstream media in Jamaica. Like reggae, the once marginalized music of African Jamaicans, much of the programming on IRIE FM celebrates African Jamaican cultural traditions such as the devalued Creole language of the black Jamaican majority.

Indeed, the name of the program has its genesis in the Jamaican vernacular. Williams-Green first thought of branding the program as "Runnings African," given the meaning of the colloquial "runnings," which signifies "current affairs," with somewhat subversive connotations of illicit activities and ideas—in this case, setting an African agenda for the program. But Williams-Green did not like the dissonant sound of "Runnings African," and so for purely aesthetic reasons she decided to make "Runnings" singular.[9] Fortuitously, the singular "Running African" encodes maroonage, a collective escape from constricting plantocratic definitions of African identity in Jamaica.

To turn from popular culture to more conventionally "academic" sites of African Diaspora studies in the Jamaica, I highlight the importance of the African Caribbean Institute of Jamaica/Jamaica Memory Bank (ACIJ/JMB), which has paid a major role in consolidating research on African continuities in the Caribbean. Located within the Institute of Jamaica, which was founded in 1879, the ACIJ was belatedly established in 1972 and the JMB in 1980. The mission of these two now integrated agencies is "to collect, research, document, analyse, preserve, and disseminate information about Jamaica's cultural heritage through the utilisation of oral and scribal sources." This mission has been accomplished through the deployment of a variety of strategies: "Apart from staging regular exhibitions on forms of African retentions in Jamaican culture, the ACIJ/JMB has led several research initiatives into areas including traditional dance forms, language, folk tales, traditional as well as popular recorded music, social movements, healing practices, and the development of villages in the Caribbean."[10] The proverb used by the Jamaica Memory Bank to define its mission is this: "An old [wo]man dies . . . a book is lost." Thus the primary objective of the Memory Bank is to ensure that the stories and wisdom of the elders are retrieved and documented for posterity.

A far-reaching project of the ACIJ/JMB is the recuperation of Marcus Garvey's legacy through the establishment in 2004 of the Kingston Liberty Hall as a multimedia museum and reference library.[11] The Liberty Hall website highlights the cultural significance of the building and contextualizes its current use:

> In Garvey's time Liberty Hall was a place for community meetings, political meetings, pre-trade union activities, an employment bureau and entertainment. It regularly held plays, concerts and dances and it had its own band and choirs. U.N.I.A. [Universal Negro Improvement Association] groups such as the Black Cross Nurses, the African Legion and the Juveniles used to meet there. After Garvey's departure from Jamaica in 1935, Liberty Hall continued as a major entertainment centre and club and nurtured the talents of the people until the early 1960s.
>
> Liberty Hall has been restored and refurbished as a living monument to Marcus Garvey. Once again it provides facilities for education, entertainment, and enrichment of spirit for people in Jamaica and visitors from abroad. Its restoration serves to remind us of Garvey's international work as well as his work in Jamaica and encourages us to develop in keeping with his philosophy.[12]

The African Studies Association of the West Indies (ASAWI), founded in 1966 by Dr. Arthur Drayton, a Trinidadian lecturer in the then Department of English at the University of the West Indies, Mona, was another important initiative in African diaspora studies.[13] Stalwart members of that association included the distinguished Jamaican lawyer and ambassador Dudley Thompson; the Guyanese Pan-Africanist historian Walter Rodney; the Trinidadian linguist Mervyn Alleyne; the Jamaican political scientist Locksley Edmondson, and the Guyanese actress and writer Jean Small. In 1973 ASAWI hosted an international seminar on Marcus Garvey, convened at the University of the West Indies, Mona. Amy Jacques Garvey and Marcus Garvey Jr. addressed the conference, which assembled Garvey scholars from the Caribbean itself, Africa, North America, and Europe.[14]

The African Studies Association of the West Indies laid the foundation for the institutionalization of the African and African Diaspora Studies program at the University of the West Indies, Mona, Jamaica. ASAWI members Maureen Warner-Lewis, a linguist/literary critic, and Rupert Lewis, a political scientist, did pioneering work to establish the innovative academic program that was introduced in the 1996–97 academic year.

The interfaculty program was conceived as multidisciplinary, and it drew on existing courses offered in the then Faculty of Arts and General Studies and the Faculty of Social Sciences. No new courses were designed for the program. This pragmatic approach makes it clear that African Diaspora Studies was not originally conceived as a discrete discipline. It was a thematic "area studies" enterprise founded on conventional disciplinary structures and strictures.

Furthermore, African Diaspora Studies was not distinguished from African American Studies or Caribbean Studies. Courses in these areas were simply incorporated into the program, as evidenced in appendix 1. In addition, the composite nature of the program—African and African Diaspora Studies—remains potentially both advantageous and disadvantageous. The advantage is that the joint conception enables understanding of the complex nature of African civilization in the centuries before the establishment of the Atlantic slave trade. The disadvantage is that distinctive features of African diasporic culture in particular contexts may be erased.

In the case of my own course on African/Diaspora Women's Narrative, which was conceived as an exploration of cultural dis/continuities, I pay close attention to the cultural autonomy of the selected literary texts in their local context as well as the potential meanings that transcend place, time, and immediate cultural specificity. The course description, which appears here abbreviated as appendix 2, invites comparison and contrast between the worldview of the texts set in Africa, the Caribbean, and African America.

The Institute of Caribbean Studies at the University of the West Indies, Mona—and, within it, the Reggae Studies Unit and the Rastafari Studies Initiative—has played a central role in consolidating the multidisciplinary field of African Diaspora Studies. Established in May 1987, the Institute has decidedly enriched the intellectual life of the Mona campus, indisputably confirming the primacy of Caribbean Studies as the University's competitive advantage in a globalized higher education market.[15] Major accomplishments include the establishment of the over-subscribed graduate and undergraduate degree programs in Cultural Studies, under the leadership of the former director of the Institute, Joseph Pereira. In addition, the Institute hosted three international conferences on (1) the distinguished work and legacy of Vice Chancellor Emeritus, Professor the Hon. Rex Nettleford; (2) the equally distinguished work and legacy of the Barbadian historian and poet Professor Kamau Brathwaite; and (3) global reggae: Jamaican popular music *a yard* [at home] and abroad.

I now conclude with a comparative critique of a dancehall song text and two traditional religious song texts that illustrates the value of a multidisciplinary approach to African diaspora studies. I draw attention to the ways in which both "folk" and contemporary popular music manifest "African" elements that can be examined from a variety of disciplinary perspectives: literature, linguistics, ethnomusicology, religion, history, philosophy, dance, geography, anthropology, and political science, for example.[16]

In their song "African Ting" [Thing], Prezident Brown and Don Yute, declaring the African genesis of contemporary popular dance forms in Jamaica, contest the censorial labeling of erotic dance as vulgar:

> [Prezident Brown]:
> It's a African ting so African people sing
> And if yu love what yu hear mek me hear yu chanting
> Well dem took we foreparents from di mother land
> Africa we from an a there we belong
> African an Jamaicans we all are one
> So mek we beat pon di drum and sing dis ya song
> Come een Don Yute come gi yu contribution
> [Don Yute]:
> If yu see a gyal a wine [gyrate] pon all her head top
> No bother put on no label like di gyal slack
> A vibes she a vibes to di sound weh she hear
> Is a African ting an she bring it down here
> It's a African ting so African people sing
> An if you love what yu hear
> Mek mi hear yu chanting
> All di dance dem weh a cause all a explosion
> All a dem a come from inna di motherland
> Bogle dancing, butterfly dancing
> An di tati dancing
> All [even] world-a-dance is a African ting

Having chanted an abbreviated history lesson on the Middle Passage, these dancehall DJ philosophers offer an ameliorative reading of the sexualized female body in contemporary popular culture that reclaims the potency of embodied spirituality. From an anthropological perspective, instructive parallels can be drawn between contemporary popular music and "traditional" religious ritual music focusing on the representation of female sexuality. In his 1956 study of African-derived Convince religious ceremonies in Jamaica, anthropologist Donald Hogg documents songs performed by "Bongo Men" to summon ancestral spirits. These men, according to Hogg, "believe that spiritual power is morally neutral—that it can be put to both constructive and malevolent purposes by spirits who have it and by persons who can influence them."[17]

Some of these Convince songs celebrate "pum-pum"—female genitalia—and its deadly power. Citing a line from one of these songs, "Pum-pum kill me dead, I make he kill me," Hogg offers this interpretation: "[It] concerns the insatiable sexual appetites of Bongo spirits. Freely trans-

lated it means, 'If too much sexual intercourse will kill me, then I'll just
have to let it kill me.'"[18] Hogg's literal minded value judgment about "insatiable sexual appetites" seems to miss the point. The song appears to
be a metaphorical acknowledgment of the efficacy of pum-pum even for
dis/embodied Bongo spirits, which, though already "dead," reclaim mate-
riality through the possession of devotees.

Hogg cites another Convince song in which the spirits beg for pum-pum:

(Chorus)	(Verse)
Whole-a-night [all night]	Me da beg him mother-in-law
Whole-a-night	Me da beg him little more
Whole-a-night	Me da beg him father-in-law
Whole-a-night	Me a want a little more
Whole-a-night	Me da beg him little pum-pum.
Whole-a-night	Me da beg him more and more.[19]

In Jamaican, "him" signifies both male and female. So the verse in English becomes:

> I am begging her mother-in-law
> I am begging for a little more
> I am begging her father-in-law
> I want a little more
> I am begging her for a little "pum-pum"
> I am begging her for more and more

These Convince songs clearly illustrate the potent spirituality of female
genitalia in African diasporic religion in Jamaica and in its contemporary
reconfigurations in dancehall culture.

In addition, from a linguistic perspective, paying attention to the African origins of certain "vulgar" Jamaican words illuminates the nature
of cultural transformation in the African diaspora. For example, the moral
censure invested in, and provoked by, those Jamaican "bad" words that allude to female genitalia and the bloody specifics of menstruation suggests
the potency of female sexuality in the culture. The female aperture, the
menstrual blood, the protective cloths, and the birthing canal alluded to
in so many Jamaican "bad" words acknowledge the dread that the regen-
erative power of the woman often engenders. It is this embodied knowledge of female authority that is invoked in the act of voicing the damning
"bad" word: *pussy hole, blood claat* [cloth], *raas claat, bumbo claat.*

The *Dictionary of Jamaican English* defines "raas" as "buttocks" and
elaborates: "The word is more often used, however, in an exclamatory way
to show strong opposition: scorn, anger, impatience, etc. It is considered
very vulgar." The entry on *bumbo* in the *Dictionary of Jamaican English*
proposes that the word is "prob[ably] of multiple derivation" and cites

Eric Partridge's 1949 *Dictionary of Slang and Unconventional English:* "Bumbo, occ[asionally] bombo . . . mid-C 18–19, West Indian; orig[inally] a negroes' word." The *DJE* also notes that "African origin is also claimed in the earliest quot[ation] (1774), and cf [compare] Zulu -*bumbu*, pubic region. However, there has prob[ably] been concurrent infl[uence] of English *bum* and perh[aps] also Amer[ican] Sp[anish] *bombo*, both meaning the buttock, rump." The *DJE* also defines bumbo as "[t]he female pudend." That Latin word *pudenda*, meaning "that of which one ought to be ashamed," intimates that sexuality is constructed as essentially shameful in Eurocentric discourses. Conversely, the brazen use of feminized "bad" words in Jamaican popular culture becomes a subversive reclamation of the contested power of the "bad" and the "vulgar."

Maureen Warner-Lewis reports her observation of erotic folk dances performed by women in Berbice, Guyana, that evoke religious ritual: "the leader of the dance circle erotically clapped one hand over her genitals while raising her other hand to clasp the back of her neck." This body language, recurring in identical form in contemporary Jamaican dancehall culture, was first articulated by men and now equally by women. Warner-Lewis recounts the significance of this posture: "The leader described her action as part of a wedding dance that highlighted the significance of fertility; while making her gesture she exclaimed the word *bombo*, a reference to the female genitals, a word much used in Jamaica as an obscenity, and which has several Central African sources."[20]

Warner-Lewis gives the following etymology for *bombo*: "the Bembe and Nyanga *mbombo* ~ *bombo* "anus, arse," the related Koongo near-synonym *bombo* "wetness, clotted matter," Mbundu *bombo* "cavity" and, even more to the point, Mbundu *mbumbu*, "vulva."[21] Like the dancing female body in Jamaican popular culture, these cognate Central African words that denote female fertility have undergone pejoration to obscenity in the diaspora.

From a literary/cultural studies perspective, I argue that Jamaican dancehall culture at home and in the diaspora is a potentially liberating space in which working-class women and their more timid middle-class sisters assert the freedom to play out eroticized roles that may not ordinarily be available to them in the rigid social conventions of the everyday. The dancehall, thus conceived, is an erogenous zone in which the celebration of female sexuality and fertility is ritualized. In less subtle readings of the gender politics of the dancehall, this self-conscious female assertion of control over the representation of the body (and identity) is misunderstood and the therapeutic potential of the dancing body is repressed. Indeed, the joyous display of the female body in the dance is misperceived as a pornographic devaluation of woman.

This erotic performance in Jamaican dancehall can be recontextualized within a decidedly African diasporic discourse as a manifestation of the spirit of female fertility figures such as the Yoruba Oshun. In *Carnival of the Spirit*, African American Yoruba priestess and cultural activist Luisah Teish characterizes Oshun in this way: "She is Maiden, Mother, and Queen. Yoruba folklore attributes many powers to her. She has numerous lovers and is known by many praise-names. . . . She is the personification of the Erotic in Nature. It is she who sits as Queen of the Fertility Feast."[22]

In Jamaica, Oshun reappears as the River Mumma of folklore and religion, both myal and revival.[23] She is described by Rev. R. Thomas Banbury in his 1894 book, *Jamaican Superstitions; or, The Obeah Book* as "the water spirit—the diving duppy." He notes the reverential appreciation of her aquatic fertility: "She is believed to inhabit every fountainhead of an inexhaustible and considerable stream of water in Jamaica. For this reason the sources of such streams were worshipped, and sacrifices offered."[24]

Nigerian cultural critic Bibi Bakere-Yusuf proposes yet another female orisha, Oya, as a model for the performance of female sexual identity in the African diaspora. In email correspondence she observed that Oya is the orisha of "masquerades and female power." Bakere-Yusuf elaborates: "Bearing in mind that in the Yoruba language the word for Spectacle—*Iron*—is the same for ancestor, the masquerade is a spectacle that celebrates the ancestors, the living and the yet to come. Oya is the deity of the *Egun Egun* (ancestral) masquerade, as well as of spectacle.[25] Both Oshun and Oya are here invoked to inform my reading of female agency and the performance of spectacular identities in Jamaican dancehall culture.

Though cultural nationalists may cringe at the comparison, I propose that it is this same spirit of the spectacular—the dancehall *bling* aesthetic—that is anticipated in Marcus Garvey's appropriation and adaptation of Eurocentric military regalia to fashion a resplendent visual identity for his African liberation movement. The capacity to recognize the cultural continuities that are manifested in seemingly dissonant discourses is a quintessential requirement of inventive African Diaspora Studies.

In both popular and academic usage the concept of the African diaspora continues to have currency in Jamaica. The formal study of Africa and the diaspora is decidedly enriched by the deployment of multidisciplinary perspectives. Cross-faculty initiatives like the African and African Diaspora Studies program at the University of the West Indies, Mona, engender complex understandings of the breadth and depth of the field. Comparative perspectives are enabled within an academic program that encompasses scholarship in the humanities and social sciences.

In addition, popular manifestations of African consciousness in Jamaica, for example, in reggae music, dancehall DJ culture, and Rastafari *livity* (not to be confused with levity), confirm the efficacy of an approach to African Diaspora Studies that bridges scholarship and lived experience. Thus the consolidation of the legacy of Marcus Garvey in the Liberty

Hall multimedia museum and research library is an excellent example of the intersection of popular and academic conceptions of African Diaspora Studies in Jamaica. Located in that liminal space between and within "education and entertainment," the Liberty Hall enterprise emblematizes the protean nature of the terrain of African Diaspora Studies. From a wide variety of disciplinary perspectives and with a broad range of cultural understandings, both the "academic" and the "popular" are fertile fields for the cultivation of the transdiscipline that is African Diaspora Studies.

APPENDIX 1. MAJOR IN AFRICAN AND AFRICAN DIASPORA STUDIES

Faculty of Humanities and Education
University of the West Indies, Mona, Jamaica

A major consists of a minimum of 36 credits in the following courses with at least 24 credits over Levels II and III.

A minor consists of a minimum of 18 credits over Levels II and III.

Level I	*(3 credits each except where noted)*
HIST1304	Africa in World Civilisation to 1800 (COMPULSORY)
GEND1101	Introduction to Comparative Caribbean Literature I: Afro-Caribbean Poetry
FREN1304	Introduction to Caribbean and African Literature In French
HIST1601	The Atlantic World 1400–1600
MUSC1099	Introduction to Music (6 credits)
THEO1401	Introduction to the Study of Religion

Level II	*(3 credits each except where noted)*
LITS2107	African/Diaspora Women's Narrative
FREN2301	African Literature in French
GOVT200	Philosophical Foundations of Slavery and Anti Slavery Resistance

GOVT2004   Sports, Politics, and Society
GOVT2005   Caribbean Political Thought
GOVT2009   Introduction to African Politics
GOVT2012   Popular Jamaican Music, 1962–82: Roots Lyrics as Socio-
            political and Philosophical Text
GOVT2017   Issues in Contemporary African Politics
HIST2301   The State and Development in Africa
HIST2302   The State and Development in Africa since 1900
LING2201   African Language Structure and History
LING2602   Caribbean Language: Socio-Historical Background
MUSC2099   Music of the English-Speaking Caribbean (6 credits)
PHIL2601   African Philosophy I
PHIL2602   African Philosophy II
THEO2404   Comparative Religion

Level III   *(3 credits each)*

LITS3701   African American Literature
GOVT3022   Garveyism in the Americas
HIST3008   Race and Ethnicity—The British Caribbean since 1838
HIST3301   Origins and Development of Apartheid
HIST3305   Culture, Religion, and Nation-Building in West Africa
            since 1500
HIST3310   Colonialism and Underdevelopment: Africa since 1880
HIST3601   Capitalism and Slavery
HIST3614   By the Rivers of Babylon: The African Diaspora in
            the West
HIST3803   African Archaeology
LING3202   Creole Linguistics
SOCI3001   Caribbean Social Thought
SOCI3025   Caribbean Culture

APPENDIX 2. LITS 2107 AFRICAN/DIASPORA WOMEN'S NARRATIVE

Course Description

Beginning with the analysis of one Southern African and one West African novel, the course defines indigenous African feminist perspectives from which to compare the diasporic African American and Caribbean texts. The authors' use of narrative conventions and modes such as autobiography, the *bildungsroman*, the romance; the quest/journey motif; dreams, visions, and awakenings suggests a tradition of female discourses that cross lines of race, class, ethnicity, and gender. These female-authored African/diasporic narratives employ "mainstream" canonical literary techniques while simultaneously sharing discursive strategies with other feminist texts that contest the hegemony of the phallocentric literary canon. Techniques of oracy, for example, constitute an alternate, privileged discourse for these African/diasporic women writers.

Prescribed Texts:

African:
> Dangarembga, Tsitsi. *Nervous Conditions*
> Aidoo, Ama Ata. *Changes*

African American:
> Marshall, Paule. *Praisesong for the Widow*
> Morrison, Toni. *Tar Baby*

Caribbean:
> Brodber, Erna. *Jane and Louisa Will Soon Come Home*
> Kincaid, Jamaica. *Lucy*

Recommended:

Boyce Davies, Carole, and Elaine Savory Fido, eds. *Out of the Kumbla: Caribbean Women and Literature*

Gates, Henry Louis, Jr., ed. *Black Literature and Literary Theory*

Harris, Joseph. *Global Dimensions of the African Diaspora*

Pryse, Marjorie, and Hortense Spillers, eds. *Conjuring: Black Women, Fiction, and Literary Tradition*

Showalter, Elaine, ed. *The New Feminist Criticism*

Wall, Cheryl, ed. *Changing Our Own Words: Essays on Criticism, Theory, and Writing by Black Women*

NOTES

1. Cited in Martin, *Marcus Garvey, Hero*, 21, 22.

2. The Rastafari neologism, *livity*, means "way of life."

3. Harris, ed., *Global Dimensions of the African Diaspora*, 5.

4. The trope of walking on water to return to Africa is beautifully rendered in the story of the flying Africans of Ibo Landing, elaborated in the novel *Praisesong for the Widow*, written by the Barbadian American Paule Marshall.

5. I am indebted to my colleague in the Department of Literatures in English, Dr. Norval Edwards, for bringing this anecdote to my attention and for his generous comments, which have enriched my argument here. For a lucid account of the politics of race and nation, see his "States of Emergency."

6. For a multilayered elaboration of this concept of continental consciousness, see Brodber, *The Continent of Black Consciousness*.

7. Martin, "Garvey and Scattered African," 243.

8. Jamaican higglers (migrant traders who are mostly female) are famous for traveling the world in search of bargains. There is story, perhaps apocryphal, of a Jamaican higgler who asked a travel agent, "Where is Taiwan?" She had noticed that a lot of the goods she was selling were made in Taiwan, and she wanted to go to the source to cut out the middleman.

9. Telephone interview with Carolyn Cooper, February 9, 2009.

10. Information brochure of the African Caribbean Institute of Jamaica/ Jamaica Memory Bank. I am indebted to Millicent Shannon, administrator at the ACIJ/JMB for research assistance.

11. The curator/director of Liberty Hall is Donna McFarlane, a PhD candidate in museology at the University of Leicester. Her dissertation project focuses on the cultural politics of establishing and maintaining Liberty Hall.

12. See www.garveylibertyhall.com.

13. I am indebted to Arthur Drayton, a quick-witted octogenarian, for this abbreviated account of ASAWI, given in email correspondence. A full history of this association needs to be written.

14. I am indebted to Tony Martin for his brief account of the seminar given in the chapter, "Underground Hero," in *Marcus Garvey, Hero*, 158.

15. I conceived the Reggae Studies Unit in 1992, and it was institutionalized in January 1994. Dr. Jalani Niaah, lecturer in Cultural Studies in the Institute of Caribbean Studies, has led the initiative in Rastafari Studies.

16. I reproduce here excerpts from my book *Sound Clash: Jamaican Dancehall Culture at Large*.

17. Hogg, "The Convince Cult in Jamaica," 4. I am indebted to Burton Sankeralli, a graduate student in Cultural Studies at the University of the West Indies, Mona, for bringing these pum-pum references to my attention, via Cecil Gutzmore, a former lecturer in the Institute of Caribbean Studies.

18. Ibid., 11.

19. Ibid.

20. Warner-Lewis, *Central Africa in the Caribbean*, 235, 236.

21. Ibid., 236.

22. Teish, *Carnival of the Spirit*, 79.

23. For this insight I am indebted to L'Antoinette Stines, Yoruba priestess, artistic director of the L'ACADCO Dance Company, and a PhD candidate in Cultural Studies at the University of the West Indies, Mona.

24. Cited in Cassidy, *Jamaica Talk*, 184, 252.

25. Bibi Bakere-Yusuf, January 13, 2003.

REFERENCES

Discography

Andy, Bob. "I've Got To Go Back Home." Track 5, *Bob Andy's Song Book*, Studio One, 1970.

Brown, Prezident, and Don Yute. "African Ting." Track 10, *Prezident Selections*, RUNNetherlands, RNN0043, n.d.

Ranks, Shabba. "Back and Bellyrat." Track 4, *Just Reality*, Vine Yard Records, VYDCD 6, 1991.

——. "Flesh Axe." Track 7, *As Raw as Ever*, Sony, 468102 2, 1991.
Tosh, Peter. "African." Track 6, *Equal Rights*, Columbia, 1977.

Print Materials

Brodber, Erna. *The Continent of Black Consciousness: On the History of the African Diaspora from Slavery to the Present Day*. London: New Beacon Books, 2003.

Cassidy, Frederic. *Jamaica Talk*. Basingstoke and London: Institute of Jamaica/Macmillan, 1961.

Cooper, Carolyn. *Sound Clash: Jamaican Dancehall Culture at Large*. New York: Palgrave Macmillan, 2004.

Edwards, Norval. "States of Emergency: Reggae Representations of the Jamaican Nation-State." *Social and Economic Studies* 47, no. 1 (March 1998): 21–32.

Harris, Joseph, ed. *Global Dimensions of the African Diaspora*. Washington, D.C.: Howard University Press, 1982.

Hogg, Donald. "The Convince Cult in Jamaica." *Yale University Publications in Anthropology* no. 58. Reprinted in Sidney Mintz, ed., *Papers in Caribbean Anthropology*. New Haven, Conn.: Human Relations Area Files Press, 1970.

Martin, Tony. "Garvey and Scattered African." In Joseph Harris, ed., *Global Dimensions of the African Diaspora*, 243–49. Washington, D. C.: Howard University Press, 1982.

——. *Marcus Garvey, Hero: A First Biography*. Dover, Mass.: Majority Press, 1983.

Teish, Luisah. *Carnival of the Spirit*. San Francisco: Harper, 1994.

Warner-Lewis, Maureen. *Central Africa in the Caribbean: Transcending Time, Transforming Cultures*. Barbados, Jamaica, Trinidad and Tobago: University of the West Indies Press, 2003.

14 SOUTH AFRICA'S ELUSIVE QUEST FOR AN AFRICAN IDENTITY: THE IRONIES OF A SOUTH AFRICA–LED AFRICAN RENAISSANCE

Xolela Mangcu

In 1959, two of South Africa's leading intellectuals, Eskia Mphahlele and Gerard Sekoto, visited the offices of the Society of African Culture in Paris. There they met with the editors of *Presence Africaine* and asked them, "Where do we come in—we, who are detribalized and are producing a proletariat art."[1] Mphahlele had just come from South Africa. He was dismissive and disdainful of negritude as just another form of "medieval clannishness." This reflected the dominant political culture of the ANC and its multiracial alliance partners: "We are aiming at a common society and to prove that multiracial societies can thrive and become a glorious reality in Africa."[2] Mphahlele wrote a scathing attack on negritude as yet a romantic representation of the African experience: "Who is so stupid as to deny the historical fact of negritude as both a protest and a positive assertion of African values? All this is valid. What I do not accept is the way in which too much of the poetry inspired by it romanticizes Africa—as a symbol of innocence, purity, and artless primitiveness."[3] He was equally dismissive of Nkrumah's "African personality" as inappropriate and irrelevant for a people trying to construct a multiracial society. David Attwell describes Mphahlele's early response to negritude as an "apology for the South African intellectual's estrangement in the face of negritude which was, at the time, the most talked-about of intellectualizations of identity in the black world."[4] However, the hardening of racial attitudes on the part of South Africa's white population, his experience as a member of a racial minority in the United States, and the emergence of black consciousness in South Africa led to a dramatic reassessment of Mphahlele's political outlook. And so in 1974 he observed that "there is something about the act of and fact of communal survival inside a situation of racism that either tones down, or lends another complexion to, the hate that is mixed with anger. Outside the situation you are on your own, you have little communal support: at best, it is intellectual. So you hate the whites you left behind with a scalding intensity. Could it be that distance creates a void and that the burning lava of hate must fill it?" But even in his embrace of negritude Mphahlele turned not to the lyricism of Senegal's Leopold Senghor but to the radical, secular ideals of Aimé Césaire. Finally Mphahlele had come around. In 1974, he declared that negritude was "the modern (cultural) equivalent of the old condition of fugitive slaves."[5]

Ngugi wa Thiong'o offers a slightly different account of why the distance of exile turns into a more radical orientation. Speaking at the Macmillan-Stewart Lectures at Harvard University, Ngugi argues that the differences can be seen in the ways in which diasporic Africans and continental Africans responded to the tremendous loss of life that occurred during slavery, colonialism, and apartheid. Whereas Africans in the diaspora were always longing for home, continental African elites have never properly mourned the deaths of slavery, colonialism, and apartheid. Ngugi argues that even though diasporic Africans lost much of their languages, they held on to what they could as a way of keeping their memory of home. They subverted the dominant languages of the New World through processes of creolization and the development of an alternative aesthetic. The result was the Negro spiritual—an aesthetic of resistance—which later led to the blues and jazz, calypso, hip-hop, and other forms of representation. He cites Aimé Césaire as someone who, even though lacking in African languages, played around with the French language, subverting and giving it a new form. Africans in the diaspora had to innovate or perish. This innovative turn is to be distinguished from the development through imitation that characterized the Europeans, who merely transplanted architectural models, place-names, and other things from the Old World to the New World. Ngugi argues that continental Africans did exactly the opposite of their diasporic brothers and sisters. They ran away from their languages and instead engaged in processes of evasion and denial. In the end Ngugi offers a psychoanalytic explanation for this obsession with European languages and memory on the part of continental Africans.[6] However, in Eskia Mphahlele's story we find a synthesis of the diasporic and continental African—someone initially suspicious of his African identity ultimately coming around to it through his diasporic experiences. Nonetheless, the fact of coming around to it is not in and of itself sufficient for as long as Mphahlele is in exile. Not only was he yearning for a place called home; he also had the option of fulfilling that yearning, albeit at the risk of alienating his political comrades. Indeed, he broke with the cultural boycott that had taken him into exile in the first place and returned to South Africa. He could not resist the yearning for home because "a philosophical accommodation to a broadly diasporic identity was not a sufficient answer to Mphahlele's longing for rootedness,

for place." He finds in his philosophy of African humanism a synthesis
of finding "a subject position within the broader African modernity"—a
way of bringing his broad experience of exile to bear on his life and work
at home.[7] The question, though, is whether the same cross-cultural synthesis of a diasporic identity existing in tension with a continental and
South African identity can be assumed for those who have returned from
exile to lead the African Renaissance. To what extent does their return
take us closer to a synthesis of our diasporic and continental identities? I
am not sure if it takes us any closer at all—for reasons of history and for
reasons imposed by the fact of returning as rulers. The historical ambivalence with black nationalism goes beyond the early Mphahlele and is re-
flective of a multiracial accommodationism that goes back to the mid-
nineteenth century.

TIYO SOGA'S MULTIRACIAL ACCOMMODATIONISM

Reverend Tiyo Soga was South Africa's first modern public intellectual.
He was also the first, at least in recorded history, to grapple with our diasporic identity. Born in 1829, Tiyo Soga entered Lovedale College—the
center of missionary education for Africans for the next 150 years—at the
relatively advanced age of 15 under the tutelage of Scottish missionary
William Chalmers. However, his education was interrupted by the wars of
resistance that spanned the entire nineteenth century.[8] In 1846, Soga was
taken to safety in Glasgow, Scotland, by his colonial minders, to return
only in 1849 as a missionary and schoolmaster. Soga returned to Scotland
at the outbreak of yet another war in 1851. He was to remain in Scotland
until his graduation in 1856—the first African to graduate from Glasgow
at the time. He returned as South Africa's first ordained minister with his
wife, a white Scottish woman, Janet Burnside, to the consternation of both
blacks and whites. When Prince Albert presented him with a beautifully
bound Bible, Soga exclaimed in gratitude: "What shall I say in admiration
of the noble qualities of the second son of our beloved Queen? My loyalty
knows no bounds." Tiyo Soga had denounced African culture as backward
and heathen, and he had refused to participate in the all-important custom
of circumcision. However, Soga's experience in Scotland had not been entirely happy, and even after he returned he was not immune to the racial
taunts of the white community, including imprisonment for not carrying
a pass, even though he was exempted from doing so because of his status.
He was acutely aware that the settler community tolerated him because
of his education and missionary standing: "The Scotch education, not my
black face, has been my passport into places where that face would not be
permitted to enter." At times he spoke out against the colonial land grabs
and killing of innocent Africans, albeit in the language of a true mission-

ary: "Warriors of noble spirit disdain to strike a foe without weapons. . . .
It is beneath the dignity of civilized men to be the formidable enemy of
naked barbarians, who cannot write and reason like themselves."[9]

SOGA'S TURN TO BLACK NATIONALISM
AND THE AFRICAN DIASPORA

Soga's politics changed radically after he read a newspaper article by one
of his fellow missionaries, John Chalmers. Just as Edward Blyden's turn to
African nationalism was triggered by Hegel's racist assertion in *The Philosophy of Culture* that black people's "condition is capable of no development of culture, and as we see them at this day, such as they have always
been," Soga's African nationalism was triggered by Chalmers's assertion
that black people were indolent and incapable of development and inexo-
rably drawn to extinction. Soga drew on the history of Africans in the diaspora to repudiate Chalmers as follows:

> Africa was of God given to the race of Ham. I find the Negro from the days
> of the Assyrian to downwards, keeping his "individuality" and his "distinc-
> tiveness," amid the wreck of empires, and the revolution of ages. I find him
> keeping his place among the nations, and keeping his home and country. I
> find him opposed by nation after nation and driven from his home. I find
> him enslaved—exposed to the vices and the brandy of the white man. I
> find him in this condition for many a day—in the West Indian Islands, in
> northern and South America, and in the South American colonies of Spain
> and Portugal. I find him exposed to all these disasters, and yet living,—
> multiplying and "never extinct." Yea, I find him now as the prevalence of
> Christian and philanthropic opinions on the rights of man obtains among
> civilized nations, returning unmanacled to the land of his forefathers, tak-
> ing back with him the civilization and Christianity of those nations (see
> the Negro Republic of Liberia). I find the Negro in the present struggle in
> America looking forward—though with still chains in his hands and chains
> on his feet—yet looking forward to the dawn of a better day for himself and
> all his sable brethren in Africa.[10]

Soga's references to Liberia and other African countries suggest he would
have known about the works of Martin Delany, Alexander Crummell, and
Edward Blyden in Liberia. Soga's biographer, Donovan Williams, thus describes Soga as the founder of black nationalism and black consciousness
in South Africa. Williams argues that Soga was caught up in the "cross-
tide of cultures." He avoided both the naïve Eurocentrism of his youth
and the nativist racial purism of someone like Edward Blyden. He faced
his existential dilemma head on by suggesting that African identity was
a matter of identification, not biology or skin color. He counseled his mu-
latto children about their identity thus: "I want you, for your future com-

fort, to be very careful on this point. You will ever cherish the memory of your mother as that of an upright, conscientious, thrifty, Christian Scotchwoman. You will ever be thankful for your connection by this tie to the white race. But if you wish to gain credit for yourselves—if you do not wish to feel the taunt of men, which you sometimes may be made to feel—take your place in the world as coloured, not as white men, as kafirs, not as Englishmen. You will be more thought of for this by all good and wise people, than for the other."[11] According to Attwell, "Soga was indeed 'a man of two worlds,' but he was also a transitional figure within Xhosa history, marking a choice that subsequent generations would have to re-make for themselves."[12]

Soga's turn to radical black consciousness was a little late, however—the seeds of a multiracial, nonracial consciousness had been laid in the African intellectual response to colonial defeat—a response of which he was the initial principal author. This was the response of accommodation. The thrust of the response is contained in Citashe's famous poem:

> Your cattle are gone, my countrymen!
> Go rescue them! Go rescue them!
> Leave the breechloader alone
> And turn to the pen.
> Load it with ink
> For that is your shield.
> Your rights are going!
> So pick up your pen.
> Load it, load it with ink.
> Sit on a chair.
> Repair not to Hoho[13]
> But fire with your pen

THE SEPARATION OF AFRICAN NATIONALISM FROM PAN-AFRICANISM IN THE ANC

Citashe's poem prefigured the turn toward the adoption and adaptation of European modernity by early intellectuals in the Eastern Hemisphere. William Gqoba's essay "Education" was the first systematic argument for turning to education as the new weapon for freedom.[14] Writing about this first generation of African intellectuals, Ntongela Masilela argues that these people stood on the border line between tradition and modernity: "They were concerned with the historical issue of what were the political and cultural facilitators of entrance into modernity."[15] Masilela divides these early intellectuals into two groups: the conservative modernizers and the revolutionary modernizers of the 1940s. However, this is where categories can fail us, sometimes ignoring the nuances among the conservative modernizers themselves. Certainly among the conserva-

tives we could include people such as John Tengo Jabavu (founder of the
first black newspaper, *Imvo Zabantsundu,* and the University of Fort Hare
and perhaps the most influential African leader since Tiyo Soga) and John
Langalibalele Dube (cofounder of the ANC, the newspaper *Ilanga Lase-
Natal,* and Ohlange Institute). But where would we put the more radical
among them: Rubusana (the first black person to become a member of parliament), Sol Plaatje (the legendary author and newspaperman), and S. E. K.
Mqhayi (the great Xhosa poet)? Even though they were all conservative,[16]
the former were more influenced by Booker T. Washington and the latter
by W. E. B Du Bois. In the end, however, Washington seems to have had
much greater influence on early South African intellectuals than Du Bois.
Many of these conservative modernizers were just frightened by Garvey's
Pan-Africanism and set out to destroy it before it gained any hold in South
Africa. These intellectuals exercised their influence through their own
newspapers. For example, the most conservative and perhaps the most influential of all was R. V. Selope Thema, who campaigned vigorously against
Garveyism in South Africa. As Masilela puts it, "Selope Thema could not
accept in many ways that the philosophy of his master, Booker T. Washington, had evolved and taken the mantle of Garveyism. To conservative
modernizers such as Dube and Selope Thema, the black radicalism of
Garveyism was viewed as a threat to their conservative and middle-class
construction of African nationalism." His attempt to bring in the African
American experience was not so much a Pan-Africanist or diasporic project as "a neutral undertaking of taking lessons from a particular black
modernity." Masilela argues that by the time of the formation of the ANC
it was "too late to bring in Du Bois to counter the deep influence of Booker
T. Washington on a substantial number of New African intellectuals."[17]
And thus began the separation of the ANC's African Nationalism from
Pan-Africanism. This partly explains the ambivalent identity of South Africans toward Pan-Africanism or the African diaspora in general, and provides the backdrop to Mphahlele's question, "Where do we come in—we
who are detribalized and are producing a proletarian art?"

PAN-AFRICANISM AND
BLACK CONSCIOUSNESS

This is not at all to suggest that South Africa did not have a Pan-Africanist
vision, only that it was never the dominant position of the liberation movement. In the 1940s there emerged a group of "revolutionary modernizers"
such as A. P. Mda, Anton Lembede, and Robert Sobukwe who sought to
connect South Africa to Nkrumah's call for a United States of Africa.
Some of these "revolutionary modernizers" broke off from the ANC in
1959 after the latter had adopted the Freedom Charter. What irked the
Africanists was the Charter's declaration that "South Africa belongs to

all who lived in it, black and white." This confirmed to them that the
ANC was no longer the custodian of African nationalism, let alone Pan-
Africanism. Seeking to take the initiative from the ANC, the PAC led
a countrywide anti-pass campaign, culminating in the Sharpeville Mas-
sacre of 1960. However, what is more interesting is not so much what happened to the PAC in South Africa after 1960—it was decimated through
a nationwide series of arrests of its leadership—as its reception in exile.
Sobukwe was kept on Robben Island for the entire decade and ultimately
released and banished to Galeshewe in Kimberley, a place with which he
had had no connection before his imprisonment—yet another example of
how apartheid dismembered black people from their places of memory
and meaning.

Meanwhile, many African governments refused to acknowledge the
ANC as the genuine representative of the South African people. They accorded that status to the PAC because only the PAC spoke the language of
Pan-Africanism. Unfortunately, the PAC was wracked by internal strife,
which ultimately led to its demise as a political force.

However, the politics of identity would be carried forward by the student activists of the black consciousness movement under the leadership
of Steve Biko. The movement emerged in the late 1960s and 1970s as a
reaction of black students to the dominant role played by white liberal
students in the liberation struggle. The rejection of white tutelage was
taking place within a broader revival of black power politics in the United
States and radical anticolonial struggles in Mozambique, Angola, and Zimbabwe. Steve Biko even wrote to Charles Hamilton and Stokely Carmi-
chael after reading their book, *Black Power*. Even though he never left
South Africa, Biko had a deep appreciation and based much of his thinking on diasporic writings, particularly the writings of Frantz Fanon and
Aimé Césaire. Barney Pityana describes Biko's diasporic consciousness as
follows:

> Black Consciousness for him was moulded by a diversity of intellectual
> forces and fountains: from the liberation history of South Africa, the
> Pan-Africanism of Kwame Nkrumah, the African nationalism of Jomo
> Kenyatta, the negritude of the west African scholars like Leopold Sadar
> Senghor, Aimé Césaire, and others in Paris. Biko taught himself a political
> understanding of religion in Africa. He devoured John Mbiti. Ali Mazrui.
> Basil Davidson. He understood the critical writings of Walter Rodney, and
> he interpreted Franz Fanon. He laid his hands on some philosophical writ-
> ings like Jean Paul Sartre and made ready use of some philosophical con-
> cepts like syllogism in logic and dialectical materialism in Marxist politi-
> cal thought. All this by a young medical student.[18]

In his writings Biko advocated a joint culture—or what Attwell calls
transculturation—that would give birth to a new South African identity
that would be at once African and universal.[19] An important legacy of

Steve Biko was the creation of a new black political identity that included Africans, Indians, and Coloreds through what Kirstie McClure describes as the "politics of direct address." This is "a quotidian politics"[20] in which individuals and communities changed their identities through horizontal, solidaristic relationships with each other. Even though Indians and Coloreds had always played a leading role in the liberation movement, this was really the first time that there was an inclusive political definition of blackness that went beyond skin color or other physical characteristics. Blacks would be defined as "all those who are by law and tradition, politically, socially, and economically discriminated against as a group and identify themselves as a unity towards the realization of their aspirations." But Biko spoke also of the need to incorporate the African experience into that collective political identity. This was "primarily a culture that accepts the humanity of the black man. . . . Sure it will have European experience because we have whites here who are descended from Europe. We don't dispute that. But for God's sake it must have African experience as well."[21] This was at least the promise of Thabo Mbeki's African Renaissance.

THABO MBEKI AND THE AFRICAN RENAISSANCE

There was a great deal of excitement among Africanists and black consciousness activists when Thabo Mbeki first signaled that he was taking the ANC toward a Pan-Africanist direction. The ANC had finally seen the light, we proclaimed. In a sense African nationalism was being joined to the broader stream of Pan-Africanism, or so we thought. It is not clear what made Mbeki take the ANC in this direction. After all, in the 1980s Thabo Mbeki was the darling of the white media and business community. On his return from exile, he was feted by leading white politicians and business leaders as the polished, urbane, suave, pipe-smoking, gray-haired intellectual—an embodiment of modern sophistication. But something must have happened to trigger this radical turn. At some point he must have come to the realization that he could not transform South African society without challenging the assumptions of the very people who had courted and supported him. They must have been just as surprised by his radical turn as he was by their resistance. As soon as he felt the sense of rejection and resistance, Mbeki increasingly called on black intellectuals to rally to his support. "Where are the black intellectuals?" he asked repeatedly and plaintively. Unfortunately, this coincided with his embrace of increasingly controversial policy positions on HIV/AIDS and the economy. This left him exposed on both flanks, so to speak, and brought about a defensive culture within the ANC. This would have implications for the prosecution of the African Renaissance. Mbeki simply turned to a limited number of trusted advisors to spearhead the renaissance project. An African Renaissance Institute was established, and conferences were organized to inaugurate the renaissance. Mbeki delivered a moving address to parliament affirming his African identity: "I am an African." It was Mbeki's best speech. It was remarkable not only for its poetic delivery but also for its assertion of African pride in a country that, in the words of Steve Biko, had always seen itself as "a province of Europe." However, the speech was equally remarkable for the fact that it said little about the African diaspora or the continent of Africa itself, except that Africa needed to be rescued from the warmongers and dictators. There was nothing in the speech about African philosophy or culture or how those might inform the project of the African Renaissance. The "African" in Mbeki's speech was the South African "African." This confirmed that our conception of ourselves as African has never gone beyond South Africa—we are Africans because we are geographically located on the African continent.

This cultural omission has not been helped by the almost exclusive conceptualization of the African Renaissance as nothing more than *a vehicle* for economic development. To paraphrase Nehru, the African Renaissance and the economic development projects that would carry it forward would become South Africa's "temples of the modern age."[22] Unfortunately, the more the African renaissance became the language of official discourse, particularly economic development discourse, the further it was removed from civil society, the universities, or the media. Very little was heard from the African Renaissance Institute, and the conferences that had been organized with much fanfare came to a halt. Instead, we saw a proliferation of "African Renaissance" commercial enterprises and consulting companies and even security companies. Apparently, putting on the badge of the African Renaissance was good for business. The whole thing had been vulgarized.

Our media is even worse. If anything, our media shows an incredible amount of not only ignorance but also willful disinterest in African cultural and intellectual matters beyond South Africa—and here I am talking about black-led and black-edited newspapers that find it difficult to cover major African thinkers and scholars when they visit South Africa. Not only is our conception of African identity limited to South Africa, but even within South Africa itself the question of who constitutes an African has been reduced to a biological essentialism and limited to those who walk a particular ideological line—those who are "distinctly African." This crude essentialism is a departure from the tradition of Tiyo Soga, Eskia Mphahlele, Robert Sobukwe, and Steve Biko. If there is any lesson from our experience, it is that the sooner the project of the African Renaissance is accorded relative autonomy from the state, the better it will be for us to revive it in civil society both within our country and across our borders. The question therefore remains, "Where do we come in—we who are detribalized, who are producing a proletarian art?"

Pallo Jordan, South Africa's former minister of arts and culture and one of the ANC's leading thinkers, located South Africa's place in the history of the African diaspora in a speech he gave in Jamaica in 2005.[23] Jordan sketched the shared history of connections among African people, and he described Pan-Africanism as "the political project inaugurated by a group of African-descended intellectuals and activists at the beginning of the twentieth century, with the aim of restoring the human rights of the peoples of Africa and those of African descent throughout the world." He spoke of the central role played by Henry Sylvester Williams in organizing the first Pan-African conference. He celebrated the role played by Haiti in lighting the "torch of freedom" for African people when the Haitians revolted and defeated the French in 1804. But he also spoke of the role played by the founding father of the ANC, Pixley ka Seme, starting with the speech he gave at Columbia University in 1906. Like Ngugi he drew attention to the different responses to slavery between those who sought to abandon the New World and return to Africa and those who sought to recast their relationships with whites in the New World while also fighting for the freedom of their people in the colonized territories back home. Over time the former lost its attractive appeal, and the latter group prevailed. Jordan noted that these two movements were not mutually exclusive. For example, those who remained in the New World—particularly African Americans—played a crucial role in providing material and strategic resources to those who were struggling for freedom on the continent: the African diaspora was destined to play a decisive supportive role, especially in the southern African theater of struggle. Many South African leaders came under the influence of people such as Booker T. Washington. Jordan drew attention to the conservative nature of the early leadership, whom he said spoke in "the cautious language of petitioners." He did not examine how this conservatism ultimately shaped the nature and evolution of African nationalism in South Africa in similarly conservative and ascetic ways in relation to the country's connection to the continent. He rightly noted that "Garveyism in the British empire found an echo in Negritude in France's Atlantic empire, Afro-Cubanismo in Cuba, Modernismo AfroBrasileiro in Brazil, and the New African movement in South Africa." Jordan spoke of increasing radicalization after the fifth Pan-African conference in 1945. By this time Africans had taken over the leadership of the struggles for independence, no longer overwhelmingly reliant on the advocacy of their kith and kin elsewhere on the globe. But it would be a mistake to argue in the case of South Africa that this political radicalization was strong enough to change the sense of estrangement between South Africa's variant of African nationalism and the Pan-Africanism taking root elsewhere in the continent. This explains why the Pan-Africanist Congress became popular with Pan-Africanists outside of South Africa, including Robert Mugabe in South Africa. Even a man of Jordan's historical expertise fell into the technocratic conception of the

African renaissance. Thus by the end of his speech he was defining Africa's regeneration in terms of Mbeki's pet project, the New Partnership for Africa's Development. He spoke of trade, trade, and more trade as the modern-day version of the challenges facing the African diaspora: "Africa has attempted its own indigenously evolved response to globalization, the New Partnership for Africa's Development, focusing on the development of infrastructure, the redefinition of trade between Africa and its principal trading partners, the exploration of intra-African trade, and the development of a new partnership among African and other developing countries." Trade, trade, and more trade would thus be the thrust and content of the African renaissance.

As a demonstration of South Africa's commitment to the diaspora, Jordan spoke about the positive role that South Africa plays in mediating conflicts in Africa, but said nothing about the monstrous rule of Robert Mugabe and the shameful role played by Thabo Mbeki in providing cover for Mugabe both at international forums and in the negotiations between Mugabe and the opposition Movement for Democratic Change. Mbeki earned the image of someone who coddled and protected dictators in the name of African nationalism. For example, there was a letter he wrote to the MDC's Morgan Tsvangirai, effectively painting a picture of him as an "Uncle Tom" who obeyed Europe's instructions at the expense of the African brotherhood in the South African Development Community (SADC). The unfortunate consequence of Mbeki's African nationalism politics was that even laudable causes were seen as part of his Africanist grandstanding while using the language of African nationalism to defend the indefensible. His excursions into African historical achievements were seen as part of a political project of the diaspora that was very different from the one Jordan provided—a political project of restoring human rights to African peoples. Mbeki's political project became closely associated with Robert Mugabe, a leader who was doing everything to undermine the human rights of his own people.

What had become a political project of freedom became a political project in defense of dictators. In January 2005, Mbeki addressed the Sudanese national assembly in celebration of that country's forty-ninth anniversary. Here again Mbeki used the language of African nationalism to invoke a shared colonial past. He lauded Sudan's pioneering role in the struggle for freedom while saying nothing about the genocidal atrocities the Sudanese government was committing against its own people. Mbeki's biographer (although *hagiographer* would be more appropriate), Ronald Suresh Roberts, argues that in that speech Mbeki made "the Pan-African imperative not merely a mark of solidarity but part of the definition of tasks to come." As a result, even some of his best initiatives were always clouded by the fact that they were used by his own supporters as proof of his African nationalism and conversely as a way of putting down perceived enemies. Thus Roberts used Mbeki's support for Haiti as an occasion to take a shot at Nadine Gordimer, with whom he had previously had a falling-out over his biography of her. In Roberts's study of Mbeki, he writes, "These slaves Nadine Gordimer described as 'the simple people of Haiti.'" His laudable decision to host Aristide and bestow on him the Supreme Order of the Companions of Oliver Tambo (Gold)—South Africa's highest national honor—was seen as part of his politics. For Mbeki, the people of the Caribbean had been the victims of American and Western interference, and that was exactly what the Americans and the West were doing in Zimbabwe. Those who criticized him on Zimbabwe, HIV/AIDS, and corruption were practicing the same old tradition of Western interference that the people of the Caribbean had so valiantly resisted. This analogy held because, in Roberts's rather elegant phrasing, the people of the Caribbean and the people of South Africa (read Mbeki) were powered by an "invisible hand of an anti-imperialist tradition."[24] The global past of shared struggle was thereby deployed to call for solidarity around the cynical political practices of autocrats on the southern tip of the African continent. This was the cynicism that informed Mbeki's approach to the renaissance, including his decision to extend his stay in political power by seeking a third term as president of the ruling African National Congress. By reaching for power this way, Mbeki went against everything he had articulated in the 1990s as the bright-eyed champion of the African renaissance. However, the ANC would have none of that.

In December 2007, the party resoundingly rejected Mbeki's reach for power by electing his anti-type—Jacob Zuma—to become its leader. In my book *To the Brink: The State of Democracy in South Africa*, I describe Zuma as the very opposite of Thabo Mbeki. Whereas Mbeki was seen as a detribalized, modernist African leader, Jacob Zuma appeared to be a conservative traditionalist. On the face of it, this might lead people to believe that Zuma would therefore have a greater affinity for the continent and the diaspora. In yet another ironic moment, Jacob Zuma was the one leader who went out to the scenes of the xenophobic violence that claimed many lives in the townships in 2008. The angry crowd asked him to leave, but Zuma stood his ground and informed them he was not going anywhere. Zuma was, of course, one of them—the uneducated herd boy. That became the source of his authenticity—as it has become to many people in the rural areas and townships of South Africa. On the other hand, the great champion of the African renaissance and the president of the republic, Thabo Mbeki, was nowhere to be found. Instead, he chose to address the nation and appeal for calm on television in a speech in English about human rights that was hardly likely to strike resonance with the rampaging crowds. Someone needed to talk to the people, face to face and in their language, and that person was Zuma. But would this of necessity redefine South Africa's understanding of its place on the continent?

There are many on the continent who see Zuma as an embarrassment. Achille Mbembe has described Zuma as the false prophet (um-profethi) who represents a millenarian movement on a path of self-immolation. He compares Zuma to the young nineteenth-century Xhosa prophetess called Nongqause, who led the mass suicide of the Xhosa people when she asked them to kill their cattle and burn their granaries as penance for their sins and in anticipation of new wealth. Nongqause prophesied that if the Xhosa did that, then all the dead would arise, and with them would come untold wealth. At the instigation of their chiefs, some people went along with Nongqause's tragic prophecy, and others refused. Thousands of people died as a result, and the foundations of Xhosa society were destroyed. This story is regarded as one of the most damaging of all the colonial conspiracies in South Africa. Zuma, Mbembe argues, promises the poor and downtrodden exactly the same kind of millenarian vision. In the end nothing will come of it, as Zuma will be proven to be the false prophet he really is, Mbembe contends. However, by resorting to metaphysics in explaining political phenomena, Mbembe relies on the stereotype of the unthinking poor. And yet the people behind Zuma represent an astute political movement supported as much by members of the middle class as by the working class. These are people and constituencies that have been the victims of Thabo Mbeki's political machinations over the past decade. Zuma has become the populist symbol around which they will get back at Mbeki.[25] As much as some of his views will make you cringe—such as saying he would take a shower after having sex without a condom to avoid contracting HIV, Zuma is not a political blank slate. And the paradoxes of a Zuma presidency may well be that of a culturally conservative presidency that nonetheless makes politically progressive changes, such as the new ANC leadership's tough actions on Zimbabwe, including holding back agricultural aid until a settlement has been reached by the ruling ZANU-PF and the Movement for Democratic Change. Nonetheless, Jacob Zuma's alienation from Africa and the diaspora is going to be different from Thabo Mbeki's. Mbeki's instincts are continental and diasporic. Like other political pathfinders before him, his desire for political power got the better of him. Zuma's political instincts are likely to be more South African, even if Africanists will continue to push for wider initiatives focused on Africa and diaspora. However, Zuma's provincial instincts may still prevail, proving yet again how even the tribalized among us are also awkwardly African.

NOTES

1. Attwell, *Rewriting Modernity*, 116–17.
2. Mphahlele, *The African Image*, 74.

3. Mphahlele, "A Reply."

4. Attwell, *Rewriting Modernity*, 119.

5. Mphahlele, *The African Image*, 2nd ed., 42, 95.

6. Ngugi wa Thiong'o delivered the Macmillan-Stewart Lectures at Harvard University on March 14–16, 2006. Abiola Irele, a professor in residence at Harvard, offered the same account of Aimé Césaire's role in the creolization of the French language.

7. Attwell, *Rewriting Modernity*, 132.

8. For a discussion of the wars of resistance, the so-called frontier wars, see Mostert, *Frontiers*.

9. Quoted in Williams's biography of Tiyo Soga, *Umfundisi*.

10. Tiyo Soga, *King William's Town Gazette and Kaffrarian Banner*, 11 May 1865. The response initially came under the pseudonym Defensor—a Reply.

11. Chalmers, *Tiyo Soga: A Page of Mission Work*, 430. Chalmers's condescending, paternalistic attitude to Soga is evident in the subtitle of the biography.

12. Attwell, *Rewriting Modernity*, 46.

13. Hoho was a section of the Amatole mountain range where the Xhosa retreated, often to counterattack against the British.

14. See Jordan, *Towards an African Literature*, for a favorable appraisal of Gqoba's influence.

15. Masilela, interview with Sandile Ngidi, 2006, unpublished ms, 63.

16. Perhaps we are talking about more than two categories here: conservatives (Dube, Selope-Thema), moderates (Pixley ka Seme, Plaatje), radicals (SEK Mqhayi), and revolutionaries (Anton Lembede).

17. Masilela, interview, 50.

18. I asked Barney Pityana to write this as part of my research on Steve Biko's biography.

19. This is the reason why black consciousness would be so attractive to Eskia Mphahlele, who sought "a conceptual frame of reference that was grounded in an intuitive loyalty to his home, but that could, nevertheless, answer to the complexity of his experience in the twenty years of exile." Attwell describes Mphahlele as someone who had "a sense of being buffeted by history, a child of modernity, but being, at the same time, in possession of a cultural code that owes nothing to modernity's bland universality." Attwell, *Rewriting Modernity*, 134–35.

20. McClure, "On the Subject of Rights."

21. Biko, *I Write What I Like.*

22. Indian prime minister Jawaharlal Nehru was disdainful of Gandhi's suggestion that the best route to Indian renaissance was through the cultures of the local people. He felt this would be divisive, and instead he sought to make development projects "the temples of the modern age." For a fuller discussion, see Tharoor, *India: From Midnight to Millennium*, and Khilnani, *India*.

23. Pallo Jordan, speech delivered at the SA-AU-Caribbean Diaspora Conference, Kingston, Jamaica, 17 March 2005, www.Dfa.gov.za/docs/speeches/2005/jordo317.htm.

24. Roberts, *Fit to Govern*, 75, 80.

25. For a political discussion of Jacob Zuma, see Mangcu, *To the Brink*, and Gordin, *Zuma*.

REFERENCES

Attwell, David. *Rewriting Modernity: Studies in Black Literary History.* Durban: University of KwaZulu Natal Press, 2005.

Biko, Steve. *I Write What I Like.* Ed. Aelred Stubbs. London: Bowerdean Press, 1978.

Chalmers, John. *Tiyo Soga: A Page of Mission Work.* Edinburgh: Andrew Elliot, 1877.

Gordin, Jeremy. *Zuma: A Biography.* Cape Town: Jonathan Ball, 2008.

Jordan, A. C. *Towards an African Literature: The Emergence of Literary Form in Xhosa.* Berkeley: University of California Press, 1973.

Khilnani, Sunil. *India.* New York: Giroux and Strauss, 1997.

Mangcu, Xolela. *To the Brink: The State of Democracy in South Africa.* Durban: University of KwaZulu Natal Press, 2008.

McClure, Kirstie. "On the Subject of Rights: Pluralism, Plurality, and Political Identity." In Chantal Mouffe, ed., *Dimensions of Radical Democracy.* London: Verso, 1992.

Moore, Gerald, ed. *African Literature and the Universities.* Ibadan: Published for the Congress of Cultural Freedom by Ibadan University Press, 1965.

Mostert, Noel. *Frontiers: The Epic of South Africa's Creation and the Tragedy of the Xhosa People.* London: Jonathan Cape, 1992.

Mphahlele, Eskia. *The African Image.* London: Faber and Faber, 1962.

———. *The African Image.* 2nd ed. London: Faber and Faber, 1974.

———. "A Reply. In Gerald Moore, ed., *African Literature and the Universities*, 22–26. Ibadan: Congress for Cultural Freedom, Ibadan University Press, 1965.

Roberts, Ronald Suresh. *Fit to Govern: The Native Intelligence of Thabo Mbeki.* Johannesburg: STE, 2007.

Tharoor, Shashi. *India: From Midnight to Millennium.* New York: Viking, 1997.

Williams, Donovan. *Umfundisi: A Biography of Tiyo Soga, 1829–1871.* Lovedale, South Africa: Lovedale Press, 1978.

15

"BLACK FOLK HERE AND THERE": REPOSITIONING OTHER(ED) AFRICAN DIASPORA(S) IN/AND "EUROPE"

Jayne O. Ifekwunigwe

> When we have made an experience or chaos into a story we have transformed it, made sense of it, transmuted experience, domesticated the chaos.
>
> —*Ben Okri, A Way of Being Free*

The story I will begin to recount is one that seeks to expand the way we think about African diaspora(s) in/and "Europe." Using broad brushstrokes, I will explore two compound problematics that stand in as distillations rather than crystallizations of relevant debates. First, why is it difficult to confine or define the African Diaspora in/and Europe, and what impact has the pioneering work of Stuart Hall and Paul Gilroy had on the emergence of a dominant Anglophone Black [North] Atlanticist approach to African Diaspora Studies in Europe?[1] Second, how might a reconceptualization of "new" transnational/extracolonial African diasporas offer a framework that unsettles the conceptual "tidiness"—as discursive formations—of "Europe," "Africa," and the "African Diaspora"?[2] Finally, I will close with some polemical thoughts about potential impediments to proper diasporic dialogue "here and there."[3]

PROBLEMATIC ONE

> Afro-Caribbeans ["African Europeans." . . .] couldn't simply be African, it was literally impossible to retrace their origins. Symbolically, they have to acknowledge they have a complex cultural inheritance. . . . Their roots are routes, the various places along the path of slavery, [(post)colonialisms] and migration.
>
> —Hall, "Les Enfants de Marx et de Coca-Cola"

I was still in London, where I was born and to which I had returned to work almost seventeen years ago, when the book editors invited me to contribute. As I write, I am now in Durham, North Carolina, to which I relocated three years ago and where I have now almost completed the process of (re)acculturation to American life in all its complexities and contradictions. There is no doubt that this current liminal phase has contributed to my producing a very different chapter than one which I would have conceived in "Europe," which in and of itself is a shifting fractured construct:

> The imaginary of Europe has been undergoing drastic changes. In the nineteenth century, Europe was represented as the heartland of civilization, progress and power. Europe, the citadel of the Great Powers, lorded over the world, as in the Berlin Congress carving up Africa. . . . During two major wars, "the lights went out all over Europe" and hegemony shifted across the Atlantic. Through the cold war, Europe was a space in-between and under the shadow of the superpowers. . . . In the 1980s, Europe recovered dynamism en route to the New Europe of 1992. 1992 came and went and the EU remains divided in the process of integration.[4]

What Pieterse encapsulates is the difficulty of defining a monolithic Europe with so much history and which keeps growing like a supranational fungus.[5] Nevertheless, in spite of the declining significance of the nation-state alongside the sustained importance of nationalisms, a nostalgic attachment to a romanticized Europe of the "Old World" does persist and is reproduced in the popular imagination of the "New World."[6]

This is not the Europe to which I will turn my attention. For the purposes of exploration, I am concerned with a partial Europe[7] that used the master tools of scientific racism to manufacture its racialized "Others" and build the industries of transatlantic slavery and imperial expansion.[8] It is this cooperative complicity under the guise of "commerce" and "civilizing" mission that literally and figuratively aligned rather than conflated the destinies of Africans—diasporic and continental (as one of many enslaved and colonized by Europeans) with diverse histories, cultures, and modes of economic and political organization, thereby forever situating them within the same unfolding dialectical macronarrative.[9] As a result, since the sixteenth century (and before), these earlier circuits of trade, processes of settlement, and political economic regimes have created co-terminal points of reference for "older" African diasporic constituents in Europe as well as the Americas and the Caribbean.[10]

As a metaphor and paradigm,[11] interdisciplinary characterizations of this story frequently privilege the narrative of transatlantic slavery (*roots*) or focus on the social and historical processes of imperialism and colonialism (*routes*).[12] Mazrui's periodization provides a synthesis:

> We must remember that historically there are two African Diasporas and not just one. There is first the Diaspora created by the slave trade, the dispersal of people of African ancestry sold as slaves both across the Atlantic

and across the Indian Ocean and the Red Sea. . . . But there is also a Diaspora created by colonialism, by movements of populations instigated or provoked either directly by the colonial experience or by the ramifications and repercussions of the colonial aftermath.[13]

By dint of historical and political circumstances, African Diaspora Studies in Europe necessitate incorporating the " both/and/[beyond]"[14] of slavery and (post)colonialisms (and colonialisms' twin: underdevelopment) as well as the latest phases of transnationalism and globalization.[15] Borrowing from the seminal essay "Unfinished Migrations: Reflections on the African Diaspora and the Making of the Modern World,"[16] African diasporas in Europe can be configured not simply as political *spaces* but also as *processes* and *conditions*. That is, first, African diasporic processes extend the links of the migration chains which originated in the historical moments of the transatlantic slave trade and the rise of European empires, wherein two adages respectively pervade the collective consciousness of these older African diasporas: "We are here because you brought us here" or "We are here because you were there." Second, African diasporas are spatially constituted wherever African (post)colonial and transnational constituents find themselves, be that "initially" in the Caribbean or West Africa and then subsequently in Europe, as were the respective trajectories, for examples, of Surinamese to the Netherlands and Senegalese to France.[17] Their spatial and "racial" locations as both gendered African diasporic agents and former black colonial, tribal, and island subjects inscribe sameness as they mobilize and politicize.[18] Finally, African diasporic conditions persist and are transformed by the interface of transnational Pan-African diasporic traditions of resistance, protest, and cultural innovation with global economic, political gendered, and racialized hierarchical structures that exclude as they appropriate and commodify.[19] Local and dynamic diasporic spaces, processes, and conditions intersect with and in fact are produced by transnational identities, translated cultural commodities, and global political strategies.[20]

However, mutually constituted and yet infinitely complex African diasporic spaces, processes, and conditions in Europe resist complete containment within either the "culture-bound" discourse of the nation-state (and more recently the supranational formation of the EU) or the transnational "imagined community" paradigm of the African diaspora.[21] This inability to entirely name African diasporas in Europe or firmly situate them within the dominant discourse of the African diaspora across the Atlantic stems from two divergent myths of "common" origin. First, in spite of the long-standing and transformative presence of their diasporic "Others," specific origin narratives of nation-states *across* Europe are predicated on differential mythologies of indigeneity and provincialism, which in turn define citizenship and deny rights to belonging: "As a result, it is difficult to translate each of these national discourses directly into the terms of another because the meaning of even the apparently common elements is structured in part by the place they occupy in the nationalized ensemble."[22] For example, as exclusionary/explanatory immigration ideologies, "race" is privileged in a British context while the notion of biological descent is favored in Germany.[23] Second, in American, Caribbean, and Brazilian contexts, the African diaspora has evolved into a potent political formation, which provides an evocative historical narrative for descendants of slaves, all of whom have a symbolic if not a spiritual link to the "Motherland."[24] In Europe, the transatlantic slave trade only explains half of the story, which is also not one that is embraced by all constituents of African descent, such as those who as colonial or (post)colonial subjects journeyed directly and more recently from continental Africa to their "Mother" countries "abroad."[25] As such, the violent imprint of (post)colonialism leaves as indelible a psychic mark on African diasporic subjects in Europe as the transgenerational emotional scars of the Middle Passage.[26]

"Cultural Identity and Diaspora" is one of Stuart Hall's foundational texts, which, while also paying homage to the *Negritude* movement, Frantz Fanon, and Pan-Africanism, eloquently addresses these fusions and fissures in Pan-African diasporic genealogies. Though he specifically engages with "the absences and presences" in Caribbean cultural identities, his formulation is instructive for my partial meditations on African diasporic identities processes in Europe. Hall suggests that there are two ways of understanding cultural identity. Within the first:

> our cultural identities reflect the common historical experiences and shared cultural codes which provide us as "one people," with stable, unchanging, and continuous frames of reference and meaning, beneath the shifting divisions and vicissitudes of our actual history.[27]

In the geopolitical context of European (post)colonial metropoles, this collective African diasporic consciousness is forged from the lived realities and the legacies of interwoven histories characterized by metropolitan racism, sexism, class discrimination, xenophobia, Islamophobia, and resistances. In a (dis)integrated Europe, where the racialized boundaries of exclusion are tightly drawn, a profound sense of (un)belonging is the end result.[28] The French-born (although marked in the press as "African" or "Arab"—"*Les beurs*") Muslim youth uprisings that erupted in October/November 2005 in the impoverished *banlieues* (suburbs) of Paris and the bombings in London in July 2005 that were carried out by a multiethnic cohort of British-born Muslims highlight the profound failings of the European multiculturalism project.[29] These recent political events also pinpoint the complexities of fluid, partial, and multiple identity politics in contemporary Europe, where lines of identification are (and always have been) drawn along more than one axis than "race."[30] The contested terrain upon which twenty-first-century Europe is attempting to limp forward is dotted with very contemporary antagonisms, whose ontological roots are firmly situated in modernity.[31]

While Hall's first definition illuminates a common heritage of institutionalized oppression that contributes to similar persistent lived social inequities for and resiliences of black communities in different metropolitan European milieux, his second conceptualization uncovers the messy lived dimensions of African diasporic identity politics in specific/local contexts:

> This second position recognizes that, as well as the many points of similarity, there are also critical points of deep and significant *difference* which constitute "what we really are"; or rather—since history has intervened— "what we have become." We cannot speak for very long, with any exactness about "one experience, one identity," without acknowledging the ruptures and discontinuities which constitute, precisely . . . uniqueness.[32]

The necessity of acknowledging the simultaneity of closure and rupture is echoed in the influential work of Paul Gilroy, particularly *The Black Atlantic*. Gilroy provides a heuristic configuration—"the black Atlantic"—which as a "transcultural international formation" links the lived experiences, political projects, and cultural products of Black Europe (Britain in particular) and Black America [and beyond]. By way of critique, Gilroy supports Hall's assertion that as a dialectical formation, the African diaspora is by definition an "unfinished" and complex entity:

> the status of nationality and the precise weight we should attach to the conspicuous differences of language, culture and identity which divide the blacks of the diaspora from one another, let alone from Africans, are unresolved within the political culture that promises to bring the disparate peoples of the black Atlantic world together one day.[33]

While Gilroy is specifically addressing the myriad challenges associated with tracing transatlantic and transnational contours of the African Diaspora based on a unified political destiny, his assertion indirectly also highlights the road blocks and detours toward the furthering of a Pan-African diasporic political project in Europe. On the one hand, despite a sustained African presence stretching back centuries, a Europe of social exclusion, which deploys different assimilation models to contain the "unmeltable" "minority ethnic" communities already there, prescribes a "common European identity" as much on the mythologization of an essentialized "white" indigeneity as on brandings of "black" alterities.[34] On the other hand, although this road is by no means without its essentialist potholes, the popular folk concept of "race" as it is imposed by "non-blacks" and politicized by "blacks" has long been a Pan-African/diasporic route to solidarity and affiliation.[35] BEST (Black European Studies Program) is one such example of the ways in which a strategic identification with "Blackness" has been mobilized in the interest of advancing African Diaspora Studies in Europe.[36] Funded by the Volkswagen Foundation, based in Germany at the Johannes Gutenberg-University Mainz, and inaugurated in October 2004, the program is intended to

> conduct empirical studies focused on the often neglected history and present of black people in Europe, and remains in close contact with the University of Massachusetts at Amherst, where another Center for Black European Studies is planned. Regional working conferences in Northwest, East, and South Europe will offer a forum of exchange for scholars and activists, establish regional networks, and offer an inventory of existing scholarship. An archive will for the first time bundle sources on black Europe, up to now scattered in archives and private collections.[37]

Although still in its infancy, BEST is a necessary and exciting intervention, whose mission echoes the solidarity in difference plea voiced by both Hall and Gilroy.[38]

In short, myriad dialectical tensions are reflected in emergent African Diaspora Studies (ADS) in Europe, which is a field and an "area" without borders. This particular conceptualization of ADS in Europe, which has morphed into an extended rumination, is influenced by both my own disciplinary moorings in Cultural Studies, Anthropology, and Sociology as well as my former location in Britain. Yet simply being positioned within a European discursive frame by no means makes me the designated authority, nor can this guarantee a perspective, which is either comprehensive or necessarily entirely representative. The existence of a common currency (more or less) but not a common language, the geographical expansiveness of our "region" as well as the paucity of Pan-European ADS institutional structures to disseminate knowledge and foster dialogue/collaboration all contribute to the conceptual challenges of ADS in Europe. Brent Edwards artfully reinscribes the difficulties of literal and figurative translation across the linguistic and geopolitical spaces between diasporic joins as *décalage* ("the kernel of precisely that which cannot be transferred or exchanged").[39] Within the context of this important book, which is primarily an analysis of evolving black internationalism in the 1920s and 1930s, Edwards also makes a point pertinent to constraints of translation as contemporary African diasporic knowledges circulate:

> The cultures of black internationalism can be seen only *in translation*. It is not possible to take up the question of "diaspora" without taking account of the fact that the great majority of peoples of African descent do not speak or write in English.[40]

Framed in another way, many Anglophone scholars of the African Diaspora do not speak or write in more than one language than English. To rigorously engage with African Diaspora Studies in Europe, in addition to the default *lingua franca* English, at the very least, one would need to be proficient in French, German, Dutch, Italian, Portuguese, and Spanish, and there are few if any of us who are such polyglots.[41] George Shepperson's seminal essay in Joseph Harris's groundbreaking anthology provides both another historical explanation for the relative dominance of Anglophone ADS and a challenging prescription for the expansion of the field beyond its current linguistic and geopolitical boundaries:

> The concept of the African diaspora . . . originated in the English-speaking world, where it received the most development to date . . . although it owes much to Anglophone influences, now has everything to gain by approaches through other languages as well as English; the European languages of the slave trade and the transplanted slave cultures; the relevant Asian languages; the African languages of the slave trade, east as well as west; and the hybrid languages that have resulted from the very complex mingling over centuries of African and non-African peoples.[42]

As already mentioned, all of these silences, absences, ruptures, and closures make African Diaspora Studies in Europe an "unfinished" project.[43]

"Finishing" ADS in Europe necessitates the simultaneous pivoting of the conceptual axes of time, space, and shifting condition: "Conceptualizations of diaspora must be able to accommodate the reality of multiple identities and phases of diasporization over time."[44] For discursive purposes, African Diaspora ("big D") is the generic, singular, temporal formation, conceptualized by Hall as the transcendent supranational common heritage derived from the shared legacies of and resistances to slavery, colonialism, (post)colonialism, racism, and other forms of structural inequalities.[45] African diaspora ("little d") signals shifting multiplicity, that is, specific, localized/spatialized, and politicized necessarily already-always "hybrid" including "mixed race," complex, and gendered configurations (e.g., English-African diaspora, German-African diaspora, Swedish-African diaspora).[46] Each of these situated African diasporic communities represents diverse outcomes to similar but not necessarily simultaneous macrosocial, economic, and historical processes, which are unifying but not unified. As such, across continua of time and space, African diasporas can be conceived of as dynamic, interlocking, and interdependent global networks of geopolitical spheres, each of whose localized intersectional constituencies are also sensitive to and impacted by the political machinations of the nation-states of which they are a part.

For example, in Britain (about which I can speak with the most privileging "authority"), and mindful of the essentialism inherent in my not acknowledging the ethnic and structural diversity within these communities (both West African and "West Indian"), between 1900 and 1960, thousands of elite West African students from Nigeria and Ghana flocked to England.[47] In 1948, the ship *Empire Windrush* disgorged 492 working-class Jamaican women and men, many veterans of World War II, at Tilbury

Docks, who were among the first of countless postwar reserve army laborers actively recruited by the British colonial government.[48] Although the objectives and trajectories of West Africans and African Caribbeans differed, the fact that their countries of origin were at the time all British colonies gave them a common destination, "Mother England," and a common destiny, that of unrelenting metropolitan racism and discrimination.[49] For the following three decades, events leading to decolonization, liberation, and neo-colonization took place on the Indian subcontinent, in the Caribbean, and in continental Africa.[50] At the same time, successive corresponding waves of (post)colonial migrants, now members of the Commonwealth, arrived in Britain only to be subsumed under the banner of discrimination and resistance, which Ron Ramdin described as "the Empire Within."[51]

As an aside, it is worth noting that there have always been inter-diasporic and extracolonial migrations of peoples of African descent such as African Americans in Paris or African students in the United States, such as Kwame Nkrumah and Nnamdi Azikiwe, which further complicates the cognitive remapping of the African Diaspora and its multiple and heterogeneous diasporas.[52] Furthermore, the long-term effects of underdevelopment in Africa as well as Latin America and the Caribbean,[53] coupled with the recent global rise of multinational/neo-imperial corporate industrial complexes and insatiable predatory capitalisms,[54] have given rise to contemporary compound African diasporas that do not necessarily or neatly correspond to former colonial European or Commonwealth status: "delocalized transnation[s] which retain a special ideological link to a putative place of origin but is otherwise a thoroughly diasporic collectivity."[55] The complexity of the constituent parts of these newer hyphenated diasporic signifiers force additional reassessment of conventional forms of diasporic space, process, and condition.[56] The recent clandestine movements of women and men from West Africa via Morocco to southern Spain, discussed in the next section, delineate further the impossibility of containing such multilayered and "overlapping" African diasporas in Europe.

PROBLEMATIC TWO

> At the heart of diaspora is the image of [a] journey. . . . The circumstances of leaving determine not only the experiences on these journeys, but also the circumstances of arrival and settling down.
>
> —Ujuris, "Diaspora and Citizenship"

Although the etymological root of *diaspora* is particular (from the Greek, to scatter and sow), its contemporary applications are now many and varied and extend beyond the classical formulations of the Jewish diaspora and the African diaspora.[57] In the latest phase of transnationalism and globalization, diaspora has become what Phil Cohen describes as "the master trope of migration and settlement."[58] The term is deployed indiscriminately to describe travelers and cosmopolitan elites as well as political refugees, economic migrants, and guest workers: "In these ways, the dispersed diasporas of old have become today's "transnational communities" sustained by a range of modes of social organization, mobility, and community."[59] With such apparent elasticity and fluidity, what constitutes the criteria for "authentic" diaspora inclusion is highly contested: "Focusing peculiarly on the ethnic axis of homelands and abroad, theories of diaspora overlook the transgressions of the national and lose sight of the new dynamics and topography of membership."[60]

Nowhere is this problematic more apparent than in classical versus contemporary conceptualizations of the African Diaspora.[61] That is, as previously mentioned, the roots and routes paradigm, heralded by Hall and Gilroy, periodizes the African Diaspora on the bases of similar lived legacies of transatlantic slavery and (post)/colonialisms, respectively.[62] At the same time, an exploration of specific ("older") African diasporic formations in Europe, which emerged as a result of these aforementioned political economic processes, demands the embrace of heterogeneity, dynamism, hybridity, and multiplicity. In the late twentieth and early twenty-first centuries, there have been "newer" African diasporas in Europe, whose origin narratives are interwoven with but not exclusively defined by either the Middle Passage or Empire and their aftermath.[63] Historian Paul Tiyambe Zeleza provides a useful typology of "contemporary diasporas" as those that have formed since the late nineteenth century, and he distinguishes them on the basis of three waves:

> the diasporas of colonization, decolonization and the era of structural adjustment, which emerged out of the disruptions and dispositions of colonial conquest, the struggles for independence, and structural adjustment programmes (SAPs), respectively . . . the diasporas of structural adjustment have been formed since the 1980s, out of the migrations engendered by economic, political and social crises and the destabilizations of SAPs.[64]

These "diasporas of structural adjustment" include reconfigured continental African migrations to Europe since the 1980s and persisting until today, which can be conceptualized not as *faux* diasporas ("economic migrations") but as new epistemologies of the African Diaspora.[65] The strategic identifications of newer and at times clandestine African diasporic communities across Europe are mired by the precariousness of their political status.[66] Cartographies of new African diasporas can contribute to a reconfiguration of gendered and racialized situated politics of belonging in Fortress Europe and beyond.[67]

In Fortress Europe, borders remain permeable for the transnational flow of capital, commodities, and information but not people. Across the

EU, "illegal" immigration control is a hot button issue that polarizes political debates and public opinions. The rallying cry from the Right is
to contain "the Others" already within and keep "those Others" out.
These outside "Others" are exemplified by clandestine movements "by
any means necessary" of the unwanted and the impoverished (as opposed
to the "brain drain" elites) from structurally (mal)adjusted West African
urban centers to economically and demographically restructured Western
and Southern European metropoles.[68] What motivates West African migrants is the promise of European Union (EU) wages "10-15 times higher
than in Africa. . . . [given] the [GDP] gap between the EU and the less-
developed non-EU Mediterranean [and Sub-Saharan] countries."[69] As was/
is the case with older African diasporic formations, at every stage of the
migration process, strategies are highly gendered.[70] That is, West African
clandestine migrant women and men may share a similar destination, but
by virtue of their glocalized structural positions, their destinies will be
very different.[71] Sassen's dialectical configuration of global cities and survival circuits demonstrates the extent to which migrant women, who are
overrepresented in the service sector laboring as nannies, domestics, or
sex workers, are integral to the growth of economies in both "the North"
and "the South."[72]

These transnational migratory processes include the smuggling of
West African (such as from Nigeria, Sierra Leone, Mali, Cameroon, and
Guinea-Bissau) and North African (particularly Moroccan) women and
men via Morocco to Southern Spain—the Gateway to Fortress Europe.[73]
Conventionally, these contemporary continental African dispersals have
been analyzed either utilizing traditional tropes of "push/pull" migration
or within the broader contexts of European asylum and immigration discourses.[74] An alternative intervention repositions recent clandestine West
African migrations as culturally specific, differentially gendered, and similarly racialized new African diasporas, which are situated within, not outside, the latest political economic circuits of global capitalism.[75] Placing
clandestine West African migrant women and men at the center provokes
a (re)examination of what constitutes volition, agency, and victimhood in
theorizing about the African Diaspora in particular and diaspora in general.[76] As agents and victims, these "unofficial" migrants deploy strategies
that demonstrate both the limits of individual agency and the exigencies
of survival. (Re)imagining "new" temporal and spatial dimensions of African diasporas in Europe, within which there are even more compound
and multiple forms, animates the ways in which, in all their specificity
and complexity, the historical ideas, economic processes, and political
projects of continental Africa and the African Diaspora are (and always
have been) mutually constituted.[77]

This continental/diasporic African interface is exemplified by clandestine movements from West Africa to Europe via Morocco and southern

Spain. Imagined by prospective migrants as "the Promised Land" but with managed and controlled borders which more approximate a "Fortress Europe," Spain is a relatively recent extracolonial destination or transit zone for former British and French colonial West African migrants and thus an underexplored area within European African Diaspora Studies.[78] Addressing undocumented African migration flows to the Western Mediterranean also shifts the traditional [Black] North Atlanticist African diasporic frame thereby highlighting older and established trade and migratory routes between North Africa and Southern Europe.[79] With reachable roots on the continent, contemporary African "irregular" migrants speak from multiple locations as transported and transplanted daughters and sons of "overlapping" diasporas.[80] Lewis is specifically addressing the American-African diaspora in a North Atlanticist frame. However, the dynamics of overlap and intersection in new temporal, spatial, and experiential configurations of African diasporas also resonate in very interesting ways in the contexts of these Southern European and Mediterranean movements.

This blurred complexity reconfigures the dynamics of inter/intra African/diasporic and transnational activities at what Yeoh, Willis and Fakhri call "the edges."[81] That is, en route to southern Europe, West Africans frequently traverse (or remain for years at a time in) former colonial French African territories, pass through (are detained for economic or political reasons in) the contested Spanish/North African enclaves of Ceuta and Melilla, and then make their way to Maghreb/Arab spaces, where (if they can raise the funds for this next stage) they cross the Mediterranean in order to enter Iberia.[82] The borders crossed are not just physical but also symbolic, economic, and political.[83] At the same time, as always, the nation-state is both extraneous to transnational identities formation and integral to the everyday policing, surveillance, management, and containment of racialized and gendered African diasporic bodies.[84]

For clandestine West African migrants en route to Spain via Morocco, a contingent state of (un)belonging is fabricated in response to both their legal and social exclusion. From a legal standpoint, most taking these treacherous journeys do not meet the criteria for refugee status outlined by the 1951 UN Convention.[85] Socially, the popular folk concept of "race" as it pertains to local Spanish and Moroccan constructions of "Blackness" and "non-Blackness" inform and impede the collective and personal projects of these "new" African diasporic agents.[86] This latest (in)voluntary transnational circulation of African peoples illuminates the complexities and politics of new African diasporic processes in the latest globalizing age and forces a realignment of the gendered conceptual relationship between continental Africa and the African Diaspora.[87] Rather than treating contemporary processes of continental African migration as separate entities outside the diaspora paradigm, this new theoretical formulation assumes their interconnectedness and demonstrates their dynamism.

This "worlding" of Africans as a "state of being 'cast out' into the world" has happened before.[88] Although these journeys are as treacherous as the Middle Passage, the difference is that these Africans are (un)wanted.[89] The sifting of the "(un)wanted" is not unique to Spain. Most European countries, including the United Kingdom, France, Germany, Italy, the Netherlands, and now Ireland, are grappling with "the asylum and immigration problem."[90] Once they land, their vulnerable status as illegal immigrants deprives them of rights and entitlements afforded citizens and designated refugees.[91] These aforementioned contemporary emigrants, most of whom have not been granted political asylum by Spain on the grounds of refugee status, should be recognized as the latest transnational manifestation of older African diasporic processes.[92] In European (and North American) metropolitan destinations, the new migrant cosmopolitanism that is manufactured also demands that we come to terms with the heterogeneous dialectics of Africanness and blackness in different diasporic frames.[93] Their consciousness of home as both continental African and diasporic is multi-sited and imagined but not imaginary and territorialized as well as both de-territorialized and re-territorialized. When we witness these more recent dispersals, we must name them as part of a historical continuum within, not outside, the African Diaspora—the latest layers. More recent migrants and refugees from continental Africa have different, shared, and specific narratives of home, community, longing, and belonging than their predecessors. The "myth of return" is to a place they recently knew rather than to a place they can only imagine. Such a repositioning forces a rethinking of the constitutive dimensions of persecution and victimhood, which have been integral criteria for "classical" diasporic membership. Such a paradigm shift politically empowers African economic (and political) refugees and relocates their struggles within a broader Pan-African diasporic framework. The persistence of globalized, racialized, and gendered inequities as manifest in the legal and social exclusion of clandestine West African migrant women and men en route to Europe affirms the importance of viewing African/diasporic formations as dynamic and historically contextualized and thus cyclical rather than static and ahistorical. The harsh economic, social, and political realities of this situated (un)belonging remind us that, spanning five centuries and still unfolding, the unique history of the African diaspora is also in part both a history of continental Africa and Fortress Europe.[94]

CONCLUSION

It is out of chaos that new worlds are born.

—Audre Lord, "Eye to Eye"

Although there are many aspects of life in London that were gratifying, the significant burden of underrepresentation and the profound isolation associated with black intellectual labor in the Belly of the (Post)-Imperial Beast necessitated regular trips back "across the pond" to participate in the recurrent interdisciplinary conferences in the United States delightfully dedicated entirely to the interrogation of African Diaspora Studies, such as those of ASWAD (Association for the Study of the Worldwide African Diaspora). I would then return home sufficiently sated. Now that I am residing in the heartland of African Diaspora Studies, I am contending with a different malaise. That is, unless they transpire at conferences specifically devoted to the African diaspora beyond the United States, such as the April 2006 conference at Northwestern on "Black Europe and the African Diaspora," debates and discussions about "other" African diasporas are relegated to the margins or nonexistent.[95] For example, at the Madison conference in March 2006, which gave birth to this important and groundbreaking collection, those of us representing "the international" dimension were gathered together in the very last session on the last day. On a positive note, this was the first time I had been grouped together with fellow African Diaspora scholars (re)presenting South Africa, Brazil, and the Caribbean, so in and of itself, this was a refreshing and intriguing development. Sounding out a more critical note, though I am certain that this was not the intention of the conveners, this particular assembly intensified the already marginalized status of African Diaspora Studies outside the United States. Within this "area studies" panel (as opposed perhaps to the earlier "disciplinary" sessions), I was also troubled by the omission of either contemporary West African or East African perspectives on African Diaspora Studies.[96] The apparent framing of the symposium in terms of U.S.–African Diaspora Studies and "its" disciplines suggests that "the United States" is not a contested "area," while unwittingly simultaneously ensuring the ontological fixity of the Caribbean, Brazil, South Africa, and Europe. This implication limits the context for any critical engagement with "constraints and possibilities of doing African Diaspora Studies" not just in Europe but also in the shadows of the institutional might of the United States.

That is, within the cartography of the African diaspora, there are "spaces" (the Americas and the Caribbean) which garner significant academic attention and others such as those in Europe that are more peripheral.[97] On the other hand, as anthropologist Lena Sawyer's ethnographic research in Sweden suggests, there are peripheries within the peripheral, such as those beyond Britain and even "continental" Europe:

> African Diasporas are not without evaluation and hierarchy; one person's periphery can be someone else's center . . . and [these] center[s] and peripheries on a hegemonic map of African Diaspora shift for people in locales (nations, regions, cities, towns) like Helsinki (Finland), Bergen (Norway), and even the northern Swedish city of Kiruna; it is possible that Stockholm is an important "center" of African Diasporas.[98]

Additional examples that broaden the scope and intensify the complexities of diasporic affiliations are Jacqueline Nassy Brown's mapping of
the "geographies" of Black Liverpool (England), Elisa Joy White's formulation of "minoritized" and "retro-global" African diasporic spaces in Dublin (Ireland), and Jacqueline Andall's examination of second-generation
African-Italian diasporic identities formation in Milan.[99] In powerful
ways, each demonstrates how—although informed by the "global"—
micropolitics of diaspora are contested and negotiated within the specific
dynamism of urban "local" (rather than necessarily European or entirely
reverential American) spaces. Finally, in Tina Campt's work on the politics of memory and Black-German identities, both her "inter-cultural address" intervention and her application of Brown's conceptualization of
"diasporic relations" provide a salve for filling these silences and absences:

> Intercultural address illuminates important tensions of diasporic relation
> through the ways in which it simultaneously contests and affirms the as-
> sumptions of similarities between . . . black communities.[100]

Hence, the considerable current and future challenges of African Diaspora Studies in Europe (and Global African Diaspora Studies in general)
include how to constitute interdisciplinary research and engage across
"international" borders in a truly dialogic manner.[101] As such, any comparative interrogations of African diasporas across Europe, within European nation-states, or for that matter encompassing those in the Americas
and the Caribbean, must be interdisciplinary, historically grounded, ethnographically situated, and mindful of institutional hierarchies and infrastructural deficits that contribute to the perpetuation of hegemonic
discourses. Only then can the rules of engagement for African Diaspora
Studies be deemed truly dialogic.

NOTES

Many thanks to Teju Olaniyan and James Sweet for their shrewd editorial assistance and collegiality as well as for inviting me to participate in the symposium,
which gave birth to this important and exciting collection. Thanks also to the two
anonymous reviewers who provided insightful critical feedback.

The section titled "Problematic Two" is an updated version of a chapter segment that was previously published. See Ifekwunigwe, "An Inhospitable Port in
the Storm: Recent Clandestine West African Migrants and the Quest for Diasporic
Recognition."

    1. Campt, "The Crowded Space of Diaspora"; Brown, *Dropping Anchor, Set-
ting Sail*; Sawyer, "Routings"; White, "Forging African Diaspora Places in Dublin's Retro-Global Spaces"; Andall, "Second-Generation Attitude?"
    2. Anderson, *Imagined Communities*; Appiah, *In My Father's House*; Mu-
dimbe, *The Invention of Africa*; Mudimbe, *The Idea of Africa*; Hine and McLeod,

eds., *Crossing Boundaries*; Okphewho, Davies, and Mazrui, eds., *The African Diaspora*.

3. Drake, *Black Folk Here and There*.

4. Pieterse, "Europe, Traveling Light," 4.

5. On May 1, 2004, the European Union "enlarged" (and is still ripe and poised for more expansion) to include fifteen more countries, for a total of twenty-five. In 2007, it expanded to include Bulgaria and Romania, increasing the estimated total population to 489 million. However, it is important to note that there are several countries, such as Switzerland, that are "geographically" part of Europe but not members of the EU.

6. Gilroy, *After Empire*; Anderson, *Imagined Communities*.

7. From the Egyptians, to the Ethiopians, to the Phoenicians, to the Moors, to the Mandingo mariners, Africans have always been migratory and thus hybridized people. See Drake, *Black Folk Here and There*. Hence a more historically accurate marking of moments of rupture could be in terms of pre-Colombian and post-Colombian African diasporas. See Ifekwunigwe, "Reconfiguring the 'African' in the English-African Diaspora." The ancient African migrations (that is, long before the fifteenth century), which led to a sustained African presence in Asia, the Middle East, and Europe map on to pre-Colombian African diasporas. See Bennet, *Before the Mayflower*; Cohen, *Global Diasporas*. On the other hand, the defining *locus classicus* moments of post-Colombian African diasporas are that of transatlantic slavery and European expansion (and their aftermaths). That said, Paul Tiyambe Zeleza reminds us that "some of the African diasporas in Asia were created during the post-Columbia [*sic*] era and some with the involvement of the same European powers that controlled the Americas." See Zeleza, "Rewriting the African Diaspora," 55. As such, like discursive formations of "Europe," any periodizations and conceptualizations of "the African Diaspora" (whether "ancient," "modern," or "new") are already necessarily also partial, overlapping, fragmented, and thus contested. See Brown, *Dropping Anchor, Setting Sail*.

8. Blakely, "European Dimensions of the African Diaspora"; Segal, *The Black Diaspora*.

9. Skinner, "The Dialectic between Diasporas and Homeland"; Echuero, "An African Diaspora."

10. Steady, "Women of Africa and the African Diaspora"; Palmer, "The African Diaspora"; Hanchard, "Black Transnationalism, Africana Studies, and the Twenty-first Century."

11. Shepperson, "African Diaspora: Concept and Context."

12. Hall, "Les Enfants de Marx et de Coca-Cola"; Gilroy, "Route Work."

13. Mazrui, *The Africans*, 302.

14. Scott, *Refashioning Futures*, 219.

15. Carter, preface to *New African Diasporas*.

16. Patterson and Kelley, "Unfinished Migrations."

17. Hargreaves and McKinney, eds., *Post-Colonial Cultures in France*; Wacquant, "Urban Outcasts"; Modood, and Werbner, eds., *The Politics of Multiculturalism in the New Europe*; Torres and Whitten, eds., *Blackness in Latin America and the Caribbean*.

18. Adi, "Pan-Africanism and West African Nationalism in Britain"; Gilroy, *Between Camps*; Obichere, "Afro-Americans in Africa."

19. Rose, *Black Noise*; Chuck D, *Fight the Power*; Campbell, *Rasta and Resistance*; Drachler, ed., *Black Homeland/Black Diaspora*; Joyce, "African-Centered Womanism."

20. Diawara, *In Search of Africa*; Drake, "Diaspora Studies and Pan-Africanism."

21. Brown, *Dropping Anchor, Setting Sail*; Ifekwunigwe, *Scattered Belongings*; Styan, "*La Nouvelle Vague!*"; White, "Forging African Diaspora Places in Dublin's Retro-Global Spaces"; Campt, *Other Germans*; Aisha C. Blackshire-Belay, "The African Diaspora in Europe"; Mazón and Steingörver, eds., *Not So Plain as Black and White*; Carter, *States of Grace*; Anjel-Anjani, "Diasporic Conditions"; Sawyer, "Routings"; Huggins-Williams, "We Are There"; Fikes and Lemon, "African Presence in Former Soviet Spaces."

22. Miles, "Explaining Racism in Contemporary Europe," 193.

23. Ibid., 189–221.

24. Echuero, " An African Diaspora."

25. Brown, *Dropping Anchor, Setting Sail*; Carter, preface.

26. Fanon, *Black Skin, White Masks*.

27. Hall, "Cultural Identity and Diaspora," 234.

28. Gilroy, *There Ain't No Black in the Union Jack*; Essed, *Understanding Everyday Racism*; Geddes and Favell, eds., *The Politics of Belonging*.

29. Small, "Racism, Black People, and the City in Britain"; Body-Gendrot, "Living Apart or Together with Our Differences?"; Wacquant, "Urban Outcasts."

30. Modood, "The Emergence of a Muslim Identity Politics"; Carter, *States of Grace*; Sawyer, "Routings."

31. Gilroy, *The Black Atlantic*; Rattansi, "'Western' Racisms, Ethnicities, and Identities in a 'Postmodern' Frame."

32. Hall, "Cultural Identity and Diaspora," 236.

33. Gilroy, *The Black Atlantic*, 34.

34. Social conceptions of "race" and thus political constructions of "blackness" are historically, geographically, and culturally specific and thus do not travel easily. As such, "blackness" and "whiteness" are shifting and thus unstable fractured signifiers of exclusion and inclusion. See Blakely, "European Dimensions of the African Diaspora"; Rattansi, "On Being and Not Being Brown/Black British." See also Hall, "The Spectacle of the Other"; Blakely, "European Dimensions of the African Diaspora"; Van Sertima, ed., *African Presence in Early Europe*.

35. The popular folk concept of "race" is a potent dynamic social and cultural imaginary, the naturalization of which attaches symbolic meanings to real or manufactured physical differences. Along with other hierarchically positioned signifiers such as gender, generation, ethnicity, religion and social class, these create, explain, justify and maintain social inequalities and injustices and perpetuate differential access to privilege, prestige, power, and ultimately belonging. See Ifekwunigwe, *Scattered Belongings*; Echuero, "An African Diaspora"; Gilroy, *The Black Atlantic*.

36. Obviously, there are other associations with a broader scope, including CAAR (Collegium for African American Research), which from its inception in 1992 has collaborated with the W. E. B. Du Bois Institute for African American Research at Harvard, and BASA (Black and Asian Studies Association), which is autonomous but receives institutional "support" from the University of London. In

2000, I was a guest lecturer for a summer program as part of the International Doctoral Programme on Black Culture and Ethnicity in Europe and Latin America, the ALFA Network, University of Amsterdam.

37. See www.best.uni-mainz.de. Since its 2004 formation, BEST has organized two international and interdisciplinary conferences in Germany. The first took place in November 2005 and was entitled "Challenging Europe: Black European Studies in the 21st Century." The second occurred in July 2006 and was entitled "Black European Studies in Transnational Perspective."

38. Hall, "Cultural Identity and Diaspora"; Gilroy, *The Black Atlantic*.

39. Edwards, *The Practice of Diaspora*, 14.

40. Ibid., 7.

41. Zeleza, "Rewriting the African Diaspora."

42. Shepperson, "African Diaspora," 44.

43. Gilroy, *The Black Atlantic*; Anthias, "New Hybridities, Old Concepts."

44. Butler, "Brazilian Abolition in Afro-Atlantic Context."

45. Hall, "Cultural Identity and Diaspora"; Herskovits, *The Myth of the Negro Past*; Segal, *The Black Diaspora*.

46. Brown, *Dropping Anchor, Setting Sail*; Ali, *Mixed-Race, Post-Race*; Ifekwunigwe, *Scattered Belongings*; Campt, *Other Germans*; Mazón and Steingröver, *Not So Plain as Black and White*; Sawyer, "Routings."

47. Adi, *West Africans in Britain, 1900–1960*; Killingray, ed., *Africans in Britain*.

48. Ramdin, *Reimaging Britain*; Fryer, *Staying Power*; Phillips and Phillips, *Windrush*.

49. Since Roman times and in fluctuating numbers from the sixteenth century to the nineteenth, there has been a black African presence in Britain. See Luke, "African Presence in the Early History of the British Isles and Scandinavia"; Rashidi, "Ancient and Modern Britons"; Gerzina, *Black England*. There are long-standing black communities in Liverpool, England, and Cardiff, Wales, that predate the mass post–World War II settlements by at least a century. See Rich, *Race and Empire in British Politics*; Brown, *Dropping Anchor, Setting Sail*. Africans, African Caribbeans, and South Asians made considerable contributions to both world wars. See Ramdin, *Reimaging Britain*. However, the sheer numbers of postwar immigrant laborers from the Caribbean, the Indian subcontinent, and Africa as well as the fact that their presence and resistance permanently altered the social and political landscape, means this period in British history garners more but still paltry academic and popular attention than other intersecting moments. See Carby, *Cultures in Babylon*; Mirza, ed., *Black British Feminism*; Brah, *Cartographies of Diaspora*; Gilroy, *There Ain't No Black in the Union Jack*; Ramdin, *The Making of the Black Working Class in Britain*; Centre for Contemporary Cultural Studies, ed., *The Empire Strikes Back*; Owusu, ed., *Black British Culture and Society*; Bryan, Dadzie, and Scafe, *The Heart of the Race*; Small, "Racism, Black People, and the City in Britain."

50. Fanon, *The Wretched of the Earth*; Nkrumah, *The Class Struggle in Africa*.

51. Ramdin, *Reimaging Britain*.

52. Edwards, *The Practice of Diaspora*; Wright, *Becoming Black*; Stovall, *Paris Noir*; Archer-Straw, *Negrophilia*; Gilroy, *The Black Atlantic*;

Marable, *African and Caribbean Politics*; Drachler, ed., *Black Homeland/Black Diaspora*.

53. Rodney, *How Europe Underdeveloped Africa*; Fanon, *The Wretched of the Earth*.

54. Mohanty, "Women Workers and Capitalist Scripts: Ideologies of Domination, Common Interests, and the Politics of Solidarity"; Alexander, "Erotic Autonomy as a Politics of Decolonization"; Grewal, *Transnational America*; Hardt and Negri, *Empire*; Alexander, *Pedagogies of Crossing*.

55. Appadurai, *Modernity at Large*, 172.

56. Carter, *States of Grace*; Al-Ali, Black, and Koser, "The Limits to Transnationalism"; Hannerz, "The World in Creolization."

57. Cohen, *Global Diasporas*; Braziel and Mannur, "Nation, Migration, and Globalization."

58. Cohen, "Welcome to the Diasporama."

59. Vertovec, "Conceiving and Researching Transnationalism."

60. Soysal, "Citizenship and Identity," 1.

61. Hanchard, "Black Transnationalism."

62. Clifford, *Routes*; Hall, "Les Enfants de Marx et de Coca-Cola"; Gilroy, "Route Work."

63. De Haas, "The Myth of Invasion."

64. Zeleza, "Rewriting the African Diaspora," 55.

65. Davies, "Reconceptualising the Migration-Development Nexus."

66. Martin, "'Fortress Europe' and Third World Immigration in the Post–Cold War Global Context."

67. Ifekwunigwe, "An Inhospitable Port in the Storm."

68. Harding, *The Uninvited*.

69. Gold, *Europe or Africa?* 133.

70. Morris, *Managing Migration*.

71. Westwood and Phizacklea, *Trans-nationalism and the Politics of Belonging*.

72. Sassen, "Global Cities and Survival Circuits"; Aghatise, "Trafficking for Prostitution in Italy"; Asale Angel-Ajani, "Diasporic Conditions"; Ifekwunigwe, "Recasting 'Black Venus' in the New African Diaspora."

73. Harding, *The Uninvited*.

74. Sadiqi, "Morocco: The Political and Social Dimension of Migration."

75. Akyeampong, "Diaspora and Drug Trafficking in West Africa"; Bashi, "Globalized Anti-Blackness."

76. Carter, preface; Bales, *Disposable People*.

77. Zeleza, "Rewriting the African Diaspora"; Ifekwunigwe, "An Inhospitable Port in the Storm."

78. Cannell, dir., *Sorious Samura's Africa: Exodus*; Harding, *The Uninvited*.

79. Bennett, "National Boundaries and the 'History' of the Black Atlantic"; Zeleza, "Rewriting the African Diaspora"; Van Sertima, ed., *The Golden Age of the Moor*; Chandler, "The Moor"; Pimienta-Bey, "Moorish Spain."

80. Lewis, "To Turn as on a Pivot."

81. Yeoh, Willis, and Fakhri, "Introduction: Transnationalism at Its Edges."

82. Corkhill, "Economic Migrants and the Labour Market in Spain and Portugal."

83. Fargues, Cassarino, and Latreche, "Mediterranean Migration."

84. Richmond, "Globalization: Implications for Immigrants and Refugees."

85. Fargues, Cassarino, and Latreche, "Mediterranean Migration"; Neumayer, "Bogus Refugees?"

86. Ifekwunigwe, *Scattered Belongings*; Sage, "Desperation at Europe's Back Gate"; Calavita, "Immigration, Law, and Marginalization in a Global Economy."

87. Bauman, *Globalization*; Crisp, "Policy Challenges of the New Diaspora."

88. Simone, "On the Worlding of African Cities."

89. Arango and Martin, "Best Practices to Manage Migration."

90. Yuval-Davis, Anthias, and Kofman, "Secure Borders and Safe Havens and the Gendered Politics of Belonging"; Angel-Ajani, "Diasporic Conditions"; White, "Forging African Diaspora Places in Dublin's Retro-Global Spaces."

91. Gilbert, "Is Europe Living Up to Its Obligation to Refugees?"

92. Sefa Dei, "Interrogating 'African Development' and the Diasporan Reality"; Mazrui, "Globalization and Cross-Cultural Values"; Mazrui, *The Africans*.

93. Mbembe, "Ways of Seeing: Beyond the New Nativism"; Styan, "*La Nouvelle Vague?*"; Stoller, *Money Has No Smell*; Holtzman, *Nuer Journeys, Nuer Lives*.

94. De Haas, "The Myth of Invasion"; Davies, "Reconceptualising the Migration-Development Nexus."

95. Increasingly, though, certain programs and departments within American institutions, such as the Program in African American and Diaspora Studies at Vanderbilt University or the aforementioned University of Massachusetts at Amherst, are carving out significant spaces within the ADS paradigm for African diasporas in Europe.

96. One of the anonymous reviewers posed an interesting challenge, which was to assess the extent to which transplanted continental African scholars have themselves contributed to the shaping or rethinking of African Diaspora Studies in the United States. Without deliberately doing so, I realized that there was quite a representative sample of such scholarship peppered throughout my chapter! A useful conceptual apparatus for understanding the particularities of this work is "bifocality," coined by John Durham Peters in "Seeing Bifocally" but invoked by Gupta and Ferguson: "social actors simultaneously experience the local and the global, possessing both 'near-sight' and 'far-sight.'" See Gupta and Ferguson, "Culture, Power, Place," 9. For example, Malian transplant (currently director of both New York University's Institute of Afro-American Affairs and the Africana Studies program) Manthia Diawara's *In Search of Africa* beautifully illustrates the ways in which he is rooted in Mali, West Africa, and how his routes have been guided by educational sojourns in Europe and North America as well as critical academic engagement with African American expressive cultures and politics.

97. Campt, "The Crowded Space of Diaspora"; Brown, *Dropping Anchor, Setting Sail*.

98. Sawyer, "Routings," 13–14.

99. Brown, *Dropping Anchor, Setting Sail*; White, "Forging African Diaspora Places in Dublin's Retro-Global Spaces"; Andall, "Second Generation Attitude?"

100. Campt, "The Crowded Space of Diaspora," 103.

101. Christian, ed., *Black Identity in the Twentieth Century*; Walcott, *Black Like Who?*

REFERENCES

Adi, Hakim. "Pan-Africanism and West African Nationalism in Britain." *African Studies Review* 43, no. 1 (2000): 69–82.

——. *West Africans in Britain, 1900–1960: Nationalism, Pan-Africanism, and Communism.* London: Lawrence and Wishart, 1998.

Aghatise, Esohe. "Trafficking for Prostitution in Italy." Concept paper presented at the Group Meeting on Trafficking Women and Girls, Glen Cove, N.Y., November 18–22, 2002.

Akyeampong, Emmanuel. "Diaspora and Drug Trafficking in West Africa: A Case Study of Ghana." *African Affairs* 104.416 (2005): 429–47.

Al-Ali, Nadje, Richard Black, and Khalid Koser. "The Limits to Transnationalism: Bosnian and Eritrean Refugees in Europe as Emerging Transnational Communities." *Ethnic and Racial Studies* 24, no. 4 (2001): 578–600.

Alexander, M. Jacqui. "Erotic Autonomy as a Politics of Decolonization: An Anatomy of Feminist and State Practice in the Bahamas Tourist Economy." In Alexander and Mohantey, *Feminist Genealogies,* 63–100.

——. *Pedagogies of Crossing: Meditations on Feminism, Sexual Politics, Memory, and the Sacred.* Durham, N.C.: Duke University Press, 2005.

Alexander, M. Jacqui, and Chandra Talpade Mohantey, eds. *Feminist Genealogies, Colonial Legacies, and Democratic Futures.* London: Routledge, 1997.

Ali, Suki. *Mixed-Race, Post-Race: Gender, New Ethnicities, and Cultural Practices.* Oxford: Berg, 2003.

Andall, Jacqueline. "Second-Generation Attitude? African-Italians in Milan." *Journal of Ethnic and Migration Studies* 28, no. 3 (2002): 389–407.

Anderson, Benedict. *Imagined Communities.* London: Verso, 1991.

Anjel-Anjani, Asale. "Diasporic Conditions: Mapping the Discourses of Race and Criminality in Italy." *Transforming Anthropology* 11, no. 1 (2002): 36–46.

Anthias, Floya. "New Hybridities, Old Concepts: The Limits of Culture." *Ethnic and Racial Studies* 24, no. 4 (2001): 619–41.

Appadurai, Arjun. *Modernity at Large: Cultural Dimensions of Globalization.* Minneapolis: University of Minnesota Press, 1996.

Appiah, Anthony. *In My Father's House: Africa in the Philosophy of Culture.* New York: Oxford University Press, 1992.

Arango, Joaquin, and Philip Martin. "Best Practices to Manage Migration: Morocco and Spain." *International Migration Review* 39, no. 1 (2005): 258–69.

Archer-Straw, Petrine. *Negrophilia: Avant-Garde Paris and Black Culture in the 1920s.* London: Thames and Hudson, 2000.

Bales, Kevin. *Disposable People: New Slavery in the Global Economy.* Berkeley: University of California Press, 1999.

Bashi, Vilna. "Globalized Anti-Blackness: Transnationalizing Western Immigration, Law, Policy, and Practice." *Ethnic and Racial Studies* 27, no. 4 (2004): 584–606.

Bauman, Zygmunt. *Globalization: The Human Consequences.* Cambridge: Polity Press, 1998.

Bennet, Lerone. *Before the Mayflower: A History of Black America.* New York: Penguin, 1984.

Bennett, Herman. "National Boundaries and the 'History' of the Black Atlantic." *African Studies Review* 43, no. 1 (2000): 101–24.

Blackshire-Belay, Aisha C. "The African Diaspora in Europe: African Germans Speak Out." *Journal of Black Studies* 31, no. 3 (2001): 264–87.

Blakely, Allison. "European Dimensions of the African Diaspora: The Definition of Black Racial Identity." In Hine and McLeod, *Crossing Boundaries*, 87–104.

Body-Gendrot, Sophie. "Living Apart or Together with Our Differences? French Cities at a Crossroads." *Ethnicities* 2, no. 3 (2002): 367–85.

Brah, Avtar. *Cartographies of Diaspora*. London: Routledge, 1996.

Braziel, Jana Evans, and Anita Mannur. "Nation, Migration, and Globalization: Points of Contention in Diaspora Studies." In Jana Evans Braziel and Anita Mannur, eds., *Theorizing Diaspora*, 1–22. Oxford: Blackwell, 2003.

Brown, Jacqueline Nassy. *Dropping Anchor, Setting Sail: Geographies of Race in Black Liverpool*. Princeton, N.J.: Princeton University Press, 2005.

Bryan, Beverley, Stella Dadzie, and Suzanne Scafe. *The Heart of the Race: Black Women's Lives in Britain*. London: Virago, 1985.

Butler, Kim. "Brazilian Abolition in Afro-Atlantic Context." *African Studies Review* 43, no. 1 (2000): 127.

Calavita, Kitty. "Immigration, Law, and Marginalization in a Global Economy: Notes from Spain." *Law and Society Review* 32, no. 3 (1999): 529–66.

Campbell, Horace. *Rasta and Resistance: From Marcus Garvey to Walter Rodney*. London: Hansib, 1985.

Campt, Tina. "The Crowded Space of Diaspora: Intercultural Address and the Tensions of Diasporic Relation." *Radical History Review* 83 (2002): 94–103.

——. *Other Germans: Black Germans and the Politics of Race, Gender, and Memory in the Third Reich*. Ann Arbor: University of Michigan Press, 2005.

Cannell, Dollan, dir. *Sorious Samura's Africa—Exodus*. Documentary. Insight News Television, London, 2000.

Carby, Hazel. *Cultures in Babylon: Black Britain and African Americans*. London: Verso, 1999.

Carter, Donald. Preface to Khalid Koser, ed., *New African Diasporas*, ix–xix. London: Routledge, 2003.

——. *States of Grace: Senegalese in Italy and the New European Immigration*. Minneapolis: University of Minnesota Press, 1997.

Chandler, Wayne B. "The Moor: Light of Europe's Dark Age." In Van Sertima, *The Golden Age of the Moor*, 151–81.

Centre for Contemporary Cultural Studies, ed. *The Empire Strikes Back: Race and Racism in 70's Britain*. London: Hutchinson, 1982.

Christian, Mark, ed. *Black Identity in the Twentieth Century: Expressions of the U.S. and UK African Diaspora*. London: Hansib, 2002.

Chuck D. *Fight the Power: Rap, Race, and Reality*. Edinburgh: Payback Press, 1997.

Clifford, James. *Routes: Travel and Translation in the Late Twentieth Century*. Cambridge: Harvard University Press, 1997.

Cohen, Phil. "Welcome to the Diasporama." Centre for New Ethnicities Research, University of East London newsletter 3 (Spring/Summer 1998).

Cohen, Robin. *Global Diasporas*. London: UCL Press, 1997.

Corkhill, David. "Economic Migrants and the Labour Market in Spain and Portugal." *Ethnic and Racial Studies* 24, no. 5 (2001): 828–44.

Crisp, Jeff. "Policy Challenges of the New Diaspora: Migrant Networks and Their Impact on Asylum Flows and Regimes." New Issues in Refugee Research, Working Paper Number 7. Geneva: UN High Commission for Refugees, 1999.

Davies, Rebecca. "Reconceptualising the Migration-Development Nexus: Diasporas, Globalisation, and the Politics of Exclusion." Third World Quarterly 28, no. 1 (2007): 59–76.

Diawara, Manthia. In Search of Africa. Cambridge: Harvard University Press, 1998.

Drachler, Jacob, ed. Black Homeland/Black Diaspora. Port Washington, N.Y.: Kennikat Press, 1975.

Drake, St. Clair. Black Folk Here and There: An Essay in History and Anthropology. 2 vols. Los Angeles: University of California Press, 1987, 1990.

———. "Diaspora Studies and Pan-Africanism." In Harris, Global Dimensions of the African Diaspora, 451–514.

Echuero, Michael J. C. "An African Diaspora: The Ontological Project." In Okpewho, Davies, and Mazrui, The African Diaspora, 3–18.

Edwards, Brent Hayes. The Practice of Diaspora: Literature, Translation, and the Rise of Black Internationalism. Cambridge: Harvard University Press, 2003.

Essed, Philomena. Understanding Everyday Racism. London: Sage, 1991.

Fanon, Frantz. Black Skin, White Masks. New York: Grove Press, 1967.

———. The Wretched of the Earth. New York: Grove Press, 1968.

Fargues, Philippe, ed. Mediterranean Migration 2005 Report (Cooperation Project on the Social Integration of Immigrants, Migration, and the Movement of Persons). Brussels: European Commission–MEDA Programme, 2005.

Fargues, Philippe, Jean-Pierre Cassarino, and Abdelkader Latreche. "Mediterranean Migration: An Overview." In Fargues, Mediterranean Migration 2005 Report, 5–31.

Fikes, Kesha, and Alaina Lemon. "African Presence in Former Soviet Spaces." Annual Review of Anthropology 31 (2002): 497–524.

Fryer, Peter. Staying Power: The History of Black People in Britain. London: Pluto, 1984.

Geddes, Andrew, and Adrian Favell, eds. The Politics of Belonging: Migrants and Minorities in Contemporary Europe. Aldershot: Ashgate, 1999.

Gerzina, Gretchen. Black England: Life before Emancipation. London: John Murray, 1995.

Gilbert, Geoff. "Is Europe Living Up to Its Obligation to Refugees?" European Journal of International Law 15, no. 5 (2004): 963–87.

Gilroy, Paul. After Empire: Melancholia or Convivial Culture? New York: Routledge, 2004.

———. Between Camps: Nations, Cultures, and the Allure of Race. London: Allen Lane, Penguin Press, 2000.

———. The Black Atlantic. Cambridge: Harvard University Press, 1993.

———. "Route Work: The Black Atlantic and the Politics of Exile." In Ian Chambers and Lidia Curti, eds., The Post-Colonial Question, 17–29. London: Routledge, 1996.

———. There Ain't No Black in the Union Jack. London: Hutchinson, 1987.

Gold, Peter. Europe or Africa? A Contemporary Study of the Spanish North African Enclaves of Ceuta and Melilla. Liverpool: Liverpool University Press, 2000.

Green, Charles, ed. *Globalization and Survival in the Black Diaspora.* Albany: State University of New York Press, 1997.

Grewal, Inderpal. *Transnational America: Feminisms, Diasporas, Neoliberalisms.* Durham, N.C.: Duke University Press, 2005.

Gupta, Akhil, and James Ferguson, eds. *Culture, Power, and Place: Explorations in Critical Anthropology.* Durham, N.C.: Duke University Press, 1999.

——. "Culture, Power, Place: Ethnography at the End of an Era." In Gupta and Ferguson, *Culture, Power, and Place,* 1–32.

de Haas, Hein. "The Myth of Invasion: The Inconvenient Realities of African Migration to Europe." *Third World Quarterly* 29, no. 7 (2008): 1305–22.

Hall, Stuart. "Cultural Identity and Diaspora." In Jonathan Rutherford, ed., *Identity: Community, Culture, Difference,* 222–37. London: Lawrence and Wishart, 1990.

——. "Les Enfants de Marx et de Coca-Cola." *New Statesmen* 126 (1997): 34–36.

——. "The Spectacle of the Other." In Stuart Hall, ed., *Representation: Cultural Representations and Signifying Practices,* 223–79. Milton Keynes: Open University Press, 1997.

Hanchard, Michael. "Black Transnationalism, Africana Studies, and the Twenty-first Century." *Journal of Black Studies* 35, no. 2 (2004): 139–153.

Hannerz, Ulf. "The World in Creolization." In Karin Barber, ed., *African Popular Culture,* 12–17. Bloomington: Indiana University Press, 1997.

Harding, Jeremy. *The Uninvited: Refugees at the Rich Man's Gate.* London: Profile Books with the London Review of Books, 2000.

Hardt, Michael, and Antonio Negri. *Empire.* Cambridge: Harvard University Press, 2000.

Hargreaves, Alec, and Mark McKinney, eds. *Post-Colonial Cultures in France.* London: Routledge, 1997.

Harris, Joseph, ed. *Global Dimensions of the African Diaspora.* 2nd ed. Washington, D.C.: Howard University Press, 1993.

Herskovits, Melville. *The Myth of the Negro Past.* Boston: Beacon Press, 1958.

Hine, Darlene Clark, and Jacqueline McLeod, eds. *Crossing Boundaries: Comparative History of Black People in Diaspora.* Bloomington: Indiana University Press, 1999.

Holtzman, Jon. *Nuer Journeys, Nuer Lives: Sudanese Refugees in Minnesota.* Boston: Allyn and Bacon, 2000.

Huggins-Williams, Nedra. "We Are There: The African-Diaspora in Hungary." *Transforming Anthropology* 11, no. 1 (2002): 49–50.

Ifekwunigwe, Jayne O. "An Inhospitable Port in the Storm: Recent Clandestine West African Migrants and the Quest for Diasporic Recognition." In Nira Yuval-Davis, Kalpani Kannabiran, and Ulrike Vieten, eds., *The Situated Politics of Belonging,* 84–99. Thousand Oaks, Calif.: Sage, 2006.

——."Recasting 'Black Venus' in the New African Diaspora." *Women's Studies International Forum* 27 (2004): 397–412.

——. "Reconfiguring the 'African' in the English-African Diaspora." In Khalid Khoser, ed., *New African Diasporas,* 56–70. London: Routledge, 2003.

——. *Scattered Belongings: Cultural Paradoxes of 'Race,' Nation, and Gender.* London: Routledge, 1999.

Joyce, Joyce Ann. "African-Centered Womanism: Connecting Africa to the Diaspora." In Okpewho, Davies, and Mazrui, *The African Diaspora,* 538–54.

Killingray, David, ed. *Africans in Britain*. Ilford: Frank Cass, 1994.

Lewis, Earl. "To Turn as on a Pivot: Writing African Americans into a History of Overlapping Diasporas." In Hine and McLeod, *Crossing Boundaries*, 3–32. Bloomington: Indiana University Press, 1999.

Lorde, Audre. "Eye to Eye: Black Women, Hatred, and Anger." In *Sister, Outsider: Essays and Speeches*, 145–75. Trumansburg, N.Y.: Crossing Press, 1984.

Luke, Don. "African Presence in the Early History of the British Isles and Scandinavia." In Van Sertima, *African Presence in Early Europe*, 223–44.

Marable, Manning. *African and Caribbean Politics*. London: Verso, 1987.

Martin, Michael T. "'Fortress Europe' and Third World Immigration in the Post–Cold War Global Context." *Third World Quarterly* 20, no. 4 (1999): 821–37.

Mazón, Patricia, and Reinhild Steingörver, eds. *Not So Plain as Black and White: Afro-German Culture and History, 1890–2000*. Rochester, N.Y.: University of Rochester Press, 2005.

Mazrui, Ali. *The Africans: A Triple Heritage*. Boston: Little, Brown, 1986.

———. "Globalization and Cross-Cultural Values: The Politics of Identity and Judgment." *Arab Studies Quarterly* 21, no. 3 (1999): 97–110.

Mbembe, Achille. "Ways of Seeing: Beyond the New Nativism: Introduction." *African Studies Review* 44, no. 2 (2001): 1–14.

Miles, Robert. "Explaining Racism in Contemporary Europe." In Rattansi and Westwood, *Racism, Modernity, and Identity*, 189–221.

Mirza, Heidi, ed. *Black British Feminism*. London: Routledge, 1997.

Modood, Tariq. "The Emergence of a Muslim Identity Politics." In Madeleine Bunting, ed., *Islam, Race, and Being British*, 19–23. London: Guardian/Barrow Cadbury Trust, 2005.

Modood, Tariq, and Pnina Werbner, eds. *The Politics of Multiculturalism in the New Europe: Racism, Identity, and Community*. London: Zed, 1997.

Mohanty, Chandra Talpade. "Women Workers and Capitalist Scripts: Ideologies of Domination, Common Interests, and the Politics of Solidarity." In Alexander and Mohanty, *Feminist Genealogies*, 3–29.

Morris, Lydia. *Managing Migration: Civic Stratification and Migrants' Rights*. London: Routledge, 2002.

Mudimbe, V. Y. *The Idea of Africa*. London: James Currey, 1994.

———. *The Invention of Africa: Gnosis, Philosophy, and the Order of Knowledge*. London: James Currey, 1988.

Neumayer, Eric. "Bogus Refugees? The Determinants of Asylum Migration to Western Europe." *International Studies Quarterly* 49 (2005): 389–409.

Nkrumah, Kwame. *The Class Struggle in Africa*. New York: International, 1970.

Obichere, Boniface. "Afro-Americans in Africa: Recent Experiences." In Drachler, *Black Homeland, Black Diaspora*, 15–42.

Okphewho, Isidore, Carole Boyce Davies, and Ali Mazrui, eds. *The African Diaspora: African Origins and New World Identities*. Bloomington: Indiana University Press, 1999.

Okri, Ben. *A Way of Being Free*. London: Phoenix House, 1997.

Owusu, Kwesi, ed. *Black British Culture and Society*. London: Routledge, 1999.

Palmer, Colin. "The African Diaspora." *Black Scholar* 30, nos. 3–4 (2000): 56–59.

Patterson, Tiffany Ruby, and Robin Kelley. "Unfinished Migrations: Reflections on the African Diaspora and the Making of the Modern World." *African Studies Review* 43, no. 1 (2000): 11–46.

Peters, John Durham. "Seeing Bifocally: Media, Place, and Culture." In Gupta and Ferguson, *Culture, Power, and Place*, 75–92.

Phillips, Mike, and Trevor Phillips. *Windrush: The Irresistible Rise of Multi-Racial Britain*. London: HarperCollins, 1999.

Pieterse, Jan Nederveen. "Europe, Traveling Light: Europeanization and Globalization." *European Legacy* 4, no. 3 (1999): 3–17.

Pimienta-Bey, José. "Moorish Spain: Academic Source and Foundation for the Rise and Success of Western European Universities in the Middle Ages." In Van Sertima, *The Golden Age of the Moor*, 182–248.

Ramdin, Ron. *The Making of the Black Working Class in Britain*. Aldershot, Hants: Wildwood House, 1987.

———. *Reimaging Britain: Five Hundred Years of Black and Asian History*. London: Pluto, 1999.

Rashidi, Runoko. "Ancient and Modern Britons: A Review Essay." In Van Sertima, *African Presence in Early Europe*, 251–60.

Rattansi, Ali. "On Being and Not Being Brown/Black British." *Interventions* 1 (2000): 118–34.

———. "'Western' Racisms, Ethnicities, and Identities in a 'Postmodern' Frame." In Rattansi and Westwood, *Racism, Modernity, and Identity*, 15–86.

Rattansi, Ali, and Sallie Westwood, eds., *Racism, Modernity, and Identity*. Oxford: Blackwell, 1994.

Rich, Paul. *Race and Empire in British Politics*. Cambridge: Cambridge University Press, 1986.

Richmond, Anthony. "Globalization: Implications for Immigrants and Refugees." *Ethnic and Racial Studies* 25, no. 5 (2002): 707–27.

Rodney, Walter. *How Europe Underdeveloped Africa*. Washington, D.C.: Howard University Press, 1981.

Rose, Tricia. *Black Noise: Rap Music and Black Culture in Contemporary America*. Wesleyan, Mass.: Wesleyan University Press, 1994.

Sadiqi, Fatima. "Morocco: The Political and Social Dimension of Migration." In Fargues, *Mediterranean Migration 2005 Report*, 225–30.

Sage, Adam. "Desperation at Europe's Back Gate." *New Statesman*, 10 October 2005.

Sassen, Saskia. "Global Cities and Survival Circuits." In Barbara Ehrenreich and Arlie Russell Hochschild, eds., *Global Woman: Nannies, Maids, and Sex Workers*, 254–74. London: Granta Books, 2003.

Sawyer, Lena. "Routings: 'Race,' African Diasporas, and Swedish Belonging." *Transforming Anthropology* 11, no. 1 (2002): 13–35.

Scott, David. *Refashioning Futures: Criticism after Postcoloniality*. Princeton, N.J.: Princeton University Press, 1999.

Sefa Dei, George. "Interrogating 'African Development' and the Diasporan Reality." *Journal of Black Studies* 29, no. 2 (1998): 141–54.

Segal, Ronald. *The Black Diaspora*. London: Faber and Faber, 1995.

Shepperson, George. "African Diaspora: Concept and Context." In Harris, *Global Dimensions of the African Diaspora*, 41–49.

Simone, Abdou Maliq. "On the Worlding of African Cities." *African Studies Review* 44, no. 2 (2001): 17.

Skinner, Elliot P. "The Dialectic between Diasporas and Homeland." In Harris, *Global Dimensions of the African Diaspora*, 11–40.

Small, Stephen. "Racism, Black People, and the City in Britain." In Green, *Globalization and Survival in the Black Diaspora*, 357–78.

Soysal, Yasemin Nuhoglu. "Citizenship and Identity: Living in Diaspora in Postwar Europe." *Ethnic and Racial Studies* 23, no. 1 (2000): 1–15.

Steady, Filomina Chioma. "Women of Africa and the African Diaspora: Linkages and Influences." In Harris, *Global Dimensions of the African Diaspora*, 167–87.

Stoller, Paul. *Money Has No Smell: The Africanization of New York City*. Chicago: University of Chicago Press, 2002.

Stovall, Tyler. *Paris Noir: African Americans in the City of Light*. New York: Mariner Books, 1996.

Styan, David. "*La Nouvelle Vague?* Recent Francophone African Settlement in London." In Khalid Koser, ed., *New African Diasporas*, 17–36. London: Routledge, 2003.

Torres, Arlene, and Norman Whitten, eds. *Blackness in Latin America and the Caribbean*. Vol. 2. Bloomington: Indiana University Press, 1998.

Ujuris, Tijen. "Diaspora and Citizenship: Kurdish Women in London." Paper presented at the East London Refugee conference, "Crossing Borders and Boundaries." London, June 25, 2001.

Van Sertima, Ivan, ed. *African Presence in Early Europe*. New Brunswick, N.J.: Transaction, 1985.

———, ed. *The Golden Age of the Moor*. New Brunswick, N.J.: Transaction, 1992.

Vertovec, Steven. "Conceiving and Researching Transnationalism." *Ethnic and Racial Studies* 22, no. 2 (1999): 448.

Wacquant, J. D. Löic. "Urban Outcasts: Stigma and Division in the Black American Ghetto and the French Urban Periphery." In Green, *Globalization and Survival in the Black Diaspora*, 331–56.

Walcott, Rinaldo. *Black Like Who? Writing Black Canada*. Rev. 2nd ed. Toronto: Insomniac Press, 2003.

Westwood, Sallie, and Anne Phizacklea. *Trans-nationalism and the Politics of Belonging*. London: Routledge, 2000.

White, Elisa Joy. "Forging African Diaspora Places in Dublin's Retro-Global Spaces: Minority Making in a New Global City." *City* 6, no. 2 (2002): 251–70.

Wright, Michelle. *Becoming Black: Creating Identity in the African Diaspora*. Durham, N.C.: Duke University Press, 2004.

Yeoh, Brenda, Katie Willis, and Abdul Fakhri Khader. "Introduction: Transnationalism at Its Edges." *Ethnic and Racial Studies* 26, no. 2 (2003): 207–17.

Yuval-Davis, Nira, Floya Anthias, and Eleonore Kofman. "Secure Borders and Safe Havens and the Gendered Politics of Belonging: Beyond Social Cohesion." *Ethnic and Racial Studies* 28, no. 3 (2005): 513–35.

Zeleza, Paul Tiyambe. "Rewriting the African Diaspora: Beyond the Black Atlantic." *African Affairs* 104, no. 414 (2005): 35–68.

CONTRIBUTORS

LATIFA F. J. BORGELIN is a doctoral student in Ecology and Evolutionary Biology at the University of Arizona. Her research focuses on the relationship between genetics and infectious disease in humans, with particular interest in determining how adaptation to infectious diseases has helped shape the genetic architecture of African-descended peoples of the New World. Her work has been presented at the National Conference on HIV/AIDS, African HIV/AIDS Conference, and Association for the Study of the Worldwide African Diaspora (ASWAD).

KIM D. BUTLER is Associate Professor of History and Africana Studies at Rutgers University. She is a historian specializing in African diaspora studies with a focus on Brazil and Latin America/Caribbean. Her major work is *Freedoms Given, Freedoms Won: Afro-Brazilians in Post-Abolition San Paulo and Salvador*. This publication won her the American Historical Association's Wesley-Logan Prize and the Association of Black Women Historians' Letitia Woods Brown Prize.

MELVIN L. BUTLER is Assistant Professor of Music at the University of Chicago. His research interests center on the dynamics of musical experience, national identity, and charismatic Christian practice in Haiti, Jamaica, and the United States. His work has appeared in *Ethnomusicology, Journal of the American Academy of Religion, Black Music Research Journal, Obsidian, Journal of Popular Music Studies*, and *Current Musicology*.

JUDITH A. CARNEY is Professor of Geography at the University of California in Los Angeles. She is a specialist in environment and development in West Africa and the African diaspora. She is author of *Black Rice: The Origins of Rice Cultivation in the Americas*, which won the Melville Herskovits Award from the African Studies Association in 2002 and the James M. Blaut Award from the Association of American Geographers in 2003. She is co-author (with Richard Nicholas Rosomoff) of *In the Shadow of Slavery: Africa's Botanical Legacy in the Atlantic World* (2009).

CAROLYN COOPER is Professor of Literary and Cultural Studies at the University of the West Indies, Mona, Jamaica. One of Jamaica's foremost cultural critics, she has hosted her own television talk show and is a frequent contributor to public debates on gender and culture in Jamaica. She is author of *Noises in the Blood: Orality, Gender, and the "Vulgar" Body of Jamaican Popular Culture* and *Sound Clash: Jamaican Dancehall Culture at Large.*

GRANT FARRED is Professor of Africana Studies and English at Cornell University. He is author of several books, most recently *What's My Name? Black Vernacular Intellectuals; Phantom Calls: Race and the Globalization of the NBA;* and *Long Distance Love: A Passion for Football.* He is the general editor of the journal *South Atlantic Quarterly.*

ROBERT FATTON JR. is the Julia A. Cooper Professor of Government and Foreign Affairs in the Department of Politics at the University of Virginia. He is author of *Black Consciousness in South Africa; The Making of a Liberal Democracy: Senegal's Passive Revolution, 1975–1985; Predatory Rule: State and Civil Society in Africa; Haiti's Predatory Republic: The Unending Transition to Democracy;* and *The Roots of Haitian Despotism.*

PAGET HENRY is Professor of Sociology at Brown University. He has taught at SUNY Stony Brook, the University of the West Indies (Antigua), and the University of Virginia. He is author of *Caliban's Reason: Introducing Afro-Caribbean Philosophy* and *Peripheral Capitalism and Underdevelopment in Antigua,* and co-editor of *C. L. R. James's Caribbean* and *New Caribbean: Decolonization, Democracy, and Development.*

JAYNE O. IFEKWUNIGWE is a Visiting Research Fellow in Africana Women's Studies at Bennett College, having previously held the position of Reader in Anthropology at the University of East London. She is an anthropologist whose research interests include feminist, (post)colonial, and transnational genealogies of the African diaspora. Among her publications are *Scattered Belongings: Cultural Paradoxes of "Race," Nation, and Gender* and *"Mixed Race" Studies: A Reader.* She is working on a new book project provisionally entitled *Out of Africa ("By Any Means Necessary"): Recent Clandestine West African Migrations and the Gendered Politics of Survival.*

FATIMAH L. C. JACKSON is Professor of Biological Anthropology and Distinguished Scholar-Teacher at the University of Maryland, College Park. She is also Director of the Institute for African American Research at the University of North Carolina, Chapel Hill. She is an expert on the biohistory of African peoples and their descendants in the diaspora and has coordinated genetics research on the African Burial Ground Project in New York City. Her articles have appeared in journals such as *Human Biology, American Anthropologist, Annual Review of Anthropology, Journal of Black Studies, American Journal of Human Biology,* and the *British Medical Bulletin.* She is co-founder of the first human DNA bank in

Africa (based at the University of Yaoundé I in Cameroon), and appeared in the BBC documentary *Motherland: A Genetic Journey.*

XOLELA MANGCU is Convener of the Platform for Public Deliberation at the University of Johannesburg and a nonresident fellow at the Brookings Institution. He has written a regular column for leading South African newspapers such as the *Sunday Independent, Business Day,* and *Weekender.* He is author of *To the Brink: The State of Democracy in South Africa.*

MOYO OKEDIJI teaches art and art history at the University of Texas at Austin. He is author of *African Renaissance: Old Forms, New Images in Yoruba Art,* and *The Shattered Gourd: Yoruba Forms in Twentieth-Century American Art.* His art has been shown in galleries and museums around the world.

TEJUMOLA OLANIYAN is Louise Durham Mead Professor of English and African Languages and Literature at the University of Wisconsin–Madison. He is author of *Arrest the Music! Fela and His Rebel Art and Politics* (2004, 2009; nominated for Best Research in World Music by the Association for Recorded Sound Collections in 2005), *Scars of Conquest/Masks of Resistance: The Invention of Cultural Identities in African, African American, and Caribbean Drama* (1995), and co-editor of *African Literature: An Anthology of Criticism and Theory* (2007, with Ato Quayson) and *African Drama and Performance* (2004, with John Conteh-Morgan).

RICHARD PRICE is Duane A. and Virginia S. Dittman Professor of American Studies, Anthropology, and History at the College of William and Mary. He is author of *Alabi's World,* for which he won the Albert J. Beveridge Award, the Gordon K. Lewis Memorial Award for Caribbean Scholarship, and the J. I. Staley Prize in Anthropology; and *Travels with Tooy: History, Memory, and the African American Imagination,* winner of the 2008 Victor Turner Prize for Ethnographic Writing and the 2009 Gordon K. and Sybil Lewis Memorial Award for Caribbean Scholarship. He has also written (with Sidney Mintz) *The Birth of African-American Culture;* (with Sally Price) *The Root of Roots; or, How Afro-American Anthropology Got Its Start;* and (with Sally Price) *Romare Bearden: The Caribbean Dimension.*

SANDRA L. RICHARDS is Professor of African American Studies and Theater with a courtesy appointment in Performance Studies at Northwestern University. She is author of *Ancient Songs Set Ablaze: The Theatre of Femi Osofisan* and numerous articles on African American and Nigerian dramatists.

THERESA A. SINGLETON is Associate Professor of Anthropology at Syracuse University. She is editor of two volumes on the archaeology of the African diaspora: *The Archaeology of Slavery and Plantation Life* and

"I, Too, Am America": Archaeological Studies of African-American Life.
She directs a research project in Cuba that involves excavation of a coffee
plantation that was known as Santa Ana de Viajacas.

JAMES H. SWEET is Associate Professor of History at the University of
Wisconsin–Madison. His book *Recreating Africa* won the American Historical Association's Wesley-Logan Prize for the best book on the history
of the African diaspora in 2004. It was also a finalist for the Frederick
Douglass Prize. Sweet is the author of more than a dozen journal and book
articles. His second book, *Domingos Álvares and the Politics of Public
Healing: An Atlantic Biography,* will be published in 2011.

OLÚFÉMI TÁÍWÒ is Professor of Philosophy and Global African Studies
and Director of the Global African Studies Program at Seattle University. He is author of *Legal Naturalism: A Marxist Theory of Law* and *How
Colonialism Preempted Modernity in Africa* (Indiana University Press,
2009). He is co-editor of *West Africa Review.*

INDEX

Page numbers in italics refer to tables.

CPSIA information can be obtained
at www.ICGtesting.com
Printed in the USA
LVHW081409240321
682324LV00027B/402